*Greenbackers, Knights of Labor, and Populists*

# *Greenbackers, Knights of Labor, and Populists*

## Farmer-Labor Insurgency in the Late-Nineteenth-Century South

MATTHEW HILD

The University of Georgia Press  *Athens & London*

© 2007 by the University of Georgia Press
Athens, Georgia 30602
Set in Berthold Baskerville by Bookcomp, Inc.
Printed and bound by Thomson-Shore
The paper in this book meets the guidelines for
permanence and durability of the Committee on
Production Guidelines for Book Longevity of the
Council on Library Resources.

PRINTED IN THE UNITED STATES OF AMERICA
11   10   09   08   07   C   5   4   3   2   1

*Library of Congress Cataloging-in-Publication Data*

Hild, Matthew.
Greenbackers, Knights of Labor, and populists : farmer-
labor insurgency in the late-nineteenth-century South /
Matthew Hild.
    p. cm.
Includes bibliographical references and index.
ISBN-13: 978-0-8203-2897-3 (hardcover : alk. paper)
ISBN-10: 0-8203-2897-9 (hardcover : alk. paper)
1. Knights of Labor.   2. Labor unions–Southern States–
Political activity–History–19th century.   3. Working
class–Southern States–Political activity–History–19th
century.   4. Farmers–Southern States–Political activity–
History–19th century.   5. Populism–Southern States–
History–19th century.   6. Southern States–Race
relations–History–19th century.   I. Title.
HD8055.K7H57 2007
322'.2097509034–dc22        2006035808

*British Library Cataloging-in-Publication Data available*

# Contents

# Acknowledgments

I would like to take this opportunity to thank my three graduate school mentors: Robert C. McMath, who supervised this study in its doctoral dissertation form; William F. Holmes, who guided me through my earliest efforts at exploring the topics covered in this study; and Douglas Flamming, who not only helped me a great deal when I was a graduate student but has continued to be very helpful to me in the years that have followed. I consider myself most fortunate to have worked closely with these outstanding scholars and teachers.

In the course of researching and writing this study in its various drafts and forms, I also benefited from the helpful advice of some other exceptional scholars, including W. Fitzhugh Brundage, Gregg Cantrell, James C. Cobb, John C. Inscoe, Barton C. Shaw, Andrea Tone, Steven W. Usselman, and Julia Walsh. I thank them for showing interest in my work and offering their valuable opinions and insights.

I must give special mention to the editors of the *Arkansas Historical Quarterly* for publishing small portions of this book as an article entitled "Labor, Third-Party Politics, and New South Democracy in Arkansas, 1884–1896" in the spring 2004 issue. Not only did the editors choose two anonymous readers who read my work carefully and provided helpful comments, but associate editor Patrick Williams was also kind enough to provide me with Arkansas county-level election data from the 1880s and 1890s that proved useful for both that article and this book.

I would also like to thank everyone at the University of Georgia Press who has contributed time, effort, and talent to the production of this book. I am especially grateful to the Press's director, Nicole Mitchell, who has patiently and enthusiastically supported this project since its inception, and project editor Courtney Denney, who has devoted great attention and care to this book as it has made its way through the editing and production processes.

Finally, I would like to dedicate this book to my parents, George and Wanda Hild, and to the memory of Helen Hild, whom I still think of often and miss sorely.

*Maps*

## THE KNIGHTS OF LABOR AND FARMER-LABOR
## PARTIES IN ARKANSAS

K = County with at least one Knights of Labor local assembly
U = County carried by the Union Labor Party gubernatorial candidate, 1888 and/or 1890
P = County carried by the Populist gubernatorial candidate, 1892
G = County carried by Greenback–Labor gubernatorial candidate, 1880

GREENBACKERS, KNIGHTS OF LABOR,
AND POPULISTS IN ALABAMA

**#** = Number of times county was carried by the Populist
(or Jeffersonian Democratic–Populist) gubernatorial
candidate, 1892–1896

**K** = County with at least one local assembly of the Knights of Labor
**G** = County carried by Greenback–Labor gubernatorial candidate, 1882

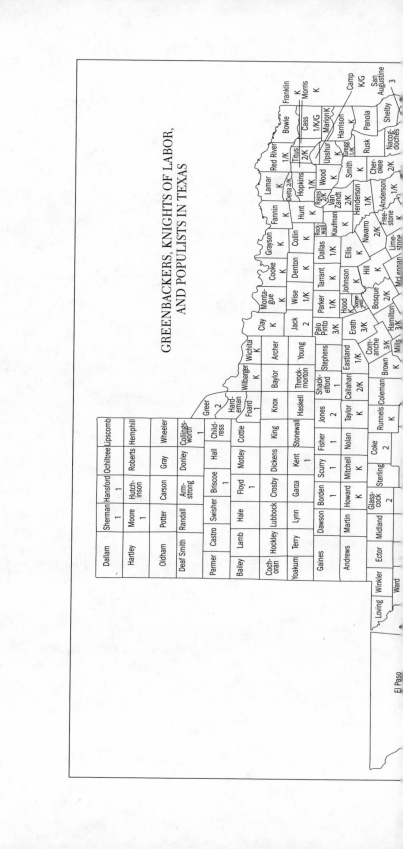

GREENBACKERS, KNIGHTS OF LABOR, AND POPULISTS IN TEXAS

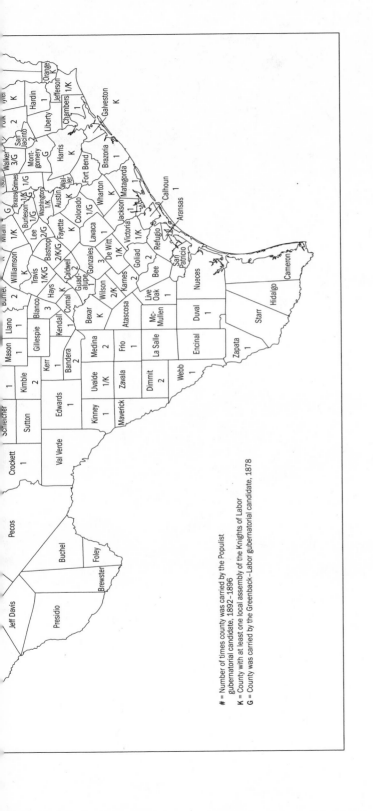

# = Number of times county was carried by the Populist gubernatorial candidate, 1892–1896

K = County with at least one local assembly of the Knights of Labor

G = County was carried by the Greenback–Labor gubernatorial candidate, 1878

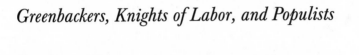

*Greenbackers, Knights of Labor, and Populists*

# Introduction

In December 1890 a worried lawyer in Greensboro, North Carolina, wrote in his diary, "The Knights of Labor, Farmers['] Alliance, Trades Unions and other laboring classes are combining to form a national political party to overthrow everything in their way[,] and the end is not yet." Of course, the dire prediction of this excitable observer that these groups might "bring about a bloody Revolution in the country" never came to pass, but the mere fact that this educated professional harbored such fears suggests that the challenge posed by united farmers and laborers as a force in southern politics during the late nineteenth century should not be taken lightly.[1] Yet historians have not given sufficient attention or credence to the political threat posed to the Democratic planter-industrial axis by the farmer-labor axis in the South during the last quarter of the nineteenth century. Historians have recounted and analyzed the agrarian revolt led by the Southern Farmers' Alliance and the People's (or Populist) Party at considerable length, and they have also examined the smaller southern labor movement led by the Knights of Labor and other organizations during this era. But for the most part historians have given only minimal consideration to the convergence or unification of these movements, the looming possibility that struck terror in the heart of the aforementioned Greensboro attorney.

Many older histories of Populism, such as *The Populist Revolt: A History of the Farmers' Alliance and the People's Party* (1931) by John D. Hicks and *Farmer Movements in the South, 1865–1933* (1960) by Theodore Saloutos, make scant mention of labor organizations other than to note briefly the secondary role played by the Knights of Labor in the formation of the national People's Party.[2] Lawrence Goodwyn paid more attention to the possibility of farmer-labor coalitions in *Democratic Promise: The Populist Moment in America* (1976) but emphasized the obstacles facing such efforts, including the lack of a "movement culture" among labor organizations such as the Knights, a characterization that labor historians would later dispute.[3] More recent studies of Populism, such as Robert C. McMath's *American Populism: A Social History, 1877–1898* (1993) and Edward L. Ayers's survey *The Promise of the New South: Life after Reconstruction* (1992), give more consideration and credence to the joint efforts of southern farmers and laborers to redress their grievances during this period, at least suggesting the promise of the topic and the likelihood of fruit to be borne by further examination. In a still more recent work that spans (and links) the Greenback, Populist, and Progressive movements political scientist Elizabeth Sanders undertakes further examination of farmer-labor political alliances. Her book *Roots of Reform: Farmers, Workers, and the American State, 1877–1917* (1999) focuses on national politics but also examines farmer-labor politics in specific regions, including the South. Sanders astutely notes that in what she calls "periphery" regions, such as the South and much of the Midwest and West, many laborers had close ties to the country and therefore "likely did not sharply distinguish their interests from those of farmers." Sanders adds that this factor made "the Populists . . . comfortable with a farmer-labor alliance."[4] But her "glossing over of the issue of race," as one reviewer put it, limits her ability to analyze farmer-labor politics in the South, given the inextricable relationship between politics and race in the region.[5]

Like students of Populism, southern labor historians only recently have begun to give serious consideration to the relationship between struggling, disaffected laborers in the late nineteenth century and their equally downtrodden agrarian brethren. Early labor historians who wrote about the Knights of Labor, like the early scholars of Populism, considered the farmer-labor relationship primarily in terms of the role played by the Knights in the establishment of the national Populist Party.[6] One scholar who gave more in-depth examination to this relationship, Gerald Grob, nevertheless also chiefly considered the interaction between the national leaders of the Knights and the national leaders of the Populist Party.[7] In a number of works published in the 1970s Melton McLaurin, the first historian to write extensively about the Knights of Labor in the South, gave some consideration to the relationship between the Knights and the white as well as the Colored Farmers' Alliance, and, to a lesser degree, that between the Knights and the Populists, although farmer-labor coalitions are not a central subject of his work.[8] Two recent works by Daniel Letwin and Karin Shapiro that focus on coal miners in, respectively, the Birmingham district of Alabama and east and middle Tennessee during this period devote considerable attention to the relationship between farmer and labor organizations. While these studies are both restricted chiefly to one category of workers in specific locations, they both show that farmers and those laborers were aware of some common interests and that some members of each group wished to unite as a political force. Letwin and Shapiro also demonstrate, however, that conflicts of interest existed between the members of each group, as did doubts about making common cause politically.[9]

No historian, however, has written a book-length study that provides an in-depth examination of biracial farmer-labor insurgency across the South during the last three decades of the nineteenth century. This book, therefore, represents the first effort at exploring this subject on such a large scale and scope. Furthermore, this study also represents a reconsideration of southern Populism as a farmer-labor movement rather than just a farmers revolt. The topic merits serious attention, given both the potential that farmer-labor activism demonstrated for reshaping southern politics and society to the benefit of the rural and urban working classes, white and black, and the long-term subjugation of those interests to those of the region's wealthier classes of whites after the demise of Populism.

This book also suggests that a great deal of continuity existed in the farmer and labor movements of the late nineteenth century. Although the southern farmer and labor movements of this period reached their apex (depending upon the state or subregion in question) between 1886 and 1894, most of the grievances that inspired them in the first place dated back to at least the 1870s.[10] This continuity of grievances manifested itself in the ideologies and platforms of farmer and labor organizations throughout this era. Goodwyn argued that a direct ideological progression developed from the National Labor Union (formed in 1866) to the Greenback Party to the Union Labor Party to the Populist Party, which represented "the final and most powerful assertion of the greenback critique of the American monetary system."[11] A similar thread of continuity ran through the major reform platforms of this era, from the Knights of Labor's Reading platform and the Greenback-Labor Party's Toledo platform (both from 1878) through the Texas Farmers' Alliance's Cleburne platform of 1886 and the Populists' Omaha platform of 1892.

Moreover, such continuity over the latter part of the nineteenth century also characterized southern farmer-labor insurgency in the states where it demonstrated the greatest strength. In Texas, Arkansas, and Alabama, three of the southern states where the third-party movement became strongest during the 1890s (or as early as 1888 in Arkansas), third-party activity began under the aegis of the Greenback-Labor Party in the late 1870s and was kept alive in the 1880s by organizations such as the Knights of Labor, the Farmers' Alliance, and the Agricultural Wheel. The efforts of these organizations led to the establishment of the proto–Populist Union Labor Party, which actually represented the formidable peak of the third-party movement in Arkansas. Not only did the third party develop significant strength in each of these three states, but it won more support from industrial or other nonagricultural laborers than in other southern states.

In two other southern states, North Carolina and Georgia, the Populists also built a strong party, but farmer-labor coalitions during the pre-Populist era had been more limited. As in the 1870s and 1880s, third-party activists failed to build true farmer-labor coalitions in these states in the 1890s. Nevertheless, in certain cities, counties, or parts of these states where the Knights of Labor had stirred farmer-labor insurgency during the mid-1880s the Populists won significant labor support.

But in southern states where no significant groundwork had been laid for farmer-labor coalitions during the 1870s and 1880s the Populists had no success at building such coalitions in the 1890s. In some of these states, such as Tennessee and, in particular, South Carolina, the Populist Party failed to develop much strength at all. In these states, however, the Populists faced far greater problems than a lack of support from labor; the party failed to win over many farmers either and had to contend with obstacles that made its failure to convert laborers seem moot. While this study does not suggest that a background of farmer-labor insurgency in a given state or part thereof was a necessary prerequisite for building a strong Populist Party, it does assert that such a background could only help Populists in achieving that goal and was indeed a necessary precondition for attracting significant labor support.

## Farmers, Laborers, and the Late-Nineteenth-Century South

Since this study deals with "farmers" and "laborers," a brief word about these terms seems appropriate. Several categories of "farmers" existed in the postbellum South. At the top of the socioeconomic ladder stood large landowning farmers or planters whose holdings "varied from a few hundred to several thousand acres." Only 2 to 3 percent of southern farmers during this era, according to historian Gilbert C. Fite, fell into this category.[12] As *Atlanta Constitution* editor and New South spokesman Henry W. Grady noted in 1881, these men were "still lords of acres, though not of slaves."[13] Therefore, the procurement of cheap, efficient labor became one of their primary concerns after the Civil War. More common than planters were small landowning farmers, with about one hundred to two hundred acres on which they grew both cash and subsistence crops and usually raised some livestock and poultry. Below the small landowner in the agricultural class hierarchy stood the renting farmer. Some renters occupied one hundred to two hundred acres, which they operated as if they were owners, though the need to pay rent, either in cash or crops, made them less prosperous than small landowners. Other poorer tenants, however, farmed as little as twenty to fifty acres, which left them barely able to make a living. Sharecroppers too generally farmed from twenty to fifty acres, but they were furnished with supplies by their landlords and usually received only one third to one half of the crops they raised. The bottom rung of the agricultural ladder belonged to wage laborers, who were paid during the mid-1880s about eight to twelve dollars per month.[14]

Some common class interests existed among all these categories of farmers. They all stood to benefit from regulation of railroads and grain elevators and warehouses, higher prices for cash crops, and, as debtors (a label that applied even to many southern planters of that era), inflated currency.[15] Yet class differences were also abundant among these groups of farmers. Historian Harold Woodman has summed up these differences succinctly by suggesting that "large-scale planters became the agrarian New South's big businessmen, the former yeomen . . . became the agrarian New South's small businessmen," and most former slaves "became part of a new working class," often as croppers on large business plantations. "The problems of small farmers," Woodman asserts, "were those of small businessmen, . . .

while the problems of croppers were those of workers." Although tenants and croppers alike often suffered from poverty, "they were nonetheless situated differently enough economically [tenants as operators and croppers as laborers] to make joint action on common solutions difficult."[16] These class differences among farmers, as we shall see, created tensions within the Farmers' Alliance, between the white Alliance and the Colored Farmers' Alliance, and between the white Alliance and the Knights of Labor.

The distinctions among southern laborers during the late nineteenth century were less complicated, although here too class differences existed, as became apparent when many skilled railroad workers refused to participate in the Southwest strike of 1886. Categories of southern laborers in this period varied according to the setting. In the rural communities or small towns that were most prevalent in the South at that time many laborers were "artisans" or "mechanics," labels that could refer to blacksmiths, leatherworkers, woodworkers, and men who could apply their skills to crafts of various sorts, the jack-of-all-trades (and master of none—or several). The Knights of Labor organized some of these workers in small communities, usually into "mixed" local assemblies that included a variety of workers of different sorts and often farmers or farm laborers as well. Domestic workers, mostly women (many of them African American), could also be found in small communities as well as cities in the late-nineteenth-century South, and the Knights sometimes organized them as well.[17]

The most common types of industrial workers in the early New South included coal miners, lumber and sawmill workers, textile mill workers (almost all of whom were white), and railroad workers. The Knights recruited and in fact led strikes among all of these groups of workers. Millhands and railroad workers often worked in urban areas, although not always. Miners and lumber and sawmill workers more often worked in rural areas, although the Birmingham district became a center of the coal as well as the iron and steel and railroad industries. Many southern industrial workers had ties to the farm, either having tilled the soil themselves or having relatives who did. Those ties, in certain parts of the South at least, would facilitate farmer-labor coalitions, although certainly not all southern laborers felt economic or cultural kinship with farmers or an inclination to vote for "farmer" candidates. Moreover, not all southern laborers (of industry or farm) were free to vote as they wished, at least not without imperiling their livelihoods or their very lives.[18]

The extent to which southern farmers of the late nineteenth century viewed themselves as having similar economic interests to those of laborers depended largely upon the type of farmer in question. Poor farmers and farmworkers sometimes identified with urban or industrial workers as fellow producers who worked hard but reaped little fruit from their labor. These farmers, despite their own gloomy financial condition, would on occasion lend not only rhetorical but also material support to striking workers, whom they sometimes joined in the ranks of the Knights of Labor as well. Middle-class farmers, landowners who ranged from slightly to moderately prosperous, also sometimes lent support to workers in the face of a common enemy, such as the much-maligned railroad monopolies. On the other hand, some farmers of this class viewed railroad strikes or organized labor's demand for an end to convict leasing as a threat to their own prosperity. No such ambiguity clouded planters' view of industrial workers and their unions. Planters identified more closely with industrialists as employers and shared their enmity and contempt for the Knights of Labor, which organized the employees of both groups.

The outlook of urban or industrial workers in the early New South toward the economic pronouncements and programs of farmers also depended largely upon the type of farmers in question. The Knights of Labor not only organized many small farmers and farm laborers but also led strikes by southern black plantation workers for higher wages.[19] The Knights gave only limited (and reluctant) support, however, to the Southern Farmers' Alliance's subtreasury plan, an inflationary farm labor and credit scheme that would have chiefly benefited landowners while potentially raising the prices of food and clothing. More generally, though, laborers shared farmers' abhorrence of monopolies and the "money power" that seemed to exacerbate the economic woes of many a poor farmer and laborer alike. In fact, many of the prescriptions of the farmers' organizations (and the Populist Party) for easing the economic woes of their constituents closely resembled reform proposals put forth in the platform of the Knights of Labor.[20]

Finally, a brief explanation seems in order about why this book focuses on farmer-labor insurgency in the South but, with the exception of the southern-western border states of Texas and Arkansas, not the West, the nation's other region of Populist strength. While it would be provincial to argue that the southern story of farmer-labor insurgency during the

Greenback-to-Populist era is more important than the western story, the unique and particularly tragic aspects of the southern story cannot be denied. As former Georgia Populist leader Tom Watson pointed out in 1910, only southern third-party activists had to contend with the looming race issue that hung heavily over every aspect of southern society, ready to explode like a dark, ominous thundercloud at any moment.[21] On a sometimes (though not always) related note, southern third-party leaders and supporters all too often faced overwhelming violence, sometimes state sanctioned. The use of state-sanctioned violence to repress strikes occurred throughout the United States during this era, but only in the South did it so often influence (or overturn) elections. And in the end only in the South did the efforts of disaffected farmers and workers to exert more influence over their government result in the disfranchisement of many of these people—most blacks and many poor whites. Thus, once biracial farmer-labor insurgency failed (or was destroyed) in the South, the "best men" who had been most threatened by that insurgency as well as, unfortunately, some disillusioned leaders of that insurgency themselves, such as Watson, eliminated the possibility of such a movement ever arising again. Indeed, the regionally unique undemocratic character of the late-nineteenth-century South explains, more than any other factor, why southern Populism failed even in those significant instances when the third party experienced considerable success in its efforts to attract support from industrial workers.

# CHAPTER ONE

# Agrarian Discontent and Political Dissent in the South, 1872–1882

In June 1873 the *Macon Telegraph and Messenger*, a Black Belt Georgia newspaper, reported that a new farmers' organization, the Order of the Patrons of Husbandry (or the Grange), was rapidly establishing local chapters throughout the state. By the Fourth of July, the newspaper noted, "as many as *one hundred granges*" would "be in successful operation." The *Telegraph and Messenger* approved of this development. "The cash system, combined credit, special rates of transportation, dealing by wholesale at headquarters with pork-packers and produce dealers, and a reduction in the ruinous rates of interest," the newspaper reported, "are the grand results which are to be accomplished." The *Telegraph and Messenger* understood that southern farmers were facing a variety of financial difficulties and seemed to place some hope in the Grange as a means of their deliverance. "Surely if the Patrons of Husbandry can do aught to relieve the distress and burdens of their brethren," the newspaper editorialized, "they should be hailed as benefactors of the human race."[1]

The *Telegraph and Messenger* saw other possible ramifications in the Grange movement, however, than concerted efforts at economic self-help by farmers. "From the present outlook," the newspaper prophesied, "this new order is destined also to be a political power in the land." Accordingly, the Democratic organ warned "politicians and old party managers" that their political survival might well depend upon how effectively they could "bend to the blast, and fraternize with, and attempt to lead and rule this crusade of the masses." So seriously did the *Telegraph and Messenger* perceive the Grange as a political threat that it declared, "We should not be surprised, if it proves the potent lever which will disrupt and rend into fragments all the old [political] organizations of the day."² When "A Patron" from Colaparchee, Georgia, indignantly informed the newspaper later that week that the Grange was a nonpartisan organization, the *Telegraph and Messenger* scoffed in reply, "He must be refreshingly verdant . . . if he thinks any great and popular combination of the masses can keep out of politics." Having reiterated its belief that the Grange would become a factor in Georgia politics, the newspaper then repeated its "wish" that the Grange "may obtain accessions of strength from our intelligent statesmen, who, from their experience and ability are well qualified to *lead* in any of the projected reforms."³

In the course of these two editorials the *Telegraph and Messenger* identified what would become two of the major public issues of the late-nineteenth-century South: agrarian discontent and political dissent. Farmers bemoaned a variety of obstacles to financial success during this period, such as monopolistic railroads, middlemen, high taxes and interest rates, tariffs that raised the costs of manufactured products, a growing shortage of circulating currency, and the crop lien system, which had become the region's prevailing credit system. The *Telegraph and Messenger* proclaimed that "experience has demonstrated that this [the credit system] is the Pandora's box which contains most of the elements of mischief and misery known to the human race." The crop lien system forced many southern farmers to plant most of their acreage in cotton, which they mortgaged to buy food and supplies on credit at exorbitantly high prices. Steadily declining cotton prices from the mid-1870s through the 1890s and the growing currency and credit crunch exacerbated their troubles, and many small landowning farmers slipped into tenancy. Farmers in the Upcountry of the South's cotton-growing region, who made the most use of commercial fertilizers, suffered the worst: by the 1890s the costs that they incurred in producing cotton exceeded their proceeds.⁴

Although the full-blown "agrarian revolt" did not begin in the South until the advent of the Populist Party in the early 1890s, that revolt took root in the 1870s. During this period farmers began to express the grievances and develop the ideologies that would evolve into those of the Farmers' Alliance and the Populists. While the Grange was avowedly a nonpartisan organization, it did not always remain detached from partisan politics. By the time of the Grange's descent in the South during the latter half of the 1870s, some farmers had begun to participate in third-party movements under the guise of "Independent" tickets or the Greenback-Labor Party (GLP).

The GLP, which emerged in most southern states in 1878 and waged its strongest campaigns in Texas and Alabama, appealed not only to farmers but to industrial laborers as well.[5] The GLP presaged both the Knights of Labor and the Populists in attempting to bridge the farmer-labor chasm and in its platform and critique of the emerging commercial, industrial political economy. Some GLP leaders (some of them prominent Grangers or former Grangers) would, in fact, subsequently play important roles in the Knights or the Populist movement or both.

The GLP served as a forerunner of the Knights of Labor, the proto–Populist Union Labor Party, and the Populist Party in more than just platform and, to a lesser degree, leadership. The successes and failures of the GLP in the South also, to an extent, foreshadowed those of these later organizations. In Texas, for example, the strong Greenback-Labor challenge was quickly followed by the rapid growth of the Farmers' Alliance and the Knights in the mid-1880s, organizations that in turn laid the groundwork for the even stronger Texas Populist Party. Similarly, the Greenback-Labor movement that developed in northern Alabama foretold and in some counties even merged directly into the Union Labor Party effort of the late 1880s led by the Knights, the Agricultural Wheel, and the Farmers' Alliance. The Union Labor Party helped to pave the way for the Populist Party, which also achieved its greatest strength in the northern part of the state.

Conversely, the failure of strong Greenback-Labor or similar Independent movements to develop in states such as Louisiana, South Carolina, and Tennessee foreshadowed the failure of the Populist movement in those states. The obstacles that prevented GLP or Independent candidates from succeeding there either reemerged to cripple the Populist Party or even precluded a serious challenge by that party altogether. Some of these same problems also confronted the Knights of Labor in South Carolina, where that organization never amounted to much, and in Louisiana, where the Knights claimed well over seven thousand members in 1887 before losing a disastrous, violent strike in the lower delta sugar fields that brought issues of race and control of agricultural day laborers to a decisive climax.[6]

Thus, the agrarian discontent and political dissent that emerged in the South during the 1870s ultimately proved more significant than its limited scope and success may have suggested at the time. During this decade the conditions that sparked the agrarian revolt of the late-nineteenth-century South began to crystallize, as did the producerist and republican ideologies that farmers developed in response. While the southern labor movement did not begin to emerge on a large scale until the 1880s, the Greenback-Labor movement also helped southern laborers in certain locales to develop and express a similar critique of the region's (and the nation's) rising commercial and industrial order. Politically, while the correlation between Greenback-Labor or Independent activity and Populism or other subsequent third-party activity has its limits, one could nevertheless argue that the relative strength or weakness of third-party efforts in various southern states during this period exerted an influence on the future successes and failures of Populism that was in some cases significant.

### The Grange and the Mobilization of Southern Farmers

The Grange served as the first step in the march of late-nineteenth-century agrarian discontent. Founded in December 1867 in Washington, D.C., by former U.S. Department of Agriculture clerk Oliver H. Kelley, the Grange entered the South about three and a half years later. The organization chartered State Granges (comprised of local subordinate Granges) in Mississippi and South Carolina in 1872 and in the rest of the former Confederate states during the following year. Despite admonitions like those of the *Southern Cultivator*, a Georgia agricultural journal, that southerners "had had 'entangling alliances' enough already with the North, to warn us against going blindfold[ed] into an organization with a great *central head* at Washington City," southern farmers flocked into the Grange. Official National Grange membership figures from 1875, when the Order was at its peak, reported that the eleven ex-Confederate states had a combined membership of 210,589, which amounted to 27.7 percent of the national total of 761,263 members. Additionally, the southern "border" state of Kentucky had 52,463 members. Among those states that had seceded, Tennessee and Texas led in Grange membership with just over 37,000 each.[7]

Who comprised these large ranks of southern Grangers? White farmers who owned small amounts of land made up much of the rank and file, although men with large planting interests usually led the organization. Although men vastly outnumbered women in the Grange, white farm women could and did join. From its inception the Grange gave them full membership privileges, unlike most earlier agricultural societies. The Grange offered women limited egalitarianism, however, maintaining a separate ritual and offices for them. One recent study of the agrarian movement in late-nineteenth-century Tennessee states that "women played a prominent role in the Tennessee Granges, though their activities remained traditional and supportive."[8] Indeed, this was the role that the Worthy Master of the Tennessee State Grange, William Maxwell, apparently envisioned for female Grangers when he declared in his annual address of 1875, "We admit woman that we may realize the benefit of her influence; that we may thereby become better men, and that we may encourage and aid her in erecting a standard of morality and conduct for man which will fit him for companionship with woman in life."[9]

Few southern African Americans joined the Grange. Dudley W. Adams, Master of the National Grange, stated in 1873 that "[t]he [Grange] Constitution is silent in regard to color. . . . If a Grange chooses to admit Negroes it may do so. . . . The matter is purely a local one." Some local Grange chapters in the northern uplands of Louisiana admitted members of both races, and in Alabama the organization eventually chartered some segregated black chapters.[10] These cases proved exceptional, though. More generally, noted one historian of the southern Grange, "[t]here seemed to be a strong tie between the Ku Klux Klan, intimidation of the Negro, and Grangers." A probably incomplete list of states where prominent Grange leaders maintained connections with the Klan includes Georgia, Mississippi, and South Carolina.[11]

Historians have painted a somewhat murky portrait of the Grange as an agent of agrarian reform. Edward Ayers, for example, has noted that "the Grange sometimes fostered radicalism as well as conservatism."[12] Lawrence Goodwyn portrayed the Grange as essentially a conservative organization while crediting it with helping to "lay the first fragile foundations of class consciousness in the nation's farming regions."[13] Thomas Woods has contended that the Grange "originated as a radical organization based on an evolving ideology that combined elements of Jeffersonian republicanism with the aggressive liberalism of the Jacksonian period and a new desire to contain individual liberty through legislative controls on monopoly capitalism." But, Woods argued, "the truly radical energy of the Grange had been largely expended by 1875," and subsequently the organization's "liberal republican critique of capitalism . . . was largely abandoned as leadership changed hands."[14]

Despite embodying this odd mix of radicalism and conservatism (which varied from state to state), the Grange did, as Woods has noted, articulate an antimonopolist ideology that depicted merchants, manufacturers, and railroad companies as greedy capitalists who "had combined to exclude competition and demand an unfair share of the worth of the farmers' labor in exchange for goods and services."[15] Like their brethren elsewhere, southern Grangers identified middlemen and monopolists as their enemies and denounced what they perceived as unfair business practices such as usury and speculating in crop futures. In 1874 the National Grange's Declaration of Purposes asserted that "we must dispense with a surplus of middle-men—not that we are unfriendly to them, but we do not need them. Their surplus exactions diminish our profits."[16] Later that year the *Georgia Grange*, the organization's official monthly publication in that state, expressed much the same sentiment: "The Patrons will seek, as far as practicable, to bring the producer to the door of the consumer, and thereby do away with a large number of agents and drummers, not because they dislike them, but because they have no use for them." The editorial also declared that "[t]he Patrons of Husbandry oppose none but monopolists."[17] Monopolies, suggested the National Grange's Declaration of Purposes, tended "to oppress the people and rob them of their just profits."[18]

The Grange in the South and elsewhere expressed similar producerist values concerning business practices such as usury and crop speculation. At the annual session of the Mississippi State Grange in September 1875 one delegate introduced a resolution declaring that any Granger found guilty of practicing usury in dealings with a Grange brother or sister would face expulsion.[19] During the same year the agent for the Missouri State Grange succinctly expressed the Patrons' attitude toward those who gambled in crop futures when he denounced them for manipulating the laws of supply and demand and hence the price of agricultural products to the detriment of farmers.[20]

Grangers sought to put their rhetoric into practice through cooperative enterprises. These included efforts that would allow Patrons to purchase farm implements and other necessities at a discount as well as agencies that would allow farmers to sell directly to consumers without interference from the maligned middlemen. Initially, most of these enterprises operated on the state agent plan, whereby Grangers would conduct their transactions through an agency that received a small commission. The Patrons of Kentucky and Tennessee, for example, established an agency in Louisville in the mid-1870s that allowed Grangers to buy farm implements and machinery at discounts ranging from 10 to 37 percent off the retail price. In return for these savings they paid a 1 percent commission to the agency.[21]

The success of Grange state agencies proved brief, though. Regular merchants, possessing more capital and business acumen than Grangers, fought the cooperatives by underselling them. Moreover, Grange cooperatives could not sell on credit due to their small reserves of capital, although the Patrons' opposition to the concept of credit purchases meant that Grange agencies would have been unlikely to do so anyway. Nevertheless, especially as the net supply of currency tightened, this policy prevented many cash-poor Grangers from using the organization's agencies. Management that ranged from ineffective to downright unscrupulous also took its toll, as in 1874, when the treasurer of the Missouri State Grange squandered $20,000 on speculative investments, forcing severe cutbacks in cooperative enterprises. The North Carolina and Mississippi State Granges both chose Farley and Company of New York as their state agent, only to discover that the company was fraudulent.[22]

By the mid-1870s the mounting failures of Grange cooperatives, including several state agencies, led the National Grange to begin supporting the establishment of cooperative enterprises modeled after the Rochdale system. Under this system, pioneered by British textile weavers in 1844, members raised the capital for the establishment of cooperative associations by purchasing stock. In order to allow as many members as possible to participate and to keep any member from assuming too large a role some associations set limits as to how many of the fixed number of shares any member could purchase. Many also operated on the principle of one person, one vote, regardless of the number of shares owned. Once established, the Rochdale cooperatives would distribute any profits in the form of quarterly dividends. Rochdale stores, however, sold goods at retail prices on a cash-only basis, thereby excluding cash-poor farmers, just as Grange state agencies had.[23]

The Grange also established cooperative marketing associations under the Rochdale model, but the limited amounts of capital raised under this system proved insufficient for the success of such enterprises.[24] The Georgia State Grange took a somewhat different approach when it organized the Direct Trade Union (DTU) in 1874 to facilitate direct trade between southern cotton farmers and British textile manufacturers. Stock in the enterprise, available only to Grangers, sold for ten dollars per share. In some ways the DTU foreshadowed the Southern Farmers' Alliance's subtreasury plan minus the governmental role: DTU members could borrow money from the association and choose to withhold their crops from the market or forward them for immediate sale. The DTU seemed promising and soon fielded agents in Liverpool, England; Norfolk, Virginia; Charlotte, New Bern, and Raleigh, North Carolina; Madison, Conyers, Savannah, Griffin, Macon, Augusta, and Rome, Georgia; and Mobile, Huntsville, and Decatur, Alabama. The DTU went bankrupt, however, in 1876 amid charges of mismanagement and disobedient agents.[25]

Among the many failed Grange cooperatives stood one notable success. The Texas Cooperative Association, based in Galveston, began operation in 1878 under the Rochdale plan. It supplied cooperative stores (155 by 1887) on a wholesale basis. It paid regular dividends and survived two depressions before it finally folded in 1900. While the Grange cooperative movement could not boast of such success overall, it nevertheless provided a model for subsequent, more ambitious cooperative efforts by the Farmers' Alliance, especially in Texas, where that organization too managed some success in cooperative enterprise, albeit more briefly.[26]

As much as they might have liked to, Grangers could not attempt to establish cooperative railroads. The resolutions passed by the Tennessee State Grange at its annual session in 1875 revealed the Patrons' ambivalence toward railroads. Grangers knew that they needed railroads to transport their produce and supported railroad development, but at the same time they refused to accept silently what they regarded as unfair treatment at the hands of railroad companies. Hence, Tennessee Grangers decided to

petition Congress to give "reasonable aid" to facilitate the "speedy completion" of the Texas and Pacific Railway, but only under certain conditions,
including "such safeguards" as would "protect the agricultural interests of
the country against unjust discriminations in the price of transportation."
Grangers from Davidson County (Nashville) submitted a petition com-
plaining of that very problem, prompting the Tennessee State Grange to
memorialize the state legislature for redress. The State Grange received
several petitions expressing another complaint against railroads that
prompted the body to recommend that Grange chapters "located in counties through which railroads pass, employ an attorney, at a stipulated sum,
to prosecute all railroads killing stock belonging to members of the Order." Then, just before adjourning, the Tennessee State Grange declared
its thanks to the several railroads that provided delegates with reduced
fares to and from the meeting site of Knoxville.[27]

But for all of the republican rhetoric emanating from Grange councils
and for all the Patrons' efforts to protect the fruits of their labor from
monopolists, middlemen, and railroad companies, the egalitarianism of
the Grange certainly possessed limits. By and large an organization of
landowning farmers, the Grange did not represent or defend the interests
of tenant farmers, sharecroppers, and farm laborers. The Grange viewed
farm laborers in particular as a class to be controlled rather than assisted.[28]

This attitude became quite evident in the Patrons' proclamations and
lobbying efforts regarding labor contracts and laws affecting the agricultural employer-employee relationship. Shortly after emancipation the
Freedmen's Bureau implemented a contract wage system that specified
minimum wages and covered provisions such as rations and time off for
illness. In the late 1860s each southern state enacted laws, either by statute
or in its constitution, that protected the rights of agricultural laborers, such
as laborers' lien laws. But as Democrats "redeemed" southern states from
Reconstruction and Republican rule, they altered those laws so as to give
landlords the upper hand in dealing with their laborers. While the extent of Grange responsibility for these laws is unclear, the organization
certainly favored and lobbied for them. In South Carolina, as historian
Stephen Kantrowitz has noted, "Grangers . . . worked to establish a common and well-regulated system of labor contracts." In 1875 the Mississippi
State Grange resolved to lobby the state legislature for "the enactment of

laws . . . as may define more clearly the relations between the employer and the employed, and such as will make it a misdemeanor, punishable by fine and imprisonment, to violate a labor contract legally drawn," as when a laborer left a plantation before the expiration of his contract.[29]

The Grange also sought the upper hand for landlords over merchants in dealing with tenant farmers. When the Georgia state legislature passed a law in 1873 that allowed merchants to deal directly with tenant farmers in granting liens, the Georgia State Grange led planters' efforts to have the law repealed. The repeal came just one year later, thus restoring to landlords the right to approve any credit arrangements made between merchants and tenants.[30]

As these lobbying efforts (and their results) demonstrated, the Grange held some political influence. That influence sometimes affected elections as well. In Arkansas, for example, although the Grange never put forth its own tickets, it nevertheless "was involved in all the political campaigns conducted during its period of strength." Granger votes often played a deciding role in local elections, and hence "candidates openly appealed to Patrons for their support."[31]

Nevertheless, the Grange claimed to be a strictly nonpartisan organization. "No grange, if true to its obligations," read the Order's Declaration of Purposes in 1874, "can discuss political or religious questions, nor call political conventions, nor nominate candidates, nor even discuss their merits in its meetings."[32] Eight months earlier, however, National Grange Chief Dudley W. Adams, while pointing out that "the discussion of partisan politics" was "forbidden" in the organization, added that Grangers were by no means ignorant of politics. He stated that they felt it "a duty" to "scan very closely the acts of our public servants" and "to see to it that the candidates of all parties be men of integrity, whose interest is the welfare of the people, and not political ring-masters." Adams justified this position in classic republican, producerist terms, asserting that "we, as producers, while we furnish food for millions, fight our nation's battles, defend its liberties in times of danger, should, of a right have an equal share as such in the making of these laws by which we are governed."[33]

Thus the Grange could hardly be deemed apolitical. The question became not *if* the organization would play a role in politics but rather what that role would be. The answer to this question varied from one state to another, depending largely upon the relationship between leading Grangers and the dominant party in a given state. Reconstruction complicated the situation in the South. As C. Vann Woodward noted, "the Grange, entering the South about 1873, had reached its peak and even started its decline in some states before Redemption had been accomplished–and therefore before Independent [or third-party] revolt could be seriously contemplated."[34]

Moreover, revolt against the Democratic Party, which assumed a position of dominance in most southern states upon Redemption (between 1870 and 1877 in various states), was the furthest thought from the minds of Grange leaders in many of these states. In Georgia, for example, the "wish" of the *Macon Telegraph and Messenger* that the Grange "may obtain accessions of strength from our intelligent statesmen" largely came to pass. Prominent members of the Georgia Grange included all three members of the so-called Bourbon Triumvirate (Joseph E. Brown, Alfred H. Colquitt, and John B. Gordon), which practically held a lock on the state's U.S. Senate seats and governor's office from 1872 until 1890, as well as future governor William J. Northen and future congressman Leonidas F. Livingston. (The latter two would be elected as "Alliance Democrats" in 1890 but remained loyal Democrats in the face of the Populist revolt.) These men represented the interests of businessmen and planters, not those of small farmers and laborers.[35]

Much the same could be said of the southern Democracy at the time. While some conflict existed between planters, merchants, and industrialists for control of the party and its policy, none of these groups had the welfare of small white farmers or laborers (and certainly not African Americans) at heart. Historian James Cobb has pointed to the existence in the postbellum South of "a common core of policies acceptable both to planters and to industrialists" that centered upon social control of the masses and the maintenance of "an adequate supply of low-cost labor."[36] To quote Woodward again, "[a]s a rule . . . the planter and industrialist Redeemers were able to compose their differences amicably and rule by coalition." This coalition favored financial and corporate interests, particularly those involving railroad promotion, merchandising, and banking, while cutting not only taxes but also government spending and hence public services. Even the Redeemers' low-tax policies tended to be regressive, and in most financial as well as class-related matters, Woodward observed, "[t]he Redeemer governments were regularly aligned against the popular side of the struggle."[37]

But as they were in Georgia, Grange leaders were sometimes more closely aligned with those Redeemer governments than with "the popular side of the struggle." In South Carolina, for example, the most prominent Granger was D. Wyatt Aiken, a member of the Executive Committee of the National Grange from 1873 to 1885 (chairman in 1875) and a Democratic congressman from 1877 to 1887. This planter's allegiance to the Democratic Party became evident during Reconstruction, when he participated in Red Shirt terrorist activities against Republicans and publicly (and successfully) called for the murder of a newly elected black Republican state senator. And although Aiken's newspaper, the *Rural Carolinian*, denounced "monopolies, rings, and middlemen" for their hostility to "the tillers of the soil," Aiken flatly rejected the invitation of South Carolina's Greenback-Labor Party chairman, W. W. Russell, to join the third party in 1882. By then, in fact, the declining South Carolina State Grange had begun holding joint annual meetings with the conservative, planter-dominated South Carolina Agricultural and Mechanical Society.[38]

Even though some Grange leaders disdained the GLP, the party offered a political outlet for the Patrons' producerist, antimonopolist views. Moreover, the party entered the South at a time when the Grange was clearly on the wane throughout the region. This decline, which occurred during the latter half of the 1870s, stemmed largely from the failure of the organization's cooperatives. As the dwindling number of Grange chapters became "little more than social and cultural clubs for rural residents," Grangers in some states began to look at the GLP with far more interest than did Aiken.[39]

## The Greenback Movement and the Greenback-Labor Party

The Greenback movement began as a protest against the national system of money and banking that had emerged by the mid-1870s. In particular, Greenbackers condemned the National Banking System, created by the National Banking Act of 1863, the demonetization of the silver dollar ("the Crime of '73" to Greenbackers), and the Resumption Act of 1875, which mandated that the U.S. Treasury issue specie (coinage or "hard" currency) in exchange for greenback currency upon its presentation for redemption beginning on 1 January 1879, thus returning the nation to the gold standard. Together, these measures created an inflexible currency controlled by banks rather than the federal government. Greenbackers contended that such a system favored creditors and industry to the detriment of farmers and laborers. Many of them also charged that this system worked to the advantage of the Northeast, then the nation's center of industry and finance, and to the disadvantage of other regions. The South in particular suffered from a lack of currency and credit. Nationally, the amount of money in circulation fell from $30.35 per capita in 1865 to $19.36 by 1880, the year after the Resumption Act took effect.[40]

The antimonopoly ideology of the Greenback movement bore some resemblance to that of the Grange. In the mid-1870s the National Grange had rejected the Greenbackers' demand that the U.S. Treasury Department issue more money; in fact, as one historian has noted, "many Grangers insisted that the government recall circulating greenbacks."[41] But as Grange cooperatives began failing, partly due to a lack of currency among members, and as the organization subsequently began to decline, its leaders reconsidered their stance on the currency issue. In November 1877 the National Grange adopted a resolution calling for the remonetization of silver and the repeal of the resumption clause of the Resumption Act.[42] Nearly two years earlier, at the fourth annual meeting of the Missouri State Grange, Worthy Master T. R. Allen had delivered what amounted to a Greenback manifesto:

At the risk of being accused of intermeddling with politics, of which I disclaim all intention, I will briefly say that all our efforts to put down monopoly will prove utterly futile, until we concentrate our forces on the foundation of all monopolies, to-wit: the money monopoly. It is that which makes all other monopolies possible. . . . [A]s long as the government persists in legislation recognizing nothing as a standard of value and medium of exchange but gold and silver [which was actually demonetized at the time], thus putting power into the hands of a few men to control the monetary affairs of the whole nation, we shall find that we fight monopolies in vain. . . . Why should a commodity [gold] be retained as the basis of all values and necessary exchanges, that at its

present standard of value does not amount to a tithe of our almost incompre-
hensibly vast productions?[43]

Other ideological similarities existed between the Grange and the
Greenback movement. For example, both the Grange and the GLP favored a national graduated income tax and proposed that public lands be
given to settlers rather than sold to land speculators. More generally, the
GLP expressed producerist, antimonopoly ideals that resembled those of
the Grange. The National (Greenback-Labor) Party platform expounded
at the party's first convention at Toledo, Ohio, in February 1878 declared
that reform of the monetary system was necessary in order to "secure to
the producers of wealth the results of their labor and skill, and muster
out of service the vast army of idlers who, under the existing system, grow
rich upon the earnings of others, that every man and woman may, by their
own efforts, secure a competence, so that overgrown fortunes and extreme
poverty will seldom be found within the limits of our Republic."[44]

The Greenback political movement may be divided into two phases.
The first unfolded between 1874 and 1877. Its strength lay primarily in the
midwestern and mid-Atlantic states. Drawing together agrarian reformers
and, in lesser numbers, labor reformers, the Greenbackers held a series
of conferences between 1874 and 1876. At a conference in Cleveland in
March 1875 they formed a new party, officially titled the "Independent"
Party but more widely known as the Greenback Party. At a party convention in Indianapolis in May 1876 the Greenbackers chose Peter Cooper of
New York as their presidential nominee. The party's Executive Committee later chose Samuel F. Cary of Ohio as its vice presidential nominee.
Cooper, an old Jacksonian (literally—he was eighty-five years old), was a
wealthy businessman and philanthropist, and Cary had been elected to
the U.S. House of Representatives in 1867 as an Independent Republican with support from the National Labor Union. (He served only one
term.) The Cooper-Cary ticket received only 81,737 votes nationwide, just
under 1 percent of all votes cast. Among the eleven states of the South,
only Arkansas and Tennessee sent a representative to the Indianapolis
convention, and only the Razorback State registered any votes for the
Greenback ticket—a meager 289.[45] Woodward suggested that the fact that
this early phase of the Greenback movement occurred before Redemption

had been fully accomplished explained why it "left the South pretty much unscathed."[46]

The same could not be said of the second phase of the Greenback political movement, which lasted from 1877 until 1884. The railroad strikes of July 1877 provided the impetus for this phase. These strikes spread from Martinsburg, West Virginia, to as far away as Galveston, Texas. They sparked violent clashes between strikers and federal troops or state militia in a number of cities. More than one hundred persons perished in the violence, and subsequently the American labor movement entered politics to an unprecedented extent.[47] Agrarian and labor reformers in Pennsylvania, a hotbed of strike activity in the summer of 1877, formed a state Greenback-Labor Party later that year. The Pennsylvania GLP's early victories included the election of a twenty-nine-year-old labor leader, Terence V. Powderly, to the mayor's office in the mining and industrial city of Scranton on 19 February 1878.[48] Three days later some 150 delegates responded to a call for a "national convention of labor and currency reformers" by meeting in Toledo, Ohio, and forming the National Party, better known as the Greenback-Labor Party.[49]

The greater presence of southern delegates at the Toledo convention as compared to the Indianapolis convention proved indicative of increased southern participation in the second phase of the Greenback political movement. Seven southern states sent representatives to Toledo: Arkansas, Georgia, Louisiana, South Carolina, Tennessee, Texas, and Virginia. (Oddly, Alabama did not send a delegate even though the Greenback-Labor movement was already well under way in the Birmingham district.) The most prominent southern delegate at Toledo, in retrospect at least, was Charles E. Cunningham of Arkansas, a State Grange officer who would play a major role in state and national third-party affairs over the next decade. The GLP composed an antimonopolist platform at Toledo that demanded that Congress issue "money adequate to the full employment of labor, the equitable distribution of products, and the requirements of business," a graduated income tax, the reservation of public lands for settlers rather than their sale to railroads or other corporations, an unspecified reduction in "the numbers [*sic*] of hours of daily toil," the establishment of national and state bureaus of labor and industrial statistics, the prohibition of contract prison labor, a ban on the importation of "servile labor" from

China, and that "no monopolies should be legalized."[50] The GLP then set its sights on the forthcoming state and congressional elections.

In several states the emergence of the GLP in 1878 would provide an early if limited test of the affinity of southern Grangers for the Democratic Party in the post-Reconstruction era. Not only did the GLP speak much the same antimonopolist, producerist language as the Grange, but its advocacy of inflationary paper currency held significant appeal for debt-ridden, credit-starved southern farmers in much the same way that the free coinage of silver would in the 1890s. In some areas of the South the GLP would also provide the first test of farmer-labor unity in politics.

## *The Grange and the Greenback-Labor Party in Texas*

All of these factors loomed significantly in Texas politics during the lifetime of the GLP. The party's national spokesmen expressed high hopes for the Lone Star State as the 1878 election season approached, and, relatively speaking, these hopes proved well founded.[51] Although the party achieved only limited success, it mounted a serious challenge to Democratic control that augured well for greater challenges to come.

In brief, the political proclivities of the Texas Grange may be summarized as follows: while the organization was growing and at its apex in the state, Worthy Master William W. Lang managed to hold the officially nonpartisan Grange within the Democratic Party despite growing political insurgency within the ranks. When the Grange began to decline sharply and swiftly in Texas after 1877, just as the Greenback-Labor movement was gaining momentum, Grange leaders became divided in their political affiliations, while many members, finding little relief in the Patrons' Rochdale cooperatives, embraced the Greenback cause.[52]

Ironically, the political ambitions of many Texas Grangers rested upon Lang himself, who refused to ever run for office as an Independent or Greenback candidate and seemed only a reluctant Democratic candidate. Grangers touted Lang for governor as early as 1874, prompting him to deny any gubernatorial aspirations. In 1875 Grangers began to promote him as a congressional candidate in the Fourth District, but once again Lang demurred. One year later Grangers pushed Lang as a candidate for the state legislature, and he finally acquiesced to their wishes. His candidacy proved successful. Although Lang received some criticism for violating the supposedly nonpartisan stance of the Grange, he joined at least eight other Democratic Grangers in the state legislature. The *Waco Daily Examiner*, the organ of the Texas State Grange, apparently did not worry about Grange rules against promoting political candidates; in the spring of 1878 it began another boom for Lang for governor. The Worthy Master declared that he would run only if he received the Democratic nomination. When the party nominated Texas State Supreme Court Chief Justice Oran M. Roberts, Lang spurned requests to run as an Independent candidate. Instead he chose to campaign for Roberts.[53]

Rumblings of third-party dissent in Texas began in 1876. Several rural Grange chapters nominated local Independent candidates that year. Marcus M. "Brick" Pomeroy, chief national organizer for the Greenbackers, appointed several organizers in Texas who formed Greenback clubs. In the Fifth Congressional District of south-central Texas G. W. "Wash" Jones ran as an Independent-Greenback candidate. Jones, a former Unionist who had subsequently risen to the rank of colonel in the Confederate army, had served as Texas's lieutenant governor as a Democrat in 1866–67. In his bid for a congressional seat Jones solicited and received Republican support. The GOP refrained from nominating a candidate in the Fifth District, and Jones garnered 46.5 percent of the vote.[54]

In 1877 the Greenbackers gained further momentum in Texas. In September they established a newspaper, the *Texas Capital*, in Austin, and one month later that city's Greenback club and workingmen's club joined in endorsing Independent candidates for local office. About half of these candidates won.[55]

The first sign of sympathy for the Greenback movement from the Texas State Grange came in January 1878. In annual session during that month the Patrons passed a resolution calling for the repeal of the Resumption Act, the remonetization of silver coinage, the payment of national bonds and interest in greenbacks, the repeal of the National Banking Act of 1863, and for greenbacks to be made "a legal tender for all debts and dues, private and public, exports and imports."[56] Also during this session leaders of the State Grange complained that members were "deserting to the Greenback party."[57] By 1880 the Grange had become nearly moribund in Texas (although it would experience a brief, limited revival in the mid-1880s), and some Grange chapters in east Texas merged with Greenback clubs.[58] Texas State Grange leadership, however, divided over the issue of supporting the Greenbackers. Lang remained a staunch Democrat, for which he eventually received the reward of a federal appointment as a consul to Hamburg, Germany. State Grange Worthy Secretary R. T. Kennedy, however, became active in the GLP, serving as chairman pro tempore at the Greenback-Labor state convention at Austin in June 1880. In January 1880 the State Grange passed a resolution endorsing the administration of Governor Roberts, but a motion to support the GLP failed by only two votes (twenty-six to twenty-four).[59] (Both of these resolutions, it might be noted, violated the National Grange's rules against involvement in partisan politics.)

The Texas Greenbackers, meanwhile, held two state conventions in 1878. The first, an "Independent Greenback" convention, met in Austin in March; it drew about forty delegates, mostly from central Texas, ten of them African Americans. The second, held at Waco in August, was the first official convention of the Texas GLP. By then the Greenback movement had spread from east and central Texas across the entire state, encompassing 482 Greenback clubs, seventy of them comprised of African Americans. Over the course of these two conventions the party developed a platform that made similar financial demands to those put forth by the State Grange in January. The Greenbackers also called for universal manhood suffrage without property qualifications and improved public schools, demands that resonated with African Americans in particular. The GLP also made several demands in the specific interests of labor, including the abolition of the contract system, which brought convict labor "into competition with honest labor," a ban on the importation of servile Asian labor, and a vague but appealing call for "cheap capital and well[-]paid labor in the place of dear capital and cheap labor."[60]

The Texas GLP, which reportedly had seven hundred clubs by October 1878, managed modest success in its maiden election campaigns that year. The party nominated W. H. Hamman for governor. Hamman had left the Democratic Party earlier in the year when its state convention refused to call for the issue of greenback currency that would be acceptable as payment for the nation's bonded debt. He finished a distant second in the election but well ahead of the Republican candidate.[61]

Wash Jones bore the GLP standard in the congressional race in the Fifth District, where the Farmers' Alliance was just starting to become active. Once again, he openly appealed for black and Republican votes and faced only a Democratic opponent. This time Jones won, receiving 51.7 percent of the vote. Although he possessed a reputation for honesty, Jones seemed an unlikely reformer. In 1867 Gen. Philip Sheridan, commander of the district that included Texas under the Military Reconstruction Act, removed Jones from the lieutenant governorship for being "an impediment to reconstruction." One year later Jones led a mob at Bastrop, Texas, that harassed black voters at the polling place, something that he probably failed to mention during his campaigns as a Greenbacker. During his four years in Congress, however, Jones proved faithful to the GLP platform. For example, he opposed a silver-coinage bill because he preferred that the federal government issue greenbacks instead, and he voted against the recharter of national banks (as did Texas Democrats). In addition to taking the Greenbacker position on these and other bills concerning currency and banking, in 1881 Jones introduced a number of petitions from constituents calling upon Congress to regulate interstate commerce, which encompassed railroads. One of these petitions came from the aforementioned R. T. Kennedy, prominent Greenbacker and secretary of the Texas State Grange.[62]

In addition to Jones's victory, the Texas GLP won ten seats in the state house of representatives in the elections of 1878, albeit none in the state senate. The ten house members served as a small farmer-labor bloc. In keeping with their party's platform, they opposed the use of convict labor outside of prisons, the dog tax, which burdened tenant farmers in particular, and the poll tax while favoring higher school appropriations, laborers' lien laws for artisans and mechanics, and an income tax that would allow for lower ad valorem taxes. But the GLP representatives found themselves, noted one historian, "too weak . . . to accomplish anything except in coalition with sympathetic Democrats."[63]

Perhaps this factor contributed to the decline that befell the Texas GLP over the next six years. Jones won reelection to Congress in 1880, and when he ran for governor as an "Independent-Greenback" candidate in 1882 he received the highest percentage of votes (40 percent) received by any non-Democrat between 1870 and 1894, although he still fell some

49,000 votes short of victory. He received fewer votes in a second attempt in 1884, however, and the GLP disappeared in Texas (as in most other states) after that campaign.[64]

Nevertheless, the GLP played a significant if brief role in Texas politics. It acclimated many farmers and laborers to the idea of turning to a third party to address their economic and political grievances; indeed, a parallel seems evident between Grangers turning to the GLP after their cooperative enterprises failed and many members of the Texas Farmers' Alliance later turning to the Populist Party after their cooperatives failed.[65] The GLP also fostered the farmer-labor unity in politics that characterized later third-party efforts in the state, most notably Populism. According to historian Alwyn Barr, "Tenants, heavily indebted farmers, and lesser numbers of organized laborers and businessmen interested in speculation or expansion formed the mass of Greenback voters [in Texas]."[66] The GLP also influenced the platforms of subsequent third parties in Texas in both demands and rhetoric. For example, Texas GLP platforms condemned the state's Democratic Party as no longer "democratic, but . . . a close corporation run by and in the interest of a syndicate of machine politicians" (1882) and declared that "the great mass of people, instead of being equals and sovereigns, have become slaves" (1884). Specific demands of the Texas GLP that would survive the party's demise included tighter regulation by Congress of telegraph lines and interstate commerce and the regulation of railroad freights by the state legislature.[67]

Finally, the GLP brought forth many of the leaders of late-nineteenth-century farmer-labor politics in Texas. Three prominent examples suffice to illustrate the point. Dr. J. D. Rankin served as chairman of the Texas Greenback state convention at Fort Worth in June 1882. He ran for Congress on the Republican, Prohibition, and Liberal tickets in 1886 and subsequently became active in the Union Labor and Populist parties.[68] Jerome C. Kearby, a prominent lawyer who would defend Knights of Labor leaders in court after the Southwest strike of 1886, ran in 1880 as a Greenback-Labor candidate for Congress in the Third District. After relocating to Dallas he ran again in the Sixth District four times between 1882 and 1894 and ran for governor in 1896 as a Populist.[69] Finally, William E. "Bill" Farmer, a native of Georgia, moved to Mineola, Texas, at age twenty-one in 1872 and took up the occupation that bore his name. He joined the Grange in 1873, played a prominent role at the state Greenback convention in 1882, became a Knights of Labor leader after joining that organization in 1885, and joined the Farmers' Alliance in 1886. After the demise of the GLP he became actively involved in just about every third-party (or even fourth-party) movement that emerged in Texas during the next two decades. His career included bids for Congress in 1886, 1888, and 1896.[70]

## The Grange and the GLP in Arkansas

In some ways the story of the GLP in Arkansas resembled its story in the Lone Star State. As in Texas, Arkansas Grange leaders divided over whether to support the third party, while many Grange members (or former members) supported the GLP. And while the GLP achieved less success in Arkansas than in Texas, it nevertheless played a similar pioneering role in the state's farmer-labor third-party movement.

John T. Jones and Simon Hughes ranked as Arkansas' most prominent Grangers. Jones had been a cotton planter in the state since the mid-1830s, twice served as a district judge, and was a Democratic U.S. senator-elect in 1866. (The Senate refused to seat him and the state's other senator-elect, Augustus H. Garland, since Arkansas was still "unreconstructed.") From the time that he contacted Grange founder Oliver H. Kelley about establishing chapters of the organization in Arkansas in June 1872, Jones served as the leader of the Grange movement in the Razorback State. Jones held the title of Worthy Master of the State Grange from 1872 until 1877, and during the last two of those years he also served as the Master of the National Grange. Hughes had once been an agricultural wage laborer, but he had become a successful lawyer by the early 1870s. The financial rewards of that profession allowed him "to engage in extensive planting interests on the side." In 1874 he won election to the office of state attorney general. Hughes succeeded Jones as the Worthy Master of the State Grange, a position that he held for two years.[71]

Both of these men remained staunch Democrats as the Greenback movement entered Arkansas in 1876. Hughes, in fact, unsuccessfully sought the Democratic nomination for governor that year. He did not officially involve the Grange in his campaign, but he drew upon Grange support.

Two years later Hughes tried again for the gubernatorial nomination, and Jones sought a U.S. Senate seat as a Democrat. By then the Arkansas State Grange no longer had the membership to be a force in state politics. Hughes remained politically active, however, and eventually served as the Democratic governor of Arkansas from 1885 to 1889.[72]

In contrast to Jones and Hughes other leading Arkansas Grangers figured prominently in the Greenback movement. Grangers comprised the vanguard of Arkansas Greenback club organizers. Charles E. Tobey, an officer in the State Grange, one of the state's first Grange organizers, and editor of the *Arkansas State Grange*, organized a number of Greenback clubs and promoted the Greenback "soft money" doctrine. When a small contingent of Arkansas Greenbackers held what they deemed a "state convention" in Little Rock on 12 September 1876, Charles E. Cunningham, another active Granger, presided. Cunningham also sponsored a resolution passed by the State Grange at its annual meeting in 1878 that placed the organization's stamp of approval upon the essence of the Greenback platform. As for the rank and file of the Arkansas Grange, one historian has averred that "former Grangers probably constituted much of the Greenback voting strength in the state."[73]

But that voting strength never amounted to much in what had been, since Arkansas' admission to the Union in 1836, "the most solidly Democratic state in the solid South," in the words of one scholar.[74] The GLP never elected a congressman or state officer in Arkansas and at its peak in 1878 elected only 7 of 124 state legislators. The state Democratic convention co-opted much of the Greenbackers' inflationary, soft money platform that year only to reverse that position shortly after the elections. Subsequently, the Arkansas Democracy consistently attacked the GLP as a threat to white supremacy and an adjunct to the Republican Party, a charge that gained some credibility in light of unsuccessful efforts at fusion between the two anti-Democratic parties in Arkansas.[75]

But as in Texas, the GLP blazed some important trails in Arkansas. The party drew support from the state's thin ranks of organized labor; later the Knights of Labor would figure prominently in third-party politics in Arkansas.[76] African Americans, particularly in Little Rock, played a significant role in the GLP, as they subsequently would in the state's Union Labor Party (ULP). GLP-Republican fusion efforts led to ULP-Republican fusion efforts that attracted significant support from Arkansas farmers and laborers of both races. The GLP drew its heaviest support in northwestern and particularly southwestern Arkansas, rural areas where farmers had to contend with rocky, unproductive soil. Farmers in both of these portions of the state continued to engage in third-party insurgency after the GLP's demise in conjunction with miners in the western Arkansas coalfields. Finally, Grange and Greenback leaders such as Tobey and Cunningham would remain active third-party leaders. The latter, who ran unsuccessfully for Congress as a Greenbacker in 1882, accepted the gubernatorial nomination of the Agricultural Wheel in 1886, and in 1888 the national ULP nominated him for vice president.[77]

## Farmers, Coal Miners, and Greenback-Independent Politics in Alabama

Grange support did not play a key role in the emergence of the GLP in every southern state in which the party achieved some strength. The GLP developed a great deal of support in Alabama despite only tenuous ties with the Grange. An early historian of the agrarian revolt in that state asserted that the GLP "grew out of the soil of Grangerism," while a later account stated that many Alabama Grangers "retreated" into this third party.[78] But another historian pointed to close ties between the Grange and the Democratic Party during and shortly after the "redemption" of Alabama from Republican rule, which occurred in 1874.[79] Undoubtedly, some truth lies in both of these assessments of the political leanings of Alabama Grangers—some became Greenbackers, while others remained Democrats (or, in the northern Alabama hill country, Republicans). But the evidence does not point to Grangers playing a significant role in forming or leading the GLP in Alabama.[80] Instead, the Alabama Greenback movement, to a greater extent than its counterparts to the west, represented a disparate group of farmers and laborers.

Northern Alabama was the heart of the state's Greenback and Independent movements. The two groups merged for district and state elections and differed little except in name. In his study of the hill country regions of Georgia, Alabama, and Mississippi, historian Michael Hyman found that anti-Redeemers usually waged Independent (or Independent Democratic) movements in predominantly white areas but rallied under the Greenback banner where black support was necessary. But hill country Independents often expressed Greenback views.[81]

Coal miners in the Birmingham district formed Alabama's first Greenback-Labor clubs. Their organizing efforts began in 1877 and resulted in twelve of these clubs by August 1878 and sixteen by fall of 1879 in Jefferson County. For these miners the GLP initially doubled as a political party and a labor organization, although the Knights of Labor would soon assume the latter role. Two GLP candidates for the state legislature from Jefferson County ran respectably in 1878, each receiving 43 percent of the vote. One of these candidates, H. J. Sharit Sr., ran for the legislature again in 1880 on a hybrid Independent Democratic–Republican–Greenbacker ticket and, after campaigning heavily in mining communities, was elected by the slim margin of seven votes. Sharit, a blacksmith and a farmer, served as an officer of Knights of Labor Local Assembly 1179 of New Castle and was, according to another local Knights officer, "a thorough Greenbacker" despite having run on this odd sort of fusion ticket.[82]

Alabama's GLP achieved its greatest strength, however, still farther north in the Tennessee Valley. In November 1878 voters in this part of the state elected GLP candidate William M. Lowe as congressman from the Eighth District. They reelected him two years later, although Lowe had to contest the election before being seated for his second term. Farmers dominated the party in this largely rural portion of the state, where Greenbackers evinced more concern with local political disputes than with their party's soft money doctrine. Such local disputes had a long history in this part of Alabama; they included quarrels between antebellum Whigs and Jacksonian Democrats and between Union loyalists and Confederates. In Lawrence County, a GLP and later a Populist stronghold, hostilities continued through Reconstruction between Bourbon Democrats and radical Republicans of both races. In the late 1870s many of these Republicans, still clinging to their belief in the free labor ideology and biracial class politics, became GLP organizers.[83] Biracialism also characterized the GLP in the Birmingham district, although Greenback-Labor clubs were segregated.[84]

The Alabama GLP made efforts at bridging the gap between farmers and laborers as well as the gap between the races. The Greenback miners of the Birmingham district tried to appeal to and organize farmers, telling them that the convict lease system and "pluck-me" company stores hurt farmers as sellers of produce by reducing miners' purchasing power. (The term "pluck-me" referred to the stores' excessively high prices, which "plucked" workers of their wages.) The GLP invited farmers' clubs and workingmen's groups to its state convention in 1880, where it incorporated the miners' greatest grievance into its platform by including a plank denouncing the convict lease system and demanding its repeal.[85] A miner from New Castle subsequently enthused in a letter to the *National Labor Tribune,* "The Bourbons are a dead cock in the pit hereabouts, and the Greenbackers will live to crow at their funeral."[86]

In the summer of 1880 the Alabama GLP waged its first gubernatorial campaign. The party nominated Rev. James Madison Pickens of Lawrence County, a Confederate veteran, Disciples of Christ preacher, publisher of religious journals, farmer, and educator who expressed great sympathy for "the oppressed and downtrodden sons of toil." Pickens stumped the state with the party's presidential nominee, James B. Weaver of Iowa, and became openly disgusted with the unscrupulous tactics of Alabama Democrats, particularly their "bulldozing" of African Americans in the Black Belt. ("Bulldozing" meant using violence and intimidation to coerce voters, before secret ballots were in use, or to prevent them from voting at all.) The Democrats' use of bulldozing and fraud certainly helped explain why Pickens received only 24 percent of the votes cast (or counted) in the gubernatorial election in August. Pickens ran against only one opponent, Democratic incumbent Rufus W. Cobb, who had been elected without opposition two years earlier.[87]

After his lopsided defeat Pickens publicly denounced Alabama Democrats for their rather undemocratic conduct in the state elections, campaigned for William M. Lowe in the congressman's bid for reelection, and made plans to begin publishing a Greenback newspaper during the following year. Pickens would be denied the chance to fulfill these plans, however; in February 1881 one of his neighbors shot him to death. Although the shooting was never proven to be politically motivated, a recent study of the case convincingly concludes that the reverend was "the target of a political assassination in 'one of the most atrocious and cowardly crimes ever committed' in Alabama." Unfortunately, the slaying of Pickens marked neither the first nor the last time that southern Democrats would take such drastic measures to silence a prominent political opponent.[88]

Despite the tragic fate of Pickens, the Alabama GLP peaked in the state elections of 1882. The party nominated James L. Sheffield, an old Jacksonian Democrat from the Upcountry county of Marshall, for governor. The state Republican Party endorsed Sheffield and the rest of the GLP state ticket.[89] Sheffield received 31 percent of the vote, the best showing made by any non-Democratic gubernatorial candidate in Alabama between 1876 and 1892.[90] One black Republican attributed Sheffield's defeat to "every species of fraud that depraved human ingenuity could devise" in the Black Belt, including "the counting out system."[91] Historian Sam Webb gives some credence to such a charge, suggesting that Sheffield might have won had it not been for the gross manipulation of the African American vote in the Black Belt.[92] Twenty-two Greenbackers or Independents won election to the state legislature in 1882, nearly all from northern Alabama. The Greenback-Independent victors included at least one African American, a man named Williams from Madison County, where the population was split evenly between whites and blacks.[93]

Despite this modest but promising success the GLP fell apart in Alabama after 1882 just as it did almost everywhere else. The death of party leader William M. Lowe in October 1882 contributed heavily to the demise of the third party in Alabama. Lowe had been a Democrat until that party denied him its Eighth District congressional nomination in 1878. After his death many of the white Democrats who had followed Lowe into the GLP apparently returned to their old party, especially as Republican-GLP fusion provided fodder for Democratic race baiting. (Despite Lowe's perhaps opportunistic conversion to the GLP, he did prove faithful to the party's platform in Congress. After the Resumption Act took effect in 1879 Lowe joined other Greenback congressmen in trying to pass legislation that would have made greenback currency legal tender for funding the national debt.)[94]

Shortly after Lowe's death the Democrats narrowly regained his former congressional seat. In 1884 there would be no Greenback-Independent state ticket or congressional candidates in Alabama. The third party did, however, retain local strength in a portion of northern Alabama ranging from Jackson and Lawrence counties on the north to Walker and Shelby counties on the south.[95] In many of these counties the GLP would yield directly to the Union Labor Party. Furthermore, all six of the counties that

Sheffield officially carried in 1882 registered majorities for the third-party gubernatorial candidate at least once between 1892 and 1896, two did so twice, and three did in all three of those elections. Three other counties in which Sheffield officially received between 42 and 47 percent of the vote— Coosa, Cullman, and Marshall, all located in the hill country—all landed in the third-party column every time from 1892 to 1896.[96]

## The Independent Movement in Northern Georgia

While the GLP's success in Alabama would not be replicated in the state to the east, a strong Independent movement developed in northern Georgia during the 1870s. In 1874 fourteen Independents (or Independent Democrats) won election to the state legislature. These included representatives from the northern to middle Georgia counties of Clayton, Gwinnett, Jackson (which elected two Independent representatives), Madison, McDuffie, Newton, and Rockdale. By 1878 the state legislature included some ninety Independents.[97]

Northern Georgia also elected two Independents to Congress. The western half of the Upcountry (Seventh District) elected William H. Felton of Bartow County in 1874, 1876, and 1878, while the eastern half (Ninth District) elected Emory Speer of Athens in 1878 and 1880. Felton was a physician and a minister, and he owned a farm, although his enemies scoffed at his efforts to portray himself as a farmer by dubbing him "Phelton: Preacher, Physician, Politician, and Pharmer." Speer, elected at age thirty, was a lawyer and had served as state solicitor general from 1873 to 1876. He had been a leading crusader against corporate privilege in Athens, particularly the granting of tax exemptions to corporations or companies.[98]

Felton and his wife, Rebecca Latimer Felton, not only were the most famous husband-and-wife political team in Georgia history but were also the leading opponents of the state's Bourbon Democrats during the last quarter of the nineteenth century. While the doctor ran for and held various political offices, his wife directed his campaigns, actively joined him in reform movements such as the temperance crusade and the campaign to abolish convict leasing, and brandished one of the sharpest political pens in the state. Her published letters to newspaper editors, which often appeared under various pseudonyms, led the *Savannah News* to accuse her

in 1879 of "step[ping] out of her proper sphere" and to suggest, "If her husband cannot or will not restrain her ambition to enter the political arena,
the press should." By then some Georgia Democrats, among them New
South spokesman Henry Grady, had come to view Rebecca as the more
intelligent half of the Felton team. Both Feltons, however, would prove to
be committed reformers in the years ahead.[99]

Whether or not he was the brainier half of the Felton team, the doctor
certainly spoke the producerist language. While campaigning in 1874 he
declared that farmers and mechanics were being robbed by a wasteful
and corrupt government and that they needed to "take the reigns [*sic*] of
government into their own hands, hurl the public plunderers from power
and elect men to office who will be *servants* of, and represent, the whole
people."[100] Rhetoric of this sort led Woodward to suggest that "[t]o a certain extent [the] early Independents [of Georgia] seem to have been influenced by the Granger movement."[101] While such an assertion would fit
with patterns of Grange-to-Greenback continuity seen in southern states
such as Arkansas and Texas, the link between the Grange and the Independent movement in Georgia seems less certain. The leaders of the Georgia
Grange, as we have seen, remained staunch Democrats. While Felton publicly supported the Grange, neither he nor Emory Speer ever joined the
organization, nor is it likely that their many African American supporters
did.[102]

Felton never joined the GLP either; he turned down an invitation from
Georgia Greenback organizer Ben E. Green of Dalton (in Felton's district)
to join the new party in 1878 even while admitting that he agreed with
its platform.[103] Indeed, Felton sounded like a Greenbacker in Congress in
November 1877 when he advocated repeal of the Resumption Act.[104] Felton decried the act as "class legislation" designed to make "monopolists,
corporationists, national bondholders and the money changers [into] . . .
the unchallenged lords of the country." He denounced corporations for
engaging in "unhallowed and fraudulent combinations to rob agricultural,
manufacturing, mining, and all the wealth-making industries of their legitimate rewards." He condemned the nation's banking and monetary system
as "a deliberate conspiracy on the part of the creditor class to rob, defraud
and impoverish the debtor class." The demonetization of the silver dollar
and the soon-to-be-implemented policy of resumption, Felton thundered,

"were as unjust and wicked as the labor strikes which have recently star-
tled and alarmed all good citizens." Like many Greenbackers, Felton railed
against New York and New England bondholders, denouncing New York
Republican congressman Samuel Chittenden, a defender of resumption,
as a "[S]hylock."[105]

Despite having waged battles against corporate privilege in Athens
Emory Speer essentially became a Republican in all but name in Congress.
He served as a protectionist member of the House Ways and Means Committee and helped to draft the tariff bill of 1883, which the *Atlanta Constitution,* a Democratic but not antitariff newspaper, denounced as "an out-and-
out fraud" and "indirect and outrageous taxation."[106] Speer lost his second
bid for reelection in 1882 to Democrat and future governor Allen D. Candler, whose Civil War injury left him with the popular moniker "The One-
Eyed Plowboy of Pigeon Roost." President Chester A. Arthur appointed
Speer as district attorney of the northern Georgia district in 1883 and as
judge of the federal court of the southern district of Georgia two years
later.[107] In the latter capacity Speer would receive praise from organized
labor and Populists for two notable prolabor rulings in cases involving
unions and became a well-known critic of chain gangs.[108]

Felton left Congress before Speer, losing his third reelection bid in 1880.
His supporters cried fraud, as suspicious voting "irregularities" occurred in
Rome (the county seat of Floyd) and perhaps Marietta (the county seat of
Cobb) as well, but he chose not to contest the election. He remained a
powerful figure in Georgia politics, though, as did Rebecca, and the pair
would eventually join the Populist ranks.[109] Although Populism would become strongest in the eastern Georgia Cotton Belt (the Tenth District), it
attracted a sizable following in the hill country as well. Populist candidates
for Congress would garner at least 40 percent of the vote in the Ninth District in 1892 and 1894, while the contest between Democrat John Maddox
and Populist Felton in the "Bloody Seventh" in 1894 ended in congressional hearings.[110]

## Daniel L. Russell and the Greenback-Labor Party in North Carolina

The GLP never amounted to much in North Carolina, due in part to the
continued strength of the Republican Party in that state after Reconstruc-

tion.[111] Nevertheless, the GLP did pull off one major success in the Tarheel State in 1878 with help from the GOP, and that victory foreshadowed joint third-party–Republican success that would occur on a larger scale in the 1890s. In fact, one man would play a central role in that success during both the Greenback and Populist eras: Daniel L. Russell.

Russell, along with G. W. Jones and William M. Lowe, became one of three southern Greenback-Labor candidates to be elected to the U.S. House of Representatives in November 1878. After announcing his candidacy under the GLP banner in the Third District, Russell subsequently received the Republican nomination as well, which helped him to defeat the Democratic incumbent by less than 900 of the 22,341 votes counted. A Wilmington lawyer who owned plantations in Brunswick and Onslow counties, Russell did not seem a particularly likely adherent to the Greenback doctrine. Nevertheless, according to his biographers, Russell "did genuinely embrace a number of reform causes, particularly those having to do with currency and the regulation of corporate enterprise." During his one term in Congress (he did not seek reelection) Russell proved to be a genuine Greenbacker. Like William H. Felton, he railed against "eastern millionaires" and "lawless capital" and "monopolists." Russell also proved to be somewhat ahead of his time in predicting that southerners would have to ally politically with westerners. When such political pronouncements became more common in the 1890s Russell would return to power, this time as a Republican in an era of North Carolina politics marked by cooperation (or fusion) between the GOP and the Populist Party.[112]

### *Foreshadowing Failure: Greenback Politics in Louisiana, South Carolina, and Tennessee*

Just as third-party stirrings and occasional successes augured well for future efforts in some southern states, however, the complete failure of third-party movements portended darkly for such efforts in others. The cases of Louisiana, South Carolina, and Tennessee all illustrate this point well. Obstacles that confronted Greenbackers and Independents in these states would continue to haunt agrarian and labor radicals during the remainder of the nineteenth century.

Initially, prospects appeared bright for the GLP and Independents in

Louisiana. Indeed, national GLP spokesmen expressed optimism for the party's chances in Louisiana in 1878, as they did for Texas as well. Such optimism seemed just as well founded for the former state as for the latter. Many Grange members or former members (though not leaders) flocked to the third-party banner in the northern hill parishes, the center of the Patrons' strength in the state. Laborers in New Orleans, meanwhile, formed a Workingman's Party with a Greenbacker agenda. The GLP and concurrent Independent movements evinced the same biracial composition (with whites in charge) in Louisiana as in Texas.[113]

This biracialism, however, prompted a ferocious barrage of intimidation, violence, and fraud from white Democrats in Louisiana, where a rather violent Reconstruction had ended only the year before when President Rutherford B. Hayes withdrew federal troops from the state.[114] Ominous signs of trouble for third-party candidates began to appear well before election day. In September 1878 a commissioner of the U.S. Circuit Court charged four Democratic clerks in New Orleans with "refusing registration to a colored man."[115] During the same month the *New York Times* reported that "[t]he reign of intimidation has already begun [in Louisiana], and the colored men have been given to understand that they must vote for the Democratic candidates or take the consequences."[116] Nor did white skin make men invulnerable to intimidation. In October the *Natchitoches People's Vindicator*, a Democratic newspaper, warned that it would be making (and perhaps publishing) a list of white men who failed to register to vote. "We regard and will treat all who do not aid us as [N]egroes," declared the *People's Vindicator*, "whether their skins be white or black."[117]

Unfortunately, white southern Democrats of this era seldom made idle threats. The supporters of the Independent "Country People's Ticket" in Tensas Parish, along the Mississippi River, learned this the hard way. This ticket represented white yeoman farmers, many of them Confederate veterans, and African Americans who opposed the Democratic Party machine that ran the parish. In October white mobs responded to the call of the parish's Democratic boss, Charles C. Cordill, to arm themselves and put an end to the Country People's Ticket, which, he suggested, might incite unwelcome behavior by blacks. Violent repression crushed the incipient biracial ticket before election day.[118] Campaign-related violence, an epidemic in Louisiana in 1874 and 1876, marred elections across the state in

1878 as well, claiming from thirty to fifty lives.[119] The violence continued well after election day. The most infamous incident occurred on 21 December. Two black men were sailing on the steamer *Danube*, bound for New Orleans, where they were to testify before a federal grand jury as witnesses regarding "election troubles." When the ship made a stop at Caledonia a constable presented a warrant for the pair's arrest, took them from the ship, and started in the direction of Shreveport. The pair never reached Shreveport; a mob seized and evidently lynched them.[120]

Such witnesses probably could have told juries a great deal. In New Orleans, for example, the Workingman's Party received only about 10 percent of the two thousand votes that a local newspaper had expected it to receive, in part at least because all of the registrars at the polls were Democrats. Violence (especially against blacks) and voting fraud would continue to be effective ways of squelching farmer and labor protest, at the polls and elsewhere, in Louisiana over the next two decades. The discouraging events of 1878 would not prevent Louisiana GLP leaders from later becoming Populist leaders, familiar obstacles notwithstanding, but they would face an uphill struggle.[121]

South Carolina's Greenback-Independent movement faced similar difficulties. As in Louisiana, Reconstruction ended in South Carolina following a bloody political campaign in 1876 and the removal of federal troops shortly after President Hayes took office.[122] When discontented whites and blacks began to unite under the Greenback banner just a few short years later, white Democrats readily revived the violent tactics of Redemption along with rhetoric about "Negro domination" and the specter of miscegenation. In 1882 the South Carolina GLP nominated Fairfield County farmer (and local Grange leader) J. Hendrix McLane for governor. The state's Republican Party endorsed his candidacy, as did President Arthur, who pursued a strategy of supporting southern GLP and Independent candidates in hopes of unseating Democratic officeholders. The Democratic terror machine responded quickly. When McLane tried to deliver an address at Winnsboro, thirty miles north of Columbia, a "crowd of Bourbon ruffians . . . attacked him before he reached the street, tore off his collar and pursued him through one of the corridors." The local Democratic boss, a former colleague of McLane, saved him from serious harm, but the mob succeeded in keeping McLane from speaking. McLane was lucky;

L. W. R. Blair, the Greenbackers' candidate for governor in 1880, was murdered for allegedly organizing and attending political meetings of "Radical Negroes" during the campaign of 1882.[123]

The worst incident occurred at Lancaster, about thirty miles south of Charlotte, North Carolina, following a speech by GLP Fifth District congressional candidate Col. E. B. C. Cash. After some black men roughed up a white Democratic newspaper editor who expressed his disapproval of Cash, several white men savagely responded by shooting six blacks, four of whom died.[124] The Democratic *Charleston News* blamed the bloodshed on "the whole brood of Greenback-Radical leaders and Independents, from the highest to the lowest. They and they alone are the criminals."[125] Even worse, insisted the *Charleston News and Courier*, the Greenbackers were promoting "social equality" between the races and "political miscegenation," loaded terms that alluded to the alleged sexual desires of black men toward white women.[126]

The intimidation, murder, and inflammatory rhetoric worked well. South Carolina Democrats also added a new weapon to their arsenal, a conveniently confusing "eight-[ballot-]box" law that required separate ballots and boxes for each of eight state offices. This law practically allowed registrars to disfranchise illiterate voters at will. This vast repertoire of dirty tactics helped Democrats outpoll the Greenback-Republican coalition statewide by a ratio of four to one and left that coalition "fractured . . . beyond repair."[127]

The Democratic destruction of South Carolina's Greenback movement amounted to a preemptive strike. Similar tactics would be revived (though, fortunately, with less bloodshed) to stamp out efforts at organizing black farm laborers in 1887.[128] Intimidation and loaded, gendered rhetoric worked well enough by then that murder need not be resorted to. And when the Populist revolt got under way in the early 1890s Governor Ben Tillman, who, like Georgia's William J. Northen, was an Allianceman but no Populist, successfully portrayed the Populists as representatives of "radical misrule" and "Negro domination." Tillman had participated in the political terror of 1876 and was still openly bragging about those despicable misdeeds in the early 1890s.[129]

In Tennessee the GLP faced less brutal but equally daunting obstacles. Historian Jeffrey Ostler, in his study of Populism in the Midwest, pointed

to the presence of a competitive two-party system in Iowa as a major
deterrent to Populist success in that state.[130] The same factor existed in
Tennessee during the brief lives of both the Greenback-Labor and Populist parties. In 1878 the GLP gubernatorial candidate managed barely 10
percent of the vote in a race against Democratic and Republican challengers. The Democrat won; two years later, with the Democrats split into
two factions over the state debt, the Republican candidate won the governor's race. The GLP candidate got buried in a four-man race, receiving
only 1.5 percent of the vote. The Democratic factions had failed to mend
their differences completely by 1882, but low-tax Democrat W. B. Bate
nevertheless emerged victorious in another four-man contest. Bate polled
about 119,000 votes, while Republican incumbent Alvin Hawkins received
92,000. Greenbacker John R. Beasley finished a distant third with 9,500
votes, and state credit Democrat Joe Fussell received a mere 5,000 votes.
This rough parity between the Democratic and Republican parties remained intact in Tennessee during the 1890s, and while the Populists fared
better in the Volunteer State than did the GLP, they never approached the
strength of the two major parties.[131]

### *The Southern Greenback-Labor Movement in Perspective*

What, then, are we to make of the Greenback-Labor movement in the
South, and, in retrospect, what did it portend for the future of farmer-labor
politics in the region? First, contrary to the notion of the "Solid South," a
term that had already come into use by 1878, the southern GLP held its
own in relation to the party's success elsewhere. In 1878, the GLP's peak
year of electoral success, the South sent three Greenbackers to the U.S.
House of Representatives. (Furthermore, Independent William H. Felton
of Georgia, reelected that year, had proven to be an advocate of Greenback ideology by then.) The more heavily populated Northeast elected
seven Greenback representatives that year, and the Midwest elected five.
No western state (save Texas) contributed to the congressional ranks of
Greenbackers.[132]

Moreover, the GLP showed that farmer-labor third-party politics held
genuine potential in certain parts of the South. This potential manifested
itself most clearly in Alabama and Texas, two states where the Populist

Party would later attract considerable support from farmers and laborers. The GLP showed some of this potential in Arkansas as well, but the lack of organized labor there made building a farmer-labor coalition difficult. This underscores an important point about the success that the GLP did achieve in the South: it occurred despite a low level of organization among farmers and a very low level of organization among laborers, suggesting that the political roots of southern Populism preceded organizations such as the Farmers' Alliance and the Knights of Labor.[133] The Grange, as we have seen, was already in decline throughout the South by 1878, while the Knights had just entered Alabama (where the organization contributed to GLP strength) at that time and would not become significant in the South until the mid-1880s. The Farmers' Alliance (and the kindred Agricultural Wheel) and the Knights would provide the organization and mobilization of farmers and laborers in the region that was largely lacking during the Greenback era.

If the modest successes of the GLP in the South hinted at greater third-party successes to come, however, the challenges that the Greenbackers faced (and often failed to overcome) foretold future difficulties. The obstacles that overwhelmed the GLP in Louisiana, South Carolina, and Tennessee also contributed to the abject failure of the Populist Party in those states. Even in southern states where the Greenbackers (and the Populists) fared better, they had to contend with charges of fostering "Negro domination" and with the Democrats' all too successful weapon of last resort, the denial of a "free ballot and a fair count." Southern Democrats used these tactics successfully in "redeeming" the South at the end of Reconstruction, and they seemed to perfect them in the face of subsequent challenges to their rule.[134]

Finally, the GLP (and, in some ways, the Grange) represented a growing sense of dissatisfaction and even resentment on the part of many southerners toward the nation's and region's rising commercial, corporate capitalist political economy. The grievances that spurred these movements included antimonopolist sentiment against railroads, corporations, and middlemen, a shortage of currency and credit, the convict lease system, and, for Greenbackers, a mounting sense of alienation from a Democratic Party that increasingly seemed to be ruled by elite "rings" in the interests of wealthy planters and industrialists, not those of small farmers and laborers.[135] While the Grange floundered and the GLP disappeared, the conditions that had spurred their initial growth did not. Thus, even as the Grange was fading into near oblivion, new farmers' organizations began to emerge with more radical critiques of what ailed the South and the nation. And as the loudly trumpeted industrialization of the "New South" proceeded, a national labor organization arrived to recruit its growing ranks of millhands, miners, railroad workers, and even farm laborers.

While many of the chieftains of the southern Democracy were perhaps glad to see the Grange fade away and certainly pleased to see the GLP collapse, their sense of relief proved premature. In fact, those organizations marked the first efforts at the collective articulation of farmers' and laborers' grievances, the organization of the aggrieved, and, in the case of the GLP, attempting to address those grievances through a third party. All of these efforts would intensify under the direction of new organizations, sometimes under the leadership of men who had played similar roles in the old ones. Further agrarian discontent and political dissent lay ahead, and organized labor would soon enter the fray.

# CHAPTER TWO

# Building the Southern Farmer and Labor Movements, 1878–1886

On New Year's Day, 1878, thirty-three men assembled at Crouse's Hall in Reading, Pennsylvania. They came from Massachusetts, Missouri, New York, Ohio, West Virginia, and, of course, Pennsylvania for the first General Assembly of the Noble and Holy Order of the Knights of Labor. All of the men represented local or district assemblies of this obscure, secret labor organization, which had been founded in Philadelphia just over eight years earlier. They met in order to establish a national organization, with a constitution, general office and officers, and organizers who could form assemblies in states and territories across the nation.

The delegates managed to accomplish all of these tasks in four days. They elected four officers—Uriah S. Stephens, one of the Order's founders, received the highest post of Grand Master Workman—and a five-man General Executive Board. The delegates also adopted a constitution and gave the Grand Master Workman the power to appoint organizers.[1]

The preamble of the Knights' constitution, known as the Reading platform, set the agenda not only for the Knights, which became the largest labor organization in nineteenth-century America, but for the agrarian movements of the next two decades as well. The Reading platform actually contained little that was new; it largely copied the preamble of the constitution of the Industrial Brotherhood of 1873–75, a labor organization whose members had included Reading delegates Robert Schilling and Terence V. Powderly. The Industrial Brotherhood's preamble in turn came largely from the platform expounded by the National Labor Union in 1866. Many of these principles could be traced even farther back to the Jacksonian labor reformers of the 1830s and 1840s.[2]

As subsequent developments demonstrated, however, these principles still resonated with millions of American laborers and farmers. The Reading platform warned that "the thorough unification of labor" was the only way to check "[t]he recent alarming development and aggression of aggregated wealth" that threatened to "lead to the pauperization and hopeless degradation of the toiling masses." The Knights, proclaimed the Reading platform, offered "a system . . . which will secure to the laborer the fruits of his toil." Specific demands encompassed by this system included the establishment of cooperative institutions, productive and distributive; the reservation of public lands ("the heritage of the people") for settlers rather than railroads and speculators; the repeal of all laws not bearing equally upon labor and capital; the adoption of measures to protect the health and safety of workers engaged in mining, manufacturing, and building; the enactment of laws compelling corporations to pay employees weekly in full and in lawful money; mechanics' and laborers' lien laws; the abolishment of the contract labor system on national, state, and municipal work; the substitution of arbitration for strikes; the abolishment of the convict lease system; equal pay for equal work for both sexes; the eight-hour workday; and the establishment and issue by the federal government of a national circulating medium (currency), without the intervention of private banks, that would "be a legal tender in payment of all debts, public or private."[3]

Many of the Knights' demands reappeared less than two months later when the National or Greenback-Labor Party issued its first platform at Toledo, Ohio. The GLP made, of course, a similar demand regarding currency, called for public lands to be "donated to actual settlers in limited quantities" rather than being granted to railroads or other corporations, called for legislation that would shorten the workday, demanded the prohibition of contracted prison labor, and, also like the Knights, called for the establishment of national and state bureaus of labor and industrial statistics.[4] The similarities between the two platforms were no coincidence. Strong connections existed between the Knights and the Greenback movement. Three of the Reading delegates (Schillings, Stephens, and Ralph Beaumont of New York) attended the Toledo convention. Richard Trevellick of Michigan, who lectured and organized for the Knights from 1878 until his death seventeen years later, served as temporary chairman of the Toledo convention. Powderly had already won election as the Greenback-Labor mayor of Scranton, and a number of other leading Knights had or soon would run for various offices as Greenbackers in Pennsylvania, New York, and Ohio.[5] By the year's end a similar connection would emerge between the Knights and the GLP in Alabama as well.

The Reading platform influenced still other major reform platforms of the late nineteenth century. Many of the Reading planks reappeared in the "Cleburne demands" promulgated by the Texas Farmers' Alliance in 1886, just before the agricultural organization swept across the South. As Texas Farmers' Alliance president Evan Jones noted in 1896, the Cleburne demands, with modification, served as the basis for the subsequent platforms of first the Southern Farmers' Alliance and then the Populist Party.[6] Again, the similarities between the Reading and Cleburne platforms could not have been mere coincidence. As historian Robert McMath has noted, during 1885 and 1886 the Knights and the Alliance possessed "such overlapping membership [in Texas] that the differences were almost moot."[7]

Indeed, given the similarities of their platforms, one would expect to find overlapping membership and a close working relationship between the Knights and the Alliance or other farmers' organizations. This would seem especially likely in the South. The region's heavily rural cast meant that, outside the handful of industrial cities in any given state, the Knights of Labor had to concentrate much of its recruitment effort on farmers, farm laborers, artisans, and mechanics in small towns and rural communities.[8] In the early 1880s neither the Knights nor the more strictly agrarian orders were well developed enough to provide a meaningful test of farmer-labor solidarity. By the middle of the decade, however, the organizations had developed enough of a base in the South that their forays into political and economic activity would provide suggestive if inconclusive tests of the affinity between farmer and labor movements.

These first tests of farmer-labor unity in the South would revolve around a series of railroad strikes in the Southwest. The strikes against Jay Gould's railroad empire during 1885 and 1886 presented farmers with the opportunity to support laborers in a battle with an organization against which both groups claimed grievances. These strikes also inspired political activism that survived the failure of the Southwest strike of 1886. In fact, while historians have argued that the outcome of that strike dimmed the future of farmer-labor politics through its harmful effects on the Knights of Labor, an examination of the specific localities affected by the strike suggests just the opposite: the strike actually served as a catalyst for farmer-labor third-party insurgency.[9]

## *The Knights of Labor Enter the South*

The Knights of Labor arrived in most southern states before the Farmers' Alliance or the Agricultural Wheel. Texas and Arkansas, the respective birthplaces of those two agricultural organizations and centers of railroad strike activity during the mid-1880s, were the lone exceptions. Texas farmers near the small town of Lampasas formed the Alliance in or around 1875, and the organization was slowly expanding in Texas by the time the Knights began organizing local assemblies in the Lone Star State seven years later.[10] A small contingent of Arkansas farmers formed the Agricultural Wheel near the town of Des Arc in February 1882, nine months before the Knights of Labor organized its first Arkansas assembly.[11] Not only did the Knights of Labor enter most southern states before the Alliance or the Wheel, but it also preceded those organizations in recruiting farmers and farm laborers.[12]

Using the powers conferred upon him by the Reading General Assembly, Grand Master Workman Stephens appointed seventy-nine organizers in 1878. Only four were southerners: Edward S. Marshall of Montgomery, Alabama; Michael Moran of Helena, Alabama; E. W. Conner of Rome, Georgia; and Peter Westgerand of Melrose, Florida. Conner only managed to organize one local assembly in Rome, which lapsed after about one year. Westgerand failed to organize any locals at all.[13]

Marshall and Moran proved more successful in Alabama. By the end of 1878 Marshall had organized two local assemblies in Mobile and another in Montgomery. The two Mobile locals were apparently "mixed," meaning that they consisted of members of various occupations. (The Knights barred only lawyers, doctors, stockbrokers, professional gamblers, bankers, and liquor dealers from membership, regarding them as "social parasites" in the "interdicted classes.") The Montgomery local, apparently a trade assembly, consisted of printers. Moran organized two local assemblies in the coal-mining town of Helena. At least one and probably both consisted of miners.[14]

During the first eight months of 1879 Stephens appointed eight more southern organizers, including three from Montgomery and two from Mobile. The Knights counted seventeen locals in Alabama that year, and the state became "the center of the Knights' southern activity until 1883." Most of the Alabama locals lay within the Birmingham district—Helena, Warrior Station, New Castle, Pratt Mines, Jefferson Mines, and Birmingham itself—and thus consisted chiefly or entirely of miners.[15] Other types of laborers belonged, though. H. J. Sharit Sr., who served as District Worthy Foreman of Helena-based District Assembly (DA) 29 and won election to the state legislature on an Independent Democratic–Republican–Greenbacker ticket in August 1880, was a blacksmith and a farmer.[16]

As in Pennsylvania and other northern states, strong connections emerged between the Knights and the GLP in Alabama in 1878. Like the Grange, the Knights of Labor professed to be a nonpartisan organization. In one of his first decisions after becoming the Knights' Grand Master Workman in 1879 Powderly proclaimed, "Our Order is above politics, and electioneering for any candidate in the Sanctuary [assembly lodge] must not be practiced."[17] Powderly himself was serving the first of three two-year terms as mayor of Scranton at the time and entertained hopes of winning a seat in the U.S. House of Representatives.[18]

Hence, Alabama Knights simply followed the trend set by their northern brethren in mixing union activity with politics. Most Greenback leaders in the Birmingham district became leading Knights as well. These included Sharit, Michael Moran, James Dye, and Willis J. Thomas, an African American. The connections between the GLP and the Knights in Alabama extended beyond Birmingham. In Montgomery Knights organizers Edward Marshall and Stephen Sykes began publishing a GLP newspaper, the *Workingman's Advocate*. In the only surviving issue the editors proclaimed, "Workingmen cannot consent to be the tools and underlings of the aristocrat Democrats, and to avoid this personal degradation, they must abandon the Democratic Party and unite with the Greenback Party, which warmly espouses the rights of the working classes. . . . The people must scourge the 'Ringites' out of power in the election of 1880, and run the State themselves." The newspaper also supported the candidacy of

Greenbacker James P. Armstrong for mayor of Montgomery. Armstrong had run unsuccessfully but respectably as a GLP congressional candidate in 1878.[19]

The early pattern of Knights organizing in Alabama also underscored the Order's close ties to the GLP. Of the nineteen local assemblies known to have existed in the state during 1880, ten were located in Jefferson County and another in adjacent Shelby County, centers of Greenbacker strength. Another local existed in Montgomery. The rest were in Mobile or its vicinity. Although this Black Belt city did not rank as a GLP stronghold, it did have a newspaper that was friendly to the third-party cause, and Greenbacker James L. Sheffield ran respectably in Mobile County in the gubernatorial election of 1882. The Knights first established Alabama locals beyond the Birmingham district, Mobile, or Montgomery in 1883 by chartering mixed local assemblies in Decatur and Gadsden. These northern Alabama towns, located, respectively, in Etowah and Morgan counties, lie in the area where the Alabama GLP claimed its greatest strength. Etowah County elected a Greenback-Independent candidate as its only representative in the state house of representatives in 1882, and Sheffield received more than 47 percent of the vote in Morgan County.[20] Thus, it appears that the GLP and Greenback clubs provided something of an organizing base for the Knights in Alabama.

Emerging in areas of Greenbacker strength, the Alabama Knights continued the GLP's efforts at organizing across the color line and building support among both city or town workers and farmers. Like the Greenbackers, however, who organized blacks and whites into segregated clubs, the Knights organized segregated local assemblies.[21] Some white Knights insisted upon this. In September 1880 William Wright, Master Workman of white coal miners' Local Assembly (LA) 1100 of Warrior (Jefferson County), informed Powderly that Warrior's African American local (LA 1376) had lapsed. Five members of the black local wanted to remain in the Order, but, Wright reported, they could not join LA 1100 because "some of the whites object to working in the same A. [assembly] with negro[e]s."[22] Powderly's reply evinced little patience for such prejudice. "[U]nder the laws of our Order," he wrote, "a brother no matter what his color is can visit any Local in the Order if he is clear and in good standing." "Can the wisest of us," Powderly asked, "tell what color *labor* is? I doubt it."[23]

Nevertheless, such prejudice persisted among the ranks of white Alabama Knights. In November 1883 the Master Workman of LA 2830 of Gadsden reported that African American men in the town were eager to be organized. He added, however, that some members of LA 2830 (an assembly of white men) had "misgivings" about blacks obtaining the same signs and passwords as those being used in the white assembly. "Could the Password given to them," he asked Powderly, "not be changed a little to prevent them get[t]ing admission to an Assembly [of whites] at work[?]"[24]

This letter also reported that "some miles from here [are] a number of farmers desiring connections with this order."[25] It is unknown if these farmers ever joined the Knights of Labor. If they did, they were probably not the first Alabama farmers to do so and were certainly not the last.[26]

As the Order began to expand in Alabama it also started to spread across the South. By 1883 Knights of Labor local assemblies existed in every southern state. The Knights counted one local in Florida and multiple locals in all of Dixie's other states. Texas and Tennessee led with seventeen each.[27]

In his seminal study *The Knights of Labor in the South*, which focused mainly upon the Southeast, Melton McLaurin contended that the Order began its organizing efforts in the region by recruiting urban workers, particularly skilled ones, first and then workers in the region's new industries, such as coal mining.[28] This pattern generally held across the entire South, although not without the occasional exception. In Tennessee, for example, coal miners in Rockwood formed the state's first local assembly, and in Mississippi the first Knights charter went to a local in the rural community of Back Creek. Arkansas' first local, Hot Springs LA 2419, initially consisted of carpenters and clerks—a mix of skilled and unskilled or semiskilled workers that typified the Knights of Labor.[29]

The Knights' early efforts among skilled urban workers in the South focused upon one group in particular: telegraphers. Beginning in 1881, telegraphers had their own district assembly (DA 45) within the Knights of Labor, and in 1882 DA 45 launched an aggressive national organizing campaign.[30] By the following year the Knights had chartered twenty-five local assemblies of telegraphers in the eleven ex-Confederate states. These included locals in Birmingham, Montgomery, Little Rock, Jacksonville, Atlanta, New Orleans, Charlotte, Charleston, Columbia, Chattanooga, Memphis, Nashville, Galveston, Houston, and Richmond. Most of these local assemblies collapsed, as did DA 45 itself, following the failure of a national telegraphers strike during the summer of 1883. Nevertheless, the telegraphers' recruitment efforts resulted in the formation of the first Knights of Labor local assemblies ever organized in Florida, North Carolina, South Carolina, and Virginia. In Georgia the Knights previously had chartered only one local assembly, the Rome local that lapsed in 1880. By April 1883 the Knights had chartered five telegraphers' locals in Georgia (in Augusta, Atlanta, Macon, Savannah, and Brunswick), more than in any other southern state. In Georgia, Virginia, and North Carolina the Knights' ranks extended beyond telegraphers by 1884, and the Order's headquarters in Philadelphia received inquiries of interest from Florida that year.[31]

Frederick Turner, the Knights' General Secretary, took notice of this increasing southern interest in the Order in his annual report in September 1884 and suggested that the Knights send "a good live organizer" to the South.[32] Accordingly, Terence V. Powderly embarked on a southern lecture and organizing tour in late January 1885. Powderly visited Richmond and Atlanta, made a number of stops in Tennessee, Kentucky, and Alabama, and visited New Orleans before concluding his tour in Mississippi. An ailing throat and exhaustion forced him to end the tour in mid-February, canceling planned appearances in Mississippi and Arkansas despite being scheduled to speak before the state legislature in the latter state. In keeping with the Knights' egalitarian creed, Powderly encouraged the organization of not only white men but of women and African Americans as well, with a modest degree of success. The tour itself was certainly a success; as a Powderly biographer has noted, it "contributed mightily . . . to southern interest in the Order."[33] That interest would soon be reflected in the number of local assemblies existing in the eleven southern states, which rose from 87 in 1884 to 317 the following year.[34] Still more growth lay ahead.

What did the ranks of southern Knighthood look like in 1885? The picture varied from one state to another. Throughout the region most of the locals were mixed. This classification fit over 80 percent of the locals in Virginia at the time. In Richmond, the center of the Order's activity in the Old Dominion, the Knights organized white cigar and cigarette makers (including an all-female local of the latter), typographers, iron molders, granite cutters, builders, machinists, and boilermakers. African American Knights in the city included tobacco factory workers, coopers, and various other laborers. Virginia workers organized by the Knights outside of Richmond by 1885 included millhands, farmhands and laborers, quarrymen, cotton screwmen, and coal miners.[35] By 1886 the Knights counted 173 locals in Virginia, a total surpassed in the South only in the much larger Lone Star State.[36]

Farther south, the Knights' membership in Georgia by 1885 included carpenters, typographers, railroad employees and car builders, cotton mill workers and others (white and black) in Atlanta, typographers and others in Savannah, and mechanics and farmers of both races in Athens. Evidence suggests that one or more of the three local assemblies in Athens was racially integrated, a rarity in the South and particularly in Georgia. Not many women belonged to the Order in Georgia at this point. LA 4394 of Roswell, north of Atlanta, included male and female employees of the Roswell Manufacturing Company, a textile mill. Atlanta's local assembly of mill workers (LA 4455) may have included women as well.[37]

Coal miners ranked as the most heavily represented workers among the Knights in Alabama and Tennessee in 1885. In both states the Knights organized miners of both races. In Alabama white and black Knights of Labor miners waged a largely successful pair of strikes during 1884 and 1885 against the Warrior Coal and Coke Company after the company brought Italian contract labor into the mines at reduced wages. In Tennessee local assemblies of skilled and unskilled workers existed in the cities of Chattanooga, Knoxville, Memphis, and Nashville. Female locals existed in at least the latter three cities and black locals in the latter two. Three mixed black locals and a white local that included cigar makers existed in Mobile, Alabama, and LA 716, a printers' assembly organized in 1878, still existed in Montgomery.[38]

Moving west, the ranks of Louisiana Knights in 1885 consisted chiefly of white mixed locals. Morgan City, however, had a black mixed local that included railroad workers. The Knights also had begun to make inroads among white railroad workers in the state, and ten locals existed in New Orleans, where the Knights had organized at least forty locals by 1890.[39]

The Knights also had established a solid base in Arkansas and, in particular, in Texas by 1885.[40] Before examining the development of the Order in these states, however, we should first consider the development of the agricultural organizations that preceded the Knights in each state. The history of these organizations and the Knights would become closely intertwined in both states.

## *The Origins of the Texas (and Southern) Farmers' Alliance*

The roots of the Texas Farmers' Alliance, which eventually became the National Farmers' Alliance and Industrial Union or the Southern Farmers' Alliance, apparently date back to 1875, although the precise year is uncertain. A similar organization began in New York at around the same time, although the order that became the National Farmers' Alliance (or Northern or Northwestern Alliance) originated in 1880 outside of Chicago. Neither the Northern nor the Southern Alliance would experience significant expansion until the latter half of the 1880s.[41]

The Texas Alliance began in Lampasas County, some fifteen miles north of the town of Lampasas, in central Texas. On 22 February 1878–the same date, coincidentally but fittingly, that the GLP held its national convention in Toledo–the county's Alliance chapters formed the Lampasas Grand County Alliance. During the next two months the Alliance also organized lodges (eventually known as subordinate or sub-Alliances) in adjacent Hamilton and Coryell counties. On 4 May 1878 delegates from these three counties organized what they ambitiously termed the Grand State Farmers' Alliance.[42]

Farmers and stockmen formed the Texas Alliance, according to historian Ralph Smith, "to clean up thieves, 'cattle kings,' and land sharks."[43] As McMath has noted, the Alliance also represented a response to "social disorganization" on the Texas frontier, where battles between Native Americans and white settlers ran rampant, as did feuds between whites with competing interests. More important, however, the Alliance represented the egalitarian, producerist values that the GLP and the Knights of Labor also embodied.[44]

Indeed, the affinity of many Texas Alliancemen for the GLP quickly became apparent. Lampasas, Hamilton, and Coryell counties all sat in the state's Fifth Congressional District, where Greenbacker G. W. Jones ran successfully for the U.S. House of Representatives in 1878 and 1880.

Lampasas County already had an active Greenback club by the time the county Alliance was formed, and L. C. Chavose, president of the Lampasas County and the Grand State Farmers' Alliances, was a Greenbacker. Under Chavose's leadership the State Alliance endorsed the GLP, albeit over the objections of some members. Jones's election to Congress did not allay the dissension over politics within the State Alliance, which fell apart in 1879.[45]

By then, however, W. T. Baggett, a Georgia native and a central figure in forming the Lampasas-based Alliance, had moved to Parker County in north-central Texas, where he replicated the organization in July 1879, "deleting only the political element from the Lampasas plan."[46] This proved easier said than done, though. As the order spread into adjacent Wise and Jack counties it soon developed strong ties with the GLP. Several men played prominent roles in both organizations, and by 1882 Alliancemen in these counties were openly supporting GLP candidates, who did well in Alliance strongholds that year.[47]

Like the Knights of Labor, however, the revived Grand State Farmers' Alliance resolved in August 1882 not to nominate or support candidates as "a distinct party," despite being heavily involved in Greenback-Labor politics. This resolution, coming just before an election season rife with Greenbacker and Independent candidacies, probably reflected a desire to protect the Alliance's growing membership; by then the organization claimed 120 sub-Alliances in 12 counties in north-central and northeast Texas.[48]

## The Knights of Labor and the Farmers' Alliance in Texas, 1882–1884

By November 1882 the Knights of Labor had issued charters to local assemblies in two of those counties, Palo Pinto (coal miners) and Tarrant (a mixed local in Fort Worth). The Knights chartered a local in another Alliance county, Cooke, in November 1883. This local, in the town of Gainesville, consisted of carpenters and laborers.[49] The Knights also organized locals in 1882 in three of the counties that Jones carried in the gubernatorial election of that year: Harris (Houston), Travis (Austin), and the less populated Navarro County, where the ranks of Knights would include farmers as well as laborers.[50] And although the Knights would not charter a local in Montague County until 1885, the *Montague Age of Progress,* a Republican-Greenback-Independent newspaper, urged Grangers, Alliancemen, Knights, and other laborers to unite in support of candidates against the Democrats in 1882.[51]

Uriah S. Stephens appointed two Knights of Labor organizers in Texas on 11 February 1879, Thomas DeLacey of San Antonio and Jerome H. Timlinson of Bryan.[52] Neither organized any assemblies. In the spring of 1882 Powderly appointed another organizer in Texas, C. R. Miller of Dallas, who delivered immediate results. On 19 May 1882 Miller organized the state's first local assembly, LA 1931 of Dallas. The membership of this mixed local included railroad workers, printers, carpenters, and general laborers, among others. It became one of the stalwart locals of the Lone Star State, remaining active for at least fourteen years. The Knights chartered fifteen more locals in Texas in 1882. In addition to LA 1931 and the other aforementioned locals the Knights also organized three locals in Galveston in 1882 (one consisting of telegraphers, one mixed local that included longshoremen, and another that included cotton workers of both sexes), two mixed locals in Sherman, and two mixed locals in Waco, one white and the other black. After that auspicious beginning the Knights grew slowly in Texas over the next two years. The Knights had twenty-two locals in Texas in 1884; despite the small increase since the end of 1882, that total still ranked second only to Tennessee's twenty-seven locals among the eleven southern states.[53]

At least the Knights were growing in Texas. The same could hardly be said of the Farmers' Alliance. By January 1884 the organization had chartered 152 sub-Alliances, but only 15 of them were known to be active. In an effort to breathe some life into the organization newly elected Alliance President W. L. Garvin appointed S. O. Daws as a full-time lecturer and organizer with the power to appoint suborganizers and sublecturers. Daws, a thirty-five-year-old Mississippi native who immigrated to Texas in 1868, had served previously as county organizer in Parker and Wise, two early Alliance strongholds. Daws, as sociologist Donna Barnes has noted, "immediately interjected a desperately needed element into the Alliance organization: a critical discussion of possible strategies to financially aid the farmer." When the Texas State Alliance met at Chico, Wise County, in February 1884 the delegates openly discussed economic strategies for the first time. The Alliance passed a resolution declaring that "we encourage the formation of joint stock companies in Sub and County Alliances for the purpose of trade and for the personal benefit of the members financially."[54]

This resolution, coming at a time when previously self-sufficient yeoman farmers were being sucked into what historian Steven Hahn has called "the vortex of the cotton economy," launched the Alliance cooperative movement and reversed the organization's sagging fortunes. County Alliances began organizing joint stock companies on the Rochdale plan (à la the Grange) and, more significantly, cooperative enterprises to market cotton, wheat, and livestock in bulk. The results proved mixed, but the cooperative movement energized the Alliance. Even when the cooperatives did not succeed, the difficulties that they encountered reinforced Daws's rhetoric about credit merchants, railroads, trusts, capitalists, and the "money power." Alliance growth became apparent when the Texas State Alliance met at Weatherford, Parker County, on 5 August 1884 with over 180 delegates present. This surpassed the attendance of any previous meeting and marked a fivefold increase over the Weatherford meeting of one year earlier.[55]

While the cooperative movement set the stage for the growth of the Farmers' Alliance in Texas, events involving Jay Gould's Southwest railroad system began to swell the ranks of the Texas Knights of Labor. In April 1884 some 450 coal miners at Gordon (Palo Pinto County) struck against the Texas and Pacific Railway, which owned and operated the mines and consumed the coal. The strike stemmed from a proposed wage cut. The miners held out for 186 days before accepting a reduced wage cut of 14 percent. The strike cost Texas and Pacific an estimated $200,000 and the strikers $150,000, a figure that was scarcely offset by the $3,500 provided to the miners by the national Knights of Labor. Nevertheless, the membership of Gordon's LA 2345 soared from 78 in July 1884 to 202 one year later.[56]

On 1 October 1884, as the miners strike neared its end, the Missouri, Kansas and Texas Railway, a Gould line in receivership at the time, announced a 10 percent reduction in wages. The workers, not well organized, submitted.[57] When the next wage cut on the Gould lines came four months later, the workers reacted rather differently. By then the Knights had grown sufficiently in Texas that the national Order had chartered (in December 1884) DA 78, based in Galveston and covering the entire state.[58]

As the farmer and labor movements began to gather momentum in Texas, similar developments unfolded in Arkansas, albeit under the guise of different farmers' organizations. Arkansas' agrarian orders would prove in some ways more inclusive than the Texas Alliance, less divided over the issue of political activity, and quicker to spread into other states—including Texas.[59]

## *Arkansas Farmers Organize: The Agricultural Wheel and the Brothers of Freedom*

The first agrarian organization in Arkansas appears to have been the Agricultural Wheel. The genesis of the Wheel occurred on 15 February 1882, when seven farmers met in an old log schoolhouse near Des Arc, Prairie County, just west of the fertile eastern Arkansas Delta, and formed the Wattensas Farmers' Club. Within about a month the organization adopted a secret ritual, perhaps influenced by the Grange, increased its membership to twenty, and changed its name to the Agricultural Wheel.[60]

This odd name reflected a purpose. Founding member W. W. Tedford explained: "No machinery can be run without a great drive wheel, and as that wheel moves and governs the entire machinery, however complex, so agriculture is the great wheel or power that controls the entire machinery of the world's industries." Yet the economic standing of Prairie County farmers hardly befitted such a central position. In 1880 Reuben CarlLee, who became a leading figure in the Arkansas Wheel, told a census taker that 90 percent of the county's farmers relied upon credit for obtaining their supplies. Tedford also explained that the name reflected the founders' belief that "we are surrounded by 'rings' of many kinds, especially political rings." The name also drew upon the biblical imagery of the prophet Ezekiel's wheel.[61]

In March 1882 the Agricultural Wheel adopted a preamble that resembled, in sentiment if not precise wording, the Reading platform of the Knights of Labor. It began:

[T]he general condition of our country imperatively demands unity of action on the part of the laboring classes, reformation in economy, and the dissemination of principles best calculated to encourage and foster agricultural and

mechanical pursuits, encouraging the toiling masses, leading them in the road
to prosperity, and providing a just and fair remuneration for labor, a just exchange of our commodities and best mode and means of securing to the laboring classes the greatest amount of good.[62]

The preamble went on to urge farmers to save their meat and bread
and raise more corn and grains and less cotton, which the Grange had also
urged farmers to do. The preamble condemned monopolies as "dangerous
to the best interests of our country, tending to enslave a free people" and
subvert the principles of the nation's Founding Fathers. The preamble also
declared that while "the laboring classes of mankind are the real producers
of wealth, . . . they are gradually becoming oppressed by combinations of
capital, and the fruits of their toil absorbed by a class who propose not
only to live on the labors of others, but to speedily amass fortunes at their
expense." The preamble also declared the Wheelers' belief in God, "the
great Creator of all things" who "created all men free and equal, and en-
dowed them with certain inalienable rights, such as life, liberty, and the
pursuit of happiness."[63]
Like the Founding Fathers of their nation, however, the founding fathers of the Wheel held a limited vision of just who counted as "free and
equal." The declaration of the objects of the Wheel limited membership
to "white males who are engaged in the occupation of farming, [and] also
mechanics who are actually engaged in farming."[64] The National Agricultural Wheel later amended the latter half of that clause to include "all
mechanics who are engaged in their respective trades" provided that they
not employ more than three hands.[65] In this respect the Wheel proved
somewhat more inclusive than the Alliance, which limited membership
to farmers, farm laborers, country schoolteachers, country physicians, and
ministers. The National Wheel also ultimately proved more inclusive than
the Southern Farmers' Alliance ever did on the question of race, declaring in 1887 that African Americans could join the Wheel provided that
"there shall be separate organizations for white and colored." (These "colored Wheels" already existed in Arkansas by then.) Although a Colored
Farmers' National Alliance began in Texas in late 1886, it remained a distinct organization from the white Alliance, whose leaders and spokesmen
sometimes frowned upon the black order. The Farmers' Alliances (North-

ern and Southern) did, however, surpass the Wheel in admitting women from their inception; not until 1887 did the National Wheel lift the gender clause from its membership requirements.[66]

Recruiting white male farmers and mechanics, the Wheel spread quickly across central Arkansas. The organization filed articles of incorporation with the Prairie County circuit clerk's office on 22 August 1882 and organized a State Wheel on 9 April 1883. The State Wheel held its first meeting at Goff's Cave on 18 July 1883, with delegates present from most of the thirty-nine subordinate Wheels organized by then. When the State Wheel met again six months later it claimed 114 subordinate Wheels and 5,000 members, despite having passed a resolution at the previous meeting barring the organization of Wheels "within the limits of incorporated towns."[67]

Another significant agrarian order emerged in Arkansas in 1882. Isaac McCracken, a Freemason, and Marion Farris formed an organization called the Brothers of Freedom in Johnson County in the northwestern part of the state. Farris remained obscure, but McCracken became the leading figure in the Arkansas agrarian revolt. Born in Huntington, Canada, in 1846 but largely reared in Lowell, Massachusetts, McCracken immigrated to Arkansas in 1870. Trained as a machinist, he initially practiced that trade in the Iron Mountain Railroad shops of North Little Rock, where he became an active member of the blacksmiths' and machinists' union. He left the trade after two years and began farming instead, but a decade later he turned his efforts at labor activism to farmers. He also eventually joined the Knights of Labor.[68]

The Brothers of Freedom resembled the Agricultural Wheel in many respects. In fact, much of the preamble of the Brothers' Declaration of Principles matched the Wheel's preamble verbatim, although no link has been established between the founding of the two organizations.[69] Some of the differences that did exist between the two organizations stemmed from the Brothers' concentration in the mountainous northwestern and western sections of Arkansas. The Brothers of Freedom probably consisted largely of yeomen or small landowning farmers. In sixteen counties where the organization was known to be active farms tended to be smaller, less valuable (as measured by value of land, fences, and buildings), and equipped with a lower value of farming implements and machinery than the state average. Farms in most of these sixteen counties also contained a lower value of livestock and yielded a higher (sometimes substantially higher) ratio of corn bushels to cotton bales than the state average. Most of these counties also had a higher percentage of owner-cultivated farms than the state average. In contrast, among fourteen Arkansas counties where the Agricultural Wheel was known to be active, only half had an average farm value below the state average, and most had a lower-than-average corn-to-cotton ratio and a lower percentage of owner-cultivated farms than the state average. Geographically, the Wheel was more widely dispersed in Arkansas than was the Brothers of Freedom. Three of these fourteen Wheel counties lay in the fertile east Arkansas Delta.[70]

Perhaps the Brothers' concentration in a section of the state characterized by small landowning farmers struggling to maintain that status on rocky, not particularly fertile soil while both corn and cotton prices fell explains why the Brothers enlisted Arkansans more successfully than did the Wheel. Membership in the Brothers of Freedom had reached thirty to forty thousand by the fall of 1885, compared to about ten thousand in the Wheel. The two organizations set similar requirements for membership. Women and African Americans could not join the Brothers, nor could merchants, bankers, or lawyers, whom the organization viewed as class enemies of the farmer. Mechanics and industrial laborers, on the other hand, could and did join. In fact, the leading historian of the organization asserted, "The Brothers intended that [their Declaration of Principles] lay the foundation for an organization open to oppressed laborers."[71]

The Brothers and the Wheel also espoused similar rhetoric and engaged in similar activities. The Brothers accused lawmakers of bowing to the money power and enacting legislation that made "labor subservient to capital and monopolies," while Wheelers condemned "the infamous trusts" that had "become an incubus upon . . . [the] body politic."[72] Both organizations called for farmers to practice diversified farming and to let "the 'all-cotton' idea be buried in the grave with our forefathers." They also called upon farmers to avoid the credit system and make their purchases with cash, although, as in the heyday of the Grange, this advice proved impractical for cash-strapped farmers.[73] Both organizations also conducted a variety of cooperative efforts. They made agreements with merchants that resulted in lower prices for members, and they established cooperative stores. Both organizations attempted to save members money by purchasing farm implements and machinery directly from manufacturers. The Brothers conducted a successful cooperative trade with St. Louis business houses and planned to expand the enterprise by investing several thousand dollars into a joint-stock company.[74]

In 1884 another similarity emerged between the Brothers of Freedom and the Agricultural Wheel in Arkansas: both entered the political arena. Neither evinced this purpose upon its founding. The founders of the Wheel were all Democrats, while the Brothers of Freedom initially prohibited partisan discussions in its lodges.[75]

The same set of conditions drove both organizations into politics. As elsewhere in the South, the men who led the Democratic Party in Arkansas "tended to represent an exclusive minority composed of the landed and business wealth in the state."[76] The Arkansas Democracy adopted the Greenbackers' "soft money" demands in 1878 and the demand of many farmers for repudiation of the state's Reconstruction debt as a means of tax relief in 1880, only to reverse those positions shortly after the elections. Meanwhile, the Democratic-controlled state legislature passed tax laws that favored railroads to the detriment of farmers and crop lien and mortgage laws that increased the hold of creditors and furnishing merchants over farmers.[77] Moreover, the Democratic Party of Arkansas, for all its fondness for linking the Republican Party to the corruption of Reconstruction, proved horribly corrupt itself. After former State Treasurer Thomas J. Churchill, a Democrat, won election to the governor's office in 1880, state investigations of his accounts revealed shortages of anywhere from $80,522 to $294,876. In 1882 the *Little Rock Arkansas Democrat* reported that the sheriff of Pulaski County was $50,000 behind with his accounts. A newspaper in rural Boone County lamented that the county government was being run "by the sharks, the gamblers, the pimps and imbeciles, instead of by the honest, moral, virtuous and brainy portion of our people."[78]

The Brothers of Freedom preceded the Wheel in taking the plunge into politics. Two old Greenbackers from Pope County, Charles Tobey and J. T. Wharton, helped lead the Brothers down the Independent political trail. (Tobey, it will be recalled, had also tried to lead the Arkansas Grange into the GLP several years earlier.) Both men portrayed the Democratic and Republican parties as the tools of what Tobey deemed the "three great monopolies"—finance, railroads, and corporations. During the spring of 1884 members of the Brothers of Freedom began calling nominating conventions for local and state offices. They did so as individuals acting without the sanction of the organization, but the artificiality of the distinction was lost on no one, including the minority of Brothers who opposed the third-party effort. The debate essentially ended, however, when the organization's president, McCracken, sanctioned the third-party effort by running for the state legislature as an Independent in Johnson County.[79]

Wheelers closely watched the Brothers' entrance into state politics. They discussed politics themselves at the Grand State Wheel meeting in July 1884. That body spurned overtures toward fusion made by three Republicans from Little Rock and Conway but not the possibility of fielding Independent tickets.[80]

When the fall campaigns got under way the Brothers of Freedom ran tickets in at least ten counties plus fusion tickets with Republicans in two others. The Agricultural Wheel ran tickets in Prairie and White counties, and the Brothers and the Wheel apparently joined each other in fielding fusion tickets in Conway and Faulkner counties. Their candidates ran on the issues of honest government and class interests, condemning the Democrats as the party of "the robber barons." They called for modification of mortgage laws and tax exemption laws that favored wealthy landowners, which would suggest that large planters exerted little influence in either organization, in contrast to the Grange. The Brothers and Wheel candidates also condemned the usurious interest rates and debt practices allowed in Arkansas.[81]

The Independent and fusion tickets won complete or partial victories in twelve of the aforementioned sixteen counties.[82] The agrarian tickets apparently won in three of the four counties in which the Wheel fielded candidates, and three of these four would give a majority of their votes to Union Labor Party (ULP) gubernatorial candidates in 1888 and 1890.[83] According to one interested observer, Arkansas Knights of Labor leader Dan Fraser Tomson, the Brothers of Freedom and the Agricultural Wheel—which he described as "organizations of farmers and laboring men"—elected 15 of the 127 members of the state legislature in 1884.[84]

## The Beginnings of the Knights of Labor in Arkansas

Tomson had hoped to become one of those 127 state legislators himself. Throughout his long association with the Knights he would vacillate on the issue of third-party politics. In January 1884 Tomson learned that some

Knights in Massachusetts were trying to promote "old Ben Butler," the former Union general, as a GLP presidential candidate. "As this order is not
a political machine," Tomson wrote to Terence V. Powderly, "I suppose of
course that you will 'nip it in the bud,' so far as the K. of L. is concerned?"[85]
Eight months later, however, he informed Powderly that the Knights of
Hot Springs and South Hot Springs, small cities in west-central Arkansas,
"had prevailed upon me to make the race on the 'Working man's' ticket
for the state legislature." Tomson's candidacy did not succeed.[86]

Tomson was one of the founding fathers of the Knights of Labor in
Arkansas. He and six other "determined men" met in a blacksmith shop
in Hot Springs on 22 November 1882 for the purpose of forming a local
assembly. They could not apply for a charter at that point, since the formation of a local assembly required at least ten charter members. On 30
December twenty-one charter members, evidently all white men, formed
the state's first local assembly, the Hot Springs Assembly (LA 2419). They
soon followed the regional norm of organizing African Americans into the
Order on a segregated basis. Members of the Hot Springs Assembly apparently helped organize the state's second local, the Freedom Assembly (LA
2447), also of Hot Springs. This local consisted entirely of African Americans. In May 1884 a member of the Hot Springs Assembly reported, "Our
colored brethren have had a poor existence so far, but they are 'turning
a new leaf' and manifesting more interest, and their meetings are better
attended than heretofore; and it is to be hoped that they will build up a
prosperous and useful Assembly." This Knight, a charter member of LA
2419, also reported that the Master Workman (Tomson) and other members of the white local frequently visited LA 2447 to "encourage and help
them along."[87]

While the founding of the first Knights of Labor local assembly in Arkansas occurred during the same year as the founding of the Agricultural
Wheel and the Brothers of Freedom, the Arkansas Knights did not grow at
nearly the same pace as the agricultural organizations. By the end of 1884
the Knights had established only eight local assemblies in Arkansas. Two
of these–a telegraphers' local in Little Rock and a mixed local outside of
Hot Springs–had apparently lapsed by then.[88] This sluggish growth likely
reflected a lack of resources for organizing rather than a lack of interest in
the Order. The previously quoted charter member of LA 2419 explained

the problem: "The Order might be built up throughout the State if it had workers in the field who could afford to spend the time and means necessary for the work, but so far no effort has been made, and but few localities [in Arkansas] know of its existence, in all probability."[89] Tomson reiterated this point four months later in a letter to Powderly. Tomson also echoed another point that his fellow charter member had made, informing Powderly that "not a single call has been made within our borders from any of our [national] leaders or even any of our brothers whatever from abroad."[90]

Tomson nevertheless hoped to see the Knights expand in Arkansas. Well aware of the Agricultural Wheel and the Brothers of Freedom, he apparently thought that these organizations might hold the key to that expansion. The three orders did, after all, espouse similar platforms and rhetoric. Moreover, not much of an urban-rural gap existed between the Arkansas Knights and the farmers' organizations. The Knights already had a local assembly of farmers in Hot Springs. According to census figures, only 4 percent of the population in Arkansas lived in "urban" communities in 1880, a figure that climbed to only 6.5 percent a decade later. (The U.S. Census Bureau then defined urban communities as those containing eight thousand or more residents.) In fact, it appears that none of the Arkansas Knights of Labor local assemblies that existed in 1884 were located in urban communities by this standard.[91]

The similarities between the Arkansas Knights and the Wheel and the Brothers seemed obvious to Tomson. In September 1884 he informed Powderly, "I am in correspondence with 'Hon. Isaac McCracken,' Clarksville, Ark., one of the leaders [of the] 'B. of F[.]' and with 'A. Walter, Esq.' of the 'Ag. Wheel,' Beebe, Ark., endeavoring to turn these bodies into the K. of L." The relative sizes of the organizations suggest that Tomson was trying to draw the horses with the cart. Nevertheless, he asked Powderly, "Can you help me? Can you not write to them [and] send them papers[?]" Powderly instructed one of his lieutenants, most likely General Secretary Frederick Turner, to correspond with McCracken and Walter.[92] Whether Turner contacted either of these men remains unknown, but within two years Powderly himself would be in contact with leaders of the Wheel, which by then had merged with the Brothers of Freedom while retaining its own name.[93]

Although, not surprisingly, Tomson failed to convince the leaders of the Agricultural Wheel and the Brothers of Freedom to merge their organizations into the Knights of Labor, he continued to try to expand the ranks of Arkansas Knights. By March 1885 Powderly had given Tomson an organizer's commission. From the 12th to the 21st of that month Tomson organized four local assemblies: LA 3646 of Little Rock, LA 3663 of Texarkana (on the Arkansas side of the border), LA 3669 of Hope, and LA 3674 of Malvern. These were all mixed locals. The Malvern local included women as well as men, although perhaps not at its inception. The Little Rock local soon came to consist primarily of workers in the railroad trades.[94]

## The Knights of Labor and the Railroad Strikes of 1884–1885

By the time Tomson organized these locals events were already under way that would trigger tremendous growth for the Knights, first among railroad workers and then among the working classes at large. In 1884 the Knights waged two successful strikes against the Union Pacific Railroad. The first strike occurred in May. Shopmen in Denver walked out in response to a 10 percent wage cut. Unorganized, they turned to Joseph Buchanan, editor of the *Denver Labor Enquirer* and a prominent figure in the Knights of Labor. Buchanan organized the workers into the Union Pacific Employees' Protective Association, and, as he later recalled, "inside of thirty-six hours, every shop from Omaha to Ogden and upon all the branch lines was on strike." Within four days the strikers won "a complete victory," as Union Pacific rescinded the wage cuts. Subsequently, Buchanan organized the Union Pacific shopmen into the Knights of Labor. Three months later Union Pacific announced a 10 percent wage cut for the first-class machinists at its shops in Ellis, Kansas, and also discharged twenty Denver machinists who had played an active role in the May strike. Two days later the Knights called a strike of all shopmen on the Union Pacific system. The Knights won the strike in five days. Union Pacific rescinded the wage cuts and rehired the Denver Knights.[95]

The Union Pacific strikes turned out to be a mere prelude to a series of larger and longer strikes on the Wabash Railroad and the Southwest railroad system. Jay Gould owned a controlling interest in these roads, which encompassed some 10,000 miles of track and employed more than 25,000 men. As the result of a recession and rate wars, the Wabash and the Missouri, Kansas and Texas Railway fell into receivership in 1884, although Gould retained managerial control over them. As a cost-cutting measure the Missouri, Kansas and Texas cut wages by 10 percent for shop-men and various other employees on 1 October 1884. Unorganized and caught off guard, the workers submitted. But in February 1885, when the Wabash Railroad announced an increase in the length of the workday from eight to ten hours while only raising the average daily wage from $1.60 to $1.80, Gould and his managers were the ones caught off guard. From the workers' point of view, a 25 percent increase in the length of the workday should have produced a 25 percent raise. Thus, the average daily wage should have risen from $1.60 to $2.00, and an average daily wage of $1.80 actually meant a 10 percent wage cut, as far as the Wabash workers were concerned.[96]

Even though most of the Wabash workers were unorganized at this point, they protested immediately. On 25 February 1885, one day be-fore the new hours and wages were to take effect, some two hundred Wabash shopmen in Springfield, Illinois, held a late-night meeting to dis-cuss the possibility of a strike. Early the next morning they held a strike vote. A large majority voted to strike, and shopmen in Chicago and De-catur, Illinois, Fort Wayne, Indiana, and Moberly, Missouri, telegraphed their agreement with the decision. By 27 February the strike had spread to Galveston, Texas, where 350 Wabash machinists quit work. Although the strike started in Illinois, it soon became most active in Missouri, Kansas, and Texas.[97]

During early March 1885 the strike spread to the Missouri, Kansas and Texas Railway, whose shopmen were still smarting from the 10 percent wage cuts of the previous autumn, and the Missouri Pacific (another South-west line), whose shopmen joined the strike wherever their lines crossed with those of the other two roads. The number of strikers on the Wabash and the Southwest system soon surpassed 4,500.[98]

No sooner did the strike begin than the Union Pacific Knights (whose lo-cals constituted DA 82) sent Joseph Buchanan to organize the Wabash and Southwest strikers into the Knights of Labor. The Union Pacific Knights also told Buchanan to inform the strikers that DA 82 would provide up to

$30,000 in financial assistance if necessary. Buchanan organized Knights of Labor locals in the Missouri cities of Kansas City, Sedalia (which became a center of strike activity), Moberly, Hannibal, and St. Louis. From there Buchanan planned to go to Texas, but the strike ended on 15 March before he had a chance to do so. Texas railroad workers did not need Buchanan's assistance anyway. Marshall, Fort Worth, Dallas, Palestine, and Denison all became centers of strike activity. The Knights already had a Texas district assembly (no. 78) and quickly organized local assemblies among railroad workers in all of the aforementioned locales as well as Bonham, Galveston, Houston, Lampasas, Longview, San Antonio, Sealy, Taylor, Texarkana, Toyah, and Tyler.[99]

The Knights of Labor did not, however, play a role in settling the strike. The parties who did included officials from the affected railroad lines, the governors of Kansas and Missouri, lesser ranking government officials from Texas, and various officials from other railroads in those three states. Nevertheless, the strikers gladly accepted the terms. The Missouri Pacific rescinded its wage cut of the previous October, and the Wabash immediately followed suit. The Southwest railroads also pledged that they would not cut wages in the future without a thirty-day notice.[100]

While the Knights did not participate in the settlement, the Order nevertheless received a great deal of credit for it. In April 1885 labor journalist John Swinton reported that Gould shopmen were joining the Knights "by thousands." In June the Knights chartered DA 93, representing Wabash workers, followed three months later by DA 101, which represented workers in the Southwest system.[101]

The settlement, however, proved short-lived. Trouble began almost immediately in the Wabash shops. The railroad laid off members of the Order in April and May and closed several of its shops on 16 June, including its largest at Sedalia. The shops reopened two days later, but management required workers to sign "yellow dog" contracts (anti-union pledges) before returning. Most Knights refused. The Executive Board of DA 93 deemed this ultimatum the equivalent of a lockout. Hence the district assembly asked the Knights' General Executive Board (GEB) for arbitration services and strike funds. The GEB denied the latter request on the basis of the Order's cumbersome rules regarding strike assistance and because, as historian Craig Phelan explains, "Powderly and his cohorts could not obtain water from a bone dry well."[102]

In late July Powderly did try to meet with A. A. Tallmage, the general manager of the Wabash. Tallmage, however, refused to meet with Powderly, just as he had refused to meet with DA 93's Executive Board a month earlier. Shortly after Tallmage snubbed Powderly the Knights of DA 101 declared their readiness to strike in support of their Wabash brethren.[103]

Stymied in efforts at negotiation, the GEB called all of the Order's Wabash workers out on strike on 18 August and issued a stunning decree that if the strike remained unsettled six days later, "all Knights of Labor in the employ of the Union Pacific and its branches and Gould's Southwestern system, or any other railroad, must refuse to repair or handle in any manner Wabash rolling stock until further orders from the General Executive Board, and if this order is antagonized by the companies through any of its [*sic*] officials, your Executive Committee is hereby ordered to call out all Knights of Labor on the above system without further action." This announcement captured Gould's attention. A strike on the Gould lines plus the Union Pacific would have affected more than twenty thousand miles of railway and equaled the scope of the railroad strikes of 1877.[104]

Gould and Tallmage met with Powderly and the GEB on 26 August in New York. Powderly and Knights General Secretary Turner met with Tallmage again in St. Louis eight days later. The parties reached a settlement that stated that the Wabash would no longer discriminate against the Knights and that all employees who were locked out on 16 June or had subsequently gone on strike would be reinstated by 1 October and before any new workers were rehired. Powderly agreed that the Knights would not call any future strikes before holding a conference with railroad officials. In his classic study of the Knights Norman Ware wrote, "This was the most important settlement the Knights of Labor ever made and was largely responsible for the growth of the Order in 1886." The *St. Louis Chronicle* expressed contemporary opinion when it declared, "The Wabash victory is with the K. of L. . . . No such victory has ever before been secured in this or any other country."[105] This victory, however, would prove ephemeral.

## The Southwest Strikes and Farmer-Labor Unity

Not only did the Gould railroad strikes of 1885 spark tremendous growth for the Knights of Labor, but they also laid the groundwork for farmer-labor unity in fighting a common enemy. This development occurred most evidently in Texas. The first Southwest strike crippled the state's two chief railroads, the Missouri, Kansas and Texas Railway and the Texas and Pacific Railway. The latter, an east-west road, passed through the east Texas cotton lands where the Farmers' Alliance was gaining strength. As Robert McMath has noted, "Texas farmers and merchants cheered" when the first Southwest strike broke out in February 1885. While the reason for their enmity toward the Gould monopoly seems readily apparent, one should not assume that their support for the strike was inevitable. As much as farmers and merchants resented the Southwest system's domination of railroads in Texas, they nevertheless relied on the railroads to ship their produce and merchandise. Had the strike occurred during the autumn cotton harvesting season, farmers might have reacted much differently. As it was, the late winter strike interfered with the shipment of cattle and foodstuffs. The supply of corn, bacon, and flour ran out in many Texas towns. Hog and cattle trading dropped sharply in St. Louis, a metropole of commerce for the Midwest and Southwest.[106] But farmers, townspeople, and even businessmen did not, for the most part, blame the strikers for the interruption in business. Instead, they supported the strikers and condemned the railroads. Citizens in Marshall and Dallas raised money to aid the strikers.[107]

The year 1885 proved to be one of great growth for both the Farmers' Alliance and the Knights of Labor in Texas. The Alliance growth that began in 1884 following the appointment of S. O. Daws as a full-time traveling lecturer and organizer continued unabated into the next year. By December 1885 the Alliance claimed some fifty thousand members among no fewer than twelve hundred sub-Alliances, some of them beyond the Texas border in the Indian Territory. The Knights of Labor, which had only 22 local assemblies in the state in 1884, chartered 112 locals in Texas in 1885. By 1886 the Knights had some 12,500 members in Texas. Railroad workers comprised the greatest number of these recruits, but farmers and farm laborers joined as well, particularly in the north Texas counties through which the Texas and Pacific Railway passed and in the mining communities of west Texas. In these areas in particular the Knights and the Alliance developed heavily overlapping memberships.[108]

Shared members, similar ideologies, and compatible goals drew the two organizations together. During the summer of 1885 the Knights and the Alliance held joint mass meetings as well as picnics and barbecues. When

the Grand State Alliance met at Decatur in August Knights officials addressed the delegates, who in turn appointed a committee to meet with a
Knights committee in Dallas "to draft resolutions to bring about effective
union of the Knights of Labor and the Farmers' Alliance of Texas." Part
of this unity of action soon centered upon joint cooperative enterprises,
although the extent to which these actually came to fruition is unclear. A
greater portent of things to come occurred in Palo Pinto County, the site of
the Knights' recent strike against the Texas and Pacific–owned coal mines,
where the Knights and the Alliance discussed the possibility of running an
Independent ticket for local offices later that year.[109]

Further evidence of unity between the two organizations came in January 1886 when the Knights' DA 78 held its annual session at Galveston.
The Knights resolved "[t]hat a standing committee of one delegate from
each county be appointed, whose duty it shall be to visit from time to
time, the different Farmers' Alliances of their respective county, for the
purpose of closer binding together the respective interests of both." The
district assembly also resolved to elect a committee of three to visit the next
meeting of the Grand State Alliance for the same purpose. The Knights
also requested the Alliance's aid in a number of ongoing battles, including
boycotts of the *Houston Evening Age* newspaper and the Mallory Steamship
Line and the Knights' efforts to have convict laborers removed from the
construction of the state capitol in Austin.[110]

The Knights' request for Alliance assistance in these matters touched
off a firestorm of controversy within the latter organization. William R.
Lamb, the State Alliance traveling business agent, expressed the support
of his Montague County Alliance for the Mallory boycott and asked State
Alliance President Andrew Dunlap to do likewise on behalf of the state
organization. Dunlap refused. Prominent supporters of Dunlap's position
included J. N. Rogers, editor of the State Alliance organ, the *Jacksboro Rural
Citizen*. Rogers composed an editorial denouncing boycotts as dangerous
to liberty, law, and order. Nevertheless, Alliances in Robertson, Palo Pinto,
Erath, and Dallas counties joined the Montague County Alliance in supporting the Mallory boycott. With the exception of Robertson, Knights of
Labor locals existed in all of these counties, and at least one local in each
county included farmers. The Knights chartered three locals in Robertson
County in 1886 that most likely enlisted farmers as well.[111]

In March 1886 Lamb explained his support of the Knights' Mallory boycott in a letter to the *Rural Citizen.* As state business agent, Lamb reminded
Alliance members of the increasing difficulty that their cooperative enterprises were having in purchasing farm tools and implements directly
from manufacturers. Lamb warned that "the day is not far distant when the
Farmers' Alliance will have to use [the] Boycott on manufacturers in order
to get goods direct[ly]" and argued that therefore the Alliance should "help
the Knights of Labor in order to secure their help in the near future."[112]

By the time Lamb's letter appeared in the *Rural Citizen* a far more important labor conflict had begun that further fractured Alliance unity while
promoting farmer-labor unity. On 1 March 1886 the second Southwest
strike began in Texas. The origins of this railroad strike remain somewhat shrouded in mystery. The most thorough historian of the strike, Ruth
Allen, suggested that Jay Gould "had accepted a Fabian failure [in 1885]
that he might triumph the more completely" in 1886.[113] Craig Phelan's
recent study of the Knights concurs that Gould "set about precipitating a
conflict to rid himself of the nuisance of a feisty work force."[114] The strike
began in Marshall, when a Texas and Pacific shop fired Charles A. Hall,
Master Workman of LA 3658, for taking three days off to attend a session
of DA 101 in that town. Hall's foreman had granted him permission to
attend the meeting, however, and Allen asserted that the firing "can be explained only as crass ineptitude or as the expression of a desire to affront
the workers with the serious possibility of forcing them to revolt."[115]

Once the Marshall local assembly struck, DA 101 Master Workman
Martin Irons, a fifty-three-year-old native of Scotland, telegraphed all of
the district's local assemblies and asked them to vote on whether to ex-
tend the strike across the entire Southwest system. When the votes came
in Irons called the entire district out on strike effective 6 March. Within
days, however, he began hearing reports from within the district that the
vote had been "dishonestly reported." Irons called a meeting of the District
Executive Board in St. Louis to review the matter, but, as Terence V. Powderly later revealed in his autobiography, an unidentified man allegedly
forced Irons at gunpoint in a hotel room to sign an affidavit reaffirming
the validity of the strike order. Allen not only concluded that the story was
true but declared the incident "a crucial moment in the history of labor in
the Southwest."[116]

Notwithstanding the firing of Hall and the mysterious incident involving Irons, many Texas Knights held grievances against the Gould railroad companies that the first Southwest strike had failed to settle. In January 1886 LA 3788 of Baird composed a Statement of Grievances against the Texas and Pacific calling for higher wages ($1.50 per day instead of the $1.15 being paid to unskilled laborers), a speedier settlement of discharges, and the expulsion of Chinese from the workforce, as the company was allegedly paying higher wages to Chinese workers than to white workers on the west end of the railway. Many other locals on the Southwest system also clamored for the $1.50 daily wage. After the Southwest strike of 1886 ended one former striker told a congressional committee that DA 101 had already determined before the dismissal of Hall that "if [the pay raise] could not be attained [in any other manner], we would go on a strike for that, together with our other grievances."[117]

Knights on the Southwest system outside of Texas seemed to have fewer grievances, however, and this differentiated the second Southwest strike from the first of a year earlier. This difference proved significant. For instance, Sedalia, Missouri, had been a major center of the first Southwest strike, when railroad workers there walked out largely due to prevailing local sentiment. In March 1886, however, they went on strike "not because of their own grievances, not because of a decline in material conditions, and not because of Jay Gould's greed. . . . They went on strike out of loyalty to a distant, centralized organization [DA 101 of the Knights of Labor]."[118] The same scenario unfolded in Little Rock. The 250 to 300 Knights who belonged to LA 3646 walked off the job at the Iron Mountain shops, but, according to historians Ralph V. Turner and William Warren Rogers, "[t]he principal cause of the strike at Little Rock was the Knights' acceptance of Irons' directives." Only about twenty-five of these Knights (trackmen) actually voiced a grievance; they were working for $1.10 per day, and, like their brethren in Texas, they wanted $1.50.[119]

The lack of local grievances outside of Texas translated into a lack of the community support that had contributed heavily to the Knights' earlier victories against the Gould railroad empire. Furthermore, important groups of railroad workers aside from shopmen and trackmen, such as engineers, firemen, brakemen, and conductors, proved far less supportive of the second Southwest strike than the first. Their participation greatly aided the success of the first strike, and their lack thereof greatly reduced the second strike's chance of success. [120]

Powderly and the Knights' General Executive Board raised $86,901 for the strikers' aid and made numerous attempts at negotiation with Gould and other Southwest system executives, but to no avail. By the end of April strikebreakers and skilled workers who had never left their jobs in the first place had the Southwest system operating at nearly full scale. A congressional committee, investigating the strike at Powderly's urging, persuaded the Knights' chief to call off the strike on 4 May 1886. The Knights suffered a total defeat. Not only did the union receive no concessions, but many strikers never got their jobs back. [121] The date 4 May 1886 went down as an infamous one in American labor history for another reason as well: the notorious Haymarket riot, which resulted in at least sixteen deaths, including those of at least eight policemen, occurred in Chicago that day. [122]

Although the second Southwest strike turned out to be a major loss for the Knights of Labor, it did serve to pull farmers and laborers closer together in the affected areas, and it further politicized the farmer-labor movement as well. As with the first Southwest strike, these effects occurred most noticeably in Texas. Farmers' Alliance chapters along railroads in north and east Texas contributed food and money to sustain the strikers. The Dallas County and Red River County Farmers' Alliances both issued proclamations supporting the strikers. [123]

Not all Texas Alliance members, however, supported the strikers. *Jacksboro Rural Citizen* editor J. N. Rogers opposed the strike just as he opposed the Knights' Mallory boycott. Rogers argued that farmers who supported the strike were acting against their own economic interests. Higher wages for railroad workers, he warned, would mean higher freight rates. Wholesalers could compensate for this by raising prices, as could merchants, but farmers would lose money if railroads raised freight rates. [124] Rogers's argument did not seem to weaken Alliance support for the strikers though. Leaders of the Texas Grange agreed with Rogers, but their decaying organization no longer carried much influence. [125]

## Farmer-Labor Politics in the Aftermath of the Southwest Strike of 1886

Before it even ended the Southwest strike of 1886 assumed political dimensions, as the Knights and the Alliance held a number of joint political meetings. This too caused controversy within the latter organization. Rogers and State Alliance President Dunlap tried to keep the organization out of politics, but here too they were fighting a losing battle. The Red River County Alliance asked the Knights "to meet us at the ballot box and help overthrow all monopolies." In Wise County, an early Alliance stronghold, the Knights and the Alliance held a Laboring Men's Convention that eventually led to the nomination of an Independent political ticket. The convention issued a platform that strongly resembled the National Labor Union platform, the Knights' Reading platform, and the Greenbackers' Toledo platform.[126] In early April 1886 Knights and Alliancemen helped elect Independent candidate H. S. Broiles to the mayor's office in Fort Worth. Bill Farmer, former GLP leader and now an officer of the Knights of Labor DA 78, actively campaigned for Broiles. Upon Broiles's election Farmer declared that "a revolution . . . has begun" and that "[t]he ballot box is our battlefield."[127]

Similar farmer-labor political coalitions emerged elsewhere in Southwest strike territory. In Sedalia, Missouri, the state GLP met in June 1886, one month after the second Southwest strike ended. The convention, cochaired by former GLP congressman T. M. Rice, nominated a St. Louis Knight for state railroad commissioner. The candidate had experience in the railroad industry; at the time, he was under indictment for charges stemming from his activities as a striker. He did not get elected, and the Missouri state GLP never met again. In May 1888, however, many of its old stalwarts met in Sedalia again for the convention of the state Union Labor Party, which drew a similar mix of old Grangers, Greenbackers, Knights, trade union members, and members of the Farmers' Alliance and the Agricultural Wheel.[128]

In Little Rock, too, farmers and laborers held political meetings in the wake of the second Southwest strike. On 14 May 1886 a committee of Little Rock Knights of Labor attended a meeting of the Pulaski County Wheel in the nearby hamlet of Mabelvale. The Knights' committee, reported the *Arkansas Gazette*, "consisted of Robert McKay, Joe Perry and three colored men." The Wheel appointed a committee to confer with the Knights' committee and discuss the possibility of the two organizations forming a political coalition and putting forth a county ticket. On 8 June the Pulaski County Wheel and the Knights met in joint "secret session" in the hall of the Brotherhood of Locomotive Engineers in Little Rock.

About 110 men were present, a fair-sized minority of whom were African Americans. Isom P. Langley, chaplain of the State Wheel and editor of the Arkansas Knights of Labor newspaper, the *Industrial Liberator*, presided. Although the meeting did not produce a county ticket, the State Wheel met at Little Rock the following day and nominated a state ticket, which subsequently underwent several changes and was incomplete by election day in September. In at least one Arkansas county—Carroll, in the northwestern part of the state—the Knights and the Wheel nominated a joint ticket that won the county elections. These limited efforts at entering county and state politics would be a mere prelude to far more serious farmer-labor political activity under the guise of the Union Labor Party two years later.[129]

The Southwest strike of 1886 served as a catalyst of sorts that brought loosely connected farmer and labor movements into closer contact in the affected areas. The strike provided the first major test of whether the similar rhetoric espoused by farmer and labor organizations would translate into unity of action in a conflict against a common adversary. In retrospect, the reluctance of some Texas Farmers' Alliance leaders to support the Knights of Labor proved telling. The shared rhetoric of the Knights and the farmers' organizations did not convince all of the members of those organizations that they shared the same interests. Some members of the Alliance would again express misgivings about the Knights of Labor, while some Knights and trade unionists would express ambivalent or even hostile opinions of the Alliance.

The Southwest strike of 1886 also forced Knights, Alliancemen, and Wheelers to consider the roles of their organizations in politics. The strike crystallized both the major points of disagreement between conservative Democrats and reform-minded farmers and laborers and the shared grievances that might form the basis of a farmer-labor political coalition. In Texas and Arkansas compliant Democratic officials sided with the Gould empire and helped crush the strike.[130] In the aftermath of the strike, as the Texas Grand State Farmers' Alliance was calling for increased taxation of railroads and the passage of an interstate commerce law that would regulate freight rates and prohibit the practices of rebates and pooling, the Texas Democratic Party nominated Lawrence Sullivan Ross, an opponent of railroad regulation, for governor. Ross's campaign manager was railroad attorney George Clark, a staunch opponent of railroad regulation who probably influenced Ross's opposition to regulation during his governorship.[131]

In Texas and Arkansas the role of Democratic officials in crushing the strike convinced many Knights that they would have to break from "the party of their fathers" if the labor movement were to survive and accomplish its goals. Many Texas Alliance members who had supported the strike came to the same conclusion regarding their own welfare, although many of them had already supported the GLP in past years. Yet many Alliancemen remembered how their organization had been destroyed by its entrance into politics in 1878 and feared that reentering politics now would yield the same result. Moreover, some Texas Alliance members, like some of the state's few remaining Grangers, were staunch Democrats.[132] In Arkansas, as we have seen, many Wheelers (including former members of the Brothers of Freedom, which had merged into the Wheel) had already engaged in third-party politics, and large-scale farmer-labor third-party efforts would emerge more quickly than in the Lone Star State.

The development of the southern farmer and labor movements in 1885 and 1886, while most visible in Southwest strike territory, extended well beyond that territory. The Knights of Labor grew remarkably following the two successful Gould railroad strikes of 1885. Nationally, official membership soared from 111,395 as of 1 July 1885 to 729,677 exactly one year later. Actual membership may have surpassed one million in 1886.[133] Membership did drop in Texas and Missouri after the Southwest strike of 1886, but it continued to rise in Arkansas and elsewhere in the South.[134] The Knights recruited industrial laborers, artisans and mechanics, and farmers and farm laborers, while the Agricultural Wheel and the Farmers' Alliance expanded across the South during 1886 and 1887.

Thus historians' portrayal of the Southwest strike of 1886 as a momentous blow to the Knights of Labor and, hence, organized labor's participation in the Populist movement does not even hold true for the region in which the strike occurred. Nor does it fit the South at large. The strike did not weaken the Knights of Labor in most of the South (nor did Chicago's Haymarket riot), and the Order remained vibrant in Texas longer than in most other states of the South and the nation.[135] Most observers at the time—friends and foes alike—did not write off the Knights or stop taking the Order seriously after the strike ended.[136] Finally, in light of subsequent events the Southwest strike of 1886 seems to have marked more of a beginning than an end to farmer-labor coalitions in the South. Such coalitions would become evident across the region over the next several years, and the potential as well as the pitfalls that the strike suggested for these coalitions would be tested on a larger scale.

CHAPTER THREE

# The Knights of Labor and Southern Farmer-Labor Insurgency, 1885–1888

On 15 August 1885 a group of workingmen met at the Odd Fellows' Hall in Athens, Georgia, a town of about seven to eight thousand residents, to organize themselves for "self-protection."[1] Seven days later they met again at the Good Templars' Hall, where Henry Jennings, a "life member" of the defunct Clarke County Grange and recently defeated candidate for the state legislature from nearby Oconee County, organized them into LA 4141 of the Knights of Labor. This mixed local consisted primarily of mechanics. In September 1885 the Knights chartered another mixed local of mechanics (LA 4273) and a local of farmers and laborers (LA 4274) in Athens.[2]

The Athens Knights of Labor, which included white and black members in apparently integrated locals, evidently viewed political activity as one type of "self-protection." They endorsed William L. Wood, one of their members, in the mayoral election held in December 1885. Wood, a city councilman, had been the first candidate to enter the mayor's race, doing so before the formation of the Athens local assemblies. While his entrance into the Knights might seem politically opportunistic, three Athens Knights informed Terence V. Powderly that Councilman Wood had done more for the laborers of Athens "than any who ever preceded him." When Wood lost the nonpartisan mayoral election by only 122 votes to Citizens' candidate R. K. Reaves, the nominee of the town's businessmen, the Knights claimed that Reaves had won on bought votes and threatened to bring charges before a grand jury. The Athens Knights also vowed to name their own tickets in the next city and county elections and, as one of their leaders put it, to "get as members all the darkeys and farmers" in order to increase their strength at the polls.[3]

The case of the Athens Knights of Labor presents a somewhat extreme but not atypical example of the direction that southern farmer and labor movements would increasingly take in the latter half of the 1880s. Although the timing and intensity of this trend varied from state to state (and even county to county), farmers and laborers across the region took the plunge—sometimes in unison—into independent or third-party politics. The same pattern emerged elsewhere, particularly in some midwestern and western states, until it finally resulted in the formation of the People's (or Populist) Party in the early 1890s.[4]

Historians have devoted a great deal of attention to the Knights' political activities during the mid- to late 1880s. In the most thorough examination of the topic, *Workingmen's Democracy: The Knights of Labor and American Politics,* Leon Fink identified 189 American towns and cities where labor tickets appeared in 1886, and his list is incomplete.[5] But in analyzing this activity historians have largely overlooked the extent to which it represented farmer-labor coalitions, at least in the South.[6] As we have seen in the case of those areas affected by the Southwest strikes, the labor tickets of the mid- to late 1880s often represented elements of agrarian orders such as the Farmers' Alliance and the Agricultural Wheel as well.

Furthermore, since the Knights of Labor recruited farmers and farm laborers as well as artisans, mechanics, and industrial workers, the Order became a bona fide farmer-labor organization in its own right, organizing tillers of the soil before the Alliance or the Wheel even reached some parts of the South. Therefore, Knights of Labor political tickets in the region often represented a farmer-labor constituency even when no agricultural organizations were involved, as in the case of Athens.

In Texas, Arkansas, Alabama, Georgia, and North Carolina the Knights of Labor, drawing on farmer and labor support, played a significant role in leading independent or third-party movements during the mid- to late 1880s. In doing so the Knights laid important and largely overlooked groundwork for strong Populist movements in these states, particularly the first three of those mentioned above. In Arkansas, in fact, the Union Labor Party campaigns of 1888 and 1890, in which many Knights were heavily involved, represented the peak of third-party activism. The Arkansas story also proved instructive in another significant sense, as it clearly illustrated how both the response of Democrats at the local or state level and the fusion with Republicans could shape the fortunes of third-party movements.

## The Knights of Labor Spread across the South, 1886

The plethora of Knights of Labor political activity in 1886 would not have been possible, of course, had it not been for the organization's remarkable growth following its two seemingly successful showdowns in 1885 with the Jay Gould railroad empire. By the beginning of 1886 the onslaught of hundreds of thousands of new recruits into the ranks of Knighthood had unnerved Powderly and other Knights leaders.[7] In a letter to Dan Fraser Tomson, Powderly wrote, "The growth we are now witnessing is unhealthy. [I]t is much . . . too feverish to be good."[8] By March 1886 the Knights' hopelessly overworked General Executive Board agreed. The board declared a forty-day moratorium on the organization of new local assemblies, calling upon organizers to devote their efforts instead to giving proper instruction in the principles and workings of the Order to existing locals. The moratorium went largely ignored, however, as organizers continued to form new locals and withheld the applications until the forty days had passed.[9]

Nowhere was the Knights' sudden growth from 1885 to 1886 more evident than in Dixie. In 1885 the Knights counted 317 local assemblies in the eleven ex-Confederate states; that figure tripled to 951 the next year. The most dramatic increases occurred in North Carolina (from 5 to 79), Georgia (14 to 99), and Arkansas (20 to 111). The Order went from having virtually no presence to a modest one in South Carolina (1 to 25), Florida (4 to 24), and Mississippi (6 to 22). The Knights organized the greatest number of locals in the South in 1886 in the two southern states in which the most locals already existed: Texas (where the number of locals rose from 131 to 236) and Virginia (68 to 173).[10]

In Arkansas the Knights' greatest gains came among farmers, white and black, across the economic spectrum. Next to mixed local assemblies, which were the most common type of local throughout the South and often included farmers, local assemblies comprised chiefly or wholly of farmers ranked as the most prevalent type in the Razorback State in 1886, as in

Texas as well. The Arkansas Knights, however, organized a more diverse array of farmers' locals than did their Texas counterparts. These included locals of farmers and farmhands, segregated by race but sometimes including women, locals of white planters, locals of black planters, locals of plantation employees, and even three locals consisting of planters and their employees.[11] The odd spectacle of employer and employee belonging to the same local assembly of the Knights of Labor underscored both the Order's dual function as a labor union and fraternal organization and how the Knights' inclusive membership policy could undermine its effectiveness in the former role. Perhaps the starkest example of this came at the Knights' General Assembly at Richmond, Virginia, in October 1886, where the delegates included a cotton mill operator, James W. Sweatt of the Eagle and Phoenix Mills of Columbus, Georgia.[12]

In Georgia and the Carolinas the Knights' greatest gains in 1886 came among farmers, farmhands, and cotton mill workers as well as tobacco workers in North Carolina. The larger ranks of Virginia Knights remained more diverse, including more female and black members and a greater variety of workers, which by 1886 included millhands, coal miners, woodworkers and carpenters, telegraphers, cigar makers, and farmers and farmhands as well as housekeepers, servants, washerwomen, and cooks. Many of these domestic workers were African American women.[13] The Knights also organized black female domestic workers in Wilmington, North Carolina, prompting the *Charlotte Home-Democrat* to warn, "White people had better begin to practice waiting on themselves more than they have been doing, for when most of the colored servants join the Knights of Labor . . . it will be almost impossible to get along with them."[14] The Knights also recruited female domestic workers of both races in rural Cobb County in northwestern Georgia.[15] The Knights' organizing efforts among poor black laborers, male and female, would cause friction both within the Order and between the Knights and the Farmers' Alliance.

Southern women often found entry into the Knights of Labor difficult regardless of their race. As historian LeeAnn Whites has noted, "the name of the organization, the *Knights* of Labor, makes one think of *men* as the honorable defenders of labor."[16] Apparently, many southerners viewed the Order this way. Mrs. Ira Campbell of Jemison, Alabama, bubbled over with enthusiasm for the Knights of Labor in a letter to the *Journal of United Labor* in January 1888, but she was "ashamed to confess" that she lived "in a community where it is considered not lady-like for [women] to become members." [17] The publication of her letter apparently altered local sentiment on this matter, for within two months thirty-one women belonged to Jemison's seventy-five-member local assembly. Nevertheless, only a handful of local assemblies in Alabama appear to have ever included women. [18]

Moreover, the initiation of women into local assemblies did not necessarily mean that they were accepted as equal members by their brother Knights. The case of LA 6307 of Van Buren, Arkansas, illustrates this point well. In 1890, after several years of efforts at and sometimes contentious discussions about organizing women, this local assembly finally succeeded in bringing them into its ranks. Once several women had joined, however, the assembly appointed a committee of four women and one man "to get up supper for [the] next meeting night." [19] As far as can be determined from the assembly's minute book, this marked the first time that it had ever appointed such a committee in its fifty-six-month history.

As elsewhere in the nation, southern men who belonged to the Order sometimes aided and encouraged the formation of all-female local assemblies. In Tennessee, for example, the organization of female locals soon followed that of male locals in East Nashville, Jackson, Memphis, and Knoxville. In Knoxville the Knights organized a mixed local assembly of women just two weeks after the formation of the city's first men's local, and the women's local was formed at the same hall where the men's local held its meetings. [20] In Richmond, Virginia, where the Knights' membership exploded in the wake of Powderly's visit in early 1885, the plethora of new locals that soon appeared included one composed of young white female cigarette makers, the first women's labor organization ever formed in the city. In all, according to historian Jonathan Garlock, the Knights chartered no fewer than thirty-two locals composed of white women and ten locals of black women in Virginia. [21] The organization of such locals, particularly the latter, often proved less welcome farther south, though. In the Raleigh-Durham area of North Carolina and in Savannah, Georgia, white men blocked the formation of black female locals. When Knights in these cities turned to Powderly to resolve the dispute, in each instance he decided that it was better to delay or forgo the organization of black women's locals than to risk alienating the white men who constituted the bulk of the Order's membership in each city.[22]

Squabbles over racial and gender issues notwithstanding, by 1886 the Knights had built enough of a membership base in several southern states to become a factor in politics. The Knights' entrance into politics that year, not just in the South but across the nation, also created internal friction, but the dissenters generally found themselves helpless to halt the stampede. In all five of the southern states in which the Knights had the most local assemblies—Texas, Virginia, Arkansas, Georgia, and North Carolina—the Order became involved in politics that year. In Arkansas the Agricultural Wheel played the leading role in these campaigns. In Texas the Knights and the Alliance both became heavily involved in these campaigns, although the independent political path proved rather divisive in the latter organization. In Georgia and North Carolina, both still untouched by the Alliance and the Wheel, the Knights drew both farmers and laborers into political campaigns. Among these five states, only Virginia's movements of political insurgency lacked a significant farmer component, partly because they were centered in urban areas. The lack of farmer involvement in Virginia's Independent campaigns in 1886 proved foretelling, however, in a state where the Populist Party would fail to develop the strength achieved by the party in Texas, Georgia, and North Carolina or by the Union Labor Party in Arkansas.[23]

## The Knights of Labor and the Farmers' Alliance in Texas Politics, 1886

Given that the Southwest strike of 1886 began in Texas and remained most heavily centered there, it should have come as no surprise that the South's most widespread and hotly contested battles between the "regular" Democracy and farmer-labor insurgents that year occurred in the Lone Star State. Some of these battles erupted within the Democratic Party. In Johnson, Lamar, and San Saba counties members of the Farmers' Alliance, the Knights of Labor, the Grange, and the Agricultural Wheel held joint meetings with the goal of building their strength within the Democratic Party. In Dallas County, where the Knights and the Alliance sponsored a joint fair in the summer of 1886 as a rival to a fair sponsored by the Dallas business elite, Rev. J. H. Jackson told his fellow members of both orders that they too should work within the Democratic Party.[24]

Jackson's advice was not entirely out of step with the rank and file of the two organizations. Several delegations of Knights and Alliancemen attended the state Democratic convention at Galveston in August 1886 and, according to one account, "possessed sufficient strength to make an impress[ion] on the acts of this convention." The platform put forth by the convention called for a "comprehensive and efficient" mechanics' and laborers' lien law and declared that "all State convicts should be confined within the walls of the penitentiary." The latter resolution amounted to a call for the abolition of the convict lease system, which the platform did not specifically mention.[25] The influence of the Knights and the Alliance at the convention possessed definite limits, though; two contesting delegations of Knights and Alliancemen from north Texas counties did not get seated, and the Knights and Alliance delegates were unable to carry their choice for the gubernatorial nomination, Marion Martin, a "staunch Alliance man" and future Union Laborite and Populist.[26]

More commonly, however, farmer-labor political coalitions in Texas in 1886 took the form of third-party or Independent movements. Such movements sprang up in at least twenty north Texas counties that year. The most successful, the oddly named "Human Party," emerged in drought-stricken Comanche County in north-central Texas, the heart of Alliance country. Thomas Gaines, president of Baggett Alliance 297, played the leading role in organizing the party. He charged that "both the old parties . . . are in sympathy with and support the capitalists" and pledged that the new party would "work for the interest of the laborer [and] do away with land thieves." The entire "Human Party" county ticket swept into office. It became the Comanche County People's Party in 1892 and remained powerful until the end of the century.[27] Just to the north in Erath County, where the ranks of the Knights of Labor included farmers and mechanics, a similar but less colorfully named Independent Party also took over the county offices. The future State Alliance president, Evan Jones, played a prominent role in the Erath County Independent Party, which became the Erath County People's Party six years later.[28]

The Dallas–Fort Worth area, situated in the state's Sixth Congressional District, witnessed some of the fiercest competition between Democrats and third-party challengers. In early April 1886, days after railroad strikers killed two deputy marshals in a shootout near Fort Worth, Knights and Alliancemen combined to elect H. S. Broiles as the city's mayor on

an Independent ticket.[29] Shortly thereafter, Fort Worth Alliancemen and
Knights formed an Anti-Monopoly Party, which the hostile mainstream
press dubbed the "Dark Lantern" Party. The party's "cry," according to a
correspondent for the *New York Times*, was " 'Down with bankers,' 'Down
with lawyers,' 'Down with the ring.' " "So serious has the situation grown,"
the correspondent wrote on the eve of the November elections, "and so
many good men have been seduced to support the 'Dark Lantern' ticket,
that the bulk of the Republicans have joined the Democrats in county
politics, and are working with them for good government."[30] The Anti-
Monopoly ticket carried the county (Tarrant) outside of Fort Worth but
lost in the city. That loss might suggest a lack of support by the members
of the city's six local assemblies of the Knights of Labor, although many
of the Fort Worth railroad workers who had belonged to the Knights in
April may have left the city by November in search of work. The Tarrant
County farmer-labor coalition did succeed in electing a state legislator in
November.[31]

By the autumn of 1886 all signs pointed to lively contests for state legislative and congressional seats in Texas, particularly the latter. In August
the Farmers' Alliance held its state convention in Cleburne and practically adopted the Knights' Reading platform, with the addition of planks
against dealing in futures in agricultural commodities and against fencing on public or school lands, a Greenbacker demand for the increased
coinage of silver and gold, and a demand for interstate commerce laws
that would facilitate railroad regulation. The convention also replaced the
antilabor *Jacksboro Rural Citizen* with the prolabor *Dallas Mercury* as the
official State Alliance journal.[32] These steps toward a political coalition
with labor, however, caused a serious rift in the Alliance ranks. In the
months following the convention the organization nearly split into two
factions, and conservative president Andrew Dunlap resigned. Into this
breach, however, stepped Charles W. Macune of Milam County, a charismatic thirty-five-year-old farmer, physician, Methodist preacher, newspaper editor, and lawyer. Not only did Macune help mend the nearly fatal
split within the Texas Alliance, but as the president of the organization he
would soon shepherd its unprecedented growth and geographical expansion.[33]

A month after the Texas State Alliance approved its modified Reading platform, Fort Worth's Independent mayor, H. S. Broiles, called a convention in that city for the purpose of organizing a state Anti-Monopoly Party. The turnout of delegates from twenty-eight counties proved too small for promulgating a platform or nominating a state ticket. Instead, the convention urged "all antimonopolists in Texas" to support candidates for Congress and the state legislature who would "come nearest [to] representing their sentiments." Future Union Labor and Populist leaders attending the Anti-Monopoly convention included J. T. W. Loe, a Knights of Labor leader from Austin, and former Greenbacker J. E. Martin of Tarrant County.[34]

The November elections for the state legislature proved anticlimactic. According to historian Alwyn Barr, "only two members of the newly elected Legislature identified themselves as Independents, and only two as Republicans, but it included at least fourteen Alliance men, ten Grangers, and two Knights."[35] The Alliancemen and Grangers, however, may well have been typical Democrats, given the conservative leanings of some members of the former organization and of most of the relatively few remaining members of the latter.[36]

The congressional elections yielded even fewer results for farmer-labor insurgents yet provided Texas Democrats with the most opposition they had encountered in these contests since the end of Reconstruction. Democrats faced opponents in eight of eleven districts, and in five of those contests an opposition candidate received at least 25 percent of the vote. Former Greenbacker J. D. Rankin of Limestone received nearly 40 percent of the vote as a Republican-Prohibition fusion candidate. Independent Labor candidates Jerome Kearby of Dallas, Bill Farmer of Mineola, Henry Clay Mack of Gainesville, and J. W. Barnett of El Paso each received between 26 and 37 percent of the vote, although Mack ran against two Democrats and Kearby against a Democrat and a Republican. Kearby and Farmer received the highest percentages among Independent Labor candidates, 37 and 31 percent, respectively. They were also the two opposition candidates with the closest ties to the Knights. Kearby, a trial lawyer, had earned the respect and gratitude of the Knights by defending destitute members against charges stemming from the second Southwest strike. Farmer was a high-ranking officer in Knights of Labor DA 78. He also belonged to the Farmers' Alliance, and at an Alliance rally shortly after the strike ended he told an audience of thousands, "If you listen to other classes you will have only three rights . . . to work, to starve, and to die."[37]

Four of these five opposition candidates in the Texas congressional elections of 1886 later became Populist leaders. (Mack was the exception.) Farmer and Rankin both played prominent roles in the proto–Populist Union Labor Party as well.[38]

## The Agricultural Wheel and the Knights of Labor in Arkansas Politics, 1886

The campaigns of 1886 also laid the groundwork for more significant efforts at farmer-labor political insurgency in Arkansas. Here the Agricultural Wheel clearly played the leading role in the third-party movement, with the Knights playing a supporting role. The Wheel, having absorbed the Brothers of Freedom in October 1885, reportedly included some 55,000 members in over 1,200 subordinate Wheels (or local chapters) in Arkansas by August 1886. In June 1886 the State Wheel nominated a state ticket headed by John G. Fletcher, a Little Rock merchant and Democratic politician, for governor. Fletcher accepted the nomination but reversed his decision a day later under a barrage of criticism and pressure from Democrats. The rest of the Wheel slate of candidates then followed Fletcher off the ticket.[39]

On 28 July 1886 the Wheel held a convention at Litchfield, Arkansas, that drew delegates from Kentucky, Missouri, Tennessee, and Texas. The delegates formed a National Agricultural Wheel and elected Isaac Mc-Cracken, president of the Arkansas State Wheel, to the same position in the "national" organization. McCracken was one of the most ardent "political Wheelers," as they were called, having won election to the state legislature as an Independent representative in 1884. In addition to McCracken, other leaders of the Arkansas State Wheel included Grand Secretary R. H. Morehead, Executive Committee Chairman Reuben CarlLee, and National Wheel lecturer (and Knights of Labor newspaper editor) Isom P. Langley. These men too were "political Wheelers," and, despite opposition from some Wheel members, they managed to put together another Wheel state ticket in early August.[40]

This ticket featured Charles E. Cunningham of Pulaski County, an old Granger and Greenbacker who had run as a Greenback-Labor Party congressional candidate in 1882, as its gubernatorial nominee. The Wheel ticket included at least one other prominent former Granger and Greenbacker, Charles E. Tobey of Pope County, nominated for state land commissioner. The *New York Times* reported that "Wheelers who are posted" predicted 20,000 votes for the ticket. This estimate proved nearly on the mark, as the ticket garnered just over 19,000 votes in the September state elections. This amounted to about one third of the State Wheel's membership and paled in comparison to the approximately 90,000 votes that the Democrats polled and the 54,000 received by the Republicans. Nevertheless, the *Times* suggested, "with a membership of 60,000, with able leaders well chosen, and with thorough organization, there is no reason why the Wheelers may not yet control Arkansas."[41]

The weak showing in the state election did not discourage Wheel candidates from running for Congress in three of Arkansas' five districts. In the Second Congressional District of central and east-central Arkansas Reuben CarlLee ran under the Wheel banner. L. H. Hitt ran as a Wheeler in the Third District of southern Arkansas, and Isom P. Langley ran in the Fourth District of west-central Arkansas.[42]

CarlLee resided in Prairie County, the birthplace of the Wheel, where he won election to the state house of representatives in 1882 and 1884, "apparently [as] a rebel from the Democratic party," according to one scholar. As a state legislator he successfully fought for the passage of a law reducing the crime of selling mortgaged property from a felony to a misdemeanor. He also introduced bills to provide increased funding for institutions for the blind, deaf, and insane.[43]

CarlLee and Hitt both faced Democratic and Republican opponents. Both finished a distant third. CarlLee received 18 percent of the vote in the Second District, while Hitt garnered only 15 percent in the Third.[44] Langley, on the other hand, only faced Democratic incumbent John H. Rogers. Rogers could hardly be considered a friend of labor, as he had ardently opposed a federal labor arbitration bill that the Knights pushed for as the second Southwest strike began to collapse. Langley apparently ran as an Independent Labor candidate, although the precise partisan label that he assumed probably meant little.[45] In September he described himself as a "Democrat–Greenbacker–Republican–Wheeler–Knight of Labor–farmer–preacher–lawyer–editor," undoubtedly hoping to appeal to as wide a base of voters as possible.[46] The limited available evidence suggests that Langley did indeed draw support from the Knights of Labor. When he spoke at the Crawford County town of Van Buren, white LA 6307, whose membership included tobacco factory workers, farmers, a railroad conductor, and men who worked as general laborers for the city, attended the speech en masse. When the supposedly forbidden topic of partisan politics arose during one of the local assembly's meetings shortly thereafter, most members declared allegiance to labor candidates. Langley received 42 percent of the vote in Crawford County, which had four Knights locals at the time. He fared best, with 56 percent of the vote, in Pulaski County. Pulaski, including the state's capital city of Little Rock, was a hotbed of Knights of Labor activity at that time, with some thirty-seven local assemblies that collectively encompassed railroad workers, sawmill hands, cotton mill hands, teamsters, and farmers and farm laborers.[47]

The fact that the Republican Party made no nomination in this contest must have further bolstered Langley's support from the Knights. As Tomson explained to Powderly in January 1887, Republicans–many of them African Americans–comprised a significant portion of the Knights' membership in Arkansas. In fact, at the annual meeting of the State Assembly of the Arkansas Knights of Labor on 3 January 1887 Tomson lost his bid for the office of State Master Workman to John W. Howell of South Hot Springs, whom Tomson described as "a bitter partisan leader, office holder + seeker, [and] chairman [of the] Co. Republican Committee of Garland County for years–a real professional politician."[48] Langley received 38 percent of the vote in his congressional bid, more than double the percentages that CarlLee or Hitt managed to attract.[49] The fact that the most successful opposition candidate in Arkansas' congressional elections in 1886 could draw upon organized farmers and laborers and Republicans who had no GOP candidate to support foreshadowed a far more significant challenge to Democratic control of the state two years later.

### *The Knights of Labor and Farmer-Labor Politics in Georgia, 1886*

The Farmers' Alliance did not reach Georgia or North Carolina until 1887, while the Agricultural Wheel entered Georgia in 1888 but never reached the Old North State.[50] Nevertheless, the Knights of Labor led a number of farmer-labor political campaigns in both states in 1886. In Georgia Knights of Labor candidates ran for the state house of representatives in the counties of Bibb (Macon), Chatham (Savannah), Clarke (Athens), Cobb (Marietta), DeKalb (Decatur), and Richmond (Augusta).[51] In Bibb County two Knights of Labor nominees, including the Knights' State Master Workman, won in the Democratic primary election and consequently the general election in October, in which Bibb voters elected three representatives.[52] In Chatham County the Knights captured a Democratic Party mass meeting on 24 September 1886 and, as the chagrined *Savannah Morning News* noted, " 'scooped in' the nominations for the Legislature with ease." Three days later the executive board of the county Democratic Party put forth its own ticket, which became known as the "regular" Democratic ticket as opposed to the Knights of Labor ticket. The Knights won a limited victory in the ensuing campaign, electing one of their three candidates. This candidate, however, was a lawyer who did not belong to the Order. Moreover, the campaign caused crippling internal dissension within Savannah's DA 139.[53]

While it is unclear if Knights candidates drew much farmer support in Bibb and Chatham counties, evidence suggests that the Order's legislative candidate received respectable support from farmers in Richmond County. Here the campaign unfolded against the backdrop of the largest textile strike the South had ever experienced. In mid-September the Knights nominated two Independent candidates (one white and one black) for the state legislature.[54] But Rev. J. Simmions Meynardie, Master Workman of the Augusta Local Assembly of mill workers, denounced the Independent ticket. He urged Knights to vote instead for the Democratic candidates, particularly former county public school system superintendent Martin V. Calvin, whom he proclaimed "cordially endorses the principles of our Order."[55] (Calvin, incidentally, would later become the chairman of the State Farmers' Alliance judiciary committee.)[56] The black Independent candidate ultimately dropped out of the race. In a four-man contest the white Independent candidate received 1,320 votes, while the three candidates who won seats in the state house of representatives received between 1,920 and 3,050 votes each. The Independent candidate made a strong showing, however, in the district that included Augusta's working-class Fifth Ward, inhabited by mill workers and farmers.[57]

The Georgia state legislative races in which Knights of Labor candidates most clearly looked to farmers as well as laborers for support occurred in Clarke and Cobb counties. In Clarke the lack of a Democratic primary election or nominating convention meant that the election was a "scrub race," in which any candidate could run under any party label.[58] Incumbent state representative Richard B. Russell, a lawyer and the father of the future Georgia governor and U.S. senator who bore his name, ran as a Democrat. Another candidate for the county's lone seat in the state house of representatives, the "successful farmer" George T. Murrell, also apparently ran as a Democrat. Murrell later became the president of the Clarke County Farmers' Alliance, but he would remain a Democrat in the face of the Populist revolt. Dr. G. W. Lowry ran as the Knights of Labor candidate, although the *Athens Banner-Watchman* reported that he "was nominated by them without solicitation." Russell received a slim majority of the votes cast, while Lowry ran a strong second. The *Banner-Watchman* reported that Lowry received "almost the solid factory vote and also the support of a majority of the white mechanics of Athens." Lowry also carried two districts outside the city limits that most likely included many farmers. Russell, the newspaper claimed, received only seven votes from white Knights in the city. African American Knights, however, reportedly "deserted" the Knights "in large numbers, and rallied around the standard of Russell."[59] This "desertion" may have reflected dissatisfaction with the Order's nominee; in late September a group of black Knights put forth Abe Tucker, described by the *Banner-Watchman* as "a man of good education and unusual intelligence" with "great influence over his people," as a candidate for the legislature. Tucker's candidacy, which the *Banner-Watchman* opposed despite its praise for him, never materialized, though.[60] This election seems to have marked the beginning of the demise of the Knights of Labor in Athens, which was apparently complete by 1890.[61]

While farmers played a significant role in the Knights of Labor in Clarke County, they played a still greater one in Cobb County, just northwest of Atlanta but largely rural at the time. Cobb became a Knights of Labor stronghold in 1886, with thirteen local assemblies by the end of the year, more than any other county in the state.[62] At least four of these Cobb County locals included farmers: LA 7492, a mixed local, LA 8283, a farmers' local, and LA 8597, a local of farmhands and cotton gin workers, in Marietta, and LA 8472, a mixed local that included renting farmers and farmhands, in Powder Springs. Two mixed locals in Big Shanty (or Kennesaw) and another in Smyrna, towns of less than a thousand residents, probably included farmers as well.[63] A letter from a member of Marietta's Gem City Assembly (LA 7492) to the *Journal of United Labor* in January 1888 discussed nothing but the economic problems of farmers and how the Order was helping to alleviate these problems to a degree.[64]

James C. Sanges, a twenty-nine-year-old Marietta carpenter, served as the Knights' chief organizer and lecturer in Cobb and, before long, other northwestern Georgia counties as well. He undoubtedly deserves some of the credit for the Knights' remarkable growth in Cobb.[65] Not surprisingly, given his importance in the Order locally, Sanges attended the Knights' General Assembly convention in Richmond in October 1886 as a representative of Atlanta-based DA 105.[66] It is unclear if Sanges attended the entire convention, but if he did, then he was absent from Cobb County while an election of much interest to him was being held. In early September he had declared himself to be a Workingman's candidate for the state house of representatives. Three other candidates vied for Cobb's two seats: incumbent Alexander Stephens Clay, who later became a U.S. senator, the "practical farmer" S. R. McCleskey, both Democrats, and "people's candidate" A. G. Dempsey. While it is unknown what issues Sanges ran upon, his frequent lectures as a Knights organizer apparently amounted to effective campaigning. Of the seven Cobb districts in which Knights locals are known to have existed at that time, Sanges was the leading vote-getter in three and finished a very strong second in two others. Sanges also succeeded where his Athens counterpart failed in receiving significant support from black voters. Overall, out of 3,136 votes cast, Sanges fell just 110 votes short of the second-place finish needed to win a house seat.[67]

While most of the Knights' bids for seats in Georgia's state house of representatives in 1886 fell short, some that did succeed produced limited but nevertheless notable results. A small but persistent labor bloc emerged in Georgia's lower house after the October elections. This bloc included Knights of Labor State Master Workman James E. Schofield and William A. Huff of Bibb County and two representatives from Richmond County, the aforementioned Martin V. Calvin and lawyer Charles Z. McCord, whose office sat near those of several textile mills on Broad Street in Augusta. (In 1888 some ex-Knights who formed a new labor organi-

zation in Augusta contended that the Knights had helped elect McCord.)
The Georgia house labor bloc did not include Savannah lawyer Phillip M.
Russell, elected on the Knights' ticket, lending credence to charges that the
former Democratic legislator was merely using the Knights as a vehicle to
return to office.[68]

The Georgia house labor bloc focused on four goals: passing a ten-
hour workday law and a child labor law, creating a state bureau of labor statistics, and abolishing the state's notorious convict lease system. All
of these goals reflected planks in the Knights' Reading platform.[69] In the
convict lease battle the labor bloc joined forces with former congressman
William H. Felton and his wife, Rebecca Latimer Felton. Dr. Felton, who
became a state legislator in 1884, began this fight in the state house, while
his wife joined the Woman's Christian Temperance Union (WCTU) and
marshaled that organization's influence in trying to eradicate (or at least
reform) the convict lease. The crusade gained some momentum after a
mutiny of convict laborers at the Dade Coal Company in northwestern
Georgia in July 1886 shed light on the horrors of the system. One of the
most powerful men in the state, U.S. Senator Joseph E. Brown, owned
these mines, however, and neither the Feltons, the Knights of Labor, the
WCTU, nor the small house labor bloc could muster the influence to
change the convict lease system at that time.[70] Similarly, the labor bloc
fell short in the rest of its goals after making an earnest fight. As an Atlanta Knight informed Powderly in early 1888, though, the introduction
of these labor bills "generated a healthy agitation[;] with that, many of us
were satisfied for a beginning."[71] The Georgia Knights eventually won one
limited legislative victory in November 1889 with the passage of an eleven-
hour workday law for factories, although it lacked effective enforcement
measures.[72]

## The Knights of Labor and Farmer-Labor Politics in North Carolina, 1886

The North Carolina Knights of Labor proved both somewhat more politically ambitious than the Georgia Knights and more successful in building a coalition of Republicans, Independents, and disaffected Democrats
in 1886. The North Carolina Knights also appealed to farmers as well as

laborers and to the poor of both races. For a brief moment the North Carolina Knights capitalized on both the split between Bourbon Democrats and poor whites and blacks that had existed since the end of the Civil War and the increasing impatience of many white Democrats with their party's failure to restore economic prosperity to the state. The Knights thus managed to achieve some significant political success in the Old North State, but the coalitions upon which this success was built would prove precarious.[73]

The Knights entered North Carolina in 1883 when telegraphers formed local assemblies in Charlotte and Wilmington. Neither of these locals survived the national telegraphers strike of that year. But by 1885 the Knights had managed to establish several locals in the cities of Raleigh and Durham, including a black mixed local in the latter city and a mixed local in the former that was briefly racially integrated but by March 1885 consisted solely of blacks except for its Master Workman.[74] From this centrally located urban area the Knights spread across the state in 1886 as the number of local assemblies in North Carolina reached seventy-nine.[75] In April 1886 the Knights claimed fifteen hundred members in Raleigh township, one fifth of them women. The *Raleigh News and Observer* reported that "nearly all" of these women were white, but in fact the Knights had chartered a mixed local of black women in Raleigh a month earlier.[76] By November 1886 the Knights had five local assemblies in Durham, at least two of which were comprised of African Americans, with a reported total membership of two thousand.[77]

Since the Raleigh-Durham area was both the center of the Knights' strength in North Carolina and "the political heart of the state," it should have come as no surprise that the North Carolina Knights' greatest push for political power came there.[78] Indeed, the Raleigh Knights included all of the basic elements of the Order's political constituency in the state—poor blacks, middle-class white Republicans, white Democrats who were becoming alienated by that party's economic policies, farmers, and a wide variety of white laborers.[79] Raleigh LA 3606, which took the initiative in forming the North Carolina State Assembly of the Knights of Labor in the summer of 1886 and provided its leading officers, also supplied the state's most notable Knights of Labor political candidate that fall. By late summer John Nichols, the Order's newly elected State Master Workman, announced that he was running for the U.S. House of Representatives as an Independent in the Fourth District.[80]

Nichols, a fifty-one-year-old native of Wake County (which includes Raleigh), enjoyed a long career of state and federal Republican patronage positions. In 1867 he joined the newly formed North Carolina Republican Party, and the following year he supported white Radical Republican leader William W. Holden's successful bid for governor. The North Carolina Republican Party, according to one scholar, "carried the banner of the 'have-nots' and promised a creed of workers' rights, public education, and a selectively egalitarian ideology," which should have made Nichols and other party regulars at home in the Knights of Labor in the 1880s. A printer by trade, Nichols served as principal of the North Carolina Institute for the Deaf and Dumb and Blind from 1873 until 1877, when the Democrats regained control of the state government. Nichols then served as a federal revenue stamp agent in Durham from 1879 to 1881 and as postmaster of Raleigh from 1881 until 1885. That job ended when Democrat Grover Cleveland assumed the presidency.[81]

The ambitious Nichols belonged to a variety of labor and civic organizations. In 1855 he joined the Raleigh Typographical Society, which later became the Raleigh Typographical Union No. 54, and became its first secretary. In 1857 he became a Mason, serving as the State Grand Master fifteen years later. In the 1880s he became the secretary of the influential State Agricultural Society and served as secretary and treasurer of the State Fair Association. In 1884 Nichols joined the Knights of Labor, "hoping," according to historian Melton McLaurin, "to use the Order to enhance his political career."[82]

While campaigning for Congress in the fall of 1886 Nichols presented a platform that seemed carefully designed to appeal to both the farmers and mechanics or urban laborers of the Fourth District. Nichols called for federal and state laws to limit the hours of labor in factories but shrewdly excluded agricultural laborers so as not to alienate the Knights' substantial base of small landowning farmers in the district. Nichols also offered laborers advocacy of child labor laws, stricter immigration laws, and protectionist tariffs, which he argued would provide jobs for laborers and markets for farmers. For farmers he also spoke of railroad regulation and land policy reform while denouncing internal revenue taxes, especially on tobacco, the district's chief crop. Nichols also likened the Knights of Labor to the Farmers' Alliance and the Agricultural Wheel, organizations that some North Carolina farmers had heard of, though neither organization had reached their state.[83]

In the November election Nichols defeated his only opponent, prominent Democratic attorney John W. Graham, by 1,437 votes, or nearly 5 percentage points. Nichols carried Wake County by about 1,500 votes and also carried the city of Durham (Durham County) by a large majority. McLaurin credited a "labor-farm-Republican coalition" with providing Nichols's majority, although in Wake County in particular many of his farmer supporters were erstwhile Democrats who were enraged by the Democratic-controlled state legislature's recent passage of a law requiring the fencing of livestock in that county. One of the three white Republican, anti–stock law farmers whom Wake County voters elected to the state house of representatives in the fall of 1886, Knight of Labor Paschal Sorrell, had been a Democratic county magistrate who switched parties because of what he perceived as "a violation of Democratic principles by that party."[84]

While it is unclear how many candidates with ties to the Knights won election to the North Carolina General Assembly in 1886, the North Carolina Knights lobbied the state legislature for some of the same demands made by the Knights in Georgia. These demands included the creation of a state bureau of labor statistics, reform of the convict lease system, and a ten-hour workday law. The North Carolina Knights relied primarily upon Republican legislators from counties with several local assemblies to introduce these bills.

In a portent of future developments in the Tarheel State, however, these bills ran afoul of agrarian legislators. Leaders of the white farmers' movement in North Carolina, such as L. L. Polk and S. B. Alexander, took an ambivalent view of laborers and labor organizations. Polk eventually adopted a more cooperative stance toward the Knights of Labor as he moved toward advocacy of a third party, but Alexander, a Democratic congressman from 1891 to 1895, never championed Populism, let alone the cause of labor. Alexander, past Worthy Master of the State Grange and future president of the North Carolina Farmers' Alliance, opposed the labor bureau bill. As a compromise, the state legislature created an autonomous bureau of labor statistics within the Department of Agriculture. The ten-hour workday bill died, however, after being reported upon unfavorably by the house agricultural committee. Only in the anti–convict labor bill did the Knights have the agrarians' support, but the Democratic lieutenant governor cast the tie-breaking vote against the bill in the state senate.[85]

## The Knights of Labor in Virginia Politics, 1886

As in Texas, Arkansas, Georgia, and North Carolina, the Knights of Labor entered politics in Virginia in 1886, but this political activity did not involve a significant farmer component in the Old Dominion. The Knights' chief political efforts in Virginia in 1886 came in the urban centers of Richmond and Lynchburg. No local assemblies of farmers or farm laborers appear to have existed in either Henrico County (Richmond) or Campbell County (Lynchburg). Mixed locals may have included some farmers or farm laborers in these counties, but Leon Fink noted that in Virginia's Third Congressional District, which included Richmond, opponents of a Knights of Labor congressional candidate (who withdrew from the race before election day) included "rural blacks untouched by the labor movement." (In contrast, African Americans composed a majority of Richmond Knights in 1886.) The Knights achieved some political success in Richmond and Lynchburg in 1886; the congressional candidate of the Lynchburg Knights, "reform Democrat" Samuel I. Hopkins, defeated an incumbent Democrat. The Knights' political success in both of these cities proved short-lived, however, partly due to internal friction created within the Order in each city by political activity. The strength and political prospects of the Richmond Knights further eroded after that city hosted the Order's General Assembly convention in October 1886, at which a biracial delegation from New York created an uproar by violating the "social [Jim Crow] customs" of the South.[86]

## Farmer and Labor Organizations and Political Prospects across the South, 1886–1888

In retrospect, the wave of labor political activity that swept across the South and the rest of the nation in 1886 "may still stand," as Fink suggested, "as the American worker's single greatest push for political power."[87] At that time, however, it was not clear that the tide had crested. Moreover, while the Knights of Labor began to decline quickly at the national level after 1886, the organization continued to grow in several southern states, including Alabama, Arkansas, Louisiana, Mississippi, and North Carolina (see appendixes 2 and 3).[88]

Furthermore, in some of the southern states in which the Knights' political activity encompassed participation by farmers, such as Texas, Arkansas, North Carolina, and Georgia, organized farmers' movements were either still growing or had not yet begun. As these farmers' movements gained momentum, the potential existed (in theory at least) for farmer-labor political coalitions to make stronger showings in these states in 1887 and 1888. Whether such promise came to fruition depended largely upon the relationship between organized farmers and organized laborers in those states.

By the end of 1886 the Agricultural Wheel had spread beyond its home state of Arkansas to Texas, Missouri, Mississippi, Tennessee, Kentucky, Alabama, and the Indian Territory.[89] Louisiana farmers had their own organization, the Louisiana Farmers' Union (LFU), formed in March 1886 from the remains of an earlier organization, the Lincoln Parish Farmers' Club. By January 1887 the LFU claimed ten thousand members, although historian William I. Hair estimated actual membership at that time to be about four thousand.[90] The Texas-based Farmers' Alliance remained almost entirely confined to that state and the Indian Territory, with a reported membership of two hundred thousand by January 1887.[91]

As part of Charles Macune's plan to solidify and strengthen the politically fractured Texas Alliance, however, the organization launched an ambitious plan of expansion in 1887. Correspondence between Macune and officers of the LFU led to the absorption of that organization into the Alliance in January. In the spring Macune sent organizers into Missouri, North Carolina, Alabama, Florida, Mississippi, Kentucky, Georgia, and Tennessee. By the end of 1887 State Alliances existed in all of these states except Kentucky and Tennessee. The fact that State Wheels already existed in both of these states probably hindered Alliance growth there, but Kentucky and Tennessee both chartered State Alliances in 1888, as did Kansas, South Carolina, and Virginia. Representatives of Indian Territory sub-Alliances (or local Alliance chapters) organized a Territorial Alliance in April 1887.[92]

Given the heavily rural cast of the Knights of Labor in much of the South, the paths of the Knights and the farmers' organizations inevitably crossed throughout the region. Whether the Knights and the Farmers' Alliance or the Knights and the Agricultural Wheel developed a complementary or even overlapping relationship or instead became adversaries varied from state to state. Which path the organized farmer-labor relationship followed in a given state generally depended upon the character of the respective organizations in that state, particularly the relative conservatism or radicalism of the farmers' organizations.

The relationship between the Alliance and the Knights in Texas illustrates this point well. The majority "radical" faction of the Texas Alliance, which passed what amounted to an expanded version of the Knights' Reading platform at Cleburne in August 1886, looked upon the Knights as allies in the struggle against the forces of monopoly (particularly railroads) and potentially at the ballot box as well. But to the minority of Texas Alliancemen who were opposed to the organization becoming involved in partisan politics and who viewed farmers and railroad workers as having diametrically opposite economic interests, the idea of an alliance between their organization and the Knights was anathema. In every state that the Southern Alliance reached, members could be found in each of these factions. The faction that held the balance of power set the tone for Alliance-Knights relations in that state, although that relationship often varied from county to county within a state. In those states where the Wheel was the leading farmers' organization, the organized farmer-labor relationship tended to be complementary if not overlapping. The Wheel, after all, tended to be more radical than the Alliance on important issues such as the organization of African Americans and direct involvement in politics. Furthermore, the Wheel's leadership, in comparison with that of the Alliance, contained less of the conservative planter element that generally opposed the Knights of Labor.[93]

## An Uneasy Alliance: Farmers and Laborers (and Race) in North Carolina, 1887–1888

North Carolina became one of the first eastern states of the former Confederacy in which the relationship between the Knights and farmers' organizations was put to the test. Initially, prospects for this relationship looked bright. As we have seen, farmers of both races constituted a significant portion of the Knights' membership in the Tarheel State, including the Fourth District, which sent State Master Workman John Nichols to Congress. When a farmers' convention in Raleigh formed the North Carolina Farmers' Association in January 1887, Nichols attended, and the Knights and the Farmers' Association exchanged fraternal greetings.[94] While the disagreement between the Farmers' Association and the Knights over the bureau of labor statistics bill ultimately proved to be a harbinger of the path that organized farmer-labor relations would take in the state, this was not yet apparent when the Farmers' Alliance reached North Carolina in April 1887.

In fact, one of the first Alliance organizers in the state, J. B. "Buck" Barry, a North Carolina native returned from Texas, was a member of the Knights of Labor himself. On 6 June 1887 Barry visited Raleigh LA 3606 and gave the Knights "an interesting account" of the Alliance's work. On 1 August Barry visited the Raleigh Assembly again and told the Knights that "against much opposition he had secured a membership of about 800 in the County."[95] This number included some of the Raleigh Knights themselves.[96] Members of the Raleigh Assembly started and ran the National K. of L. Cooperative Tobacco Company, which purchased tobacco from local farmers and did well for several years, remaining in business as a cooperative enterprise until at least 1890.[97] In the spring of that year, when the Alliance opened a cooperative store in Raleigh "for the purpose of supplying its members with goods at cost except a small amount added for freight [and] drayage," the Alliance invited the Knights to do business at the store on the same terms.[98]

Elsewhere in North Carolina, too, signs pointed to a mutually supportive relationship between the Knights and the Alliance. In January 1888 the *Fayetteville Messenger*, the official newspaper of the North Carolina Knights of Labor, editorialized: "The principles of [the Farmers' Alliance] and the Knights of Labor are closely allied and they alone will save the poor farmers of this country from a system of tenant farming. Let every farmer read and study its principles, and he will become convinced that it is his duty to join the Alliance."[99] In April 1888 the *Messenger* printed a letter from an anonymous Alliance member from Winnie, North Carolina, that stated that "it would be wise for the two orders [the Alliance and the Knights] to stand shoulder to shoulder in the grand work of emancipating the farmer and wage-worker. Let us stand firmly together and a glorious victory awaits us."[100]

Such evidence of Knights-Alliance unity in North Carolina, however, does not tell the entire story. The differences in the racial and class orientations of the two organizations caused considerable friction between them. No one felt this rift more than the landowning farmers who led the all-white Alliance or the black farm laborers who belonged to the Knights. As members of the latter group grew in number, McLaurin noted, "the opposition of white farmers [primarily those who owned land] to the Order increased."[101] In a letter to the *Journal of United Labor* the recording secretary of a local assembly of farmhands and renters in rural Northampton County wrote, "The 'landlords' in this section of the country are bitterly opposed to the Knights of Labor, so much so, that some of them have said that no member of the Order should stay on his land."[102] When John Bryan Grimes, a young white planter and Alliance leader in Pitt County, learned that some of his black farmhands had joined the Knights, he tried to plant a spy in their local assembly in hopes of destroying it. Grimes, described by one historian as a "planter aristocrat," would remain faithful to the Democratic Party during the Populist revolt and eventually became North Carolina's secretary of state.[103]

While Alliance planters had little use for the Knights of Labor, black farmhands who belonged to the latter organization took an equally dim view of the Farmers' Alliance. A member (perhaps the Master Workman) of a local assembly of farmhands, washerwomen, cooks, and laborers in the north-central North Carolina hamlet of Lawsonville condemned the Alliance's treatment of farm laborers. "It has slipped out here," he wrote, "that the so-called Farmers' Alliance . . . is instructing its members to pay no more money to wage-workers. They are to be paid off in orders on stores." Denouncing this "nefarious plan," the writer added, "We fear that this so-called Farmers' Alliance in our State means nothing more nor less than oppression and death to the laborer."[104] A spokesman for the state's "Negro exodus," which peaked when some fifty thousand African Americans left North Carolina in 1889, also condemned the Farmers' Alliance as "an oppressive institution to the colored laborer."[105]

*Deepening Dissent in the Heart of Dixie: Farmer-Labor Politics
in Alabama, 1886–1888*

In contrast to North Carolina, in Alabama the influence of the Agricultural
Wheel and, in the northern part of the state, the legacy of decades of political struggle helped to produce a more unified farmer-labor movement.
Although the Wheel and the Alliance both achieved and maintained significant size and strength in Alabama until the two organizations merged
in August 1889, the Wheel preceded the Alliance in establishing a state
body there. Both organizations entered Alabama in 1886 in the Tennessee
Valley, where these past political conflicts had been the most widespread
and intense. By January 1887 the Wheel held a state convention in the old
Greenbacker stronghold of Lawrence County and published a newspaper, the *Alabama State Wheel*, in adjacent Franklin County. By the following
spring the Alliance too had established a state organization. [106]

Although the Knights of Labor had first arrived in Alabama nearly a
decade earlier, its most significant period of growth in the state coincided
with that of the Wheel and the Alliance. After reaching an early peak of
nineteen local assemblies and perhaps as many as seven hundred members by May 1880, the Alabama Knights went into a steady decline, partly
because of members' unwillingness to pay dues. By late 1885, however,
the Knights began to grow considerably in Alabama, as in the rest of the
nation, after the Order's successful skirmishes against Jay Gould's railroad
empire. The Knights chartered ten local assemblies in Alabama in 1885
and an additional thirty-four the following year. By then the Alabama
Knights included coal miners, dry goods salesmen, woodworkers, machinists, cotton mill workers, ironworkers, and farmers. As the Order continued to grow in Alabama it recruited landowning farmers, renters, and farm
laborers of both races. In keeping with the biracial political tradition of
the northern part of the state, where "colored Wheels" became nearly as
common as white chapters, the Knights' recruitment of African Americans does not seem to have engendered much opposition there. (Like the
Wheel, the Alabama Knights organized blacks into segregated locals.) In
Tuscaloosa County, however, just north of the state's Black Belt, a member
of Washington LA 10092, a local of black farm renters in Stewarts Station,
reported that "the white people in the vicinity are opposed to the Order."

Blacks became well organized into the Knights of Labor in the southern Alabama cities of Montgomery and Mobile, though.[107] Nevertheless, the Agricultural Wheel built more of a biracial organization in Alabama than did the Knights. Black local assemblies of the Knights of Labor represented a relatively small percentage of the total number of local assemblies in the state, in contrast to the significant portion of "colored Wheels." Not until the late 1890s, it appears, did the Knights form any racially integrated locals in Alabama.[108]

Many Alabama Wheelers and Knights, regardless of race, shared a common bond of economic hardship and increasing dissatisfaction with the Bourbon Democracy's rule of the state. The Wheel developed its greatest strength in the northern part of the state, an area of hilly terrain and relatively unproductive soil that demonstrated marked anti-Democratic political proclivities. Lawrence County became the greatest Wheel stronghold in Alabama, with at least forty subordinate Wheels. Not only was Lawrence "a traditional center of political and economic unrest where the Greenback and Independent movements had been strong," but declining cotton prices and increasingly worn soil intensified the economic distress suffered by the county's farmers as well as their receptiveness to anti-Democratic, class-based political movements by the late 1880s. Similar conditions spurred the Wheel's growth in the adjacent counties of Colbert, Cullman, Franklin, Lauderdale, and Morgan.[109] Not far to the south in the Birmingham district the Knights of Labor could by 1887 claim a nearly decade-long legacy of political agitation and strikes revolving around such issues as convict labor, alien contract labor, unsafe working conditions, and low and irregular pay that sometimes came in scrip redeemable only at company stores.[110]

Having been heavily involved in Greenback-Labor politics several years earlier, the Birmingham Knights not surprisingly participated in the wave of labor politics that swept (if only ankle deep) across the nation in 1886. The Knights supported a "workingmen's ticket" in the city's municipal elections that year, while a local labor newspaper endorsed the county's two Republican legislative candidates, a Knight and a member of the Brotherhood of Locomotive Engineers. The Knights' support proved insufficient on election day, however, as the Order could not deliver the solid support of skilled white workers, to whom local Democrats gave some aldermen's positions, or black workers, whose locals constituted only two of the twelve that formed Birmingham's DA 173 on 16 October 1886.[111]

In contrast to Arkansas, in Alabama the Agricultural Wheel made the first overtures to the Knights of Labor. In the summer of 1887 the *Alabama State Wheel* suggested, "The Knights of Labor, Wheelers, Farmers' Alliance, Grange, Patrons of Husbandry [*sic*–the latter two organizations were one and the same] and all of the trades unions are striving for the self-same object–that is, the abolition of class legislation, stop[ping] the importation of pauper labor, the elevation of the toiling masses, the education of the rising generation, the equalization of taxation and the entire obliteration of the misnamed Democratic and Republican parties."[112] The accuracy of this assertion remained to be seen, but members of all the organizations named would soon put it to the test.

The first vehicle for doing so would be the Union Labor Party (ULP). This party never amounted to anything nationally, although it demonstrated strength in several states. More important than its own level of success (or lack thereof), however, was the role that the ULP would play as a bridge between the loosely organized farmer-labor political activity of the mid-1880s and the Populist Party of the 1890s.

The brief career of the ULP began in February 1887, when anywhere from three hundred to six hundred delegates attended the Industrial Labor Conference in Cincinnati. This conference, chaired by veteran Greenbacker and Knight of Labor Richard Trevellick, formed the new party. The platform composed at the conference clearly reflected the influence of the Knights' Reading platform and old Greenback platforms while presaging the Populist platforms of the 1890s. Among other demands, the ULP called for a graduated land tax "on all large estates"; governmental ownership of the means of communication and transportation; the issue of a sufficient quantity of full legal tender directly from the federal government to the people, which might also be "loaned [to] citizens upon ample security at a low rate of interest"; the free coinage of silver; a graduated income tax; a constitutional amendment establishing direct popular election of U.S. senators; and the prohibition of Chinese immigration, the convict lease system, and "the employment of bodies of armed men by private corporations." Significantly, the platform demanded women's suffrage, a demand that the Populist Party would leave out of its Omaha platform in 1892 at the insistence of southern delegates. Every state in the Union sent at least one delegate to the Cincinnati conference except California, Louisiana, Maine, Nevada, South Carolina, and Vermont.[113]

The Industrial Labor Conference established a Union Labor national executive committee, which included members from twenty-five states and territories. These members also served as state or territorial organizers. The four southern appointees were Sam Evans of Texas, J. R. Mills of Tennessee, J. R. Winston of North Carolina, and J. J. "Jonce" Woodall of Alabama.[114]

Woodall could already boast a fairly accomplished career as an agrarian reformer. He was a leading member of the Grange in Morgan County, where the Patrons remained strong until being largely superseded by the Wheel and the Alliance in 1887. When that happened Woodall became the secretary of the Morgan County Wheel. He was also active in the Greenback and Independent political movements.[115]

In July 1887 Woodall issued a call for a Union Labor Party state convention to be held in Birmingham in September. The convention drew about one hundred delegates to the city's Sublett Hall, although the *Alabama Sentinel* charged that unspecified "persons had misled many who intended [on] being present by circulating a report that the meeting would be held elsewhere."[116] Aside from Woodall, Birmingham Knights played a leading role at the meeting. About one third of the delegates, however, belonged to the Wheel. Future Populist state legislator O. M. Mastin of Chilton County, where the Knights and the Farmers' Alliance were both strong and closely allied, joined Woodall and Birmingham Knights leaders on the five-man committee on permanent organization. Among the three committee members from Birmingham was one African American. The convention issued a platform similar to that of the national party while placing more emphasis on opposition to the convict lease system (not surprisingly, given the particular concern of the Birmingham Knights with that issue). The Alabama ULP platform also called for the establishment of a state bureau of labor and a law compelling "companies employing more than twelve men to pay their employe[e]s every two weeks in lawful money" rather than in scrip to be used at company stores, "more commonly known as 'grab-alls' and 'pluck-mes.'" This demand too reflected the influence of Knights of Labor coal miners in the Birmingham district.[117]

What amounted to a second meeting of the Alabama Union Labor Party occurred six months later, when many of the same delegates reconvened in the hall of the House of Representatives in Montgomery for a state convention of organized labor called by Knights State Secretary J. T. Lavery. Over eighty delegates attended. The committee on business included one delegate from each organization represented: George F. Gaither of the Farmers' Alliance, future secretary and general manager of the State Alliance Exchange; Alfred Taylor, a Birmingham Knight of Labor; E. Q. Norton of the Land and Labor Club; B. Andrews of the Carpenters' Union; Dr. J. T. Masterson of the Agricultural Wheel; and T. H. Weafer of the Tailors' and Typographical Union. African Americans served on some committees; the *Montgomery Advertiser* observed, "These men call each other 'brother,' all of them, without distinction of race or organization or employment." The convention put forth a platform similar to the ULP platform of six months earlier, adding planks calling for mechanics' and mercantile employees' lien laws, demanding that "the cotton tax be paid back to the farmer," and demanding that election laws provide "a free ballot throughout the State," recommending the Australian (secret) ballot system in particular. The convention also chose a new party name, the Labor Party of Alabama.[118]

The Labor Party of Alabama did not run a state ticket in 1888, but it fielded tickets in a number of counties. Leading Knights headed the Jefferson County ticket. Democrats defeated this ticket, though, by adopting a strategy later used to beat back the Populist challenge throughout the South: co-opting key issues (in this case, opposition to convict leasing, company stores, and scrip payment) while charging the Labor Party with promoting black political power.[119] Elsewhere, however, the Labor Party managed some victories. In the Gulf Coast county of Baldwin, where the Knights primarily consisted of turpentine farmworkers of both races, the Labor ticket won every county office except for three commissioners' seats.[120] Labor Party candidates (sometimes calling themselves Independents) also scored some successes in the hill country counties of Chilton, Cullman, and Shelby, electing a state representative in each of the former two counties and some county officers in the latter. In Chilton County a rift temporarily developed within the Farmers' Alliance after some members attended the Labor Party convention in Montgomery, which some local Alliancemen denounced as a "Socialist" meeting. This breach healed in time for the Independent-Labor ticket (described by a local editor as "Al-

liance, labor or third-party or whatever") to win the county's legislative
race as well as those for sheriff, tax collector, and county treasurer.[121]

In other Alabama Alliance chapters, however, the anti-insurgents prevailed. The Auburn Hill Alliance of Colbert County, in the Tennessee Valley, passed a resolution in May 1888 "condemn[ing] the effort that is being
made to form a third political party of the Farmers' Alliance and Agricultural Wheel, together with other labor organizations."[122] Dissension of this
sort would continue to fester within Alabama Alliance ranks over third-party coalitions with the Knights of Labor.

Nevertheless, despite the minor scale and success of farmer-labor third-party efforts in Alabama during the late 1880s and the rancor that they
sometimes produced, these efforts served as an important bridge between
the Greenback-Labor activity of the late 1870s to mid-1880s and the state's
Jeffersonian Democratic/Populist campaigns of the early to mid-1890s.
The lists of delegates at the two state labor political conventions of 1887
and 1888 bear testimony to this point, as they include leaders of the earlier
period, such as Jonce Woodall, and of the later period, such as George F.
Gaither, whom historian William Warren Rogers called "the first prominent Allianceman in the state to advocate a total break with the Democrats."[123]

### Lost Momentum: Labor Politics in North Carolina and Georgia, 1888

Union Labor and other third-party efforts occurred elsewhere in the South
in 1888. But in states where the Farmers' Alliance dominated the farmers'
movement and remained firmly tied to the Democratic Party, these efforts
failed to amount to anything. In North Carolina the Knights of Labor,
with only a small measure of Alliance support, tried to establish a Union
Labor Party, but the few local tickets that the party fielded foundered.
John Nichols, still the Knights' State Master Workman, narrowly lost his
congressional seat to a Democratic cotton mill owner after facing an intensely racist campaign in which the Democratic press denounced him as
"a Southern man with Northern principles." Nichols's marked tendency
to vote with the Republican Party, particularly against the low-tariff, anti–
internal revenue tax Mills Bill, may have lent some credence to this image.
Another factor in his defeat emerged when factory workers in Alamance,

in Nichols's district, and elsewhere made allegations that they were being denied the right to vote as they wished under the "job lash," or threat of being fired.[124]

In Georgia, too, the Knights' political strength declined in 1888. A member of the Order did capture the mayor's office in Savannah in January 1889 on a "Citizens' Club" ticket, but this was an isolated victory.[125] In Augusta the Independent Order of United Workingmen, largely consisting of former Knights, tried with little success to influence the Richmond County Democratic Party nominating process in the summer of 1888. In the fall the United Workingmen put forth an Independent candidate for the state legislature, but he lost badly, partly due to a county voter registration law that had helped push the organization into political activism in the first place. Nevertheless, some of the United Workingmen's leaders later became local Populist leaders.[126] In Cobb County Knights of Labor leader James C. Sanges ran again for the state legislature in 1888. This time he campaigned before at least one joint meeting of the Knights and the Farmers' Alliance. Sanges made less of a showing at the polls than two years earlier, though, despite running well in Kennesaw (Big Shanty), where the Knights may have still had two local assemblies, and in Post Oak, where he had spoken before members of the Alliance and the Knights.[127] (Kennesaw and Post Oak, incidentally, had both been William H. Felton strongholds during his failed bid for reelection to Congress eight years earlier.)[128] Overall, no evidence exists of how many Cobb Alliancemen voted for Sanges in 1888, but it should perhaps be noted that when the Farmers' Alliance ran its own county ticket in 1890 "its slate of office seekers swept Cobb."[129]

## Union Laborites and "Nonpartisans": Farmer-Labor Politics in Texas, 1888

While the vast majority of Alliancemen in the Southeast were still loyal Democrats in 1888, many of their brethren in the western states of the former Confederacy had already left the party's ranks. As in Alabama, the Union Labor movement in Texas represented a continuation of Greenback-Labor and Independent farmer-labor political activity and foreshadowed the Populist revolt that would soon engulf the state. But because so many Texas Alliancemen and Knights of Labor had mobilized in support of

Independent political activity in the wake of the Southwest strikes of 1885–86, the Union Labor Party found a ready base of support that allowed it to make a greater impact on Texas politics in 1888 than it did in any southeastern state.

Historians have traced the founding of the Texas Union Labor Party to a convention held on 5 July 1888 in Fort Worth.[130] In fact, though, the genesis of the Texas ULP occurred exactly one year earlier in Waco. As the recording secretary of Knights of Labor LA 10510 of Bruce, Texas, wrote in a letter to the *Journal of United Labor* three weeks later, "The meeting [at Waco] was a large one, composed of delegates from all over the State, but we do not have hopes of doing much for several years."[131]

Since 1887 was not a state or national election year, the ULP did not become active in Texas until the following summer. By then popular support for third-party activity seemed to be rising in the Lone Star State. The *Journal of United Labor* published several letters from Texas Knights attacking the old parties and favoring a third party. In one such letter a Knight from rural Willowhale, where the Order claimed "about one hundred members," wrote that "the laboring people here are opening their eyes and beginning to . . . think and act for themselves" and that "the sentiments of the people generally are for the united labor party."[132] The terms "Union Labor" Party and "United Labor" Party were sometimes used interchangeably at the local level in the South, although nationally they were separate parties, the latter consisting of the proponents of Henry George's "single tax" on land.[133]

As in 1886, not all Texas Alliancemen expressed the same opinion of the Knights or vice versa. The recording secretary of a Knights of Labor local assembly in east-central Texas explained in fall 1887:

> A short time ago I attended a meeting of the Farmers' Alliance, in Limestone County, and, to my astonishment, I found a number of the members who thought [that] the Knights of Labor was not a fit organization for a farmer to be connected with. On visiting another meeting in my own county the conditions were reversed, and there the Order was looked upon as being the salvation of the workingman, no matter if he labors on a railroad, in a shop or on a farm. We realize the fact that, as workers, we stand or fall together–the farmer and the mechanic being mutually dependent each upon the other.[134]

The aforementioned recording secretary of LA 10510 in Bruce offered still another perspective, claiming, "The Order is growing here among the farmers, who seem to like it better than they do the Alliance."[135]

Whether a white farmer preferred the Knights or the Alliance (if he did not belong to both) depended to some degree upon his economic status. In Texas, where Bill Farmer claimed in 1889 that 50 percent of the agricultural population were tenants, the Alliance seems to have consisted of at least as many tenants as landowners. In the Southeast, by contrast, a majority of Alliance members apparently owned farms. Even in Texas the Alliance's cooperative exchanges were operated by and for landowners; most tenants lacked the cash to participate.[136] As an Alabama Allianceman explained in 1888, "The State Exchange has been introduced at our Alliance with which we are in sympathy, but we have not yet voted. We are poor people, and even a small amount of money is hard for us to raise."[137] Nor was the Alliance free of internal class conflict. "Renter" from Texas complained in a letter to the *Dallas Southern Mercury*: "The Alliance was invented for the benefit of the laboring men, and you hear men who own good farms crying, 'oppression,' and at the same time they will charge the renter from fifty to one hundred percent for the use of a cabin and piece of land for one year." The writer went on to suggest that "if the Farmers' Alliance is for the betterment of all classes, it is time they were about it" before renters such as himself slipped "into bondage."[138]

The Knights of Labor, in contrast, seemed more in tune with the interests of renters, sharecroppers, and farmhands. These landless farmers made up a considerable portion of the Order's membership in Arkansas and North Carolina, particularly after the arrival of the Farmers' Alliance in the latter state.[139] Knights of Labor locals that included landless farmers were not uncommon in the predominantly white western half of the Georgia Upcountry (especially in Cobb and Paulding counties) and could be found in every southern state.[140] Next to mixed local assemblies, some of which included farmers, farmers' locals were the most common type in Texas, and many of these included landless farmers.[141] Clearly, however, many landowning farmers belonged to the Knights as well. A cotton planter from Alabama attended the Richmond General Assembly in 1886, and a number of Arkansas locals included planters.[142] In Winnsboro, Texas, the fact that four local assemblies were able to purchase their own cooperative cotton gins and grist mills suggests that they probably included landowners.[143] Bill Farmer, the Texas Knights' State Master Workman from 1887 through 1890, owned a farm in Mineola, although he probably spent more time lecturing and politicking than farming.[144]

Variations from one county to another notwithstanding, the relationship between the Farmers' Alliance and the Knights remained strong enough in 1888 to once again make their combined forces felt in Texas politics. On 15 May 1888, pursuant to a call published in the *Dallas News* and the *Southern Mercury*, some three hundred delegates from seventy counties attended a Convention of Farmers, Laborers, and Stock Raisers in Waco, the birthplace of the state ULP, "for the purpose of considering what steps, if any, should be taken in the approaching campaign." In his compilation of platforms of political parties in Texas, Ernest Winkler wrote that "Alliance men were most numerous" at this convention, but "the Knights of Labor secured control of the organization." Some Wheelers and Grangers attended as well, although the Worthy Master of the State Grange, A. J. Rose, staunchly opposed third-party efforts.[145]

The convention chose H. S. Broiles, who had been reelected as mayor of Fort Worth with the support of the Knights and the Alliance, as chairman. Bill Farmer served on the committee on platform, which declared "independence [from] all political parties, rings, bosses, and cliques." The platform contained few surprises; it made the familiar Greenbacker demands regarding banks and currency, declared that "the means of transportation and communications should be owned or controlled by the people," called for the direct election of the president, vice president, and U.S. senators, and demanded "a free ballot and fair count." The platform also expressed "favor" for the enactment of a national usury law. The convention did not name any political candidates.[146]

Some Texas Alliancemen still remained opposed to a farmer-labor third party. In May 1888 the secretary of Sanches Creek LA 1472 of Parker County, an early Alliance stronghold, wrote to the *Southern Mercury*: "One brother wants new parties, another wants to purify the old. One is in favor of joining with the Knights of Labor, and mak[ing] a union labor party; another wants nothing to do with them."[147] By autumn, however, letters favoring the third party had become more common in this Alliance paper, which itself supported the third-party ideal while maintaining an officially nonpartisan stance. A self-described "old" man and former Democrat from Colorado County wrote one of the more impassioned letters favoring the third party, declaring, "I have seen enough for my half dollar in both parties, and if I think more of any party than I do the interest of myself, wife and children, and the Farmers' Alliance, I do not deserve the name of a free man."[148]

On 2 July 1888 a small Nonpartisan convention, called by Broiles, met in Fort Worth in anticipation of the Union Labor convention scheduled to meet there three days later. William R. Lamb, one of the leading Alliance proponents of unity with the Knights in 1886 and a Knight himself, served as chairman. This convention practically preempted the ULP convention by composing a platform much like the one promulgated at the May convention, with some added planks (such as a call for term limits for public officeholders), and by nominating a state ticket. The ULP convention, attended by about 110 delegates from 47 counties, simply approved this ticket, adopted the platform, and endorsed the national ULP platform. The endorsement of the national platform, however, came with one explicit and significant exception: the Texans refused to endorse the women's suffrage plank. Later the Texas Populists would help keep that plank out of the national People's Party platform.[149]

The Texas ULP convention attracted many of the state's established third-party or Independent leaders. Old Greenbackers like Dr. J. D. Rankin, J. E. Martin, and former congressman and gubernatorial candidate Wash Jones attended. Others present included Lamb, Dallas Knights of Labor leader J. T. W. Loe, Sam Evans, another old Greenbacker who had declined the ULP vice presidential nomination in May, and R. M. Humphrey, a Baptist missionary and the white cofounder and "general superintendent" of the Colored Farmers' National Alliance, which had begun to expand across the South that spring. The names of several of the state candidates approved by the ULP also bore a familiar ring. The party nominated State Alliance President Evan Jones for governor, Broiles for lieutenant governor, and Jerome Kearby for chief justice of the state supreme court.[150]

Jones reluctantly refused the gubernatorial nomination, fearing that to accept it would cause division in the ranks of the State Alliance, which would meet in August and was already under the strain of a faltering state cooperative exchange. Kearby also declined his nomination. In late August the ULP and Nonpartisan executive committees held a joint meeting in Dallas and decided to support Prohibition Party candidate Marion Martin, an advocate of railroad regulation, for governor and named new candidates in place of Kearby and others who had declined nominations. The Union Laborites and Nonpartisans also replaced the prohibitionist Broiles with a German Alliance lecturer in an effort to placate nonprohibitionists. The Republican Party announced its support of the ULP state ticket in September, and organized labor "strenuously campaigned" for the Martin ticket, but to no avail. The Democratic state ticket won a resounding victory, as incumbent governor Lawrence Sullivan Ross defeated Martin by a ratio of more than 2.5 to 1.[151]

The ULP nominated congressional candidates in five of Texas's eleven districts. Only three of these candidates drew anything approaching a respectable share of votes. Bill Farmer ran again in the Third District and received 32 percent of the vote, barely more than he did two years earlier. Sam Evans drew 31 percent of the vote in the Sixth District, 6 percentage points fewer than Jerome Kearby had received in that district in the previous election. In the Second District, which included Houston, R. M. Humphrey polled just under 30 percent of the vote. Each of these three candidates faced only one opponent (Democratic), unlike the ULP candidates in the First and Eighth districts.[152] Therefore, the ULP presidential vote may have reflected more accurately the party's strength in Texas. The ticket of A. J. Streeter of Illinois, the president of the National (Northern) Farmers' Alliance, and his running mate, Charles E. Cunningham, the Arkansas Wheel's gubernatorial candidate in 1886, received 29,459 votes in Texas, or 8.2 percent of the presidential votes cast in the state. While this figure might seem minuscule, it represented 20 percent of the third party's national vote. Only Kansas registered a larger Union Labor vote.[153] In many of the Texas counties where Independent tickets ran in local contests in 1886, Nonpartisan or Union Labor candidates ran in 1888. These counties included Red River, Navarro, Robertson, Lampasas (birthplace of the Texas Alliance), and Dallas, where J. T. W. Loe served as chairman of the ULP executive committee.[154]

## *"The Fraudulent State Government of Arkansas":*
### *The ULP and Southern Democracy, 1888*

While the ULP made a stronger showing in Texas in 1888 than in any southeastern state, it drew still more support in Arkansas. In fact, although nobody could have realized it at the time, in Arkansas the Union Labor challenge turned out to be the apex of the third-party crusade. The story of the ULP in Arkansas would also foretell obstacles that the third-party movement would face in other southern states to a greater or lesser extent during the decade that followed.

The official voting returns—all of which were rendered suspect in Arkansas in 1888 by outrageous fraud at the ballot boxes—credited the Streeter-Cunningham ticket with 10,613 votes in the Razorback State. This figure represented 6.8 percent of the state's presidential vote and the fourth-highest total of ULP votes, behind Kansas, Texas, and Missouri.[155] Fusion with the Republican Party in state and congressional elections, however, under the ULP banner allowed the third party to make a far more serious challenge in those Arkansas contests.[156]

Even before the Arkansas ULP held its first state convention on 30 April 1888 in Little Rock, members of the Agricultural Wheel and the Knights of Labor began making plans for the fall elections. Members of the two organizations were already cooperating in other ways. In Woodruff County, located just within the Arkansas Delta, where tenant-operated farms slightly outnumbered owner-operated farms, the Knights and the Wheel petitioned landowners for a 25 percent reduction in land rent in late 1887.[157] In the small town of Waldo, in the southwestern part of the state, Wheelers and Knights established a cooperative building association in February 1888 that in its first month built a barbershop and started work on a music hall and ten residences. The Knights' local in this town included sawmill hands, farmhands, railroad section hands, clerks, and cooks.[158] In early April 1888 the *Marianna Index* reported that "a kind of joint convention of Wheelers and Knights of Labor" had made either "the nomination or recommendation" of L. P. Featherston for Congress in the First District. Featherston, president of the State Wheel, was then serving in the state house of representatives, having been elected the previous year on a Democratic ticket. He quickly established himself as an advocate of farmers' interests, particularly railroad regulation and reform.[159]

Some fifty delegates attended the state ULP convention, representing twenty-two of Arkansas' seventy-five counties. Prominent Wheelers at the meeting included Reuben CarlLee, Isom Langley, and Isaac McCracken, who presided as chairman. Three or four black delegates attended, all but one of whom were reportedly Knights of Labor. The convention wrote a platform advocating "legislation as will secure the reforms demanded by the Agricultural Wheel, the National Farmers' Alliance and the Knights of Labor." The specific demands resembled those of other ULP platforms. One exception came in the form of a plank calling for laws regulating mining and providing for proper ventilation in mines.[160] The Labor Party of Alabama had made a similar demand in its platform several weeks earlier, calling for an inspector of mines.[161]

The Arkansas ULP convention nominated a state ticket headed by former state senator Charles M. Norwood, a one-legged Confederate veteran, for governor. The *St. Louis Post-Dispatch* reported that Norwood was "regarded as a strong man," but the bitterly partisan *Arkansas Gazette* ridiculed him as "probably the most ignorant man who ever aspired to high position in Arkansas."[162] The convention also selected six men to attend the national ULP nominating convention to be held in May in Cincinnati. These delegates included CarlLee, Charles E. Cunningham, and an African American, P. M. Thompson. The Arkansas convention instructed the delegates to support A. J. Streeter for the presidential nomination and Terence V. Powderly for the vice presidential nomination. Cunningham would ultimately receive the latter nomination.[163] Powderly undoubtedly would have declined it anyway. The Knights' General Master Workman refused to endorse the Union Labor Party or any other party, informing readers of the *Journal of United Labor*, "There is no Knight of Labor ticket in the field anywhere in the United States."[164] Privately, Powderly bargained with leaders of both major parties in hopes of being offered the position of U.S. commissioner of labor, but he ultimately broke off negotiations with both parties and maintained a position of neutrality throughout the campaign.[165]

While nobody expected Streeter and Cunningham to be moving into the White House in March 1889, Norwood's chances of moving into the governor's mansion in Little Rock rose significantly when, as was expected by then, the Republican state central committee gave its stamp of approval to his campaign in July 1888. Democratic politicians and newspapers predictably responded by warning that a vote for the ULP would be a vote to return the state to the alleged Republican misrule of Reconstruction. As the annual meeting of the State Wheel approached a week later, the *Arkansas Gazette* warned Wheelers not to fall for this Republican "scheme" or to be led astray by "political farmers who farm with their mouth[s]."[166]

In keeping with their official nonpartisanship, neither the State Wheel nor the State Assembly of the Knights of Labor endorsed Norwood.[167] Both organizations, however, clearly supported the ULP. State Wheel President L. P. Featherston, in fact, ran for Congress that year as a Union Labor candidate.[168] The Arkansas Knights, too, exhibited strong interest in the ULP campaigns. Just weeks earlier the *Journal of United Labor* had reported, "Two district assemblies will be organized in Arkansas within the next 30 days–one in the first and one in the third congressional districts."[169] These were the state's two districts, located, respectively, in eastern and southern Arkansas, in which the ULP fielded candidates in the congressional elections that year.[170] The only set of minutes known to be available for any Arkansas Knights local assembly in 1888, those of Van Buren LA 6307, clearly reveal third-party sentiment in that local. In February H. H. Dill delivered a speech before his brother Knights in which he accused the two major parties of allowing "corners on produce [and] money" and showing "indifference . . . to the laboring people." Dill concluded his speech by declaring that "he would neither support the Democrat[ic] or Republican party," to which Master Workman W. F. Stocker said, "Amen."[171] Many Arkansas Knights certainly had reason to be discontented. Several letters from Arkansas Knights published in the *Journal of United Labor* in 1888 spoke of hard times for farmers and laborers.[172] In June the Knights' State Executive Board had to issue an appeal to the locals in behalf of State Master Workman Dan Fraser Tomson "to keep his homestead from being sold at mortgage sale."[173]

Charles Norwood understood the financial difficulties confronting many of his state's farmers and laborers. He exhorted them to "strike decisive blows for the emancipation of enslaved labor in the upcoming campaign." He excoriated capitalists and their allies in government for "withholding from the honest producer and laborer the full and just reward of their toil and sweat."[174] A. J. Streeter, Charles E. Cunningham, and six other national ULP leaders stumped the state for Norwood in August. One party leader stated, "We will carry Arkansas for the Union Labor party if we can get a fair count, and we are taking steps to secure a fair count." Streeter later claimed, however, that just before the September state election leading Arkansas Democrats told him "they were going to carry the state, fairly if they could, but violently and fraudulently if they had to resort to such measures to seat their candidate." [175]

This warning, if actually delivered, proved all too prophetic. The official count gave Democratic gubernatorial candidate James P. Eagle 99,229 votes to Norwood's 84,223. [176] Fraud and intimidation, however, ran rampant in this election. Union Laborite Reuben CarlLee wrote to an acquaintance in New York City:

> I am just from Arkansas. If the people of the United States only knew half [of] how we have been treated Congress would wipe out the fraudulent State government of Arkansas and grant us a republican form of government as guaranteed by the federal constitution.
>
> In Arkansas county they robbed us of the ballot box at two townships with over 500 majority for us. In Union county Gov. Hughes armed the Democratic clubs with the State Winchesters on the night before the election (Sunday). They paraded over the county and whipped over twenty colored men, some of them so badly that they had to keep [to] their beds. On Monday they shot and killed seven Union Labor men and wounded over 20 more, and at Eldorado, the county seat, they took the poll books away from the judges and burned them before the eyes of the people and then held a new election at which no Union Labor men were permitted to vote.

CarlLee's letter went on to charge Democrats with having taken at least eighteen other counties through fraudulent and sometimes violent methods and concluded, "We undoubtedly carried the State and have been counted out." He stated that only the federal government could ensure Arkansas "an honest election." "Until then," he wrote, "the shotgun and Winchester rifle in the hands of [D]emocratic clubs, backed by the State officials, . . . rule in Arkansas and not the people." [177] While CarlLee can hardly be considered a nonpartisan source, historians have agreed that this election was clearly marked by the type of despicable measures and methods that he described. One recent study suggests that Norwood "would probably have won the governor's race had not election fraud prevented him."[178]

The Arkansas Democrats repeated this formula for victory in two of the state's five congressional elections. Four of these races featured a Democrat and one opponent: Union Laborite Featherston in the First District; John M. Clayton, a Republican who "was supported as a fusion candidate by the Wheel," in the Second District; Union Laborite John A. Ansley in the Third District; and National Wheel Grand President Isaac McCracken, who despite his prominent role at the state ULP convention apparently ran as an Independent in the Fourth District. The Fifth District pitted two challengers, an Independent and a Republican, against Democratic incumbent Samuel W. Peel, who easily won reelection. Ansley and McCracken each received slightly more than 40 percent of the votes in their districts, according to official figures. Those figures showed much narrower victories for Democratic candidates in the First District of eastern Arkansas and the Second District of eastern and central Arkansas.[179]

Norwood, Featherston, and Clayton all attempted to contest their defeats. The results proved mixed. J. W. Dollison, a ULP state legislator and Master Workman of the Knights' Paragould-based DA 223, introduced a petition from Norwood in the state house of representatives requesting a state investigation of the election. The house consented, but the state senate decreed that Norwood must first put up a forty-thousand-dollar bond to be forfeited if the state legislature did not find in his favor. This demand ended Norwood's contest.[180] Featherston and Clayton faced a far more favorable legislative body—the Republican-controlled U.S. House of Representatives—but this did not mean that their contests would be easy. The House declared Featherston the winner by eighty-six votes in the First District, but by the time he took office on 5 March 1890 half of the term of the 51st Congress had already passed. Not until 5 September 1890 did the House rule that Clayton had won in the Second District. By then, however, Clayton had been dead for more than nineteen months, having been assassinated by one of a ring of leading Conway County Democrats while gathering evidence for his case. Clayton's murder would forever be an unsolved "mystery," although historian Kenneth Barnes has recently concluded that several prominent local Democrats, heavily involved in election day chicanery, planned and executed Clayton's shotgun murder.

While the assassination of a man as prominent as Clayton, the younger brother of Arkansas Democrats' greatest enemy, Reconstruction Republican governor Powell Clayton, would prove rare, the general methods used by Arkansas Democrats in 1888 would not.[181] Such methods had proved effective in securing the "redemption" of the South from Republican rule and would be resurrected in numerous southern states to beat back the Populist challenge.

## The Union Labor Party in Perspective

The Arkansas and Texas campaigns of 1888 ranked as the ULP's strongest in the South and, indeed, among its strongest in the nation. Outside these two states the Streeter-Cunningham ticket received more than 10,000 votes in only Kansas (37,788) and Missouri (18,589).[182] In both of these states, too, Grangers, Greenbackers, Alliancemen, Knights, and, in Missouri, Wheelers all played roles in building the ULP. The few victories achieved by the Kansas and Missouri Union Labor parties occurred at the local level. In Missouri one of the chief problems faced by the ULP foretold one of the chief problems that the state's Populists would soon face: a competitive two-party system that made it difficult for a third party to attract supporters. ULP congressional candidates ran in nine of Missouri's fourteen districts in 1888, but only one received barely more than 10 percent of the vote. Populist congressional candidates in Missouri would fare little better. In Kansas, however, "a one-party dominant political system" in which Republicans held a lock on power created more of an opening for a third party, and the ULP laid the groundwork for a successful state Populist Party.[183]

Overall, though, the ULP campaigns of 1888 betrayed a lack of effective national or even regional organization. Nothing illustrated this problem more convincingly than the failure of the Streeter-Cunningham ticket to garner as many as ten thousand votes in any state outside of these four nearly contiguous states of the Midwest to Southwest.[184] Clearly, farmer and labor insurgents would have to develop a more coherent third party if that party were to have any chance of making a significant impact at the national or regional levels.

The third-party efforts of 1888 revealed more than just a lack of effective regional or national party organization. These efforts also revealed a lack of unity among reformers and reform organizations. Third-party supporters were divided into two third parties, the Union Labor Party and the United Labor Party. No formal unity existed between the Northern Farmers' Alliance, the Southern Farmers' Alliance, the Colored Farmers' Alliance, and the Agricultural Wheel or between these organizations and the Knights of Labor. In 1889, however, leaders of these organizations began efforts to bring them closer together. Although the results proved mixed, these efforts nevertheless helped lead to the formation of a more viable third party, the People's (or Populist) Party. In constructing this new party reformers would build upon previous third-party efforts and already existing biracial farmer-labor coalitions, but at the same time they also would have to confront the same obstacles that hindered those earlier attempts at biracial farmer-labor political activism.

# CHAPTER FOUR

# Toward a Third Party in the South and Nation, 1889–1892

In December 1888 the National Agricultural Wheel and the Southern Farmers' Alliance held a joint meeting at Meridian, Mississippi, at which "a consolidation of the two Orders [was] effected, subject to ratification by the organized States." The merger agreement gave the organization a new name, the Farmers' and Laborers' Union of America, and installed Texas State Alliance President Evan Jones as president and National Wheel President Isaac McCracken as vice president.[1] Ratification from the necessary number of state bodies had occurred by September 1889, although antagonism between "conservative" Alliancemen and "radical" or "political" Wheelers in Texas and Arkansas delayed the merger in these states until 1890 and 1891, respectively. But while the merger would eventually unite white Southern Alliance and Wheel members, it would not encompass African American members of agricultural organizations. Until the National Agricultural Wheel merged with the Southern Alliance its membership included African Americans, usually in segregated "colored Wheels" that were attached to the national organization. The National Wheel, however, ceased to exist with the ratification of the Alliance-Wheel merger, and the Farmers' and Laborers' Union did not allow black members. Hence, African American agrarians could only join the distinctly separate (and in many ways subordinate) Colored Farmers' Alliance.[2]

As the Southern Farmers' Alliance and the Agricultural Wheel moved toward consolidation in 1889, leaders of both organizations contacted Terence V. Powderly. Charles W. Macune, president of the Southern Alliance until the completion of the merger, wrote to Powderly in January, expressing a "desire to see you on matters of importance."[3] In June Reuben F. Gray, associate editor of the Southern Alliance's national journal, the *National Economist* (and also a member of a Texas Knights of Labor local assembly), wrote to Powderly, an "old-time acquaintance" of his. Gray requested that Powderly stop at the *National Economist* office to visit with himself and editor Macune when next in Washington, D.C. "We as farmers," Gray wrote, "hope to secure more intimate relations with [the] K. of L." "Many leading members of the Alliances are Knights," Gray noted, "and the qualifications for membership are almost identical, all productive laborers being alike eligible in each."[4] Later in June 1889 Isaac Mc-Cracken, still president of the National Agricultural Wheel, also wrote to Powderly, asking if the Knights would be interested in sending delegates to a farmer-labor reform meeting in St. Louis later that year. Pointing out that he (like Powderly) was a former machinist, McCracken told the Knights' leader, "I feel warranted in making the assertion that there is no antagonism existing between the wage workers and agriculturalists. We have a common organized enemy to fight."[5] Powderly, it will be recalled, had sent a letter to McCracken some three years earlier at the meeting of the Arkansas State Wheel that gave birth to the National Wheel. In that letter Powderly pledged the Knights' assistance "in securing needed legislation, and the repeal of obnoxious laws."[6]

This contact between leaders of the farmers' movement and Powderly helped pave the way for a series of reform conferences held between December 1889 and July 1892 that resulted in the formation of the national People's (or Populist) Party. In addition to the Southern Farmers' Alliance and the Knights of Labor, the Northern Farmers' Alliance and the Colored Farmers' Alliance both sent representatives to some of these conferences as well. (In fact, both Union Laborites A. J. Streeter of the Northern Alliance and R. M. Humphrey of the Colored Alliance would be among the staunchest advocates of forming the People's Party.) The platforms that emanated from these conferences clearly reflected the influence of the Knights' Reading platform (1878), the Greenback-Labor Party's Toledo platform (1878), and the Texas Farmers' Alliance's Cleburne platform (1886), all of which embodied the "producerist" ideology that seemed to hold the promise for bringing farmers and laborers together in political as well as economic cooperation.

Yet even as national leaders and representatives of the farmer and labor movements constructed the framework for a third party, economic and class conflicts, racial tensions, and mistrust and suspicion between and within the movements undermined the potential for building a biracial coalition of the producing classes. These problems became evident at the aforementioned national conferences and were visible in the South as well. Southern Alliancemen took a dim view of activism by the Knights of Labor and the Colored Farmers' Alliance among black farmworkers, while the Knights sometimes found Southern Alliance support lacking for key labor demands such as the abolition of the convict lease system (itself a racial as well as class issue) and the regulation of working conditions in factories or mines.

The salience of these conflicts in various states and how or whether they were resolved greatly affected the prospects of farmer-labor political alliances in those states. In southern states such as Texas, where such issues did not emerge as serious obstacles to farmer-labor unity, farmers and laborers made common cause in significant efforts that laid the groundwork for a strong People's Party. In other southern states such as Tennessee disagreement between farmers and laborers over these fundamental issues would severely curtail the prospects of building a farmer-labor third-party movement. In every southern state, of course, Populists had to confront the omnipresent race issue. This meant not only trying to appeal to black voters without alienating white voters—no easy task in the post-Reconstruction South—but also dealing with the sensational, inflammatory race baiting that such efforts were sure to provoke from the southern Democracy. Other race-related obstacles would emerge in certain southern states in the early 1890s as well, although their impact was not always immediately apparent. Indeed, during the early 1890s the Populists seemed to have a strong chance of building farmer-labor coalitions in a number of southern states, particularly those where the foundation for such a coalition had already been laid, such as Texas, Arkansas, and Alabama.

### *The Potential Value of a Declining Ally: The Knights of Labor after the "Great Upheaval"*

As historians have noted, one obstacle to the creation of a farmer-labor third party at this time, not just in the South but nationally, involved the declining strength of the Knights of Labor. The entreaties of Alliance and Wheel leaders to Powderly came at a time when the organization that he led, beset by employers' counteroffensives after the "great upheaval" of the mid-1880s as well as internal dissent, was clearly on the wane. The Knights' self-reported membership fell dramatically from 729,677 in mid-1886 to 220,607 just three years later. This precipitous decline has led scholars to suggest that by the late 1880s the Order had little to offer the farmers' organizations aside from a diminishing membership base.[7]

Such a skeptical appraisal of the Knights' potential input, however, rests upon the assumption that the organization could only contribute to a farmer-labor political coalition through its members' votes. What else, then, did the Knights have to offer? For one thing, the Order had been operating a Washington lobbying agency, the National Legislative Committee, since 1885. The Knights' lobbying successes went farther back than that, contributing to the creation of the U.S. Bureau of Labor Statistics in 1884, the Foran Anti–Contract Labor Law of 1885, and, to the Order's ultimate discredit, the Chinese Exclusion Act of 1882.[8] Since the Southern Alliance expressed many of the same demands as the Knights in its platform and would soon present a significant new one (Macune's subtreasury plan), it too would need to establish a Washington lobbying presence to have any chance of influencing federal legislation.

Moreover, some leaders of the agricultural organizations such as McCracken insisted that farmer and labor organizations would have to present a united front "to make . . . demand[s] on our National Lawmakers." "We have as seperate [*sic*] organizations made our demands," he lamented to Powderly, "and I am sorry to say made but poor success."[9] And while the American Federation of Labor (AFL), organized in December 1886, already had begun to challenge the Knights for supremacy in the American labor movement, the new organization presented a much less likely partner for the agrarians. The AFL, under the leadership of the veteran trade unionist Samuel Gompers, advocated voluntarism and "pure and simple unionism," which meant that the organization rejected third-party politics and the Knights' broad reformist agenda in favor of building a disciplined network of trade unions focused on raising wages, reducing working hours, and protecting craft traditions.[10] Thus the Knights, which in 1889 still had more members than the AFL, seemed a much more compatible choice for Alliancemen or Wheelers looking for allies in organized labor.[11] Furthermore, as we have seen, the Knights and the agricultural organizations already had a history of working together in some areas. In some of those locales where the Knights had been politically active in the 1880s the organization retained a core of experienced political organizers and activists into the 1890s, even as its membership tumbled.[12]

The likelihood of the Knights and the farmer groups cooperating on a larger scale increased in July 1889 when the labor organization chose Atlanta, an area of considerable Southern Alliance strength, as the site of its annual General Assembly meeting to be held the following November.[13] Powderly invited Col. L. F. Livingston, president of the Georgia Farmers' Alliance, and other Alliance officials to address the Knights. On the first day of the convention Powderly told the press, "I will use my best efforts to promote the alliance" between the Knights and the Farmers' Alliance. On 15 November Livingston, Reuben F. Gray, and Henry Brown, editor of the *Southern Alliance Farmer* of Atlanta, spoke before the General Assembly. All three men urged cooperation between the Knights and the Farmers' Alliance, and Gray suggested that the Knights send a committee to the joint convention of the Northern and Southern Alliances in St. Louis early the next month.[14] (Northern Alliance Vice President H. L. Loucks had already issued the same invitation to Powderly a month earlier.)[15] Powderly and two members of the Knights' General Executive Board, A. W. Wright of Canada and perennial third-party man Ralph Beaumont, attended the St. Louis convention.[16]

## A Confederation of Sorts: The Knights, the Southern Alliance, and the St. Louis Agreement

Southern Alliance leaders hoped to achieve a consolidation of their organization and the Northern Alliance at St. Louis. Some of the more radical Southern Alliancemen, such as Evan Jones of Texas, also hoped for an amalgamation or at least a confederation of sorts with the Knights of Labor. Hopes for a merger between the two Alliances quickly evaporated. Northern Alliancemen objected to the Southern Alliance's official name, the Farmers' and Laborers' Union, its refusal to admit black members, and its secret rituals. The Southern Alliance thus changed its name to the National Farmers' Alliance and Industrial Union and offered to allow each

State Alliance to make its own decision regarding black members, provided that none would be elected to the National Supreme Council. The Southern Alliance delegates also indicated willingness to compromise on the secrecy issue.[17]

Northern Alliance leaders had other concerns, however, about which their southern counterparts could do or would do nothing. The fact that about two hundred Southern Alliance delegates attended the convention as compared to about seventy-five Northern Alliance delegates reflected the relative strength of the two organizations, and Northern Alliance leaders feared a loss of influence in a merger. Moreover, while both Alliances were farmer groups, they did not share entirely compatible economic interests. The Northern Alliance consisted largely of dairy farmers who opposed the use of synthetic food products such as oleomargarine and vegetable lard, while Southern Alliancemen favored the use of these products because they were made with cottonseed oil. The subtreasury plan, introduced by Macune at this convention, also caused conflict between the two Alliances. The plan called for the federal government to build warehouses in heavily agricultural counties in which farmers could store excess nonperishable crops, allowing them to sell the crops later at higher prices rather than glutting the market at harvesttime. The plan also called for the federal government to loan farmers 80 percent of the local market price for their crops upon storage at an annual interest rate of 1 percent. The Northern Alliance delegates rejected this plan, correctly perceiving that it would provoke considerable opposition from those outside of Alliance ranks while failing to help northern dairy farmers and livestock raisers. These obstacles prevented the consolidation of the Northern and Southern Alliances.[18]

Talks between Southern Alliance leaders such as Macune and Evan Jones and the three Knights of Labor representatives proved more productive. Although Powderly and Beaumont both clearly stated that they (like the Northern Alliance leaders) opposed the consolidation of their organization with the nearly million-member Southern Alliance, Powderly did, on the other hand, harbor hopes that a partnership of sorts with the agrarian reform organizations would revitalize the waning Knights.[19] Moreover, the Knights and the Southern Alliance, easily the largest agricultural order, made many of the same demands in their platforms. Thus on 6 December

1889 Powderly, Beaumont, and Wright and the nineteen members of the Southern Alliance's committee on demands signed an agreement pledging the two organizations to "act in concert before Congress for the purpose of securing the enactment of laws in harmony with the demands mutually agreed." The agreement also declared that "we will support for office only such men as can be depended upon to enact these principles in statute law uninfluenced by party caucus." The seven demands contained in the agreement encompassed the familiar Greenbacker planks for the abolition of national banks and bank notes and the issue by the federal government of legal tender money in sufficient volume to meet the business needs of the nation; federal laws prohibiting the dealing in futures of all agricultural and mechanical products; the free and unlimited coinage of silver; federal laws prohibiting alien landownership and opening more land to settlers; stringent taxation and economically and honestly administered government; and government ownership of the means of communication and transportation. The joint Alliance-Knights demands did not include the subtreasury plan.[20]

## The Effects of the St. Louis Agreement

The agreement between the Southern Alliance and the Knights of Labor produced two significant and immediate results. One of these results occurred in the nation's capital, while the other took place in a number of states across the South. Both ultimately pushed the Southern Alliance and the Knights closer to forming the Populist Party.

Within two weeks of the St. Louis agreement Charles Macune and Alonzo Wardall of the Southern Alliance joined Ralph Beaumont and Florida Knights leader J. J. Holland in Washington as lobbyists. By April 1890 the Knights had presented bills calling for the free coinage of silver and government ownership of telegraph lines with Southern Alliance support, while the Alliance lobbyists submitted the subtreasury bill with the support of the Knights, even though Beaumont and Powderly both privately expressed reservations about the scheme. All three of these bills failed, but the Alliance lobbyists learned the craft from the more experienced Beaumont, who had been engaged in this work since 1886. Furthermore, the failed lobbying efforts made some Southern Alliance leaders, including newly elected president L. L. Polk of North Carolina, realize that neither of the two major parties would grant the organization's major political demands.[21]

The St. Louis agreement also brought the Alliance and the Knights closer together in a number of southern states and reinvigorated the latter organization to a modest but nevertheless noticeable degree. In North Carolina, where prominent Democratic attorney David Schenck worried about the Knights, Farmers' Alliance, and trade unions "combining to form a national political party to overthrow everything in their way," the Alliance and the Knights held a joint meeting at the town of Tarboro some seven weeks after the St. Louis convention. George Tonnoffski, an officer in the still-active Raleigh LA 3606, spoke for the Knights before an "overflowing" crowd at the local opera house. Elias Carr, president of the North Carolina State Farmers' Alliance, spoke for that group. Of the Knights of Labor Carr said, "If conducted upon wise and judicious principles it will be of good" while suggesting that the organization should not "engender strikes." Tonnoffski spoke of land reform (one of Powderly's favorite issues) as an important measure that both the Knights and the Alliance should support, asserting that "millions of acres of land have been stolen from the people" by railroad companies and speculators. A state senator from Pitt County (a stronghold of both the Alliance and the Knights) who either did belong or had belonged to the Grange said that "the Farmers' Alliance and Knights of Labor sprung from the Grangers—that the Grangers were their fathers and he as a father must love the children," drawing laughter from the audience.[22] The Knights chartered twenty-six local assemblies in North Carolina in 1890, the highest total in any southern state and the sixth highest among all states that year. All of these assemblies were rural, which suggests that many of them included farmers or farm laborers and that close relations with the Alliance would not boost the Knights' sagging fortunes among urban laborers.[23]

The national Knights–Southern Alliance rapprochement seemed to have a similar effect in other southern states as well. From Georgia, where the State Assembly of the Knights of Labor and the State Farmers' Alliance had announced plans in June 1889 to establish cooperative cotton oil mills together, James C. Sanges informed Powderly, "I have an engagement to organize two new Local[s] in Decatur County [in the state's southwest-

ern corner] composed wholly of Farmers' Alliancemen all growing out of
Bro. Livingston meeting the GA [Knights' General Assembly] while in session at Atlanta."[24] While the organization of such new locals gave a much
needed lift to the Knights' faltering membership figures, the Alliance could
not hope to build a coalition with nonagricultural or urban laborers when
the Knights were organizing farmers and farm laborers—especially when
those people already belonged to the Alliance.[25]

Even in a city such as Baton Rouge, Louisiana (population 10,478), the
effects of "the glorious St. Louis Convention" were much the same. Outside of New Orleans the disastrous sugar plantation workers strike of 1887
had left the Knights discredited and decimated in Louisiana. By 1890 the
two local assemblies in Baton Rouge "were languishing in every respect."
But after the St. Louis meeting "the farmers" began "taking an interest"
in the Order. To capitalize on this interest, the Baton Rouge Knights held
a public meeting that featured a speech by Daniel Morgan, an Alliance
delegate to St. Louis and former Worthy Master of the Louisiana State
Grange. Morgan sang praises of the Knights and extolled Powderly and
Beaumont as "peerless statesmen." After this meeting the Baton Rouge
Knights immediately began receiving applications for membership.[26]

The St. Louis agreement merely reinforced the direction that relations
between the Farmers' Alliance and the Knights were already taking in Alabama, although one scholar may have overstated the case by asserting,
"The marriage of the Knights and Alliance set the immediate stage for
the real Populist movement in Alabama."[27] In the summer of 1889 the
Alabama State Assembly of the Knights of Labor extended fraternal greetings to the State Alliance, noting that the two organizations held "identical"
aims and objects.[28] Two weeks later the State Alliance returned the favor by
pledging to assist the Knights "in their endeavor to have laws enacted for
the benefit of labor."[29] Shortly before the St. Louis convention the Knights
and the Alliance held joint meetings at Clanton, which the *Alabama Sentinel* called "a veritable Alliance and K. of L. stronghold," and Mentone,
located near the state's northeastern corner. The assemblage at Clanton
heard an Alliance organizer and a former Jefferson County Labor Party
candidate for the state legislature speak of the need for the two orders to
join in taking "independent political action." The latter speaker, Dr. F. L.
Fielder, denounced railroad syndicates, "mining kings," and the nation's

financial system, which worked to the detriment of the "wealth producers of the land." At Mentone Knights State Master Workman Dennis Canning told Knights and Alliance members "how the wages of a miner and other wage workers regulated prices of farm products" and how "the money men of Wall Street" manipulated both wages and crop prices.[30]

Unity between the Alliance and the Knights in Alabama also existed south of the state's hill country before the St. Louis meeting. In Selma, where the Knights' state lecturer had been recently elected mayor, many members of the Knights belonged to the Alliance as well, and some of these dual members suggested that "it would be well if the K. of L. generally would identify itself with the Alliance." Knights of Labor State Secretary-Treasurer and *Alabama Sentinel* editor T. H. White opined, however, that the two orders could accomplish more in the way of reform and legislation by working together as separate organizations than by merging into one, much as Powderly and Beaumont would in St. Louis.[31]

As one might expect, the St. Louis agreement only encouraged this close relationship between the Knights and the Farmers' Alliance in Alabama. Canning reported that "great enthusiasm is manifested throughout the country by members of both the Alliance and the Knights of Labor at the fusion effected in St. Louis."[32] More joint gatherings of Knights and Alliance members occurred in Alabama in 1890 at which those present discussed the need for political action. At Mentone members of the two organizations unanimously resolved to "cut loose from all party ties and vote an independent ticket" comprised of those "who will serve the people and not the money power."[33] While accounts of these meetings make no mention of African Americans, who were barred from joining the white Alliance, Terence V. Powderly and Alabama Commissioner of Agriculture Reuben F. Kolb both attended the convention of the Colored State Alliance in January 1890. "The aim of both men," according to one scholar, "was to secure the Negro vote for the anticipated revolt."[34] As it turned out, the revolt would have to wait for two more years. Kolb did not receive the Democratic gubernatorial nomination that he sought in 1890, despite being the recognized favorite before the nominating convention began. He did not, in 1890, choose to bolt the party after it denied him that honor.[35] The story would be different two years later.

As in 1888, however, some Alabama Alliancemen still opposed any association with the Knights. As the St. Louis convention approached the *Montgomery Alliance Journal* declared that the Knights included "the worst elements of our population," a "large number" of whom "opposed . . . our laws and the principles of our government" and posed a threat to property ownership.[36] The St. Louis agreement did not change the journal's position. Commenting upon the Knights in early 1890, the *Alliance Journal* insisted that the "only relation they sustain to agriculture is being a tax upon it."[37] Nor did the journal have any use for the Colored Alliance, expressing hope that "there will be no more of these organizations effected."[38] Both of the journal's editors were staunch Democrats who strongly opposed Alliance involvement in politics. By 1891, though, this stance was so out of step with the Alabama Alliance that one of the journal's editors was expelled from the organization; the journal then took a new name and became the mouthpiece of the State Grange, which was virtually dead outside of the wire grass region of southeastern Alabama.[39]

A similar controversy erupted involving the official journal of the Alabama Knights, the *Alabama Sentinel.* In April 1890 the *Sentinel* endorsed Democratic gubernatorial candidate Joseph F. Johnston, a Birmingham banker and industrialist, instead of Kolb, the favored candidate of the Alabama Farmers' Alliance, claiming that Johnston, if elected, would work to eradicate the state's convict lease system.[40] The Alabama Knights of Labor State Assembly responded to this endorsement by censuring *Sentinel* editor T. H. White and reaffirming the Order's intent to cooperate with the Alliance.[41]

In Arkansas, too, the St. Louis agreement only served to bolster the close ties already existing between the Knights and the farmer organizations. In the summer of 1890 the Arkansas Knights and the Arkansas Farmers' and Laborers' Union (as it still called itself) jointly issued a series of "demands for State legislation" and agreed "to act before the State Legislature, in order to carry out these demands." In addition to some of the planks in the St. Louis agreement the Arkansas Alliance members and Knights also called for a weekly cash payment law for miners, an anti–child labor law, an anti–convict labor law, a law for uniform school textbooks provided by the state "at the actual cost of production," and, perhaps most important of all in light of the events of 1888, the adoption of the Australian (secret ballot) system of voting.[42] Early indications suggested much cause for concern over this issue in 1890 as well. In the spring an Arkansas Democrat allegedly told Knights (and future Populist) leader John H. Robertson, in reference to black voters, "If we can't beat them any other way, we will bulldoze and scare them our way. . . . If democracy is to flourish in Arkansas, we must keep the nigger under our thumb."[43]

## *"The Political Agitators of the Union Labor Party" Try Again: The Arkansas Elections of 1890*

Although the National Union Labor Party disintegrated after its poor showing in the elections of 1888, the Arkansas branch not only remained active enough to hold a state convention in Little Rock in June 1890, but it figured to play a major role once again in the state's campaigns. Most of the demands that had just been put forward by the joint meeting of Arkansas Alliance members and Knights made their way onto the Arkansas ULP platform, which was composed and ratified by approximately fifty delegates (including two African Americans) from thirty-three counties at the Little Rock meeting. While Arkansas Democrats may have been encouraged by the small turnout, they also knew that it did not fully represent the ULP's voting base; as the *Arkansas Gazette* laconically commented, "the political agitators of the Union Labor party are looking to the Republicans to do the voting, [thus] it matters not to them whether there is any [party] organization in more than twenty-five counties or not."[44] Familiar names in attendance at the convention included ULP Congressman L. P. Featherston, Charles Cunningham, Isom P. Langley, Isaac McCracken, Reuben CarlLee, and former Greenbackers L. H. Hitt (a congressional candidate in 1886) and Isaac Gillam of Little Rock, who declared that "all men of his color would support" the ULP ticket, since the party promised to improve the black man's condition.[45]

The ULP nominated a full state ticket headed by Napoleon Bonaparte Fizer of White County, a thirty-seven-year-old Mississippi native who served as a presiding elder in the Methodist Church. Others on the ticket included John Pittman, a druggist and probate judge in Nevada County who accepted the party's nomination for secretary of state after state party chairman W. Scott Morgan declined it; O. S. Jones, a property-owning farmer and blacksmith, for auditor; the aptly named *Conway County Wheel* publisher and editor G. B. Farmer for commissioner of agriculture; and for land commissioner schoolteacher Charles M. B. Cox, a Knight of Labor who switched from the Democratic Party to the ULP after a state convention of the former treated his request to endorse Knights of Labor and Agricultural Wheel demands "with scorn."[46]

As in 1888 the Arkansas Republican Party endorsed the ULP state ticket. The Republicans also gave the ULP a clear field on which to battle the Democrats in the First Congressional District, where Featherston was seeking reelection, and in the Second District, in which the U.S. House of Representatives removed Democrat John Breckenridge from office in September after declaring the late John Clayton the rightful winner of the previous election. Isom P. Langley, who had run as an Independent Labor candidate in the Fourth District in 1886, ran against Breckenridge both in the election for the 52nd Congress and in a special election to fill the vacant seat for the remainder of the 51st Congress.[47]

The Arkansas Democrats responded to the ULP challenge by naming State Wheel Vice President D. E. Barker to their platform committee and virtually stealing the Union Labor platform. The Democrats announced similar demands regarding land reform, railroad regulation, convict labor, school textbooks, and, ironically, the secret ballot, even though John Robertson claimed that just weeks earlier a Democrat had smugly assured him that "the Democrats of this State want no secret ballot now, and, as we always have the majority in the Legislature, we can keep her down."[48] Voters who remembered how the state Democratic Party had adopted Greenbacker demands only to repudiate them after the elections passed may have doubted the Democrats' sincerity.

In the end, though, how voters felt (or voted) may not have mattered, as "once again violence and intimidation were used to ensure a Democratic victory."[49] Incumbent Governor James P. Eagle defeated Fizer by a percentage margin of 55.5 to 44.5.[50] The Democrats also swept the congressional races. They denounced L. P. Featherston as "Force Bill" Featherston because he (not surprisingly) supported the Lodge Election Bill, which would have facilitated federal supervision of presidential and congressional elections.[51] The State Wheel president could, however, point to a strong record of trying to help the state's farmers, despite the fact that his need to contest the election of 1888 before being seated kept him from entering the 51st Congress until it was half over. Featherston introduced several bills to provide for agricultural relief and protection of farmers' products, another "to increase the volume of money on a real estate and gold and silver basis," and another calling for the direct election of U.S. senators (a perennial Knights and Alliance demand). He also introduced petitions on behalf of the Arkansas Alliance and Wheel against the passage of the Conger Lard Bill, which many southern farmers opposed, since it would have placed taxes and restrictions upon the production of vegetable oil–based lard substitutes, including those using cottonseed oil.[52]

Featherston's record most likely would have won him reelection in a fairly and honestly conducted election. Instead he lost in 1890 by about the same scant margin that the original return had shown two years earlier. In the second district as well Breckenridge defeated Langley in both the special and regular elections by about the same margin. Although the defeated ULP candidates had ample reason to contest the results, they declined to do so. The murder of John Clayton during his bid to contest the Second District election of 1888 may well have discouraged Featherston and Langley from filing contests in 1890, but an even larger factor lay in the shift in power in the U.S. House of Representatives produced by that year's congressional elections. The Democrats wrested control of the House away from the Republicans, which meant that anti-Democratic challengers who filed election contests would face an expensive and time-consuming uphill battle.[53]

The role of the Knights of Labor in the Arkansas elections of 1890 is somewhat unclear. On the one hand, former third-party advocates such as Dan Fraser Tomson and H. H. Dill soured on "partisan politics" after the elections of 1888, claiming that the Knights' involvement in the campaigns had led to a sharp drop in membership.[54] Tomson's organizing and lecturing efforts restored the membership of the Knights' State Assembly, which encompassed most but not all of the state's locals, to 3,500 by the summer of 1890, only 250 less than where it had stood in the fall of 1888. In keeping with the Order's official nonpartisan stance, Tomson told a reporter covering the State Assembly convention in August 1890, "Mr. Fizer is not a representative of the Knights of Labor, and we had nothing whatever to do with his candidacy, and will certainly not ratify him as a body." Tomson added that members of the Order were free to vote for the candidate of their choice. Tomson also resigned as State Master Workman at this session, to be replaced by Michael Woods of Coal Hill. The State Assembly also chose Woods as the chairman of a new Knights of Labor state legislative committee.[55] Whether Woods was a Union Laborite is unknown, but other prominent Arkansas Knights such as Charles Cox, J. W. Dollison, Langley, McCracken, and Robertson were all known Union Laborites by this time.

### The "Alliance Yardstick" of 1890 and "Pseudo *Reform Leaders*"

In most southern states, however, the Farmers' Alliance attempted to work within the Democratic Party in 1890 by measuring prospective candidates by the "Alliance yardstick," or their acceptance and endorsement of Alliance demands. As several historians have noted, this strategy seemed to work well at first. In Georgia, for example, Alliance Democrats elected the governor and six of ten congressional representatives in 1890 as well as a large majority of state representatives and senators. The new legislature, however, got off to an inauspicious start in the eyes of many Alliancemen by electing a member of the old Bourbon Triumvirate, John B. Gordon, to the U.S. Senate despite this recent Alliance convert's opposition to the subtreasury plan and other Alliance demands. Furthermore, the legislature's inaction on crucial issues such as taxation, the crop lien, and the regulation of railroads and out-of-state corporations left one of the Alliance legislators himself grumbling to Terence V. Powderly about the "*pseudo* reform leaders" in the legislature. The performance of Georgia's "Alliance Legislature," in short, convinced a good many (though hardly all) Georgia Alliancemen of the need for a third party devoted to the enactment into law of Alliance demands.[56]

The same scenario unfolded in other southern states as well. In South Carolina the Farmers' Alliance helped elect Democrat Ben Tillman as governor in 1890, but the State Alliance formally repudiated him by a unanimous vote the next year after he failed to get behind railroad regulation and denounced the subtreasury plan as a potentially dangerous tool of federal power.[57] In Texas the Alliance, the Knights, and the Grange all helped James S. Hogg reach the governor's office despite the initial opposition of most of the state's urban newspapers, who, like Jay Gould, expressed concern about Hogg's support of a railroad regulatory commission. At first, the farmer and labor groups applauded the Hogg administration's accomplishments, which included the creation of the railroad commission, a law against landownership by foreign syndicates, and efforts at abolishing the convict lease system. But some Alliancemen soured on Hogg when he mandated that the railroad commission be appointive rather than elective and then failed to appoint any Alliancemen. In 1891 the Texas Alliance split into pro- and anti-Hogg factions.[58]

### *"Start the Ball Rolling": Laying the Foundations of the People's Party*

At the national level, meanwhile, the Southern Alliance, the Colored Alliance, and the Knights of Labor moved closer to forming a third party. Powderly refused to let the Knights take the lead in this movement. In April 1890 he expressed his suspicion to Knights General Secretary-Treasurer John W. Hayes that "the Farmers' Alliance would like to have us start the ball rolling [for a third party] and wreck us so that there would be but one industrial organization existing."[59] The Knights' Washington lobbyist, Ralph Beaumont, continued to advocate the formation of a third party, however, and polls conducted by the national Order through a circular and the *Journal of the Knights of Labor* in the fall of 1890 indicated strong support for Beaumont's position. In November 1890 the Knights' General Assembly, meeting in Denver, voted fifty-three to twelve to endorse independent political action "upon the principles of the preamble of the Knights of Labor." Powderly, Beaumont, and A. W. Wright all attended the Southern Alliance's convention in Ocala, Florida, in December 1890 at the invitation of L. L. Polk. The trio came with Knights General Executive Board member and Populist congressman-elect from Kansas John Davis, a symbolic gesture that represented both the potential of Knights-Alliance political unity and the Knights' own growing third-party sentiment.[60]

The Ocala convention issued a modified version of the previous year's St. Louis platform. The Ocala platform included the organization's first official endorsement of the subtreasury plan, which was already all but dead in Congress. Despite the fate of the subtreasury bill, however, most southern delegates refused to be swayed by the arguments of Kansans and other western delegates for launching a national People's Party, although many Colored Alliancemen supported the idea. As he had several years earlier

in Texas, Charles W. Macune engineered a compromise, this time by suggesting that a conference of "industrial" (farmer and labor) organizations
be held in February 1892 to discuss the possibility of creating a national
People's Party. Macune also suggested that a "Confederation of Industrial
Organizations" meet in Washington in January 1891 to develop a plan for
political education. This confederation would include representatives from
the Southern Alliance, the Colored Alliance, the Farmers' Mutual Benefit
Association of Illinois, the Knights of Labor, and the National Citizens' Alliance, a newly formed "Knight-Alliance hybrid." This latter organization,
formally assembled at Ocala, brought into the Southern Alliance political
fold those persons who supported the Ocala platform but were ineligible
for Alliance membership. Citizens' Alliance officers included Kansas Allianceman J. D. Holden as president and two of the Knights' most prominent third-party advocates, Beaumont and L. P. Wild of Washington, D.C.,
as secretary and treasurer, respectively.[61]

The Confederation of Industrial Organizations met as planned in Washington in January 1891. Delegates elected Texas Allianceman Ben Terrell
as the organization's president and Macune, Colored Alliance chief R. M.
Humphrey, Powderly, and Beaumont (as the Citizens' Alliance representative) to its executive committee. Since only two of these men (Beaumont
and Humphrey) were committed to the third-party cause at this time, the
confederation would not be the catalyst for starting a national third party.[62]
Midwestern third-party advocates, however, had already called for a convention that would be held in Cincinnati on 19 May 1891 "in order to,"
as Lawrence Goodwyn put it, "erect the preliminary organizational scaf-
folding of the new party."[63] Powderly refused to endorse the conference,
and the *National Economist*, edited by Macune, responded to the call by
insisting, "The time for hurrah conferences is at an end."[64]

But when it became apparent that many members of the Southern Alliance and the Knights would attend the Cincinnati conference, many of
the organizations' leaders decided to do likewise despite their misgivings.
More than fourteen hundred recognized delegates attended, the vast majority of them from Kansas, Ohio, Illinois, Nebraska, and other midwestern
states. Powderly and several other prominent Knights attended, including
Beaumont and Congressman John Davis. Few southerners attended; those
who did included veteran third-party men such as Charles Cunningham

of Arkansas, who served as temporary chairman, and anti-third-party men such as Congressman L. F. Livingston, president of the Georgia Farmers' Alliance. Livingston, an Alliance Democrat, told the press that he came "for the purpose of breaking up the third party." L. L. Polk did not attend, but he sent a letter to the convention urging delegates to wait until 1892 before taking any third-party action. Powderly made such a vague and weak endorsement of the third-party movement that A. J. Streeter, former Northern Alliance president and Union Labor presidential candidate, publicly denounced the Knights' leader as "no good."[65]

The Cincinnati conference issued a platform that focused on the familiar trinity of finance, land, and transportation, appointed a national executive committee, and chose the name "People's Party" as the name of the national third party. (The party would soon become commonly known, however, as the "Populist Party.") To placate Polk and anti-third-party leaders such as Livingston and Macune, the Cincinnati delegates agreed to postpone any further action until the conference already scheduled by the Southern Alliance for Washington's Birthday of the following year. Nevertheless, the Cincinnati conference laid the foundation for the national People's Party. Southern states represented on the national executive committee included Arkansas, Florida, Georgia, Louisiana, Tennessee, and Texas.[66]

## The Birth of Southern Populism: Texas Farmers and Laborers Take the Lead

Not surprisingly, given the strength of farmer-labor politics in Texas since 1886, the Lone Star State was well represented in Cincinnati. William R. Lamb, Thomas Gaines, and James "Cyclone" Davis, Farmers' Alliance leaders and veteran insurgents, all attended the conference and became the state's members of the Populist national executive committee. Texans Bill Farmer and P. H. "Patrick" Golden, longtime Knights of Labor leaders, attended as well, as did R. M. Humphrey. Some of these men had also been present for an Alliance convention in Waco in April 1891 at which Texas Alliance radicals, with the help of national third-party leaders such as Henry Vincent of Kansas and the ubiquitous Ralph Beaumont, further developed the state's third-party propaganda network.[67]

Many of those present at the Waco meeting reconvened in Dallas in August 1891, when Texas became the first ex-Confederate state to organize a People's Party. The Populist convention coincided, not coincidentally, with that of the State Alliance. Lamb, Gaines, and H. S. P. "Stump" Ashby, a Knight of Labor and former Methodist minister whose radicalism cost him that position in 1888, served as officers at the Populist convention. Golden and another veteran Knights leader, J. T. W. Loe, played prominent roles as well, as did third-party veterans such as the old Greenbacker J. M. Perdue. Leaders among the Fort Worth Independents who had twice elected Knight of Labor and Allianceman H. S. Broiles to the mayor's office attended as well. The Colored Farmers' Alliance and urban black trade unions also sent delegates.[68]

The platform written at the Dallas convention reflected this diverse composition of delegates. Aside from reaffirming the Ocala platform, the Texas Populists also called for an eight-hour workday for state and municipal workers, a laborers' and mechanics' lien law, a law compelling railroads to pay their employees monthly in "lawful money," and "a reformation in the punishment of convicts."[69] Melvin Wade, a longtime leader among African American Knights in Dallas, expressed doubts at the convention about how the party's white leadership would treat blacks, but he soon joined the Populist ranks. Another important African American leader, John B. Rayner of Robertson County, informed Charles Macune in November 1891 that he was ready to organize some 150 black men into the Knights of Labor as a stepping-stone for bringing them into the People's Party, or, as he put it, "the Labor party." (Rayner apparently mistook Macune for a Populist.)[70]

### Southern Populist Prospects amid Farmer-Labor Discord

While prospects appeared bright for building a biracial, farmer-labor third party in Texas, the outlook seemed dimmer in other southern states. In Georgia, Alliance Democrats sought the Knights' support in the Fifth and Seventh Congressional District races in 1890. Knights in each district wrote to Powderly, however, asking if they should believe the claims of these candidates (Livingston in the Fifth and R. W. Everett in the Seventh) to be the workingmen's candidates. In the Seventh District the Knights and the

Alliance had discussed the possibility of jointly running a congressional candidate two years earlier. The fact that William H. Felton was running as an Independent in 1890 presented workingmen with an attractive alternative to the Alliance candidate, however; Felton had recently led the unsuccessful attack on the convict lease system in the state house of representatives. In the Fifth District John T. Braud of Lithonia queried Powderly as to why a laborer should vote for a candidate who favored the subtreasury plan. "I can not see where the . . . Worke[r]s are to be benefitted at," Braud wrote, "only to pay hire [higher] prices for all they git." Powderly failed to answer either of these letters, although his coolness to the subtreasury plan suggests that he may well have agreed with Braud. The Alliance Democrats nevertheless won in both the Fifth and Seventh districts. [71]

The actions of the Georgia Alliance legislature, while failing to satisfy many Alliance members, must have only increased the doubts of many Knights and the laboring classes in general about a political alliance with the farmers. Whereas Felton and Knights of Labor legislators had battled against the convict lease system in the mid-1880s, the Alliance legislature actually expanded the exploitative system by passing a law allowing counties to lease misdemeanor convicts. The bill passed by a vote of ninety-eight to zero. Furthermore, while the previous legislature had passed an eleven-hour workday law for factories, the only sops that the Alliance legislature gave to labor were laws limiting the workday for railroad trainmen and engineers to thirteen hours and making Labor Day a legal holiday. The Alliance-controlled legislature of North Carolina established a similar record on labor legislation in 1891, when the House judiciary committee killed a ten-hour workday, anti–child labor law. [72]

A far more serious conflict emerged between the Alliance legislature and the Knights in Tennessee. On 14 July 1891 "scores of miners" marched upon the Tennessee Coal Mining Company's prison in Briceville, overwhelmed the guards, and released forty prisoners. The mining company had imported these prisoners for the purpose of replacing free miners whom it had locked out. After the state militia promptly brought the convicts back to Briceville, some two thousand miners descended upon the mines and released the prisoners again. The miners then proceeded to nearby Coal Creek and released 117 prisoners. Two more miners rebellions of this sort would occur in Tennessee in October 1891 at Briceville and in August 1892 in the middle Tennessee counties of Grundy and Marion.[73]

As in Georgia, the Farmers' Alliance in Tennessee ostensibly controlled the state government at this time. In the elections of 1890 State Alliance President John P. Buchanan won the governorship, and Alliance Democrats won a plurality of seats in the state legislature. According to the most thorough study of the Tennessee miners rebellions, the rise of the Alliance to power in the state government may have actually encouraged the miners to take such bold measures, since Alliance leaders and newspapers had promised to put an end to the convict lease.[74]

But when the rebellions forced the issue, the Alliance legislators (and governor) wavered. Not all Alliance members opposed the use of convicts as coal miners. When the *Nashville Weekly Toiler* published a letter from Knights of Labor leader Thomas F. Carrick, a Tracy City miner who later joined the Alliance, in November 1888 requesting that members of the two organizations stand together in opposing the use of convicts in the mines, a farmer in Tipton County, far from the state's mining regions, offered a less than cooperative response. "Convicts should be worked (and worked hard too) at anything in which their labor will come into competition with the smallest number of honest laborers," wrote the farmer, who suggested that coal mining fit the bill. "I do not think it right that a thief should steal my horse and have the State tax me to support him in idleness or at an easy job."[75]

Alliance legislators expressed similar concerns during a special session of the state legislature, called by Buchanan to consider the convict lease issue, in September 1891. Alliance Democrats and Republicans held enough seats in the General Assembly to eradicate the convict lease system. In the lower house all twenty Republican legislators, chiefly from east Tennessee, voted to consider a bill that would have ended the convict lease immediately, but thirty-one of thirty-five Alliance Democrats voted to table the bill, which therefore never reached a vote. The failure of Alliance legislators to support the miners' position stemmed from their reluctance to align themselves with the "black Republicans," their commitment to industrial development, and their unwillingness to raise property taxes to pay for new prisons. The occurrence of two more miners rebellions in the next year demonstrated the continued dismay of free miners with the convict lease. While miners disapproved of Governor Buchanan's use of the state militia to return convict laborers to the mines, conservative Democrats criticized him for trying to appease vigilante miners. The miners rebellions of 1891–92 and their immediate outcome boded poorly for both the chances of building a farmer-labor political coalition in Tennessee and for the likelihood of Buchanan winning reelection.[76]

## Southern Populist Prospects amid Racial Discord

The convict lease, of course, transcended mere economic interests. As the *Macon Telegraph* noted in 1886, "The preponderance of colored convicts makes it [the convict lease] a phase of the [N]egro problem."[77] Additional race-related problems would emerge in the early 1890s that suggested the difficulty of building biracial farmer-labor coalitions in the South.

Nowhere did these obstacles become more apparent than in Arkansas. In 1888 and 1890 Democrats in the Razorback State engaged in electoral fraud, intimidation, and murder in order to turn back the Union Labor–Republican challenge. But after 1890 the state's biracial farmer-labor movement faced still more challenges. In September 1891 Colored Farmers' Alliance chieftain R. M. Humphrey issued a call for a strike of African American cotton pickers after planters in some parts of the South, including Memphis and Charleston, held conventions at which they decided to pay pickers no more than fifty cents per hundred pounds. The strike failed to materialize on any significant level except in one locale–Lee County in the east Arkansas Delta. African Americans in this county had developed a long legacy of protest against exploitation by whites that stretched from the 1860s to the 1930s. An African American labor organizer from Memphis apparently started organizing efforts in Lee County in September 1891, but local blacks soon assumed control of the movement.

The results, however, proved disastrous. Strikers killed two black cotton pickers and a white plantation manager, and at least fifteen black strikers were subsequently murdered by a white-led biracial posse. Even in southern states where no strikes occurred, Humphrey's strike call and the events in Lee County received a great deal of attention and triggered the demise of the Colored Alliance, which virtually disappeared within a year. Thus the only organization that existed (besides the declining Knights of Labor) for the mobilization of African American farmers and farm laborers sank from about one million members in 1890 into oblivion just as the Populist crusade began. Furthermore, the strike underscored a major divergence of economic interests between members of the white and black Alliances, namely, that many members of the former employed members of the latter to pick their cotton.[78]

This fact became apparent in Georgia in 1889, when one county Alliance decreed that its members not lease land to African Americans, who instead should be hired as farmworkers. Further differences between the white and black Alliances arose in 1891, when Georgia's Alliance legislature passed a Jim Crow law for railroads, another that prohibited black and white prisoners from being chained together, and another to reinstate the use of the whipping post in chain gangs. The Colored Alliance of Georgia protested against all of these bills before they became laws. The whipping post bill passed by a vote of ninety-six to eight in the state house, and the only representative to speak against the bill was Lectured Crawford of McIntosh County, an African American Knight of Labor and a leading figure in the state's Colored Alliance.[79]

Still another race-related obstacle to building a biracial farmer-labor coalition emerged in Mississippi in 1890 and in Arkansas one year later. The tenor of race relations in Mississippi became gruesomely apparent in 1889, when Mississippi National Guardsmen combined with local whites in murdering at least twenty-five African Americans in Leflore County. They did so under the guise of quelling a race war that the victims were supposedly plotting, but in reality, according to historian William F. Holmes, the massacre occurred because the activities of the Colored Alliance in Leflore County posed a threat to whites' total dominance over blacks.[80] Similar concerns motivated the new voting laws written (with white Alliance input) at the Mississippi constitutional convention of 1890, which effectively disfranchised African Americans by, among other provisions, requiring all prospective voters to demonstrate their "understanding" of the state constitution to the satisfaction of a presumably white registrar.[81] In 1891 the Arkansas state legislature, delivering the secret ballot that Democrats had promised the year before, devised a new type of ballot that made voting quite difficult for those who lacked literacy. This meant a great deal in a state where, according to the census of 1890, 13.4 percent of white men and 55.8 percent of black men age twenty or over had not learned to read or write.[82]

## *The Outlook for Populism in the South and Nation, 1891–1892*

Thus while leaders of the farmer and labor movements established the institutional apparatus for a national third party in 1891, the future of this party seemed uncertain. The platforms enunciated at conventions at St. Louis, Ocala, and Cincinnati certainly owed a great deal to the Reading and Cleburne platforms of, respectively, the Knights of Labor and the Texas Farmers' Alliance, and the Knights and the Alliance (or the Agricultural Wheel) had already collaborated in third-party politics with varying degrees of success in a number of southern states, particularly in Texas, Arkansas, and Alabama. Leaders of both the Southern Alliance and the Knights ran the National Citizens' Alliance, which attempted to unite farmers and urban or industrial laborers in support of the Ocala platform. But on the other hand, some leaders of both the Southern Alliance and the Knights expressed reservations or even opposition regarding the formation of a third party. Leaders and members of the Knights expressed doubts about the subtreasury plan, which most third-party men in the Alliance stronghold of Georgia viewed as "the linchpin of reform."[83] For their part, some Southern Alliance legislators, as we have seen, failed to take a strong stand against the convict lease system. This occurred despite pronouncements like that of the Tennessee State Alliance, which declared its opposition to working convicts in competition with free labor just a month before the special legislative session that addressed that matter.[84] Moreover, the ongoing decline of the Knights of Labor and the fact that AFL chief Samuel Gompers attended the Cincinnati conference of May 1891 but failed to take any part in or publicly comment upon the proceedings raised further doubts as to whether urban or industrial laborers would join the Populist crusade.[85] The fact that neither the Alliance nor, by 1891, the Knights possessed much strength in the vote-rich Northeast certainly did not bode well for the party at the national level.[86]

Within the South, of course, the outlook for the third party varied from state to state. Initial prospects for a biracial farmer-labor third party looked brightest in Texas. The situation seemed somewhat promising in Alabama, where the ULP had at least developed a network of farmer and labor third-party activists (including some blacks) in 1887 and 1888 and where the St. Louis convention of December 1889 inspired some additional Alliance-Knights political agitation during the following year. A biracial farmer-labor coalition had elected Knights State Master Workman John Nichols to Congress in North Carolina's Raleigh-Durham area in 1886. Nor was the idea of biracial farmer-labor political cooperation totally foreign in Georgia, and it was not immediately apparent how the new voting system would affect such cooperation in Arkansas. In other southern states, such as Tennessee and Mississippi, recent events left prospects for a Populist Party looking rather bleak, as did the strength of both major parties in the Volunteer State. In all cases, the ability of the white farmers who led the Populist movement to appeal to nonagricultural laborers and (in the South) African Americans would figure significantly in the fate of the new party.

The two national Populist conventions of 1892 left this ability in doubt. The first convention, held in St. Louis in February as the Conference of Industrial Organizations that Charles W. Macune had proposed fourteen months earlier, in fact amounted to the true founding convention of the People's Party, with considerably greater participation from Southern Alliancemen than the Cincinnati convention of the previous year. Southern Alliance delegates, in fact, dominated the St. Louis conference, although the Northern Alliance, the Colored Alliance, and the Knights of Labor were all well represented. Conflicts marred the conference, though. Some prominent Southern Alliancemen, among them Georgia Democratic congressmen L. F. Livingston and Charles Moses, continued to oppose the formation of a third party.[87] Disagreements emerged between Southern Alliance and Knights of Labor delegates as well. The Knights (and the Northern Alliance) acceded to the desire of the Southern Alliance to include a plank in the conference's platform calling for the subtreasury plan "or some better system." Southern Alliance delegates, however, failed to show the same spirit of compromise when the Knights, at the urging of Woman's Christian Temperance Union President (and Knight) Frances Willard, tried to add a woman's suffrage plank to the platform. Southern Alliance delegates flatly refused this request, and the Knights had to settle for the passage of a resolution in support of woman's suffrage separately from the platform. When this resolution passed by a slim majority, many disgruntled delegates accused the secretary of the conference, John W. Hayes of the Knights of Labor, of deliberately miscounting the vote. The *St. Louis Post-Dispatch* subsequently emphasized Knights-Alliance tensions at the conference with the headline, "Master Workman Powderly and His Friends Trying to Get Control of Things and Opposed by the Country Element."[88]

Conflict and controversy also emerged regarding the role of the Colored Farmers' Alliance at the St. Louis conference. When the Georgia delegation of the Colored Alliance, which was not friendly to the third-party cause, learned that R. M. Humphrey, their organization's white national leader, had given white Georgia third-party advocate J. L. Gilmore the power to cast their votes by proxy, they stormed out of the convention hall. Most Colored Alliance delegates from other states followed them. Humphrey, a well-established third-party man, then granted Gilmore the power to vote as a proxy for the entire Colored Alliance.[89] Whether Humphrey and Gilmore truly represented the sentiment of the Colored Alliance's dwindling rank and file seems highly doubtful, though, and this episode hardly could have endeared that rank and file to the Populist cause.

Nor did the Populists' national nominating convention, held in Omaha, Nebraska, in July 1892, convincingly demonstrate the party's appeal to laborers or African Americans. According to historian Gerald Gaither, only four black delegates attended the Omaha convention. This figure probably represents an undercount, but nevertheless, the presence of only a handful of African Americans at a convention attended by nearly fourteen hundred delegates boded poorly for the Populists' prospects among black voters.[90] A much greater number of delegates with ties to organized labor attended the Omaha convention; members of the Knights of Labor filled a train that the Order chartered from Chicago.[91] As in St. Louis in February, however, labor delegates constituted only a small minority of the entire delegation. Past or present Knights came from several southern states, including Texas, Arkansas, and Georgia.[92] Well-known Knights leaders such as John W. Hayes, Hugh Cavanaugh, and, of course, Terence V. Powderly attended as well, although Powderly did not come as an official delegate. In fact, the General Master Workman had refused credentials as an at-large delegate from the Pennsylvania People's Party.[93] Nevertheless, true to his flair for the dramatic, Powderly entered the convention hall on the first day "side by side" with the prominent Iowa Populist James B. Weaver, drawing "prolonged cheers, lasting several minutes," according to the *Journal of the Knights of Labor.*[94]

The Populists made a clear effort to appeal to labor at the Omaha convention, but tensions remained apparent. The convention approved a series of resolutions that were clearly aimed at attracting urban or industrial laborers. These included demands for more effective laws against contract labor, the abolition of Pinkerton armies, and stricter penalties for violation of the eight-hour workday law on government work.[95] Certainly, these issues affected very few farmers. Many delegates balked, however, at the introduction of a resolution endorsing the Knights' boycott against the Rochester combine of clothing manufacturers. Even William R. Lamb of Texas, a proponent of farmer-labor unity since the Southwest strike of 1886, opposed this resolution. It took a rousing speech by one of the Populists' most skilled orators, Ignatius Donnelly of Minnesota, to convince the delegates to adopt the resolution by acclamation.[96] These resolutions in behalf of labor were not part of the Omaha platform itself, however, which focused on the familiar trinity of finance, transportation, and land, and it seemed uncertain how much labor support the resolutions would attract.[97] Even though those Knights who were present at Omaha supported Weaver, who won the Populists' presidential nomination, Powderly had already privately stated that Weaver's nomination would be "unwise."[98] Moreover, the Populists would soon learn that even Powderly's limited support for their cause exceeded that of the man who had replaced him as the nation's most important labor leader, Samuel Gompers.[99]

On the other hand, the edicts of national labor leaders such as Gompers and Powderly would have less impact upon laborers' receptiveness to Populism than would the specific circumstances in a given state, congressional district, county, or city, particularly those regarding race (at least in the South) and previous efforts at building farmer-labor coalitions. Even in some locales where those circumstances did not look promising for the People's Party, the Populists still seemed to have a reasonable chance of attracting laborers' votes. In Tennessee, for example, where erstwhile leaders of the moribund Union Labor Party (not Alliancemen) founded the state Populist Party in May 1892, some workingmen evinced willingness to support the new party despite the strain placed upon the relationship between the Farmers' Alliance and organized labor by the miners rebellions and the convict lease issue.[100] A letter published in the *Nashville Weekly Toiler* at the beginning of that month illustrates this point well. "W.F.," a self-avowed "organized wageworker" and ten-year veteran of the Knights of Labor, declared his contempt for the man who would soon receive the Democrats' nomination for governor, state supreme court Chief Justice Peter Turney. "W.F." declared that "many [laborers] will never vote for [Turney]," who was supported by the state's industrial interests. "I shall fight Pete Turney to the bitter end," he added, "and in this district we will sit down on Pete with a thud." While "W.F." gave no indication of whom he would support instead of Turney—and neither a Populist candidate nor even a state Populist Party yet existed—he did make one statement that hinted at support for the soon-to-be-formed third party. "I wish I was able to put a copy of the *Toiler* in the hands of every laboring man here," he wrote, "that the mist might be cleared from their eyes."[101] By this point the *Toiler*, the official journal of the Tennessee State Farmers' Alliance, was clearly moving into the vanguard of Volunteer State Populism.[102]

CHAPTER FIVE

# Southern Labor and Southern Populism, 1892–1896

Despite some apparent tensions between Southern Farmers' Alliance and Knights of Labor delegates at the St. Louis conference of industrial organizations in February 1892, Tom Watson's *People's Party Paper* of Atlanta assured its readers weeks later that "the Knights of Labor will vote the People's Party ticket almost to a man, and their influence will bring thousands of other laboring men to the polls to vote the People's Party ticket also."[1] The latter half of this sanguine prediction was especially important, since the Knights of Labor only had about 125,000 dues-paying members across the nation by this time, contrary to the insistence of the *Journal of the Knights of Labor* that the Order still had 275,000 members. If the Populists hoped to secure support from the American Federation of Labor, Samuel Gompers soon made it clear that he had other ideas. In an article that appeared in the *North American Review* in July 1892 the president of the AFL, which claimed 255,000 members at this time, declared that his organization would "maintain as a body a masterly inactivity" in the forthcoming political campaigns. Gompers refused to give the Populists even a mild endorsement. "Composed, as the People's Party is, mainly of *employing* farmers without any regard to the interests of the *employed* farmers of the country districts or the mechanics and laborers of the industrial centers," Gompers wrote, "there must of necessity be a divergence of purposes, methods, and interests."[2]

Thus the Populists continued to look to the Knights of Labor to deliver labor votes. Tom Watson's optimism notwithstanding, the prospect could not have been comforting. As historian Melton McLaurin has noted, "By the time of the 1892 presidential election, the Knights of Labor had few members to support Populist candidates, either in the South or in the nation at large."[3]

Nevertheless, in those southern states where the Populists were most successful the Knights of Labor already had served and would continue to serve the third party well. In Texas, Alabama, and Arkansas and in certain parts of Georgia and North Carolina the Knights had helped lay the groundwork for biracial farmer-labor political coalitions over the preceding half-dozen years, in some cases building upon the work of the Greenback-Labor Party. Although Populist strength in the South would not be confined to localities where the Knights had been politically active among farmers and laborers in the mid- to late 1880s, the People's Party would emerge as a serious threat to Democratic control in most of those areas. In this sense the Knights' impact upon Populism lived on even as the labor organization itself declined. Moreover, in the aforementioned states the Knights retained a cadre of experienced organizers and political agitators who played an important, although all but forgotten, role in launching the People's Party at the local and state levels.

Another factor that mitigated the negative effects on Populism of the Knights' decline in the South lay in the unusually close economic and cultural ties between farmers and laborers in the region. Many southern industrial workers came to the factory or mines from the farm, to which some returned as well. Many southerners worked seasonally both on farms and in mines or cotton mills. Southern industrial workers and farmers sometimes belonged to the same churches or even the same local assemblies of the Knights of Labor.[4] As historians have recently pointed out, the close ties between some farmers and industrial laborers in the late-nineteenth-century South may even have tempered the aversion of some of the latter to the subtreasury plan, which, if implemented, seemed likely to raise the prices that consumers would have paid for cotton goods and foodstuffs.[5] This is not to suggest, of course, that cultural and economic conflicts did not exist between southern farmers and laborers (or, for that matter, between different classes of southern "farmers"). Many farmers without direct ties to the cotton mills looked down upon millhands as "factory rats" or "lintheads," and some identified more closely with factory owners as employers than with factory workers.[6] Many industrial workers, conversely, did indeed view the subtreasury plan as antithetical to their own interests, causing Southern Alliance and Populist journals to try to explain how the multifaceted scheme would help them too.[7] Nevertheless, the cultural and economic boundaries between farmers and laborers tended to be relatively fluid and amorphous in the late-nineteenth-century South, which could have only helped Populists in trying to appeal to members of the latter group.

In some instances southern Populists succeeded in their appeal to laborers. In Texas and Alabama, two of the southern states where the Populists received the most votes, the third party won considerable support from labor. In the two other southern states in which the Populists won significant support, North Carolina and Georgia, the party proved less successful in building farmer-labor coalitions but nevertheless benefited from substantial labor support in certain key locales. In Arkansas the Populists drew labor support just as the Union Labor Party had, but state disfranchisement laws kept many would-be Populist voters away from the polls. In all five of these states the Knights of Labor already had been politically active among farmers and laborers, and before that the Greenback-Labor Party had been active in all of these states except Georgia.[8] In other southern states where the GLP and the Knights had not done much to mobilize farmers and laborers politically, the Populists failed to attract labor support, although in many of these states the Populists faced greater obstacles.

## The Knights of Labor and the Birth of the People's Party in the South

In many southern states the People's Party came into being during the interval between the St. Louis conference of February 1892 and the Populists' presidential nominating convention at Omaha on Independence Day. During these months southern Populist leaders worked on mobilizing their own communities, building county and state organizations and selecting delegates to Omaha. This process occurred with particularly noticeable labor involvement in Texas, Alabama, and North Carolina.

In Texas, of course, the process of mobilization and organization had already begun with the first People's Party state convention in Dallas during August of the previous year. Three weeks before the St. Louis conference the party held its second state convention in Fort Worth. About

150 delegates from north and northeast Texas attended. They included familiar veteran reformers from the ranks of the Greenback-Labor Party, the Farmers' Alliance, the Knights of Labor, and the Union Labor Party, such as H. S. P. "Stump" Ashby, who served as chairman, Thomas Gaines, Sam Evans, Dr. J. D. Rankin, J. M. Perdue, William Lamb, Patrick Golden, and Bill Farmer. The convention endorsed the Cincinnati national Populist platform and the state Populist platform of 1891, with some amendments to each. Amendments to the state platform included one calling for the state to employ convicts in the construction of double track railroads to be owned and operated by the state and another requiring railroads to continue operations during a strike "regardless of the cost of labor, until the strike ends, or forfeit [their] charter."[9]

The voice of labor spoke more clearly at the next Populist state convention in Dallas on 23–24 June 1892. Over a thousand delegates from throughout the state attended this convention, including some of the men who had attended a conference of "Jeffersonian" Democrats in Dallas in mid-February. These men had been read out of the state Democratic Party because of their support of the subtreasury plan, and most of them soon moved into the Populist ranks. The June Populist convention nominated a complete state ticket and put forth a new state platform with numerous labor planks, calling for a laborers' lien law, an eight-hour workday law, a state bureau of labor, and a state board of arbitration to settle labor disputes.[10] The delegates approved these planks despite or perhaps as a reaction to the loss of Patrick Golden, secretary-treasurer of Knights of Labor District Assembly 78 and president of the recently formed Texas State Federation of Labor, to the Democratic Party. The Democrats nominated Golden for a seat in the state house of representatives in May 1892; he won the seat later in the year and promptly introduced an eight-hour bill and helped secure the passage of a laborers' lien law, although he was dissatisfied with its final form.[11]

Organized labor also played a role in the formation of the People's Party in Alabama; in fact, the Knights of Labor figured more prominently in this process than historians have recognized. In the spring of 1892 no Alabama state People's Party existed. In March the State Assembly of the Alabama Knights of Labor convened at the small town of Echo in the wiregrass region of the southeastern part of the state. At the end of the convention the leaders of the State Assembly asked the delegates "to keep their seats a few minutes for the purpose of taking or expressing some political action." The delegates then adopted a resolution "calling upon the members of the Order everywhere to the support of the People's Party Platform." That night some five hundred people attended a public speech given by the Knights, an impressive figure in a town of 1,525 residents.[12]

Weeks later, State Farmers' Alliance President Samuel M. Adams issued a call for an Alliance Labor conference to be held on 30 May 1892 in Birmingham. The meeting would be held "to consider what action is to be taken on the People's Party Platform adopted at St. Louis . . . in February last." The *Journal of the Knights of Labor* published the call and declared, "This is the time for action. All Local Assemblies [in Alabama] should send one delegate at least."[13]

While a skeptic might question just how many local assemblies still existed in Alabama in 1892—and the number, while unknown, was certainly well below the reported peak of 150 in mid-1888—the Knights had not faded into oblivion in Alabama. Although the Order had been completely eclipsed by the AFL-affiliated Birmingham Trades Council in that city, the Knights remained active in Mobile and Montgomery as well as smaller cities or towns such as Maysville, Decatur, Huntsville, Clanton, Anniston, Calera, Selma, and Bay Minette. Farmers and farm laborers made up some of this membership, of course, but a variety of industrial workers still belonged to the Order in Alabama as well, including blacksmiths, brickmasons, lumber and turpentine workers, textile mill workers, and limestone quarrymen and lime kiln workers. African Americans constituted a perhaps sizable minority of this membership. Conversely, AFL trade unions had practically no presence in the smaller cities or towns of Alabama, except for Anniston, which like Birmingham had a city trades council.[14]

Moreover, the Alabama Knights, like the national organization, could boast of a cadre of experienced political agitators. In fact, in the late 1880s the Order had achieved electoral successes in most of the aforementioned cities or towns where it remained active in 1892. While the Farmers' Alliance played the most prominent role at the Birmingham Alliance Labor conference, Knights of Labor delegates also figured in the proceedings. State Master Workman A. J. Henley of Clanton served as assistant secretary of the conference. The Colored Alliance also sent delegates. Only two trade union delegates attended, one from the Anniston Trades Council and another from the Birmingham Trades Council. The latter, Jere Dennis, was not pleased when delegates denied his request to endorse the boycott of Birmingham Typographical Union No. 104 against the *Alabama Christian Advocate* newspaper and job printing office, but he later became an important Birmingham Populist nevertheless. The Alliance Labor conference endorsed the St. Louis platform after "considerable discussion." In light of the resolution passed by the Alabama Knights after the close of their State Assembly meeting, one would expect that their delegates voted to endorse the St. Louis platform, although no record exists of how individual delegates voted. After the Alliance Labor conference adjourned, third-party supporters held a mass meeting and formed a People's Party state executive committee. The position of chairman on that committee went to George F. Gaither, who in March 1888 had played a prominent role at the Labor Party of Alabama conference called for by the Knights. Gaither announced the first state convention of the Alabama People's Party, to be held on 23 June 1892.[15]

In eastern North Carolina, too, the Knights of Labor came out in support of the People's Party before a state party existed. This part of North Carolina was then largely rural, with only a few small cities, such as Goldsboro and New Bern, none of which had as many as eight thousand residents. Agriculture—particularly cotton and tobacco—constituted the economic lifeblood of the region, which was populated to a large extent by African Americans. The eastern North Carolina Knights of Labor reflected these characteristics. Local assemblies in this part of the state included renting farmers, farmhands, and day laborers, white and black, male and female, as well as mechanics and building trades workers.[16] The large element of landless farmers among the ranks of eastern North Carolina Knights might seem to support historian Gerald Grob's characterization of pro-Populist western and southern local assemblies as "more appendages of farm groups than bona fide labor organizations," but such a dismissive assessment is perhaps a bit hasty.[17] These assemblies, after all, consisted of many agricultural laborers who did not belong to the Farmers' Alliance. (Indeed, many of these Knights probably worked for Alliancemen who opposed the Order's efforts among farm laborers.) Therefore, these local assemblies offered the Populists a bloc of voters that the Alliance did not. Moreover, this part of North Carolina did not include large numbers of industrial workers to organize. The Knights nevertheless found some of them, even in some sparsely populated hamlets, remaining active among building trades workers in Saratoga and black sawmill and railroad hands in Woodland, for example, well into the 1890s.[18] The Knights' membership in this part of North Carolina simply reflected the heavily rural, agrarian composition of the labor force.

Some of those laborers expressed their political views on 16 January 1892, some five weeks before the St. Louis conference, when eastern North Carolina Knights "of several counties" held a convention at Elm City in Wilson County, a Knights stronghold during the late 1880s and well into the 1890s. The delegates passed resolutions asking their representatives in the U.S. Congress to compose and present a bill that would require the government to issue a national circulating currency directly to the people and also to support a bill for the free coinage of silver. The Populists' Cincinnati platform of May 1891 included both of these demands. The Knights also resolved at Elm City "to support no man of any party who will not pledge himself to labor with his ability to have the above, together with other sections of our principles, enacted into statute law." The convention also endorsed the joint Knights-Alliance demands promulgated in St. Louis in December 1889 and reaffirmed one year later at Ocala and pledged to cooperate with the Farmers' Alliance "in endeavoring to get the farmers of our organization, as well as those out of it, to plant less cotton and raise their own supplies."[19]

Four months later Local Assembly 581, a black local in Greenville, issued a call for a convention of all locals in eastern North Carolina's First Congressional District "for the purpose of taking action in support of the demands of the People's Party Platform, and other matters pertaining to the interests of the Order in the State." This meeting occurred on 12 May 1892, six days before the meeting in Raleigh that gave birth to the state People's Party. The Knights of North Carolina's First Congressional District met again at a smaller town in Pitt County on 17 June, just after the Populists had organized at the county and congressional district levels.[20]

### *The Knights of Labor, Homestead, and the Weaver-Field Ticket*

The People's Party campaigns of 1892 got under way after the Omaha convention of early July. The party's national ticket of James B. Weaver, a former Union general from Iowa, and his running mate, James G. Field, a former Confederate general who had lost a leg during the war and had later served as a Democratic attorney general of Virginia, proved somewhat disappointing to southern Populists. Southerners (and many Populists outside the region) had been expecting Southern Alliance President Col. L. L. Polk to receive the presidential nomination, but he died from a hemorrhage of the bladder on 11 June 1892, depriving the party of probably its most charismatic and influential leader.[21]

Weaver was hardly a candidate who would excite urban laborers. He came from a predominantly rural state, and his dismal performance in the presidential election of 1880 as the Greenback-Labor candidate (3.3 percent of the popular vote and no electoral votes) hardly inspired confidence in his second quest for the White House. Although Terence V. Powderly declared himself "satisfied with Weaver" during the campaign, privately the General Master Workman expressed little hope for the Iowan's success.[22]

No sooner did the Omaha convention end, however, than fate handed the Populists an opportunity to bolster their appeal to industrial laborers. The prolabor resolutions adopted by the Populists at Omaha on Independence Day included one calling for the abolition of Pinkerton armies. Two days later bloody violence erupted at Homestead, Pennsylvania, between locked-out steel workers and three hundred Pinkerton mercenaries, hired by Carnegie Steel, who sailed into town on two barges to protect strikebreakers. A quite literally heated battle ensued that included the use of guns, dynamite, and the rather unique spectacle of flaming oil slicks on the Monongahela River. Seven Pinkerton men died in the melee, as did eleven strikers or spectators. Dozens were wounded. The Pinkertons surrendered, but within a week Democratic governor Robert Pattison sent eighty-five hundred militiamen into Homestead. The troops protected strikebreakers, who soon enabled the steel plant to resume production.[23]

One southern Populist could rightfully observe the Homestead tragedy with a sense of indignant vindication. On the floor of the U.S. House of Representatives on 7 July Congressman Tom Watson of Georgia recalled that "as far back as February 9 . . . I introduced a bill which would have made the keeping of such a standing body of men [the Pinkertons] or their employment illegal, and would then have struck at the source of the trouble, by putting down this body of men." "If this Congress meant to do anything to protect the laborers," he lectured, "it could have been done [then]."[24] The lawless violence at Homestead prompted a congressional investigation, but the conduct of that investigation satisfied neither Watson nor the trio of Knights of Labor General Executive Board members present. The Knights accused Judiciary Committee Chairman William C. Oates (an Alabama Democrat) of showing favoritism to Pinkerton company representatives and their attorneys during the hearings. The *Journal of the Knights of Labor* commented, "The conduct of the Subcommittee of the Committee on Judiciary in its inquiry into the methods and doings of the Pinkerton Agency is calculated to bring Congressional investigations into contempt." "Mr. Oates' conduct," the *Journal* fumed, "has neither precedent nor parallel in the history of Congressional investigations."[25] The *National Economist* aptly summarized Watson's grilling of Oates on the House floor with the headline "Hon. Thomas E. Watson, of Georgia, Scorches the House Judiciary Committee and Its Chairman, Mr. Oates, of Alabama." Predictably, little came of the congressional hearings. "Let the campaign cry of the People's Party," suggested Watson, "be 'remember Homestead.'"[26]

After the Omaha convention and the massacre at Homestead, the *Journal of the Knights of Labor* expressed unbridled support for Watson in his bid for reelection and for the Weaver-Field ticket as well. Powderly, on the other hand, played little role in the presidential campaign.[27] He did appear, however, at a New York People's Party rally shortly before national Election Day at which he called the Omaha platform "the platform of every true Knight of Labor."[28]

Nationally, the Knights of Labor played only a minor role in the Weaver-Field campaign. Historian Norman J. Ware asserted that most of the labor vote for the Populist ticket "probably [came] from the Knights," but since that ticket received barely one million popular votes, or 8.5 percent of the total, obviously it drew no more than minimal labor support. In fact, the Weaver-Field ticket made a pathetic showing in the most heavily urban, industrialized states. Only 2.5 percent of the popular vote in Illinois, for example, went to the Populist ticket. The figure was less than 2 percent in New York and Ohio and not even 1 percent in Powderly's home state of Pennsylvania. All twenty-two of Weaver's electoral votes came from states west of the Mississippi River, all of them sparsely populated except for Kansas.[29]

The Populist campaigns of 1892, however, encompassed more than just the presidential election, and while the Knights of Labor and its leaders in general contributed negligible support to the Weaver-Field ticket, they had more support to offer and greater roles to play in other Populist campaigns that year. This would become evident in all five of the southern states where the Knights had helped mobilize farmer-labor political insurgency during the mid- to late 1880s: Texas, Arkansas, Alabama, Georgia, and North Carolina.

*Farmers, "the Laboring Element," and the Effects of "Election Reform": Populism in Arkansas, 1892*

In no state did the Populists begin their maiden campaign with a greater background of preexisting farmer-labor political cooperation than Arkansas, where the People's Party was not so much a new party as a successor to the Union Labor Party.[30] At least four of the seven members of the Arkansas People's Party campaign committee in 1892 were members of the Knights of Labor at the time, including chairman and treasurer Thomas Fletcher and Knights State Secretary-Treasurer John H. Robertson.[31] On the Fourth of July 1892 the Knights and the Farmers' Alliance held a joint picnic at the Ozark Mountain community of Cushman. Members of each organization delivered speeches before "a large concourse of people," and the Populist candidate for state auditor delivered "a special oration."[32]

Leading Arkansas Populists were well aware of the need to cultivate support from labor. Days after the St. Louis conference of February 1892 Populist J. B. Suttler, managing editor of the *Arkansas Farmer* and a member of the Knights, informed W. B. W. Heartsill that the Arkansas delegation at St. Louis had chosen Heartsill as the party's nominee in the Second Congressional District of western and south-central Arkansas.[33] Long active in farmers' organizations such as the Brothers of Freedom, the Agricultural Wheel, and the Farmers' Alliance, Heartsill was also sympathetic to laborers.[34] In fact, in August 1890 a Little Rock printer, claiming to be speaking in behalf of not only himself but other trade union members as well, wrote a letter to Heartsill urging him to run for Congress as "an independent

Democratic . . . or Alliance candidate."[35] Heartsill, who five years earlier had claimed to "have *always* been a consistent [D]emocrat," declined the suggestion.[36] But in March 1892, just after being informed of his nomination by the Populists, he joined the three-week-old local assembly of the Knights of Labor in his hometown of Greenwood.[37] Later that month Suttler advised Heartsill to "see that the workingmen of the towns (like F[or]t Smith) have representation on your county ticket. We must unify all of the laboring element and the day is our own." Suttler added that he was "sanguine of being able to do a great work in this direction" in Pulaski County (Little Rock).[38] Later in the year Suttler informed Terence V. Powderly: "I believe if this Republic is to be saved from destruction it must be done by organized labor." Suttler also told Powderly that "the K. of L. is the institution which should amalgamate all others."[39]

Suttler continued to court organized labor throughout the campaign. In August 1892 he helped arrange for veteran Knight of Labor and third-party man Ralph Beaumont to join James G. Field, the Populist vice presidential candidate, on the stump circuit in Arkansas.[40] In September Suttler spoke at an open meeting held by the Knights in Little Rock just after the close of the eighth annual session of the Arkansas Knights of Labor State Assembly, which had unanimously endorsed Suttler's *Arkansas Farmer.* (State Master Workman Ed Harns and Southwest strike leader Martin Irons also addressed the open meeting.)[41] When the Knights' state legislative committee began circulating a petition in October calling for the abolition of the convict lease system, the petition was endorsed not only by the Little Rock Trades and Labor Council but also by Central Union No. 48 of the Farmers' Alliance of Little Rock, whose president was a Knight.[42] The Arkansas Populist platform, put forth in June, called for the "barbarous" convict lease system to be replaced by a state penitentiary farm and for surplus prison labor to be utilized in the maintenance of public roads. The Arkansas Democratic Party, which had already proven adroit at appropriating third-party demands, subsequently joined the Populists in condemning the convict lease system.[43]

Abolition of the convict lease system held particular appeal not only for free laborers who had to compete with convict laborers but also for African Americans in general. Blacks, after all, were far more likely than whites to be condemned (often after being convicted of trumped-up charges) to toiling interminably long hours in a coal mine or turpentine camp while enduring whippings, near starvation, and probably the filthiest living conditions on the North American continent.[44] Arkansas Populists also spoke on another issue of particular concern to African Americans. The party's state platform of 1892 accused Arkansas Democratic lawmakers and law enforcement officers of showing "a disregard of justice and law" that had "engendered a spirit of mob law." The platform made no direct mention of lynching, but its antilynching message was readily apparent.[45] Arkansas Democrats quickly seized upon this plank with all the low vulgarity they could muster. One Arkansas Democratic newspaper declared that "no one can make us believe that the plain, practical [white] farmers . . . who have been raised in the South . . . have suddenly become [N]egro lovers, or defenders of [N]egro rapists and criminals."[46]

This despicable tactic of equating the defense of black humanity with an unmanly negligence of the sacrosanct duty of protecting white womanhood was a favored method of Democrats not only in Arkansas but throughout the South. The Knights of Labor of Oxford, North Carolina, learned this the hard way in 1887. The Order had unseated local Democratic officeholders by building a biracial coalition of Republicans and Independents. The Oxford Knights hardly offered African Americans complete equality. White men held most of the political offices captured by the coalition, and a white man served as the Master Workman of the town's otherwise all-black local assembly. Nevertheless, when a prominent white woman of Oxford charged a black man with attempted rape, and when African Americans drew blame for a fire that destroyed the town's business district, Oxford's Democratic leaders and newspaper pointed an accusatory finger at the Knights for organizing and allegedly promoting unrest among blacks. Soon Oxford Knights of both races became the targets of white vigilante mobs, one of which nearly lynched a white Master Workman. "They pointed at us with scorn," complained another white Oxford Master Workman, "and kept crying 'Nigger! nigger!' until the two words 'nigger' and 'Knight' became almost synonymous terms."[47]

Southern Populists, however, often fought fire with fire where gendered racial rhetoric was concerned. Texas Populist James "Cyclone" Davis, who toured the stump circuit in both his own state and Arkansas in 1892, delivered this none too subtle counterattack against Democratic propaganda that summer: "The worst sight of social equality to be seen in this land is the sight of a sweet white girl hoeing cotton on one row and a big, burly [N]egro in the next row. Talk of [N]egro equality when your industrial system forces a good woman's precious Anglo-Saxon girl down on a level with a burly [N]egro in a cotton row. Oh, my God! And this in free America."[48] In short, white southern Populists shared the same basic racial mores as white southern Democrats. Even when they denounced lynchings or the inhumane treatment accorded to predominantly black convict labor forces, they did not offer African Americans social or political equality. To do so not only would have run counter to the common racial mores of the era but would have been political suicide. Instead, as historian Carl Degler has observed, white southern Populists "simply were willing to ignore some old prejudices in exchange for a chance to defeat the Bourbons."[49]

As the Arkansas campaigns of 1888 and 1890 demonstrated, though, merely putting aside "some old prejudices" would not be enough to defeat that state's Bourbon Democrats. Arkansas Democrats resorted to intimidation, violence, and fraud to stamp out the Union Labor Party's challenge to their dominance in those campaigns, and to circumscribe future challenges they passed an "election reform" law in 1891 that disfranchised significant numbers of black (and, to a lesser degree, white) voters.[50] Thus the Arkansas People's Party faced daunting obstacles, close ties with the Knights of Labor notwithstanding.

One of these obstacles involved a partial breakdown of cooperation between the third party and the state Republican Party. Whereas the Arkansas Republican Party had endorsed the Union Labor state ticket in the previous two contests, the GOP nominated its own slate of candidates in 1892. The *Faulkner County Wheel*, an Arkansas third-party newspaper, laconically commented that "the [state] Democratic committee will doubtlessly pay them well for the privilege of using their names as Republican candidates," predicting that "when [President Benjamin] Harrison is reelected he will appoint these martyrs to fill the post offices in this state."[51] A bigger obstacle, however, lay in the significant effects of the new election law. After Democratic gubernatorial candidate William M. Fishback received 58 percent of the votes in a three-man race, a higher percentage than the victorious Democratic candidate received in the previous three gubernatorial elections, the state People's Party chairman told James B. Weaver that fifty thousand voters had been disfranchised by the new election law. In fact, only thirty-six thousand fewer voters cast ballots in the state elections of 1892 than two years earlier, but that was still enough to take a heavy toll on opposition to the Democratic Party.[52]

The Arkansas Populists' congressional campaigns in 1892 also suffered the consequences of the election law. In the elections for the U.S. House of Representatives the third party and the Republicans continued their practice of not competing with each other.[53] But whereas the elections in the First and Second Congressional districts of eastern Arkansas had been virtual dead heats in both 1888 and 1890, only one anti-Democratic con-gressional candidate managed even 40 percent of the vote in Arkansas in 1892.[54] Populist J. E. Bryan, who had served as State Farmers' Alliance lecturer in 1891, garnered 43 percent of the vote in the Fifth District of northwestern Arkansas. This area was the birthplace and former stronghold of the Brothers of Freedom, which had been politically active in 1884 before merging into the Agricultural Wheel one year later.[55]

That close ties with organized labor could not help the Arkansas Populists overcome their difficulties became all too apparent in the Second District congressional campaign in 1892. Populist W. B. W. Heartsill, a delegate to the Knights of Labor State Assembly meeting at Little Rock in September, received only 29 percent of the vote in that district, which now encompassed western and south-central Arkansas. Western Arkansas, including the state's coal-mining region, had become the center of the Knights' strength in Arkansas by then. In the town of Van Buren in 1892 a Knight of Labor won election as a Populist to the state legislature, where he found only nine other members of his party.[56] Heartsill, however, bore the burden of waging a "pauper campaign," still another obstacle that confronted the third party. Heartsill lacked campaign funds, and the state People's Party campaign committee failed to be of much assistance. J. B. Suttler, the committee's secretary, informed Heartsill in early October that "I . . . tried to get some money for you, but failed." Days later Suttler wrote to Heartsill again with news that he had procured $8.50 in campaign funds. "Now, old man," Suttler enthused, "you must hump yourself and make a stiff fight."[57] While the state election law of 1891 would have made even well-funded campaigns difficult for Heartsill and other Populist candidates, the added weight of their party's poverty only further decimated their hopes of victory. A state poll tax, which won the approval of voters in September 1892 and took effect seven months later, sealed the demise of the Arkansas People's Party.[58]

## *Divided Reformers: Populism in Texas, 1892*

The People's Party also represented the culmination of years of farmer-labor political agitation in Texas, where the Populists did not have to contend with the disfranchisement of illiterate voters in 1892. Lone Star State Populists, however, faced their own set of obstacles. The governor's race featured five candidates. Incumbent James S. Hogg again received the Democratic Party's nomination, at which point prominent railroad attorney George Clark, with support from business, banking, railroad, and newspaper interests, also announced himself as a Democratic candidate. The Populists nominated Thomas L. Nugent, described by historian Alwyn Barr as "a slight, mild-mannered, former Democratic district judge of Confederate background." The Prohibition Party also entered the fray, nominating D. M. Pendergrass of Limestone County, while the "Reform" or "lily white" Republicans nominated A. J. Houston of Dallas County. The state Republican Party, at the urging of black leader N. W. Cuney, endorsed Clark.[59]

Hogg, it will be recalled, had ascended to the governor's office in 1890 with the support of the Farmers' Alliance, the Knights of Labor, and the Grange. In 1892 he still retained the support of some Alliance members, Knights and other laborers, and virtually all the leadership of the declining State Grange. Although Hogg had alienated many of his Alliance supporters by making the state railroad commission appointive rather than elective, the commission did reduce rates for shipping grain, meal, flour, and cotton within state lines. Hogg promised more railroad reform in 1892. Hogg also had succeeded in getting the state legislature to pass an "anti-alien" land bill that prohibited aliens from obtaining title to land in Texas. The Alliance had strongly supported this bill. In 1892 Hogg pledged to prohibit land corporations in Texas if reelected. These reforms appealed to many laborers as well as farmers. The Hogg Democracy platform denounced, on the other hand, the subtreasury plan and government ownership of railroads and telephone and telegraph lines.[60]

Nevertheless, Hogg retained significant support among farmers in 1892, especially in the more prosperous farming counties of north, east, and central Texas. Labor votes helped Hogg carry the cities of Houston and Fort Worth, where the Knights of Labor had helped elect the Independent H. S. Broiles as mayor twice in the mid- to late 1880s. Hogg won reelection with 43.7 percent of the vote in 1892, far more than the 30.6 percent received by Clark and the 24.9 percent received by Nugent. The Populist candidate's total vote (108,483), noted one scholar, "amounted to roughly one half of the [Texas] Alliance membership at its height." Labor support was apparently split between Hogg and Nugent. Nugent carried several counties that either were then or recently had been centers of Knights of Labor strength, such as Comanche, Delta, Erath, Lampasas, Navarro, Palo Pinto, and Titus. Nugent ran a distant third in both the city and county of Dallas, however, despite the fact that the city's Knights of Labor (which still consisted of at least three local assemblies) had pledged their allegiance to the Populists in the spring of 1892, even declaring their resolution not to participate in any Democratic primaries. Nugent carried seven counties in the heart of Alliance country, stretching from Lampasas (the organization's birthplace) northward through Jack.[61] The failure of Nugent to attract more farmer and labor votes stemmed not from the unwillingness of these groups to vote for reformers but rather from the presence of two candidates who could claim with some credibility to be reformers. Many Texas farmers and laborers still had faith in the Hogg Democracy as an agent of reform.

The more troubling aspect of Nugent's defeat, from the Populist perspective, lay in the fact that "virtually no blacks" voted for him. The declining strength of both the Knights and, especially, the Colored Farmers' Alliance could not have helped the Populists in this respect, but, as historian Jack Abramowitz pointed out, the chief problem for Texas Populists in trying to attract black voters in 1892 "was the able and vigorous leadership given the Texas Republican party by a corps of Negroes, particularly Norris Wright Cuney." Cuney, the most prominent African American politician in Texas at the time, was leading the state GOP's black leadership against the "lily white" faction for control of the party, and, suggested Abramowitz, "many

Negroes who might otherwise have joined the People's Party felt compelled to aid Cuney in his losing battle." The Texas Populists, by contrast, had yet to recruit or cultivate African American leaders whose advocacy of Populism could counteract the powerful opposition of Cuney.[62]

### *"Anything to Beat Kolb": Populism in Alabama, 1892*

Few of the complications that confronted Arkansas or Texas Populists in 1892 seemed evident in Alabama that year. The scourge of disfranchisement had not reached Alabama yet, and the governor's race involved only two candidates, incumbent Democrat Thomas G. Jones and Reuben F. Kolb, who ran as the candidate of the "Jeffersonian" Democrats and the Populists. As in 1890, Kolb sought the Democratic nomination in 1892 only to see Jones win it by questionable means. After acquiescing to Jones's nomination in 1890 Kolb broke from the Democratic Party in 1892 to challenge Jones directly in the general election.[63]

During the campaign Kolb became, as one historian put it, "the spokesman for the submarginal tenant farmers and for the increasing number of laborers, miners, and factory workers."[64] Kolb, the former state commissioner of agriculture, unquestionably had strong support from the Farmers' Alliance, which still counted some seventy-five thousand members in Alabama as late as 1891, and he offered an important promise to laborers, particularly coal miners.[65] As the *Alabama Sentinel* reminded its labor readership, Kolb had pledged "at the very outset of the campaign . . . to annul the present [convict lease] contract if elected to the Governorship." Jones, on the other hand, "says he will do it legally and by request, which means that he don't intend to do it at all."[66] Kolb also made a stronger appeal to African American voters, calling for the protection of blacks in their legal and political rights in addition to his pledge regarding the convict lease. The state's Democratic press attacked these planks as the "nigger rights section" of the Jeffersonian platform and deemed them a threat to white supremacy.[67] The *Alabama Sentinel*, however, saw such tactics for what they were. "Never forget that this is a White Man's Government, and can never be anything else, and never will be anything else, and no one has the slightest intention of making it anything else," the *Sentinel* advised readers. "It is merely a matter of anything to beat Kolb . . . just as twenty-five years ago it used to be anything to beat [Ulysses S.] Grant."[68]

Kolb's appeals to laborers and African Americans (most of whom *were* either agricultural or industrial laborers) largely succeeded. But the Alabama reform coalition met the same fate in 1892 as did Arkansas anti-Democrats in 1888 and 1890: their would-be governor was counted out. The official results in Alabama in 1892 gave Jones a majority of 11,345 out of over 240,000 votes cast in the two-man contest. But as historian William Warren Rogers has convincingly shown, Jones's majority came from manipulated returns in the Black Belt. "Fraud on such a scale had not been seen since Reconstruction," Rogers wrote. "Incongruously, the organized Democrats had upheld white supremacy by using the votes of black-belt Negroes."[69] Kolb carried most of the counties that had given majorities to Greenback-Labor candidates (congressional, gubernatorial, or legislative) in the late 1870s or early 1880s or to GLP, Independent, or Labor Party of Alabama legislative or county candidates in the mid- to late 1880s. Kolb also carried four of the state's five chief coal-mining counties: Walker, Tuscaloosa, Bibb, and Shelby. Jones retained the Democratic Party's traditional control of Jefferson County (Birmingham), although Kolb carried at least half of the county's mining beats.[70]

### "Will You Knights of Labor Help the Farmers?" Populism in Georgia, 1892

In Georgia and North Carolina farmer-labor politics had been more limited in scale and scope during the era between the end of Reconstruction and the advent of the People's Party. Not surprisingly, this trend continued into the Populist era. Nevertheless, in each of these states the Populists attracted significant labor support in certain areas where the Knights of Labor had helped lay the groundwork for farmer-labor political cooperation.

One such area in Georgia was Richmond County (Augusta). Here Tom Watson, elected as the congressman from the state's "Terrible Tenth" District in 1890 as an Alliance Democrat (though he did not belong to the Alliance), sought reelection in 1892 as a Populist. His fate would depend largely upon the results in Augusta, by far the district's largest city. During 1892 organized labor in Augusta demonstrated considerable support for Watson. Watson's labor supporters included the remaining members of Knights of Labor LA 5030, which had led some three thousand millhands in the infamous strike-lockout of 1886. In February 1892, after Watson introduced his anti-Pinkerton bill in the House of Representatives, LA 5030 sent him a letter of gratitude and support for publication in his *People's Party Paper*. The letter commended Watson as "a champion for the workingman, both of city and country, . . . who has the welfare of the laborer truly at heart, and . . . the courage of his convictions." The Knights gave Watson their pledge "to sustain you to the utmost limit of our power."[71]

Watson's working-class supporters in Augusta transcended the reduced ranks of the Knights of Labor. Also during February 1892 the citizens of Augusta's Fifth Ward ("composed principally of wage-workers, who make an honest living by the sweat of our brow") held a meeting at the Knights of Labor Hall at which they pledged their support for Watson and approval of his recent decision not to enter the Democratic caucus in the House of Representatives. The meeting also "bitterly denounce[d] the seeming intention of our city council to employ convict labor in improving the streets of our city, while free labor stands by, looks on and wants." The political discussion at the meeting, which drew "at least 300 voters," showed "the connection of interest existing between the city and country people," according to one enthusiastic participant. "It should go to show that an injury to one is the concern of all," he added, quoting the motto of the Knights of Labor. Judge M. M. Conner, a notary public and justice of the peace, presided over the meeting as chairman. In 1886 Conner had served on the executive board of LA 5030 during the textile strike.[72]

Watson's actions in Congress during the summer of 1892 only enhanced his standing among laborers. The violence at Homestead enabled him to capitalize upon his efforts to have Congress investigate and curb the use of Pinkertons as strikebreakers earlier in the year. Furthermore, just five days before the Homestead tragedy Watson alone among Georgia representatives voted in favor of an eight-hour bill for laborers and mechanics employed upon public works by the federal government. President Harrison signed the bill into law on 1 August 1892, and, as national Election Day approached, Watson reminded laborers of his solitary status among Georgia representatives in supporting the bill.[73]

Watson continued to court the labor vote avidly throughout the campaign. He spoke of class conflict that pitted "the farming interests" and "the laboring classes" against their wealthier Democratic oppressors. Dur-

ing the summer of 1891 he had asked an audience of workers, "Will you
Knights of Labor help the farmers and laborers in the field of their fight
on the common enemy?" In the fall of 1892 Watson told a reported crowd
of four thousand in Augusta's working-class Fifth Ward, "Don't take my
word for it, that I have stood by you, but write to Powderly . . . or any of
your Knights of Labor men in this county." (Watson and national People's
Party Chairman Herman E. Taubeneck both wrote to Powderly themselves
in October 1892, asking him to come to Augusta and campaign for Watson, but Powderly ignored their requests.) In contrast to Watson, his opponent, Democrat Maj. James C. C. Black, deemed it "un-American and
un-Christian" to promote class antagonism and declared himself "a friend
of all classes." Struggling farmers, however, may not have shared Black's
benevolent assessment of himself. In 1890 he had publicly denounced the
Farmers' Alliance, and during the campaign of 1892 he insisted that the
distress of farmers was "exaggerated."[74]

Watson's class-oriented appeals apparently struck a chord with farmers
and industrial workers alike. He won in eight of the eleven counties in
his district, which was largely rural outside of Richmond County. C. Vann
Woodward suggested that the Democrats carried the two rural counties by
fraud and that fraud clearly gave Black his overwhelming majority in Richmond (10,776 to 1,782), which in turn resulted in Black's election. The massive use of fraud in Augusta could hardly be denied, as the number of votes
counted there vastly exceeded the number of eligible voters. Nevertheless,
the official results point to significant working-class support for Watson in
his district's one sizable city. He drew 42 percent of the votes in Augusta's
working-class Fifth Ward. Not surprisingly, given his appeal to farmers,
he carried a relatively rural district within the city limits and ran well
in another. In addition to fraud, the "job lash" limited Watson's support
from Augusta laborers. Managers of at least one of the city's textile mills
warned employees not to vote for Populist candidates and subsequently
discharged some employees who were caught disobeying this edict. This
evidence came to light in a congressional investigation when Watson contested Black's election. The Democratic-controlled House of Representatives, however, ruled in Black's favor. Nobody would have stood less
chance of receiving a favorable ruling than Watson. During the previous
summer he had caused a furor by publicly accusing an Alabama Demo-

cratic congressman of being incoherently drunk while speaking on the House floor. The committee that investigated the election issued a report that Woodward characterized as "a whitewash."[75]

Like Richmond County, Clarke and Cobb counties, which include Athens and Marietta, respectively, both had been strongholds of the Knights of Labor and farmer-labor political activism during the mid-1880s. But in contrast to Richmond County, the Knights no longer maintained a.presence in either Clarke or Cobb by the early 1890s. In Cobb County the Order ran into trouble with the Roswell Manufacturing Company in 1889 and collapsed after its leading lecturer, organizer, and political candidate (in both 1886 and 1888), James C. Sanges, left Georgia for Alabama in 1890.[76] The Cobb County Farmers' Alliance subsequently proved less inclined to challenge the Democratic Party than the Knights had; although Alliance Democrats swept to victory in the county in 1890, Populists never did well there.[77] In Clarke County the legacy of the Knights' failed political campaigns of 1885 and 1886 and the bitter backlash that ensued may have precluded any chance of Populist success.[78] After the Southern Farmers' Alliance and the Knights of Labor formed their loose confederation at St. Louis in December 1889, one Athens Alliance spokesman denounced the coalition, insisting that trying to unite the two organizations was "like trying to mix oil and water." When the Populist Party sought their support less than three years later, most Clarke County Alliancemen remained Democrats.[79]

But in a number of rural Georgia counties where the Knights of Labor had been active during the latter half of the 1880s and where its ranks had included farmers, the Populists won considerable support. One such county could be found just to the west of Cobb: Paulding County, where the Knights organized railroad laborers and farmers and farm laborers (among others) and remained active well into the Populist era.[80] As in Lawrence County, Alabama, a center of strength for both the Agricultural Wheel and the Populists, a culture of oppositional politics in Paulding County went back to at least 1860. Paulding County, which included only 129 slave owners (out of a white population of 6,490) in 1860, only one of whom owned more than twenty slaves, elected two cooperationists, or opponents of secession, to Georgia's secession convention in January 1861. Although Paulding County sent its fair share of soldiers into the Confederate army, antiwar and Unionist sentiment remained strong in Paulding throughout the war.[81]

The Civil War left most Paulding County citizens destitute, and economic recovery proved painfully slow. When the Knights of Labor swept across Georgia in 1886, its organizers met an enthusiastic reception in Paulding. The Knights chartered four local assemblies in the rural county that year.[82] The Farmers' Alliance soon followed the Knights into Paulding and became "quite strong," establishing a cooperative store there by 1889.[83] Relations between the Knights and the Alliance in Paulding initially proved strained, most likely due to the fact that the Knights' membership there included farmhands and laborers who probably worked for Alliancemen. But by mid-1888 local Knights leader James F. Foster reported, "The Farmers' Alliance has grounded its arms and quit fighting the Knights. . . . We expect to elect either a Knight of Labor or a member of the Farmers' Alliance to congress for this district (7th) in the fall."[84]

Nothing came of these plans in 1888, as Democratic incumbent Judson C. Clements defeated longtime Republican Zachary Hargrove in Georgia's Seventh District congressional contest. The Paulding County Knights remained allied with the Farmers' Alliance, however, and, subsequently, with the Populists. The bond between the Knights and the Alliance here probably lay in the shared economic hardship and cultural sameness between the two groups. The socioeconomic, ethnic, and religious composition of Paulding County was fairly homogeneous, dominated by native-born white Baptists or Methodists of working-class or yeoman status. The relative lack of industry in late-nineteenth-century Paulding County meant that there were few industrial laborers, although the labor force did include railroad hands, carpenters, mechanics, and a few factory workers.[85]

The Paulding County Knights, which still consisted of at least two local assemblies in 1892, came out in support of Populism even before the county's first Populist convention. In August 1892, one month before that convention, James F. Foster informed Knights General Secretary-Treasurer John W. Hayes, "we will vote for Weaver for President." Furthermore, he added, "I am satisfied we will elect everything in this fall's election." While Paulding County Knights sometimes proved negligent about attending their local assembly meetings, Foster reported, "when the signal is given for a political rally the laboring men of farms and factory join hands and march in unbroken columns to the [site] of action."[86]

Foster's prediction proved accurate. The Populists swept Paulding in the national, state, and county elections in 1892 and early the following year. In addition to Foster's pledge of Knights of Labor support for the Populists, further evidence of the Order's role in Paulding County Populism came when the third party put forth its county ticket in November 1892 and gave the position of surveyor to O. F. Brintle, a fifty-eight-year-old Confederate veteran who had just completed a term as the Knights' State Master Workman. The Knights remained active in Paulding County until at least 1894, and the Populists followed their initial success in the county by "taking nearly every contest for the next three years."[87]

Except in Augusta, however, the Populists failed to attract much labor support in urban Georgia.[88] Atlanta Populists chose H. N. Cramer, a prominent Knights of Labor political activist in the city since the mid-1880s, as the president of the People's Party Club No. 1, and Cramer played a prominent role at the Populists' Fifth District congressional convention. Cramer, however, was a controversial figure even among leading Atlanta Knights, and his views could hardly be considered representative of organized labor in the city. By this time, trade unions had eclipsed the Knights almost completely in Atlanta, and their leaders did not become involved with the People's Party. The Populist-Republican-Prohibition candidate in the Fifth District, the Reverend Sam Small, failed to unseat Democratic incumbent L. F. Livingston, past president of the State Farmers' Alliance, and he ran particularly poorly in the county that includes Atlanta (Fulton). Small received only 30 percent of the vote in Fulton County as compared to 45 percent in the rest of the district. In the two wards of Atlanta that could be clearly identified as "working class," the Third and the Fifth, Small received 43 and 28 percent of the vote, respectively.[89]

Nor did the Populists fare well among laborers in Savannah. The Savannah Knights of Labor had been active (and sometimes successful) in politics during the latter half of the 1880s, although that political activity contributed to the internal dissent that nearly destroyed the city's DA 139 by the middle of 1890. In July 1892 a Populist from nearby Screven County who had served as a delegate at the Omaha convention implored Terence V. Powderly, "If you will send some[one] down to Sava[nna]h and reorganize the Knights of Labor, we can beat [the Democrats]." Powderly stamped the letter "NO ANSWER REQUIRED," but he did respond to a letter from M. J. Lee of Savannah in August in which Lee asked how to go about forming a local assembly of street car motormen and conductors. During the same month, however, a Savannah Knight wrote a letter to the *Journal of the Knights of Labor* claiming that the once healthy attendance of "workingmen" at Populist Party meetings in the city had plummeted since workers began receiving threats that "if they attend People's Party meetings they will be discharged."[90]

## Prelude to Fusion: Populism in North Carolina, 1892

In comparison to Georgia, Knights of Labor support for the Populists proved more widespread and significant in North Carolina, although here too limited to certain parts of the state. Local assemblies of the Knights existed in at least thirty-eight of North Carolina's ninety-eight counties at some point during the 1890s. Twenty-eight of these counties were in the eastern half of the state, including industrialized counties such as Wake and Durham as well as the heavily rural, African American counties that comprised the First and Second districts of northeastern North Carolina. In the First District, where the Knights already had displayed strong Populist leanings, People's Party candidate Reddick Gatlin received 44.7 percent of the vote in 1892, the best showing made by any Populist in the state's congressional contests that year. While many Knights probably did vote for Gatlin, the endorsement that he received from the Republican Party certainly weighed as a greater factor in his near success. The Knights also pledged support for the People's Party in the Fourth District, where William F. Strowd, a Chatham County farmer and former Alliance Democrat, bore the Populist standard against Democratic incumbent and textile mill owner Benjamin Bunn as well as Republican and Prohibition candidates.[91] In Raleigh Knights leaders John Ray and George Tonnoffski both became active Populists, but the Order no longer carried the influence in the city that it had six years earlier, when State Master Workman John Nichols won the district's congressional seat.[92] Bunn won reelection with 48 percent of the vote to Strowd's 43 percent. The Populist and Republican votes combined would have defeated Bunn, however, a fact not lost upon leaders of the two opposition parties, as the next campaign would illustrate.[93]

As in Texas, the North Carolina Populist state ticket ran as one of three legitimate contenders in 1892. The Populist ticket finished third, with 17 percent of the official tally, although, significantly, anti-Democratic votes outnumbered Democratic votes. The state election returns suggest Knights of Labor support for the Populists. The Knights remained active in the 1890s in seven of the eight counties where the Populist state ticket fared best. In one of these counties, the Knights and Alliance stronghold of Wilson County, a member of the Order had declared before the election, "The old-party Democrats don't like the Knights of Labor, and there isn't much love lost between us." As for the Republicans, this Knight insisted, "the South won't turn from one of Wall Street's parties to the other one. When the People's Party vote is counted this fall it will be seen how the farmers and workingmen of North Carolina vote."[94] Unfortunately for the Populists, however, not enough members of either group voted for the third party in 1892.

## *The Presidential Election of 1892 and the Demise of the Farmers' Alliance and the Knights of Labor*

While the Populists' failure to elect either a congressman or a governor in the South in 1892 could be attributed to creative ballot counting by Democrats, as in the elections involving Tom Watson and Reuben F. Kolb, the Populist presidential ticket did not even come close to victory in any southern state. Weaver and Field carried Colorado, Idaho, Kansas, and Nevada but managed a marginally respectable showing only in Alabama among the former Confederate states. Weaver received 37 percent of the vote in Alabama, as opposed to 59 percent for Democrat Grover Cleveland, who won a second nonconsecutive term, and a paltry 4 percent for Republican incumbent Benjamin Harrison, a figure that resulted in part from the state Republican committee's endorsement of Weaver. But while this endorsement harmed Harrison, it may, ironically, have alienated some Alabama Populists, who feared that by voting for Weaver instead of Cleveland they might increase Harrison's chances of winning the election.[95] In North Carolina Republicans in some districts apparently agreed to support

Populist congressional candidates in return for Populist votes for Harrison. Weaver received only 15.8 percent of the vote in North Carolina, while Populist candidates received 24.5 percent of the votes cast in the state's congressional elections.[96] Overall, Weaver received only 15.7 percent of the votes cast in the presidential election in the ex-Confederate states. Nationally, he received a paltry 8.5 percent of the popular vote.[97]

In some ways the campaign of 1892 marked the last hurrah of both the Southern and Northern Farmers' Alliances as well as the Knights of Labor. All three of these organizations played active roles in the formation of the Populist Party and in its maiden campaign, and their willingness to subvert their supposed nonpartisanship spoke volumes about the ineffectiveness of their other efforts by that point. After the elections of 1892 none of the three organizations would ever again figure prominently in national politics or as farmer or labor organizations. In his classic study of the Farmers' Alliances and Populism John D. Hicks asserted that "the Alliance, Northern as well as Southern, emerged from the campaign of 1892 sadly shattered."[98]

The Knights of Labor clearly faced its own thanatopsis even before the elections of 1892. Dues-paying membership in the national Order began to drop sharply in the spring of that year after two and a half years of hovering around 110,000 to 140,000. As historian Richard Oestreicher has noted, "Why the Knights . . . began to fall apart in the spring of 1892 is unclear."[99] Certainly, the Order had lost all effectiveness and credibility as a collective bargaining agency. Its last major strike, the New York Central Railroad strike of 1890, ended in total defeat. (Adding insult to injury, the railroad company had precipitated this strike by firing Knights, including the Master Workman of DA 246.) Competition from trade unions and the Knights' ongoing battle with the AFL undoubtedly took their toll as well. The Knights' involvement with the Populist Party also did some damage, renewing the same internal political strife that had damaged the Order during the campaigns of 1888.[100] When the Knights started losing members once again in the spring of 1892, Terence V. Powderly began to fear the worst. In May 1893 he told General Secretary-Treasurer John W. Hayes of "the suspicion that . . . I unwillingly allowed myself to become possessed of more than a year ago, viz.: that the Order was in the throes of dissolution."[101] The decaying organization's internal affairs soon became mired in, as one scholar put it, "intrigue, chicanery, and malfeasance," and Powderly resigned as General Master Workman in November 1893 at a General Assembly session in Philadelphia. An unlikely coalition of midwestern agrarians and eastern socialists essentially forced his resignation, and a leader among the former group, James R. Sovereign of Iowa, became the Knights' new chief. In contrast to his predecessor, Sovereign was a self-pronounced Populist, but his support would mean little if the Knights' membership continued to erode.[102]

By the spring of 1894 the Sovereign administration reported that the Order's membership was on the rise, but the available evidence does not support this brave claim, which the now suspended Powderly dismissed as "mere bluster." The number of members paying dues to the national Order sank below fifty thousand by the year's end.[103] From Georgia, Knights State Secretary-Treasurer James F. Foster of Paulding County, where the Knights remained active, informed Hayes in February 1894 that "it is rather a gloomy prospect for our Order in Georgia," with only "some 18 or 20 Locals" still active.[104] In the spring, acknowledging that "the Order in Georgia is in a bad way," Hayes sent a member of the General Executive Board to try to organize a district assembly in the west-central Georgia town of Thomaston, but this effort failed. Plans to form a district assembly in Waycross also came to naught.[105] In Alabama the Order's once "famous and strong State Assembly," as one Knight later recalled it, lapsed in 1893. By the following year the Knights could barely claim any presence in Alabama.[106] While the Arkansas Knights still claimed thirty-three local assemblies in 1894, fourteen of them had been suspended for chronic failure to pay dues, and four more had missed their last one or two payments. A local assembly near Hot Springs lapsed, and "the whole body" subsequently joined the Farmers' Alliance. A similar fate befell a Knights local in rural Cross County, where one ex-Knight blasted the Order's "do-nothing" policy.[107]

## Labor Troubles and Politics: Arkansas and Alabama, 1894

The decline of the Knights of Labor in Alabama and Arkansas did not mean, however, that the labor movement was dormant in those states. National strikes by coal miners and railroad workers reached both states in 1894.[108] Some fourteen hundred Arkansas miners joined the national United Mine Workers of America strike in May 1894, despite the facts that few of them belonged to the union and that the Knights' State Executive Board refused to sanction the strike. The strike collapsed in Arkansas after one month, and the miners collectively lost $100,000 in wages.[109] Many Arkansas railroad workers belonged to the American Railway Union (ARU) and participated in the Pullman strike in the summer of 1894; some of the strikers belonged to the Knights as well. The strikers succeeded for a short time in obstructing traffic on the Iron Mountain Railroad, but, in a replay of the events of 1886, the strike ended soon after the Democratic governor sent the state militia to Little Rock and Fort Smith, where violence erupted.[110]

The Arkansas People's Party tried to capitalize on workers' discontent, and the Knights remained in the Populist camp. The party's platform of 1894 demanded that the state government make further reforms regarding convict labor. The Democratic-controlled legislature had abolished the convict lease system in 1893, but the state continued to work convicts in competition with free labor. The Populists also called for a state board of arbitration to settle differences between corporations and their employees and for vagrancy laws to be modified "so as to prevent the prosecution of industrious laboring men while in a condition of enforced idleness."[111] The nationwide depression that began in 1893 hit Arkansas hard.[112] Months before the miners or railroad strikes Knights State Secretary-Treasurer John H. Robertson reported that nearly two thousand workers were "idle" in Little Rock. In April 1894 Knights attended the People's Party county convention in the mining county of Sebastian, and the recording secretary of one of the county's local assemblies reported in a letter to the *Journal of the Knights of Labor*, "Every intelligent farmer and miner is strictly in line and means business." At the beginning of May Knights State Worthy Foreman Charles T. Foster of Eureka Springs reported, "Taxes are paid and it has absolutely drained the county of money. . . . Deep and bitter are the curses of the men who voted for (hush, whisper it) Cleveland." Foster added, "We are organizing P.P. [People's Party] Clubs all over the county." Prominent Knights such as Robertson and J. W. Dollison continued to play leading roles in the Arkansas People's Party.[113]

But the Populist moment had passed in Arkansas. The disfranchisement measures of 1891 combined with the first application of the poll tax of 1892 to produce the smallest voter turnout in fourteen years in the state election of 1894. The Democratic candidate for governor received 59.6 percent of the vote, far ahead of the modest totals received by the Republican and Populist candidates. Populist congressional candidates ran in three of Arkansas' six districts, but none received even 20 percent of the vote, despite the fact that the party's candidate in the first district faced only one opponent, the Democratic incumbent.[114]

The labor troubles in Arkansas in 1894 paled in comparison to those in Alabama. The decline in demand and prices for coal wrought by the panic of 1893 spelled particularly bad news for the Birmingham district, where miners soon faced irregular employment and wage cuts. In August 1893 miners at Dolomite struck when mine operator A. H. Woodward slashed wages from forty-five cents per ton, the district contract rate, to thirty-four cents. Woodward then hired "scabs" or "blacklegs" to work in the mines and locked out the strikers. The conflict remained unresolved when thirty-nine delegates, representing nearly five thousand miners, convened at Bessemer on 14 October 1893 and formed the United Mine Workers of Alabama, which was not affiliated with the national UMW. The newly formed union raised money to sustain the strikers at Dolomite, but the strike ended in failure on 20 March 1894.[115]

By then, however, conflict between miners and mine operators had spread across the district. On 30 March 1894 the UMW of Alabama met in state convention at Birmingham and appointed a committee to meet with managers of the district's coal-mining companies. The union representatives offered to accept a 10 percent wage reduction from the current contract rate, but the operators countered by demanding a 22.5 percent reduction. The union responded by calling all of its members out on strike on 14 April, and some sixty-five hundred miners, roughly half of whom were black, heeded the call. Within two weeks the number of strikers approached nine thousand. By then the national UMW had also declared a strike over the same problems confronting Alabama miners.[116]

Inevitably, the strike assumed major political dimensions in Alabama, with state elections looming ahead in August. As we have seen, Alabama already had a legacy of significant biracial farmer-labor political activism that dated back to the Greenback-Labor era. Major southern strikes of the past decade, such as the Southwest strikes of 1885–86 and the Augusta textile strike of 1886, only seemed to promote farmer-labor political insurgency in the affected communities. In Alabama, therefore, the miners strike seemed likely to bolster an already formidable Jeffersonian Democratic–Populist movement. The supporters of Reuben F. Kolb, once again the gubernatorial candidate of these two intertwined parties in 1894, realized this, viewing the labor turmoil as an opportunity to win greater support for their candidate in the mining districts than two years earlier. In February 1894 the Jeffersonians put forth a platform that contained several demands aimed directly at winning miners' votes: the removal of convict laborers from the mines, lien laws for miners, a state inspector of weights and measures to ensure that miners were paid fairly, the election of mine safety inspectors, and a law prohibiting children under thirteen from working in the mines. Later that month a convention of miners met in Birmingham, endorsed Kolb, and nominated two candidates for the state legislature on the Jeffersonian Democratic–Populist ticket. In March Alabama Populists and UMW representatives met and pledged mutual aid. Also that month new Knights of Labor chieftain James R. Sovereign stopped at Birmingham while on a southern lecture tour and spoke in behalf of the Jeffersonian Democrats. Sovereign exhorted laborers to be politically active–which they had been in Birmingham nearly since the city's inception–and endorsed "candidates pledged to the removal of [the] curse [of convict labor] from Alabama." [117]

The miners strike boded far less well for Alabama Democrats. On 25 May 1894, after several attacks upon mine property and "blackleg" miners (including the murder of a black man who was recruiting other strikebreakers), Governor Thomas G. Jones acceded to the request of Jefferson County Sheriff George M. Morrow to send the state militia to Camp Forney at Ensley, a central location in the Birmingham district. Troops would remain in the district for nearly three months. While the Alabama Farmers' Alliance provided the strikers with material aid, Governor Jones reportedly warned them that "men who wanted to work . . . would be protected . . . if he had to lay a dead miner on every cross tie between Birmingham and Pratt mines." On 18 June a convention of at least eleven hundred miners at Adamsville (just northwest of Birmingham) unanimously passed a resolution reaffirming their support for Kolb. Two days later two of the district's largest mining companies, which had a vested interest in seeing the conservative antilabor, anti–Farmers' Alliance, anti–free silver Democrat William C. Oates elected as the next governor, offered to pay transportation costs for any striking miner who would leave Alabama.[118]

On 6 July 1894, as the miners strike continued, the Pullman strike reached the Birmingham district, where the ARU had rapidly enrolled fourteen hundred members. Within one day the strike virtually halted railroad traffic in Birmingham. The striking miners cheered this development, since it meant that mining companies would not be able to ship their coal. The miners' cheers quickly turned to curses, however, when Governor Jones sent state troops into Birmingham on 9 July, ostensibly to prevent "general bloodshed" and property damage but also to break the railroad strike. The troops allowed nonunion switchmen, brakemen, and firemen to replace the strikers. Even though the ARU managed to recruit three hundred more members in Birmingham on 9 July, the strike effectively ended three days later. Many strikers lost their jobs.[119]

As the miners strike continued, along with sporadic outbursts of violence, all eyes turned to the state elections, to be held on 6 August. The miners pinned their last hopes upon a Kolb victory, and a Pinkerton spy working for Governor Jones reported that Populist politicians were trying to keep the strike alive and the strikers in Alabama at least until the election. James R. Sovereign returned to Alabama the week before the election to organize local assemblies of the Knights of Labor and deliver speeches in behalf of Kolb.[120]

As in 1892, however, Kolb lost due to "political machinations in the Black Belt."[121] He again carried four of the state's five mining counties (Walker, Tuscaloosa, Bibb, and Shelby), and he lost Jefferson County by only twenty-two votes. Kolb undoubtedly would have carried Jefferson had it not been for the self-serving generosity of the two mining companies that gave willing strikers free transportation out of the state. Even that effort failed to prevent Kolb from carrying all of Jefferson's major mining beats. The biracial composition of Kolb's support among miners reflected that of the state UMW itself. "Most black miners," historian Daniel Letwin has noted, "showed a Populist leaning comparable to that of white miners."[122]

After the state elections the strike quickly crumbled. (The national UMW strike already had come to an unsuccessful end.) The strikers won some minor concessions, but the mine operators clearly retained the upper hand. By the time of the next state elections two years later the Alabama UMW, by then affiliated with the national union, carried little clout in the coalfields.[123] The Alabama Populists, meanwhile, found some consolation in the congressional elections of 1894, in which their candidates won in the Seventh District in the north Alabama hill country and, after an election contest before the Republican-controlled U.S. House of Representatives, the Fifth District, which spanned the hill country and the Black Belt.[124]

## *Farmers, Laborers, and Republican-Populist Fusion: North Carolina, 1894*

No major strikes occurred in North Carolina in 1894, but Tarheel Populists found a formula for success through vote trading, ticket splitting, and ticket sharing (or "fusion") arrangements with Republicans. The two anti-Democratic parties engaged in fusion at the congressional level in six of the state's nine districts, including the coastal First District, the Fourth District, which included Raleigh, and the Sixth through Ninth districts, which collectively encompassed the western half of the state.[125] "The fusion movement" in North Carolina, according to historians Jeffrey J. Crow and Robert F. Durden, "was strongest in the East and West and weakest in the Piedmont," where rising business and industrial interests supported national Republican economic policies and viewed Populist economic policies as anathema. In western North Carolina the relative scarcity of African Americans meant that Democratic propaganda equating fusion with "Negro domination" carried little credibility. In the eastern part of the state, however, the architects of fusion had to overcome some significant obstacles. Sixteen counties in this part of the state contained black majorities and usually landed in the Republican column on Election Day. Furthermore, one of the leading advocates of fusion in this part of the state, former Greenback-Labor congressman-turned-Republican Daniel L. Russell, had alienated some influential black leaders by publicly suggesting that the GOP curb its nomination of black candidates for public offices.[126] The Knights of Labor probably played a helpful role in facilitating Republican-Populist fusion in eastern North Carolina by mobilizing African Americans into the Populist ranks.

In 1894 the fusionists, as Crow and Durden put it, "engineered a virtual revolution in North Carolina politics." The congressional elections resulted in victories for three Populists, two Republicans, and two candidates who bore the standard of both anti-Democratic parties. Only two Democrats won House seats.[127] Populists and Republicans also took control of the state legislature. The death of incumbent U.S. Senator Zebulon Vance, a Democrat, meant that both of the state's Senate seats were vacant, and the legislature appointed People's Party State Chairman Marion Butler (a Knight of Labor and the president of the Southern Farmers' Alliance) to a full term and Republican Jeter C. Pritchard to serve the remainder of Vance's term.[128] Greensboro attorney David Schenck, who had worried earlier about farmers and laborers forming a new "national party and bring[ing] about a bloody Revolution in the country," now lamented that the state government had fallen into the hands of "all the sore heads, extremists, and desperate political characters, who advocate every wild notion in politics."[129]

As Schenck had feared, laborers contributed to the rise of this Populist-Republican coalition, which used its control of the state legislature to cap interest rates at 6 percent annually, increased expenditures for public education, raised taxes on railroads and businesses, and enacted what one scholar called "probably the fairest and most democratic election law in the post-Reconstruction South."[130] One recent study identifies "small farmers, mountaineers, workers, and virtually the entire African American voting population" as the participants in this class-based coalition that unseated the "wealthy Democrats who controlled the state," while another contends that North Carolina Populism "was as much a political and social protest among the lower classes as it was a revolt of economically disadvantaged farmers."[131]

The North Carolina Knights of Labor still encompassed both of these categories. The supposedly moribund Order reported "steady growth in membership throughout the state" in September 1893 and formed two district assemblies in the eastern part of the state one year later: DA 80, with headquarters in Greenville, and DA 81, with headquarters in New Bern.[132] Evidence about the composition of the locals that constituted these districts is limited, but they definitely included unprosperous farmers (some of them landowners) and farm laborers. Some of the latter earned as little as thirty cents per day when they were fortunate enough to find employment. The eastern North Carolina locals also included unskilled nonagricultural laborers, such as stevedores, semiskilled mechanics who earned as much as $1.25 per day, and skilled mechanics, such as carpenters and bricklayers, who earned over $2.00 per day.[133] Most, though certainly not all, eastern North Carolina Knights of this period were probably black. Women participated in this Knights revival, too; Ellen Williams served as one of the Knights' chief North Carolina organizers during the 1890s, and many rural assemblies included women, as had many lodges of the Grange and the Farmers' Alliance.[134]

As we have seen, many eastern North Carolina Knights declared themselves Populists in 1892, and they probably remained so two years later. In September 1893 the Knights held a convention of local assemblies in Greenville, North Carolina. This convention, reportedly attended by "a large number of delegates," adopted resolutions in favor of the free coinage of silver and "decided to support at the polls only those candidates for public office who were favorably disposed toward the platform of the Order."[135] Much of the Populist platform came from that of the Knights of Labor.[136] Marion Butler established contact with James R. Sovereign in 1894 and subsequently reminded laborers that the Knights' chief wanted them to work for reform by voting rather than waging strikes.[137] Much of the eastern North Carolina Knights' strength in 1894 lay in the state's First Congressional District, which elected Populist Harry Skinner, and the Third, where Populist Cyrus Thompson finished a close second to the Democratic candidate in a three-man contest.[138] The hearings in the U.S. House of Representatives that resulted from Thompson's unsuccessful contest of the election produced anecdotal evidence of laborers (including former Knights) voting Populist. In the Fourth District, which included Raleigh, William F. Strowd, who narrowly lost as a Populist candidate in 1892, won in 1894 as a Populist-Republican candidate. Former Raleigh Knights of Labor leaders John Ray and George Tonnoffski were active Populists. Former State Master Workman and Independent congressman John Nichols had returned to the Republican Party, but he advocated fusion with the Populists despite taking a dim view of their economic doctrines. Nichols won election in 1894 as a city magistrate in Raleigh on a fusion ticket.[139]

## *Farmer-Labor Unity in Texas, 1894*

Perhaps in no other southern state did the Populists receive more support from labor than in Texas. Organized labor helped form the People's Party in the Lone Star State, and in his classic study of Texas Populism Roscoe Martin deemed it "a fact of indisputable validity . . . that most of the wage earners supported the cause of Populism and voted for the candidates nominated by the People's Party."[140] In 1892, however, these votes did not amount to enough. No Texas Populist won election to Congress, although three received more than 40 percent of the vote in two-man contests against Democrats, including Knights of Labor ally Jerome C. Kearby, who had defended Southwest railroad strikers in court and made bids for Congress as a Greenback-Labor candidate in 1880 and as an Independent Labor candidate in 1886. Not only did the Texas Populist gubernatorial candidate finish third in 1892, but the party won only eight seats in the state house and only one in the state senate.[141]

The small Populist contingent in the Texas state legislature did, however, make some efforts in labor's behalf, supporting a bill that would have established a state bureau of labor statistics (a Knights of Labor Reading platform demand) and introducing a bill for a mechanics' and laborers' lien law that eventually passed, although not in the form hoped for by Democratic house member and Dallas labor leader Patrick Golden.[142] The Populists' efforts did not go unnoticed by organized labor. In August 1893 the newly formed DA 21 of the Knights of Labor, encompassing six counties to the north of Dallas, held a five-day camp meeting with the Farmers' Alliance at Lannius that amounted to a Populist rally. "The average daily attendance was fully 10,000," District Master Workman S. L. Willyerd reported, "and we knocked the props from under the purse-proud plutocrats." The list of speakers over the five days read like a who's who of southwestern and midwestern Populism: Stump Ashby, Harry Tracy, Bill Farmer, congressman John Davis of Kansas, veteran Knight and third-party man Ralph Beaumont, who would run for Congress as a Populist in the Oklahoma Territory in 1894, and Cyclone Davis.[143] Weeks later, Pioneer Assembly 2379, one of the oldest Knights locals in Galveston, unanimously supported a resolution endorsing two Greenbacker and silverite currency bills presented by Populist senator William A. Peffer of Kansas (a

Knight himself) and pledging "to support no man who votes against" the two bills.[144]

The hard times and labor strife of 1894 only added to the ranks of Populist laborers in Texas. The Pullman strike drove many Texas railroad workers into the People's Party, especially in Dallas, where a People's Party club enrolled fifty members in one night at the apex of the strike.[145] The depression made even more impact. In March 1894 the statistician of Pioneer Assembly 2379, M. J. Gomes, reported miserable conditions in Galveston. Unemployment stood at a staggering 95 percent among wharf workers and at 90 percent in the building trades. Cotton and woolen mill workers, some two hundred of them children, earned from 25 cents to $1.25 per twelve-hour day. The Santa Fe Railroad had closed its Galveston shops five months earlier, leaving over six hundred employees out of work. "It is a well-known fact all over the country," Gomes declared, "that since the Democratic party got in power over two millions of honest workingmen were thrown out of employment." Gomes argued that the only solution was to "free our country from this irresponsible aristocracy by the intelligent use of the ballot."[146]

Many Texas Knights agreed and believed that "intelligent use of the ballot" meant voting Populist. In January 1894 J. P. Diffey of El Paso advised his fellow Knights to "let the old party 'scabs' look out for themselves—we have nursed them on a sugar teat long enough."[147] Another Knight from Roberts, Texas, called upon "farmers, mechanics, miners and laborers of every kind who want relief" to "arise and declare your manhood at the polls this fall by giving your suffrage to men who have been and are still advocating reforms." "I was born and cradled in the lap of Democracy fifty-four years ago," he added. "Have cast my last vote for it."[148] By June Gomes had decided that both the Democratic and Republican parties "should be treated with contempt, and their leaders should be treated as George Washington did John Andre and Benedict Arnold."[149] W. I. Bralley, a Knight from rural Fannin County, declared his support for the Populists while denouncing the Cleveland administration as "one of the most damnable administrations that has ever disgraced the annals of American history."[150]

While the Knights of Labor still maintained enough strength in Texas to matter, with three district assemblies and active locals in most larger cities, not all members were Populists.[151] Miles Crowley, a Knight and former longshoreman from Galveston, won election to the state senate in 1892 and to the U.S. House of Representatives two years later as a Democrat. In December 1892 Crowley informed Terence V. Powderly that he would be working for the passage of a bureau of labor statistics bill in the state senate.[152] After supporting labor bills in the state house as a Democrat, Patrick Golden of Dallas, still an officer in DA 78 of the Knights of Labor, was elected by the city council in 1894 to a two-year term as the city's street superintendent as a "Jacksonian Democrat," according to his fellow Knights and Texas State Federation of Labor leader James Fitzgerald. Fitzgerald, like Golden, had been a pioneer in the Dallas Populist movement but found himself denounced as "an enemy to labor" when he left the third-party ranks. In March 1894 Fitzgerald defiantly declared, "I don't propose to wear any party collar, be it Republican, Populistic or Democratic, but to hold myself prepared at all times to kick the traces when old or new party hacks are put to the front for my indorsement." Later that spring he barked that "the Populists of Texas are not all saints."[153]

But by August Fitzgerald seemed to be souring on the Democratic Party in light of President Cleveland's use of federal troops to break the Pullman strike in Chicago. "I want to say that the perfect unanimity with which the Democracy of the South has indorsed the President's action in this regard has stunned me, an old-time State's right advocate as I was," Fitzgerald wrote. Their action had "almost taken my breath away," he added, and left him with grave doubts about the party's credibility. "I am loath to confess that the doctrine of State's rights was merely a shield with which the planter sought to ward off the blows of the abolitionists, a pretext to perpetuate chattel slavery, or the right to traffic in human flesh and blood, and that there was nothing honest about their professions whatever."[154]

Fitzgerald apparently supported the Populists in the fall of 1894, and, as Roscoe Martin asserted, most other organized Texas workingmen probably did the same.[155] James R. Sovereign, ARU chief Eugene V. Debs, and Kansas Populists Mary Lease and William A. Peffer drew an audience of over ten thousand when they spoke at a labor celebration at the Texas State Fair in Dallas on 31 October.[156] But labor support proved to be of no avail. Populist gubernatorial candidate Thomas Nugent attracted more votes from organized labor and African Americans than he did two years earlier, aided with the latter group by the efforts of a corps of black organizers led by the African American teacher and preacher John B. Rayner of Robertson County. Nevertheless, Nugent still received nearly sixty thousand fewer votes than Democrat Charles Culberson, who had alienated organized labor by refusing to denounce President Cleveland's deployment of troops to Chicago. The Texas Populists elected twenty-two state representatives and two state senators, an improvement over 1892 but still too few to exert much influence. In the state's congressional elections five Populist candidates (in thirteen districts) ran extremely strong races, receiving more than 45 percent of the official vote counts.[157] Two Populists, Jerome Kearby and Cyclone Davis, contested the results but without success.[158] Historians of Texas Populism have agreed, however, that several Populist congressional candidates, including a Populist-Republican fusion candidate who ran as an Independent in the Eleventh District of south Texas, were counted out.[159] Knight of Labor W. I. Bralley commented, "The Democratic officeholders spent money freely and without limit, while the Populists had neither money nor liquor."[160]

## *Aiming for the Middle Class: The Populists in Georgia, 1894*

The Populists made greater gains in Georgia in 1894. In contrast to their Texas brethren, the Georgia Populists began to turn away from labor in search of middle-class voters.[161] This strategy probably made sense, as the only labor organization in Georgia that had demonstrated support for the Populists, the Knights of Labor, had all but collapsed in that state. Still, the Georgia Populists continued to call for the abolition of the "infamous convict lease system," suggesting that convicts be put to work on public roads and bridges instead of competing with free labor. The Populist gubernatorial candidate, the prominent Atlanta attorney James K. Hines, received 44 percent of the vote in a two-man contest, and the Populists elected about fifty state legislators, more than three times as many as in 1892. The Populists claimed that Democratic fraud had cost them the governor's office and more than twenty seats in the legislature, and some Democrats agreed.[162]

The Populists also waged strong contests in six of the state's eleven congressional districts, including all of the districts of north Georgia. The Populist candidate who officially received the highest percentage of the vote was none other than the old Independent warhorse (and former congressman) William H. Felton.[163] Felton opposed the subtreasury plan and ran unsuccessfully as an Independent against Alliance Democrat Robert W. Everett in 1890, but by 1894 the Georgia People's Party had lost much of its initial enthusiasm for the subtreasury, while Felton had stopped opposing it. Therefore, when the Populists tapped Felton as their nominee in the Seventh District that year, the seventy-one-year-old doctor accepted. His wife (and perennial campaign manager), Rebecca, advised him not to, and poor health clearly hampered Dr. Felton's effort, but the People's Party gave him an irresistible platform for espousing the same arguments he had made twenty years earlier. Once again he took to the stump denouncing "eastern money sharks," calling for inflated currency, and assailing his Bourbon Democratic enemies.[164] Once the subtreasury plan fell by the wayside, Populism represented nothing new to Felton. The official results of the election were nothing new to the doctor, either; he lost by a similar narrow margin as in his last two congressional bids in 1882 and 1890.[165]

Felton the Populist probably received less support from laborers in 1894 than had Felton the Independent four years earlier, though. In the two Cobb County districts that included concentrations of city or town workers, Marietta and Roswell, Felton officially received 82 and 48 percent of the vote, respectively, in a two-man contest in 1890. Four years later he received only 22 and 32 percent of the votes in these districts, still only facing one opponent. Felton carried Paulding County in 1894, probably the only county in his district where the Knights of Labor still remained active, but with too few members to be considered a voting bloc.[166] After Felton's supporters charged fraud in most of the counties that he lost, Felton contested the election (once again disregarding his wife's advice), but to no avail.[167]

The official returns in the Tenth District indicated that Tom Watson received only 39 percent of the vote in a two-man contest with Democratic incumbent J. C. C. Black. As in 1892, however, an impossibly large margin of victory in Richmond County won the election for Black. Even so, Watson carried Augusta's working-class Fifth Ward, Harrisburg. Rather than contest the election, Watson accepted Black's offer to resign and submit to another election. In that election, held in October 1895, returns showed fewer votes cast in Richmond County than in the previous two contests, but Black received 86 percent of these votes and returned to Congress. Watson once again carried the Fifth Ward, though.[168]

## The AFL and Populism, 1893–1896

Tom Watson's popularity among millhands and other laborers notwithstanding, by 1896 southern Populists' opportunity for building a farmer-labor coalition had largely passed. The Knights of Labor, which by January 1895 claimed no more than sixty-five thousand members nationally, practically ceased to exist in the South outside of Texas and eastern North Carolina. When the Knights' General Assembly convened at Washington, D.C., in November 1895, only five of the forty-five delegates came from ex-Confederate states: Lewis S. Forbes, a farmer from Greenville, North Carolina; Michael T. Judge, a brickmason from Mobile, Alabama; N. C. Murray, a ginner from Kingston, Texas; John H. Robertson (the Arkansas Populist stalwart), a journalist from Little Rock; and General Master Workman James R. Sovereign, who had just moved to Sulphur Springs, Arkansas, from Des Moines, Iowa.[169] The United Mine Workers lost much of its membership not only in Alabama but in coal-mining districts across the nation after the strike of 1894, while the ARU fell apart soon after the Pullman strike of that year.[170]

The AFL, meanwhile, could only claim some 265,000 members in 1896, little more than one third of the Knights' official membership ten years earlier.[171] Moreover, unlike the Knights in 1886, the AFL, a federation of trade and craft unions, had very little presence in the South in 1896. The annual convention of the AFL in Cincinnati in December of that year was attended by 117 delegates. Four of them came from Nashville. Unless one counts Kentucky, which sent three, no southern state besides Tennessee sent any delegates.[172] A printed list of sixty-one city central unions affiliated with the AFL in January 1897 includes only six from southern cities: Asheville, North Carolina; Birmingham; Fort Worth; Nashville; and Jacksonville and Tampa, Florida. (Louisville and Paducah, Kentucky, also appear on the list.) A list of some 380 local unions that were affiliated directly with the AFL at that time rather than through an affiliated national or international union includes only ten from the South, five of them from Texas.[173]

Moreover, even if the AFL had been stronger in the South, that strength would not necessarily have translated into labor support for Populism. For a brief period during 1893 and 1894 it appeared as if the AFL might be moving toward the Populist camp. A coalition of Populists, mostly from the Midwest, and Socialist Labor Party supporters, mostly from the East, submitted an eleven-plank political platform at the Boston convention of the AFL in December 1893 for the consideration of member unions. The preamble called for the formation of an independent political party, while the eleven-point platform, based upon that of the Independent Labour Party of England, made some typical labor demands, such as an eight-hour workday law and the mandatory inspection of mines and workshops, as well as some of a decidedly socialistic character. In particular, the controversial plank ten called for "the collective ownership by the people of all means of production and distribution." The platform also called for government ownership of telegraphs, telephones, railroads, and mines, and many delegates interpreted the preamble and platform as a step toward unity with the People's Party. The AFL convention of December 1894 would decide whether to adopt the "political programme," as it came to be known. In the interim, over three hundred AFL union members ran for public office in the fall of 1894, most of them as Populists. In the South these included candidates in Birmingham, New Orleans, and Waco, Texas.[174]

Only six of these three hundred–plus candidates won election, all as Populists, and while the AFL convention of December 1894 ratified most of the planks of the "political programme" (but not plank ten), it rejected the preamble, which called for third-party action. Samuel Gompers played a key role in defeating both the preamble and plank ten, and supporters of those measures retaliated by helping to elect UMW president John McBride of Ohio, an active Populist, as the new AFL president. After the collapse of the UMW strike, McBride had formed an Ohio labor party that quickly merged with the state People's Party. Upon assuming leadership of the AFL, McBride spoke of labor placing "a presidential candidate in the field." But unfortunately for the Populists, Gompers recaptured the AFL presidency (defeating McBride by a vote of 1,041 to 1,023) at the next AFL convention in December 1895. That convention also passed a resolution stating that "party politics[,] whether they be democratic, republican, socialistic, populistic, prohibition or any other, should have no place in the conventions of the A.F.L." [175] Thus ended any chance of the AFL joining the Populist movement. In 1896 Gompers voted for William Jennings Bryan, the Democratic-Populist presidential candidate, but refused to endorse him publicly. [176]

### In Search of a "Full Dinner Pail": Labor and the Presidential Election of 1896

Eugene V. Debs and James R. Sovereign both openly supported Bryan in 1896; the Knights' chief served on the Populist national executive committee and established a Bryan Free Silver Campaign Labor Bureau in Chicago. But neither Debs nor Sovereign spoke to as large a labor constituency as did Gompers. [177] Terence V. Powderly, on the other hand, may have still been the best-known labor leader in America in 1896, even though he was in fact an ex–labor leader by then. Powderly, however, who had been a Republican before the emergence of the Greenback-Labor Party and always seemed a somewhat reluctant Populist, returned to the GOP after ending his career as General Master Workman. In 1894 he campaigned actively for Republican local, state, and congressional candidates in Pennsylvania. Powderly increased his efforts for the GOP two years later, when the party nominated William McKinley for the presidency. Powderly and McKinley had established a friendship in 1876, when the latter provided legal defense for thirteen Knights of Labor miners in Ohio, and Powderly stumped heavily for McKinley twenty years later. The former Knights leader apparently stayed out of the primarily Democratic South but spoke throughout the Northeast and Midwest to mostly labor audiences. In Kansas City Powderly spoke to some one thousand railroad workers, many of whom had participated in the Southwest strike a decade earlier. [178]

Ironically, Powderly, the deposed ex–labor leader, proved to be more closely attuned to the political inclinations of most working-class Americans than did the current chiefs of organized labor. During the presidential campaign of 1896 McKinley ran as the candidate of the gold standard and high tariffs, while the Nebraskan Bryan had firmly fixed himself in the minds of voters as the "free silver" candidate on the basis of his famous "Cross of Gold" speech at the Democratic national convention in Chi-

cago. While Bryan insisted that the free coinage of silver was supported
by the "producing masses" and "toilers everywhere," the Republican Party
ran a shrewd campaign–supported by industrialists both financially and
rhetorically–that told workers that a vote for McKinley meant national
prosperity and a "full dinner pail," whereas a vote for Bryan meant more
of the shut-down industries and lost jobs that had characterized Democratic incumbent Grover Cleveland's second term. While Bryan swept the
eleven states of the "Solid South" and carried most states west of the Mississippi River, McKinley swept New England, the mid-Atlantic states, and
much of the upper Midwest. "Democrats," one scholar has recently noted,
"ran badly everywhere the industrial and commercial workforce lived." [179]

## Farmer-Labor Populism in the South, 1896

While only a small minority of the nation's industrial and commercial
workforce lived in the South in 1896 and relatively few of those southern workers belonged to labor organizations, the Populists nevertheless
won labor support in some parts of the South. In the states of North Carolina, Alabama, Arkansas, and Texas what remained of the Knights of Labor continued to support Populism, as other elements of organized labor
clearly did in Alabama and Texas. The persistence of hard times undoubtedly helped the Populists in this regard. District Assemblies 80 and 81
remained active in eastern North Carolina in 1896, and during the summer a member of a Woodland local assembly of African American farm,
sawmill, and railroad hands reported, "Conditions awful. Wages almost
nothing, no demand for product. People's Party very strong and growing." [180] Other similar reports from eastern North Carolina appeared in the
*Journal of the Knights of Labor.* [181] The Populists won five of the state's nine
congressional seats that year (three others went to Republicans), and the
two parties combined to dominate the state elections. Former Greenback-
Labor Congressman Daniel L. Russell, now a Republican, won election
to the governor's office, handing the North Carolina Democrats their first
defeat in a gubernatorial contest since 1872. [182]

In Alabama the few remaining Knights also supported the Populists.
These evidently included Knights in Talladega and in the southern Alabama wiregrass county of Conecuh, where lumber and sawmill work-

ers and farm laborers belonged to the Order. Knights in both locales bemoaned hard times, and the recording secretary of a Conecuh County
local observed, "I see no hope of any better times while we have such
men running our finances as we have at present; they seem to make bad
worse instead of better."[183] From the former Knights-Alliance stronghold
of Jemison (Chilton County), one-time staunch Knight of Labor Mrs. Ira
Campbell ardently supported the Populist presidential ticket of Bryan and
Tom Watson rather than the Democratic ticket of Bryan and Arthur Sewall.
She implored U.S. Senator and national People's Party Chairman Marion
Butler to try to convince the Democratic Party to drop Sewall in favor of
Watson. "The National, State and individual necessities demand the aid of
our own true populist, Mr. Watson," she wrote. "Otherwise our cause is
not only jeopardized but lost. It will be McKinley's gain and our country's
ruin."[184] In Birmingham the Knights of Labor had (for the time being) dis-
banded, but AFL trade union leaders supported the Populists. Jere Dennis,
founder of the trade union organ *Labor Advocate*, AFL organizer, and participant in the Alliance Labor conference of June 1892, publicly supported
the Bryan-Watson ticket and ran for the state legislature himself in 1896 as a
Populist. He appeared to win the seat, but when his Democratic opponent
contested the election, the Democratic-controlled state house of representatives ruled in favor of its own party member, producing outraged cries
of fraud among Populists. *Labor Advocate* editor J. H. F. Moseley, who had
formerly edited the *Alabama Sentinel* (a Knights newspaper) and helped
form the Birmingham Trades Council in 1889, served on the Alabama
Populist campaign committee. The Populist state ticket, which lost again
in 1896, received 45 percent of the vote in Jefferson County and carried
Chilton, Conecuh, and Talladega counties, among others.[185]

The Knights of Labor still remained active in Texas in 1896, with at
least two district assemblies, and remained in the Populist camp.[186] In May
1895 Knights and State Federation of Labor leader James Fitzgerald (who
by then had moved from Dallas to College Station) announced a conference of the Farmers' Alliance, the Knights, and trade unions to be held
at Lampasas Springs during the summer. "To say that I sympathize with
the movement," Fitzgerald wrote, "but mildly expresses what I feel at this
time."[187] From Celeste, where LA 3666 overlapped with the local People's
Party club, Knight of Labor R. D. Cross announced a summer encamp-

ment of Populists from Delta, Fannin, and Hunt counties. "Something must be done," declared Cross. "[W]e cannot stand the oppression of the two old parties much longer."[188] In January 1896, when DA 78 held its annual session at Waco, its District Master Workman told a reporter that "the Knights of Labor are practically all [P]opulists" and that they were "virtually unanimous" in their support for Populist (and longtime Knights ally) Jerome Kearby for governor.[189]

Texas Populists reciprocated labor's support. Meetings of the Farmers' Alliance and the People's Party denounced the imprisonment of Eugene V. Debs (who served six months in an Illinois jail for a contempt conviction stemming from the Pullman strike) and declared their support and admiration for him.[190] In the state legislature the Populists continued to support labor legislation, including bills against allowing convict labor to compete with free labor. While these efforts, according to Roscoe Martin, proved "almost completely unavailing," they nevertheless paid off in terms of labor support in 1896. According to another scholar, an "increase in labor support helped [Kearby] carry Dallas and Austin and win over 40 percent of the votes in Texas's seven major urban areas."[191] Perhaps predictably by this point, however, Kearby lost the gubernatorial election, essentially a two-man contest, by a margin of 11 percent, while the four strongest Populist congressional candidates lost by similar margins, including the old Greenbacker and Knights of Labor leader Bill Farmer.[192] The Texas Populists once again elected only two state senators, while their number of representatives in the house plummeted from twenty-two to six.[193] Kearby blamed "a [Democratic] campaign of slander, defamation, intimidation and fraud," especially where black voters were numerous, for the Populists' defeat. While this charge bore some truth, complicated and controversial fusion arrangements in a presidential election year did not help.[194]

In contrast to Texas, Arkansas had neither a strong labor movement nor a competitive People's Party by 1896, but, as in earlier campaigns, what remained of the former supported what remained of the latter. In August 1895 Knights State Secretary-Treasurer John H. Robertson informed State Master Workman W. B. W. Heartsill that "we are holding our S.A. [State Assembly] charter under dispensation, having only eight locals in actual good standing with [the] G.A. [General Assembly]." The Knights' defeat in a coal miners strike at Huntington during the following winter hardly could

have helped reverse the downward trend. But in rural Polk County, where
the Knights remained active in 1896 and were self-avowed Populists, the
third party controlled the county offices.[195] At the state level Robertson
reported that eight of the twenty-seven Arkansas delegates to the national
Populist convention in St. Louis in July 1896 came from the ranks of the
Knights. Robertson was one of those delegates, and he insisted that "had
it not been for the K. of L. in the St. Louis convention, Tom Watson would
never have been nominated [for vice president], [and] had it not been for
the K. of L. (and Louisiana was the only delegation that did not have K.
of L. in it), [Democratic vice presidential nominee Arthur] Sewall would
have been endorsed."[196]

Some organized Arkansas laborers outside of the Knights may have supported the Populists as well. In late 1894 a "leading union man of Hot
Springs" condemned the local Democrats who controlled the county government "as one of the rottenest political rings on the face of God's green
earth." He insisted that organized labor was not to blame, for "what can an-
gels do when court is held in h— and the D— is presiding judge?" "That,"
he lamented, "is virtually the way in which our ballot box is controlled."[197]
Such control of the ballot box was one of several factors that had left the
Arkansas third party a faint shadow of its former self by 1896; the party
did not nominate any congressional candidates that year, and its gubernatorial candidate, A. W. Files, ran a distant third with less than 10 percent
of the vote. Files carried only one county, Polk in western Arkansas, the
aforementioned late-in-the-day center of Knights of Labor and Populist
persistence.[198]

## The Importance of Farmer-Labor Groundwork to Southern Populism: Three States as Counterexamples

Arkansas farmers and laborers had at least once built a strong third party,
although it was reduced to a shambles by 1896. Their counterparts had
done likewise in Texas and Alabama and in parts of North Carolina and
Georgia. In all of these areas the Knights of Labor (and, in some instances,
farmers' organizations such as the Agricultural Wheel and the Farmers'
Alliance) had laid the groundwork for farmer-labor activism years before
the birth of the People's Party. How did the Populist revolt differ in those

southern states where this groundwork was not laid? In those states the Populists failed to win as much support from labor or as much support overall. Certainly, the weakness of the People's Party in those states did not stem entirely or even primarily from a lack of labor support. In states such as South Carolina, Louisiana, and Tennessee the failure of Populism went far beyond an inability to build a farmer-labor coalition. In South Carolina, Alliance Democratic Governor Ben Tillman led the state Democratic Party in adopting the entire Ocala platform of the Farmers' Alliance in 1892 while using the same rhetorical attacks that he and other Democrats had used against Greenbackers a decade earlier to "successfully cast the Populists as the latest incarnation of 'radical misrule,' 'Bourbon' incompetence, and 'Negro domination.' " As a result, official returns indicated only 2,407 votes for the Weaver-Field ticket in South Carolina, 0.23 percent of its national total.[199]

In South Carolina, then, the Populists failed to win support from farmers, let alone laborers. In Louisiana the Populists failed to attract much labor support in New Orleans, a bastion of organized labor where, by conservative estimates, some twenty thousand workers participated in a three-day general strike called by the AFL's Workingmen's Amalgamated Council in November 1892. "Because of its close association with the Democratic machine" that ran city politics, explains historian Joy Jackson, "New Orleans labor was not in a position to cooperate fully with the Populists."[200] The Populists tried to secure the Knights' support in Louisiana, but by 1891 the Order had very few members in the state outside of New Orleans, where AFL trade unions dwarfed Knights of Labor DA 102.[201]

The larger problems confronting Louisiana Populists, however, recalled those that faced the state's Greenbackers and Independents (including some of the same third-party leaders) in 1878.[202] White Louisiana Democrats engaged in intimidation, violence, and fraud to a degree that was shocking even by the standards of the late-nineteenth-century South. In the 1890s Democratic newspapers in Louisiana encouraged voting fraud as a means to party victory, and newspapers and Democratic politicians subsequently boasted and joked about their success in stealing elections. Victims of such fraud included at least one or perhaps two Populist congressional candidates in the hill country districts in 1894 and the Populist-Republican gubernatorial candidate two years later. While these techniques were hardly unique to Louisiana, only Arkansas Democrats came close to their Louisiana brethren in their use of violence. White and black Louisiana Populists suffered attacks on their persons (sometimes fatal) and property in 1896; Democrats in St. Landry "unmercifully whipped" African American women with barbed wire as a means of squelching Populist-Republican activism. Still worse, twenty-one known lynchings occurred in the state that year, most of which were connected to political campaigns and elections. This figure represented 20 percent of the known lynchings in the nation that year.[203] In sum, the failure of Louisiana Populists to build a farmer-labor coalition represented only one of many reasons for the party's failure, and hardly the most tragic or consequential one at that.

The inability to build a farmer-labor coalition did not rank as the greatest weakness of Tennessee Populists either, but it proved more vexing to them in light of their efforts to build such a coalition in 1892. The miners rebellion against convict labor, of course, greatly hindered these efforts from the start. State Farmers' Alliance leaders tried to overcome this obstacle by playing prominent roles at the first meeting of the State Labor Congress (the brainchild of the Nashville Central Labor Union) in late February and early March 1892, over two months before the formation of the Tennessee People's Party. The first plank on the Labor Congress platform was "the abolition of the penitentiary lease system, and the working of convicts in a manner [so] that they will be self-sustaining." Alliance Democratic Governor John Buchanan, however, probably failed to restore the faith of labor delegates at the Congress by declaring that when "any class or organization violates the written law of the land [as in, for example, the miners rebellions] . . . there should be universal condemnation."[204] In August 1892, when more miners rebellions occurred in east and middle Tennessee, Buchanan once again sent the militia to the mines. By then the Tennessee Democratic Party had denied Buchanan renomination, and he was running for reelection as an Independent with the Populists' endorsement.[205] The Knights of Labor had little use for Democratic nominee Peter Turney, whom one member of the Order denounced as "a plutocrat and penitentiary lease man," but as historian Roger Hart has noted, "The Knights of Labor would hardly rally to the governor who had sent troops to the mines" either.[206] Nor did they support the Weaver-Field ticket, which received only twelve votes in the east Tennessee mining community of

Newcomb.[207] Most east and middle Tennessee miners, and probably most east Tennessee workingmen in general, voted for the candidates of the party that had made the greatest effort to eradicate the convict lease system: the Republicans.[208]

While the miners rebellions and the failure of Alliance Democrats to help eradicate the convict lease system greatly hindered the efforts of Populists to win labor votes in Tennessee, another problem lay in the fact that earlier organizations had not laid the groundwork for a Populist-labor alliance. The Greenback-Labor Party had been weak in the Volunteer State, and the Knights of Labor, the Agricultural Wheel, and the Farmers' Alliance did not engage in third-party-building activities in Tennessee as they did, for example, in the neighboring state of Alabama.[209] The Tennessee Knights did not avoid the wave of labor politics of the mid-1880s, but their involvement proved fairly minimal. The elections of 1884 sent three Knights to the Tennessee state house of representatives, but two of them were Republicans and the other was a Democrat.[210] In 1886 the Chattanooga Knights nominated candidates for the state legislature and some city offices, and one of those candidates, an African American machinist, won election to the position of circuit court clerk.[211] Overall, however, Tennessee Knights showed more inclination for lobbying lawmakers than for nominating labor candidates.[212] At any rate, Tennessee Populists faced greater problems than a lack of support from labor. Although postbellum Tennessee did not have a true two-party system (Republicans dominated the eastern part of the state, while the Democrats controlled middle and west Tennessee), the Republican Party was nevertheless, as one scholar has noted, "strong enough to end the hopes of the Populists."[213]

## The Legacy of the Knights of Labor to Southern Populism

Even though a lack of labor support did not rank as the Populists' biggest problem in Louisiana or Tennessee (let alone in South Carolina, where the People's Party scarcely existed), that lack of support in these states as compared to Texas, Alabama, and Arkansas nevertheless underscores the importance of Knights-Alliance-Wheel groundwork in setting the stage for later Populist-labor coalitions. In the latter three states the Knights of Labor and the farmers' organizations laid the foundation for farmer-labor third-party activity before the formation of the People's Party or, more to the point in the case of Arkansas, the Union Labor Party. The Greenback-Labor Party also had been active in each of these three states, and from its ranks came future third-party leaders. In Georgia and North Carolina, by contrast, the Knights played a pioneering role in stirring farmer-labor insurgency before the Farmers' Alliance even reached those states. While labor support for the Populists was less widespread in Georgia and not as discernible in North Carolina (except in the eastern part of the state) as in Texas, Alabama, or, in their Union Labor incarnation, Arkansas, the Knights nevertheless deserve much credit for what labor support the Populists did attract in Georgia and North Carolina. The Knights clearly paved the way for—and provided support for—the Populists in the Georgia counties of Richmond and Paulding, in conjunction with the Farmers' Alliance in the latter. In North Carolina the Knights helped to sustain the political rift between Bourbon Democrats and the poor of both races that had existed since the end of the Civil War. This old split, of course, reemerged more forcefully in the 1890s, when the Populist-Republican coalition assumed political dominance in the state with the assistance of the Knights in the heavily black, rural counties in the eastern part of the state.

The impact of the Knights of Labor upon southern Populism went beyond merely planting the seeds of labor support for the movement. In those states of the South where the Knights led or contributed to farmer-labor insurgency in the 1880s the subsequent third party not only received more labor support than in other states but developed more overall strength as well. This does not mean that Knights of Labor political insurgency was the determining factor in Populist strength in any given state. But Knights insurgency (or the lack thereof) clearly formed an important part of the background of or the prelude to the Populist revolt, and the Order played a larger role in the history of that revolt than historians have acknowledged or understood. While this role was not confined to southern states, as shown by the story of Kansas Populism, the Order's bent for organizing across the color line magnified its importance as a forerunner of and participant in southern Populism.[214]

After 1896, however, most of the already greatly diminished ranks of the Knights of Labor soon disappeared, a fate in which the moribund Farmers' Alliances (Northern and Southern) shared.[215] Having tied its fortunes to those of William Jennings Bryan, the People's Party soon met the same fate. Southern Populism had not perished, but its downward spiral was painfully apparent to party leaders such as Tom Watson and Jerome Kearby, and the idea of a biracial coalition of farmers and laborers with a voice in politics would soon become, as Arkansas native C. Vann Woodward would say, a "forgotten alternative."[216]

# CHAPTER SIX

# Southern Farmer and Labor Movements after the Populist Defeat of 1896

After his defeat by questionable means in the Texas gubernatorial election of 1896, Populist candidate Jerome C. Kearby lamented that the opportunity for reform had been "lost." "I trust it may appear again; I fear not," predicted the veteran reformer as he announced his retirement from politics.[1] In Georgia, defeated Populist vice presidential candidate Tom Watson declared, "Our party . . . does not exist any more."[2]

The pessimistic views of Kearby and Watson proved essentially correct. The elections of 1896 destroyed the People's Party for all intents and purposes, and the last remaining vestiges of the National Farmers' Alliance and Industrial Union (the Southern Alliance) and the Knights of Labor went with it. When these organizations perished, so too did the last best chance for a biracial coalition of working-class southerners of the farm, mine, and factory. Some of the very means that southern Democrats had used to destroy biracial farmer-labor insurgency, including disfranchisement, race baiting and Jim Crow, state-sanctioned violence, and anti–labor union laws, made its resurrection extremely improbable, as did Democrats' adoption of the less radical Populist demands and the gradual emergence of less inclusive and egalitarian trade unions in the South. Thus the door to social justice for the region's have-nots, which had seemed partially open during the struggles of the Greenback-to-Populist era, appeared to slam shut as the nineteenth century ended.

No story better illustrates this tragic turn of events than that of post-1896 North Carolina. In the elections of 1894 Republican and Populist fusionists won control of the state government. They subsequently enacted "a sweeping reform program" that included democratic reform of election laws and county home rule, increased expenditures for public education, usury laws, and increased taxes on railroads and businesses.[3] In 1898, however, North Carolina Democrats mounted a vicious white supremacy campaign and resorted to intimidation and violence to recapture control of the state legislature. (Republican governor Daniel L. Russell was in midterm at the time but was nevertheless nearly lynched at the state capital of Raleigh on election day.) Two days after the state elections the Democratic "best men" of Wilmington, who had resurrected the Reconstruction-era Red Shirts terrorist organization, instigated a "race riot" in that city. Members of a "White Labor Union" apparently participated, encouraged by leading businessmen who supported the newly formed union and promised to replace black laborers with whites. Business leaders clearly led the "riot," however, which resulted in the deaths of as many as thirty African Americans. Prominent fusionists of both races fled Wilmington, and the mayor and aldermen resigned in midterm out of fear for their lives. Col. Alfred M. Waddell, a Confederate veteran, former U.S. congressman, and leader of the Red Shirts, became the city's new mayor.[4] The new state legislature segregated railroad cars in 1899 and effectively disfranchised African Americans one year later through an amendment to the state constitution.[5] The number of registered black voters in the Tarheel State plummeted from about 120,000 in 1896 to a mere 6,100 six years later.[6] Poor and working-class whites also found their voting rights restricted, and the resultant one-party system, as one scholar has observed, "provided the vehicle for the nearly undisputed power of an oligarchy of landlords, commercial leaders, and industrialists."[7]

The Populist administration of Grimes County, east Texas, met a similar violent end in 1900. Leading Democrats formed the White Man's Union to wage a campaign of violence and intimidation against the biracial Populist coalition that controlled the county government. Several black Populists and whites of both parties died in shootings before and after the county elections, which restored the Democrats to power. Once again, the "best people" of the South had destroyed a biracial democratic coalition, and by 1904 disfranchisement measures would ensure that such a coalition would not arise again in Texas.[8]

By 1908 every ex-Confederate state had enacted disfranchisement measures that almost eliminated black voting and restricted poor white voting as well. (The U.S. Supreme Court gave tacit approval to such legislation in its *Williams v. Mississippi* decision of 1898, which affirmed the legality of literacy tests and poll taxes as qualifications for voting.)[9] At the same time, the first two decades of the twentieth century witnessed what C. Vann Woodward called "the mushroom growth of discriminatory and segregation laws" in the South.[10] This codification of racism accompanied a general deterioration of southern race relations, as the harsh white racism that historian Joel Williamson described as racial "Radicalism" became pervasive in the region during the final years of the nineteenth and early years of the twentieth centuries. Two of the harshest proponents of this virulent racism were U.S. Senator Ben Tillman of South Carolina, the state's former Alliance Democratic governor, and Rebecca Felton of Georgia, the anti–Bourbon Democrat who advocated reforms such as temperance, woman's suffrage, and the abolition of the convict lease system.[11]

In addition to disfranchisement and worsening race relations the South's dying third-party movement faced other problems as the nineteenth century drew to a close. One significant obstacle occurred at both the national and state levels: Democratic co-optation of the Populists' milder demands. Nationally, the Democrats' endorsement of the free coinage of silver and nomination of Bryan in 1896 virtually preempted the Populists' chances of playing a significant role in the presidential election. Yet the Populists once again gave their nomination (barely relevant by then) to Bryan when he made another run as the Democratic nominee four years later.[12] In individual southern states Democrats more aggressively seized upon Populist demands. By 1894 little difference existed between the programs of Georgia Democrats and Populists. The former wavered on the issue of ending the convict lease, a Populist demand, but they took a stronger stand against lynching than did the Populists.[13] In Arkansas the Democratic Party continued its practice of selectively stealing from third-party platforms, which it first developed in beating back the Greenback-Labor challenge. In 1893 the Democratic-controlled state government abolished the convict lease system, albeit in imperfect fashion, and by 1896 the state Democratic platform included most of the Populists' chief demands.[14] In Texas, too, the Democrats took planks from the third-party platform.[15] Democrats never endorsed the subtreasury plan, nor did they ever endorse government ownership of the means of communication and transportation, the most radical planks in the Populist platform. Some Populists, including Watson, had backed away from these demands by 1896, though, and even the National Farmers' Alliance and Industrial Union dropped the subtreasury plan from its platform that year, apparently drawing protests only from Texas.[16]

The virtually moribund condition of the Farmers' Alliance by 1896 represented still another problem for the third-party movement. The Southern Alliance (and the Agricultural Wheel, which it absorbed in 1889) had been, as Robert McMath put it, the "Populist vanguard." But by 1892, as the People's Party began its first national campaign, the Alliance started to disintegrate. The efforts of national Populist chairman Herman Taubeneck to replace the Alliance with a new order called the Industrial Legion proved futile. Hence the Populists soon found themselves without organized networks of farmers to draw upon. During the latter half of the 1890s and the first years of the twentieth century the Alliance virtually disappeared, although an increasingly innocuous North Carolina State Alliance continued to hold meetings until 1941.[17]

The Knights of Labor followed much the same trajectory. The Order actually managed brief but significant turn-of-the-century revivals in western Florida and Alabama, but these represented exceptions to the regional and national trends. National membership fell somewhere in the range of twenty to fifty thousand as the twentieth century began, while the total membership of unions affiliated with the American Federation of Labor (AFL) reportedly surpassed one million by 1902.[18] The Knights of Labor finally closed its national headquarters in Washington, D.C., and ceased publication of the *Journal of the Knights of Labor* in 1917. The last known local assembly of the Knights, consisting of Boston motion picture operators, remained intact until 1949, when it merged into an AFL union.[19]

## *Trade Unions and Union Busting in the Turn-of-the-Century South*

But while the AFL experienced significant national growth around the turn of the century, little of that growth occurred in the South.[20] In 1904 a delegate from the Georgia State Federation of Labor to the national AFL convention reported that "the South Atlantic ports and southeastern section is [*sic*] poorly organized."[21] Economist Mercer Evans estimated that the total membership of Georgia trade unions in 1900 amounted to 6,850, only about three fourths of the roughly 9,000 members that the Knights of Labor had in the state fourteen years earlier. By 1910 the number of trade unionists in Georgia had risen to 10,800, but the percentage of non-agricultural workers belonging to unions only increased from 2.01 to 2.55 during that ten-year span.[22] In North Carolina the state Bureau of Labor and Printing identified eighty-seven trade union locals in 1901 in compiling a "partial list" of such bodies. Unless the list was only half complete, fewer trade union locals existed in the state at that time than the 161 Knights of Labor local assemblies known to have been active in North Carolina thirteen years earlier.[23] Trade union growth also came slowly in Texas, once one of the bastions of southern Knighthood. The Knights had some 12,500 members in the Lone Star State in 1886; membership in unions affiliated with the Texas State Federation of Labor did not reach that figure until 1910.[24] By then the state's population was 74 percent larger than it had been twenty years earlier.[25]

Alabama represented an exception to the slow southern growth of trade unions during this period. Birmingham trade unions had formed the Birmingham Trades Council in June 1889, and that organization affiliated with the AFL during the following year. In 1891 Birmingham hosted the first national convention of the AFL to be held in the South.[26] The national economic recovery that began in 1898 combined with revivals in Alabama's chief industries—coal and iron in the northern part of the state and lumber in the south—to spur significant union growth. Alabama trade unions formed a State Federation of Labor in 1900, which by 1902 reportedly represented forty thousand organized laborers.[27]

The atypical case of Alabama notwithstanding, several factors contributed to the slow growth of trade unions in the turn-of-the-century South. Southern labor organizers worked at great peril. When Hiram F. Hover began lecturing and organizing among white farmers and laborers for the Knights of Labor in North Carolina in 1886 (despite lacking an organizer's commission), the state press widely denounced him as a communist and anarchist. Even some of the state's leading Knights believed the charges until they heard him speak.[28] By early 1887 Hover had begun organizing black farmworkers in South Carolina, where he met with harassment from police. When he carried these efforts into Georgia, they ended with a shotgun blast that dislodged one of his eyes and disfigured his face.[29] Many other southern labor organizers would suffer violent attacks well into the twentieth century, even when their efforts were confined to white workers.[30] Another southern antilabor tradition—union-busting laws—also took root during the era of the Knights of Labor. Between 1885 and 1890 at least five ex-Confederate states (Alabama, Louisiana, Georgia, Texas, and Mississippi) enacted laws designed to impede the organization of unions.[31] In 1888 an Augusta, Georgia, union spokesman lamented that the state's Interference with Employees law, passed in 1887, "made [it] a crime punishable in the penitentiary for any person or persons, single [*sic*] or together, to agitate a strike or boycott, or to agitate in the least that is calculated to mar the smooth progress of the mill company's business." He added that the law represented the Democratic Party's attempt "to cut off every avenue of escape from almost absolute slavery."[32] In Alabama, once the inadequacy of the state's anti–labor conspiracy laws of 1885 as a union-squelching measure became apparent, the state legislature enacted a stronger antiboycott law in 1903 that would undermine organized labor for decades.[33] These laws later gave way to the "right-to-work" laws that became endemic to the South by the middle of the twentieth century.[34]

Violence and antilabor laws alone, however, do not explain the slow growth of trade unions in most of the South during the late nineteenth and early twentieth centuries. To a considerable extent the exclusionary nature of the AFL contributed to the problem. While trade unions of unskilled workers, such as hod carriers and streetcar railway workers, could and sometimes did affiliate with the AFL, as did semiskilled factory workers' unions and the United Mine Workers of America, skilled workers' unions represented most of the AFL rank and file. The AFL made far less effort to organize unskilled workers than had the Knights of Labor, and in the South in particular those workers constituted a large majority of the industrial workforce.[35] Furthermore, the Knights had organized women and African Americans in limited but nevertheless substantial numbers. The AFL, however, did not follow suit. During the 1890s, according to historian Bruce Laurie, the "hardening of white male chauvinism, racism, and xenophobia in the context of trade autonomy all but slammed shut [AFL] doors to women, blacks, and eastern Europeans." While the last of these groups was relatively scarce in the South circa 1900, the first two were quite plentiful. But prejudices and the relative scarcity of those two groups in the skilled trades (a scarcity that AFL unions sometimes worked to ensure) meant that few women or blacks joined the ranks of the AFL.[36] Unlike the Knights, the AFL did not organize domestic workers or farmers of any sort.[37] The exclusion of the latter, of course, meant that the AFL trade union movement would not emulate the Knights of Labor as a farmer-labor movement.

## The Farmers' Union

Southern farmers across the economic spectrum, however, soon formed a new organization of their own, albeit for whites only. Former Alliance organizer and Populist–turned–Bryan Democrat Newt Gresham, a rather unprosperous farmer and newspaper publisher, launched the Farmers' Educational and Cooperative Union (better known as the Farmers' Union) in 1902 in Rains County, northeast Texas, "a hardscrabble county of small farmers and high tenancy."[38] The Farmers' Union established a "national" organization in 1905 and soon formed state bodies across the South. The Farmers' Union eventually reached thirty-three states, with state organizations in twenty-six of them, primarily in the cotton-, wheat-, and tobacco-producing states.[39]

The Farmers' Union essentially revived the cooperative and lobbying efforts of its predecessors, the Grange and the Farmers' Alliance, while avoiding partisan politics. The organization engaged in cooperative buying and selling, built some sixteen hundred warehouses in the cotton states by about 1910, and tried to limit the supply and control the marketing of cotton. It established cooperative gins, stores, fertilizer factories, flour mills, oil mills, and banks. Accurate membership figures for the organization do not exist, but national membership may have reached about nine hundred thousand during the century's first decade.[40]

Perhaps not surprisingly, the Farmers' Union helped to revive farmer-labor coalitions of sorts in Texas and Alabama, the two southern states where those coalitions seemed strongest and most enduring. In Texas the Farmers' Union, like the Farmers' Alliance two decades earlier, participated in union boycotts and provided assistance during strikes. In response, the AFL vowed to help the Farmers' Union establish "agencies, exchanges, or commission houses to aid the consumer in securing products at equitable prices and relieving farmers from unjust treatment at the hands of the middlemen."[41] Members of the Texas Farmers' Union and the State Federation of Labor attended each other's conventions, and in 1908 AFL president Samuel Gompers addressed the National Farmers' Union convention in Fort Worth by invitation. The Texas Farmers' Union later passed resolutions denouncing convict labor in competition with free labor and calling for an eight-hour workday law.[42] The Farmers' Union, the State Federation of Labor, and the railroad brotherhoods helped elect progressive Democrat Thomas M. Campbell, a protégé of former Alliance Democratic governor James S. Hogg, to the governor's office in 1906, along with what one scholar has called "the most reform minded legislature in Texas history." Its accomplishments included progressive legislation regarding education, health, business, taxation, and labor.[43] The panic of 1907 caused membership in the Texas Farmers' Union to plummet, however, from a reported 120,000 just two years earlier to a mere 11,000. The organization never recovered in Texas, and, according to historian James R. Green, its decline "all but eliminated the progressive influence of farmer-labor coalitions."[44]

In Alabama the coalition between the Farmers' Union and the State Federation of Labor emerged more slowly and with less results, but it also suggested an unusually long-lived farmer-labor alliance. In 1910 the Alabama Farmers' Union expressed willingness to join the State Federation of Labor in lobbying efforts. Six years later the State Federation of Labor, the railroad brotherhoods, and the Farmers' Union jointly formed Labor's Volunteer Cooperative Citizenship and Educational Committee in order to provide laborers and farmers with information about political candidates and issues. In 1920 Alabama labor unions and the Farmers' Union made an impressive display of political unity, especially in the northern part of the state, that fell just short of unseating the antireform, antilabor incumbent U.S. Senator Oscar Underwood in the Democratic primary election. During the mid-1930s the Alabama Farmers' Union made overtures to organized labor; Farmers' Union locals in several hill country counties even chose to affiliate with the Congress of Industrial Organizations in 1937. During the 1940s the Alabama Farmers' Union, which by then included

African Americans, advocated reforms such as abolition of the poll tax, improvements in rural health care, low-interest loans to tenant farmers, and adequate living wages and collective bargaining rights for labor. Organized labor leaders served in the Alabama Farmers' Union hierarchy, including one O. H. Mastin of Gadsden. Some fifty years earlier one O. M. Mastin had belonged to the Knights of Labor and the Farmers' Alliance and served as a Populist state legislator from Chilton County, which in 1947 boasted the largest Farmers' Union membership of any county in the state. In 1951, however, the National Farmers' Union revoked the Alabama organization's charter, either because of dwindling membership or, by some accounts, increasing radicalism that did not sit well with the national organization's leaders in the era of McCarthyism.[45]

## Southern Socialism in the Post-Populist and Progressive Eras

As the increasingly radical agenda of its Alabama branch suggests, however, the Farmers' Union could not solve the problem of farm tenancy, which became steadily and sharply more prevalent across the South between 1880 and 1930.[46] In the Southwest in particular this problem drove some old Populists in a more radical direction than the progressive Democratic-oriented Farmers' Union of the early twentieth century. Although the Socialist Party never approached the strength of the Populist Party in the South, it nevertheless served as a vehicle for the more radical elements of the farmer and labor movements in Texas, Arkansas, and Oklahoma, which entered the Union in 1907.[47] In 1897, as the Populist Party crumbled, the Texas Social Democratic Party met in Fort Worth. Dr. G. B. Harris, one of the wealthiest men in the central Texas county of McLennan, where he was the Populist county chairman, became the Social Democratic Party's state secretary. Described by one historian as a "country doctor–turned–agitator," Harris promptly began organizing Social Democratic clubs. To assist him in this task he hired the leader of the by then legendary Southwest strike of 1886, Martin Irons. Despite poor health and even worse financial condition, the sixty-year-old Irons remained devoted to the reform cause. Upon arriving in McLennan County in 1897, he became active in a still functioning Knights of Labor local assembly in Waco, and by 1899 his zeal for Socialism would win accolades from another noted railroad strike leader, Eugene V. Debs. As frustrated Texas Cotton Belt farmers began to engage in barn burnings and other forms of "night riding" against landlords, Harris and Irons began organizing farmers under the slogan of "antimoney rent," with particular (if short-lived) success in McLennan, Bell, and Falls counties. Debs toured Texas for the Socialist Party in 1899, recruiting old American Railway Union members.[48]

Other Texas Populist-labor leaders soon joined the Socialist cause. These included longtime third-party and Knights of Labor leader Bill Farmer and the Rhodes brothers, Jake and Lee. In 1908, while Lee was trying "to bring together night-riding tenant farmers in a secret cotton-growers' union," Jake received 8,100 votes for governor as the Socialist candidate. In 1912 and 1914 the Texas Socialist gubernatorial candidate finished a distant second; in the latter contest E. R. Meitzen, an organizer for the renters' and typographers' unions and the son of Populist leader–turned–Socialist E. O. Meitzen, received 11.7 percent of the total vote, more than double what the Republican candidate polled.[49] Political scientist Roscoe Martin found that most of the counties in which the Texas Socialist candidate for governor fared best in 1912 had "cast a very heavy Populist vote" in gubernatorial elections during the 1890s.[50] While the Texas Socialist Party advocated a far more proactive role for government than the Populists had, the Socialists did adopt a number of Populist demands, such as an eight-hour workday for laborers, the initiative and referendum, a graduated income tax, and "the loaning of money at the lowest possible rate of interest by the State on cotton and other imperishable farm products," a demand that partially resembled the old Southern Alliance/Populist subtreasury plan.[51]

In Arkansas, too, the Socialist Party provided a new home for some of the more militant Populists, although the Socialists attracted less support in the Razorback State than in Texas. W. Scott Morgan, historian of the Agricultural Wheel and Populist gubernatorial candidate in 1898, joined the Socialist Party after the demise of the People's Party, as did many Union Labor or Populist leaders in Sebastian and Pulaski counties.[52] In the latter, which includes Little Rock, close connections developed between the Socialist Party and trade unions. The Socialists' endorsement of the new Industrial Workers of the World in 1906 strained those ties, since many Little Rock trade unions were affiliated with the AFL, but Socialists nevertheless received noticeable support in Pulaski County, particularly in the railroad town of Argenta.[53] Sebastian County, where the Knights of Labor had organized coal miners and farmers in the 1890s, became the Socialist stronghold of the state. Two of the party's gubernatorial candidates came from Sebastian County: Dan Hogan, who ran in 1906, 1910, and 1914, and George E. Mikel, the party's standard-bearer in 1912. Both men had belonged to the Farmers' Alliance and were active in the UMW. Mikel also had been a Knights of Labor leader in the 1890s, and in September 1912 he became the president of the State Federation of Labor.[54] The Sebastian County coal-mining town of Hartford elected Socialist Pete Stewart, president of UMW District 21, to the mayor's office that year as well.[55]

Socialist organizers in Arkansas initially focused their efforts on coal miners and urban laborers. The arrival of the Farmers' Union in Arkansas in 1906 commanded the Socialists' attention, though. By August of that year the Farmers' Union claimed sixty thousand members in Arkansas and reached an agreement with the State Federation of Labor to "respect one another's labels and assist one another in other ways." By 1907 Socialist organizers had greatly increased their efforts in the state's agricultural areas. On a campaign tour through Arkansas in 1908 Socialist presidential candidate Eugene V. Debs's stops included Pine Bluff, where he addressed "a farmer audience." These efforts among farmers bore some fruit; the Socialist Party received support in rural Polk and Scott counties in western Arkansas, where the Populist Party had been strong in the 1890s, and in some of the agricultural counties of the central and northeastern parts of the state. This support did not amount to much, though. Mikel received only 13,384 votes, 7.9 percent of the total cast, in 1912, the Socialist Party's peak year in Arkansas and nationally. Debs received only 8,153 votes in Arkansas in the presidential election that year.[56] As in Texas, many former Arkansas Populist leaders returned to the Democratic Party, and with them went many of the former third-party rank and file who could still vote.[57] Polk County, however, later became the home of Commonwealth College, which trained communist and socialist activists who worked with the biracial Southern Tenant Farmers' Union during the 1930s.[58]

In the Southeast the Socialist Party failed to develop even the modest strength that it displayed in the Southwest. In 1912 Debs garnered a grand total of only 16,417 votes in the eight states of Alabama, Florida, Georgia, Mississippi, North Carolina, South Carolina, Tennessee, and Virginia, only 63 percent of the number of votes that he received in Texas. He barely received a thousand votes in each of the former Populist strongholds of Georgia and North Carolina and polled just over three thousand votes in another old bastion of Populism, Alabama.[59]

The Birmingham district and surrounding Alabama hill country seemed to be potentially ripe territory for Socialism in the early twentieth century. The area contained the same basic ingredients that spurred Socialism in Texas and Arkansas: coal miners and railroad workers who had waged strikes that drove them away from the Democratic Party and steadily increasing rates of farm tenancy throughout the late nineteenth and early twentieth centuries.[60] The Socialists made some headway in the Birmingham district between the late 1890s and World War I, and a number of former Knights of Labor and Populist leaders joined their ranks. These included former North Carolina Knights leader (and Populist supporter) John Ray, who was arrested in Birmingham in July 1903 for preaching the Socialist Party doctrine on a city street, and *Birmingham Labor Advocate* editor J. H. F. Mosely. Mosely, who named a son after Eugene Debs, gave his newspaper's endorsement to Socialist mayoral candidate Clement Wood in 1913, as did the Birmingham Trades Council. Wood made a respectable showing at the polls, losing to the Democratic candidate by only 10 percent of the votes cast. Clearly, Wood received substantial support from beyond the ranks of organized labor, but Socialists were active in Birmingham unions.[61]

Socialism found fewer followers, however, in the rural counties of the Alabama hill country and adjoining Tennessee Valley, although the Socialist Party became active in some old centers of farmer-labor anti-Democratic insurgency, such as Lawrence, Shelby, and Chilton counties.[62] Like its counterparts elsewhere, the Alabama Socialist Party adopted a number of Populist demands, but, as one study has noted, "Socialist efforts to recruit leaders from among the Populists in Alabama produced no tangible results."[63] Unfortunately for Alabama's Socialist Party, the same could be said of its efforts to recruit voters from the state's substantial base of former Populists.

## *Populism, Progressivism, and the Demise of "Producerism"*

One significant obstacle to the Socialists' efforts in northern Alabama lay in the vibrancy of the progressive wing of the Republican Party in that part of the state after the Populist Party disintegrated. Historian Samuel Webb has convincingly demonstrated this point through his detailed analysis of hill country election returns in 1912, when the Socialist Party peaked. In the presidential election that year Progressive Republican (or Bull Moose) candidate Theodore Roosevelt "consistently defeated" Republican incumbent William H. Taft and Democrat Woodrow Wilson (as well as Debs) in formerly loyal Populist precincts of hill country counties. In the Chilton County community of Jemison, a former hotbed of Knights of Labor, Farmers' Alliance, and Populist activism, Roosevelt received eighty-four votes, while Wilson garnered fifty-two, Taft, twenty-five, and Debs, nineteen. After the demise of the Roosevelt-centered Bull Moose Party, many former Alabama Populist leaders worked for reform through the "regular" Republican Party, which many of them had done before 1912 as well.[64]

In Georgia, too, many of the Populists who remained politically active into the twentieth century sought to achieve reform through a "regular" party. In the Peach State, however, they did so through the only party that would ever control the governor's office or the state legislature during that century–the Democrats. (The old Populist stronghold of Paulding County represented an exception to this rule; Republican or third-party candidates carried Paulding in the first six presidential elections of the twentieth century, including Tom Watson in his hopeless campaign as a Populist in 1904, but no Socialists.)[65] Georgia Populists never exhibited much interest in Socialism; in fact, most of the state's Populist leaders (especially Watson) took pains to reject Socialism in the mid-1890s, as the People's Party tried to appeal to Georgia's middle-class voters. Historian Barton Shaw found that only one notable Georgia Populist, J. B. Osborne, "the party's leading labor leader," became a Socialist.[66] The Socialists failed, however, to convert many Georgia laborers. Socialists became active in the trade unions of Atlanta and Augusta during the late 1890s, even "controlling the Federation of Trades and the labor press in both cities," according to one scholar.[67] But such success within the trade union movement did not translate into success at the ballot box. In 1906 Osborne ran for governor on the Socialist Party ticket but received a meager 148 votes.[68]

By then many Georgia Populists had returned to the "party of the fathers." Seaborn Wright of Floyd County, the Populists' gubernatorial candidate in 1896, won election in 1900 as a Democrat to the state house of representatives, where he fought for child labor laws, ballot reform, regulation of lobbyists, and statewide prohibition.[69] By 1906 James K. Hines, the Populists' gubernatorial candidate in 1894, urged Tom Watson, "Let us take charge of the Democratic Party in Georgia and make it the People's Party." Hines and Watson subsequently threw their support behind progressive Democrat Hoke Smith against conservative Democrat Clark Howell in the Democratic gubernatorial primary that year. Smith, an anticorporation lawyer, had joined Wright and Watson in unsuccessfully supporting a child labor bill in the state house of representatives four years earlier. Most old Populists followed Watson's lead in supporting Smith, who won the primary and subsequently the general election.[70] The Smith administration proceeded to enact a number of Populist demands, including increased state regulation of railroads and public utilities, the abolition of the convict lease system, statewide prohibition (a leading Populist issue in the state campaign of 1896), and electoral reforms. The latter, unfortunately, included a literacy test for voting that, combined with the already existing state poll tax, virtually ended black voting in the state. Watson himself championed this measure, though. "Thus a legislature which had been elected to no small extent by the old Populist vote and which contained a number of ex-Populist members," wrote historian Alex Arnett, "had enacted a considerable part of the program of the People's Party."[71]

Just as some scholars have seen continuity between Populism and progressivism in southern Populist strongholds such as Texas, Alabama, and Georgia, some have argued that the movements were closely linked at the national level as well.[72] Historians and political scientists have lined up on both sides of this debate. In one of the more recent works on the subject political scientist Elizabeth Sanders asserts that "the progressive reforms of 1909–17 had their roots in programs advocated by a long succession of Grangers, Antimonopolists, Greenbackers, Farmers' Alliance members, Populists, and Farmers' Unionists." Portraying the Democratic Party as the farmer's savior, Sanders adds that "by the end of the Progressive Era" that party "had delivered almost every item on labor's legislative wish list."[73]

Few southern laborers would have known. Many union demands that could be traced back to the Knights of Labor's Reading platform of 1878 remained unfulfilled in the South throughout the Progressive Era.[74] Many southern industrial laborers, among them miners, millhands, and lumber workers, continued to receive pay in scrip redeemable only at company stores, which often compounded such robbery by charging steep prices. The convict lease system would not disappear from the South until 1928, when it was finally abolished in Alabama after a half-century of agitation by various unions. Federal child labor legislation enacted in 1916 and 1919 died at the hands of the U.S. Supreme Court. Final passage of such legislation would have to await the New Deal, although labor market forces and, in some cases, state law had reduced markedly the prevalence of child labor in the South by then. The eight-hour workday and forty-hour workweek would remain almost unheard-of in the South until mandated by federal New Deal legislation.[75] The prevalence of major strikes in the southern textile industry during both the Progressive and New Deal eras would suggest that neither was a golden age for workers in that industry.[76]

While some southern farmers experienced greater prosperity in the first two decades of the twentieth century than in the 1890s, a steady increase in world demand for cotton for two decades after 1898 probably had more to do with such prosperity than did progressive reforms. The Progressive Era witnessed the watered-down passage of some major Populist demands, such as increased governmental regulation of railroads instead of government ownership and the Warehouse Act of 1916 and various farm loan plans in lieu of the subtreasury plan. Farm credit problems persisted, though. The Populist (and Knights of Labor) demand for land reform—the reclamation by the government of unused lands owned by railroads and other corporations and of alien-owned land for use by "actual settlers"—remained ignored.[77] The failure of progressive reform to help most southern farmers significantly became all too apparent during the 1920s. While the decade was generally one of American prosperity, southern farmers (like laborers) reaped little of the bounty. In the autumn of 1928 a prominent South Carolinian noted a rash of bank failures, which he blamed upon the "persistent absence of farm profits the past nine years." After stabilizing between 1910 and 1920 the rate of farm tenancy in the South resumed its ascent in the decade that followed.[78]

While some connections certainly existed between Populism and progressivism, a biracial southern farmer-labor movement did not participate in Progressive Era reform efforts. For that matter, the failure of farmer-labor insurgency in the late nineteenth century occurred at the national level as well. Such movements failed even to materialize outside the South and some western or midwestern states. Reformers who tried to build farmer-labor coalitions in those regions faced some of the same problems as in the South. In predominantly rural Blue Earth County, Minnesota, for example, the farmer-labor coalition was undermined by ambivalence between city and country folk, real or perceived differences in their respective economic interests, and the decline of the Knights of Labor as well as the Farmers' Alliance by the time of the formation of the People's Party.[79] In Kansas City, Kansas, too, argues historian Leon Fink, the demise of the Knights seriously hindered the Populists' efforts to attract working-class support. The diverse ethnic and racial composition of Kansas City also limited the appeal of Populism, as many immigrants did not look favorably upon the movement's "intrinsically Protestant, moral reform character."[80] Ethnic diversity among the white population probably did not hurt the Populists in the South, considering the region's failure to attract immigrants during the late nineteenth century.[81]

Southern Populists did, however, face some unique challenges. While stolen elections plagued the political process across the United States during the late nineteenth century, only in the South did they so frequently involve violence and murder.[82] Parallels to the assassination of John Clayton or the Wilmington coup d'état simply cannot be found in other regions of the nation. Such violence bore a connection to another distinct obstacle facing southern reformers. As Tom Watson noted in 1910, "Bryan [a Nebraskan] had *no everlasting and overshadowing Negro Question to hamper and handicap his progress*: I HAD."[83]

The race question ultimately inspired one of the most significant and tragic aspects of the southern Democratic response to late-nineteenth-century farmer-labor insurgency: disfranchisement. The demise of the Farmers' Alliance and the Knights of Labor, often a farmer-labor organization itself in rural areas or small towns, dealt a severe blow to farmer-labor insurgency everywhere that it had or might have occurred, but disfranchisement profoundly affected the nature of politics (and hence society) in the South for decades to come. Some two decades after the demise of the People's Party the Minnesota Farmer-Labor Party would achieve a degree of success that the state's Populists had only dreamed of.[84] Disfranchisement of most African Americans and many poor whites as well made such a revival of farmer-labor politics impossible in the South. Sadly, some disillusioned southern Populists, such as Watson, encouraged or participated in this disfranchisement of many who had supported the People's Party.[85]

Disfranchisement hung heavily over the South for much of the twentieth century in a variety of ways. Obviously, it foreclosed the possibility of a biracial coalition of discontented farmers and laborers again challenging the rule of the self-anointed "best men" of the Democratic Party. Moreover, as Lawrence Goodwyn pointed out, after disfranchisement "it was no longer in the interest of white politicians to provide minimal guarantees for people who could not help elect them."[86] Because southern politicians could ignore the needs of poor blacks and, to a lesser degree, poor whites with impunity, they governed in a way that not only did ignore but even exacerbated those needs. Hallmarks of southern state governments for much of the twentieth century would include poorly funded public schools (especially for African Americans), regressive taxes that weighed most heavily on the poorest citizens, and generous tax breaks for businesses.[87] These traits stood in stark opposition to the reforms enacted by the one anti-Democratic state government of the South in the 1890s, North Carolina's Republican-Populist regime, which enacted laws against usury, significantly increased spending on education and public services, raised taxes on railroads and businesses, and democratized the election process.[88]

As corporate capitalism engulfed American culture in the early twentieth century, the ideological foundations of the great reform platforms of the late nineteenth century—Reading, Cleburne, and Omaha—and the movements that produced them became outdated, perhaps even quaint. Terms and notions such as "republicanism" and "producerism" lost much of their former meaning and resonance.[89] Yet the principal mottoes of these movements—"equal rights to all, special privileges to none" or the Knights' insistence that "an injury to one is the concern of all"—have not lost their meaning. For all the flaws that clouded their vision, such as racism that could never be fully overcome, a sometimes narrow view of class interests, and a lamentable tendency to engage in petty bickering and infighting, the leaders of these movements and many of their followers evinced faith that the democratic process and civic participation could bring about a better society that would be characterized by the social justice that their own world so sorely lacked. With the possible exception of the less inclusive and more specifically focused civil rights movement of the 1950s and 1960s, neither the South nor the nation has seen a movement since the Populist era that inspired either such active civic participation or such faith in the democratic process. In an era of 50 percent voter turnout in presidential elections, of political campaigns that raise (and, one suspects that the Knights or Populists would have said, squander) unfathomable sums of money, and in which third parties have been more or less relegated to novelty status, the long battle waged by Greenbackers, Knights of Labor, Populists, and their compatriots in the late nineteenth century, particularly in the face of such grave obstacles in the South, takes on a significance that some of its leaders feared it would as it ended.[90] It truly marked the valiant but failed last stand of a democratic movement that, had it succeeded, may well have produced a more egalitarian nation and certainly a far more egalitarian South than that inhabited by that generation or generations of its descendants.

## The Failure of Southern Populism Reconsidered

With the historian's benefit of hindsight, the concerns expressed in December 1890 by North Carolina attorney David Schenck, quoted at the beginning of this study, seem prescient only in a sadly ironic sense. "The Knights of Labor, Farmers['] Alliance, and Trades Unions and other laboring classes," wrote Schenck, might "bring about a bloody Revolution in this country."[91] Schenck's prediction of a bloody revolution came true in his own state before the end of the decade, but it was waged by the Democratic "best men" of Wilmington against the very elements that Schenck feared. The means to which North Carolina Democrats resorted in 1898 to restore white rule in the interests of the upper classes attest to just how much the biracial coalition of the state's farmers and laborers had accomplished. The despicable events that destroyed that coalition, however, also underscore the limits of biracial farmer-labor political insurgency in the late-nineteenth-century South.

Nevertheless, as Schenck had understood (if in an overzealous manner), common ground did exist to unite farmers and laborers in his home state and elsewhere. Certainly, southern farmers and laborers of that era had more in common, both in terms of culture and class interests, than many historians have realized. In his magisterial study of American Populism Lawrence Goodwyn summed up the failure of urban Populism by contending that "the Alliance organizers looked at urban workers and simply did not know what to say to them—other than to repeat the language of the Omaha Platform."[92] But in southern cities where class and cultural ties existed between farmers and laborers and where the Populists could build upon previous efforts at farmer-labor political activism, the People's Party won substantial support from workers. Cities that fit this description include Augusta, Birmingham (and its surrounding coalfields), and Dallas. In all three of these cities the Knights of Labor had facilitated farmer-labor unity by speaking a republican, producer-based language that appealed to many laborers and small or landless farmers alike.

As we have seen, these earlier attempts at building farmer-labor coalitions proved crucial to the Populists' chances of doing the same. It is not coincidental that in the three southern states where the third-party movement became strongest—Texas, Arkansas, and Alabama—these efforts began with the Greenback-Labor Party and continued with the Knights of Labor, the Agricultural Wheel, and the Farmers' Alliance before reaching a climax under the guise of the People's Party, or, in Arkansas, the Union Labor Party.[93] Again, not coincidentally, southern Union Laborites or Populists also drew the most labor support in these states.

Conversely, in southern states where the Populists lacked this foundation of farmer-labor activism to build upon, their party failed to win significant labor support. The case of Tennessee, where Populists tried in vain to win labor support, illustrates this point well. The failure of the state's farmers and laborers to build a coalition also reflects two other factors that could hinder such efforts. Class conflict sometimes arose and created a rift between farmer and labor organizations, as when Tennessee Alliancemen and Alliance legislators balked at abolishing the convict lease system partly due to concern that doing so would require raising property taxes to build prisons. Also, as the miners rebellions demonstrated, local circumstances could sometimes work against the development of farmer-labor coalitions, just as the Southwest strikes, in contrast, promoted such coalitions in many of the areas that they reached.

Racial conflict loomed as an even greater obstacle than class conflict in efforts to build a legitimate third party in the South. Of course, racial conflict and class conflict were often so closely intertwined that the distinction between them was scarcely discernible. Some of the activities of the Colored Farmers' Alliance, for example, particularly the cotton pickers strike of 1891, provoked such fierce opposition from white Alliancemen not only because they represented black assertiveness but also because they threatened the economic interests of white Alliancemen who employed members (or prospective members) of the Colored Alliance.

Even when issues of race and class were not so closely connected, race-related matters still presented third-party activists with formidable problems. Populist and other third-party candidates had to give African Americans tangible reasons to vote for them, particularly given the dangers that might be involved in doing so. Yet making open appeals to African Americans incurred the risks of alienating potential white supporters and allowing Bourbon Democrats to saddle the third party with the imaginary yet powerful specter of fostering "Negro domination." Ironically, then, the defeat of Reuben F. Kolb in Alabama's gubernatorial elections of 1892 and 1894 demonstrated still another race-related problem for third parties: Democrats could fraudulently manipulate black votes to ensure Democratic victories. This sad fact partly explains why Tom Watson and other disillusioned, embittered southern Populists eventually supported the disfranchisement of African Americans.

Yet for all the class-related and race-related difficulties confronting biracial farmer-labor coalitions in the late-nineteenth-century South, the fraudulent elections involving Kolb point to an even greater obstacle: the willingness and ability of many southern Democrats to subvert the democratic process. The fate of the third-party movement in Arkansas serves as a tragic case in point and helps to explain the failure of southern Populism. As historian Barton Shaw has noted, "Populists everywhere . . . dreamed of a union between the toilers of the country and city."[94] But the Arkansas story demonstrates that building that union could not carry the third party to victory in the South. In order for Union Laborites or Populists to seize power they had to unseat Democrats. Arkansas Democrats, however, proved determined to maintain power at all costs, whether by exploiting their control of the election machinery and the state legislature or resorting to intimidation and violence. When two opposition candidates dared to contest such methods after the congressional elections of 1888, Arkansas Democrats responded by murdering one of them. Since such tactics were hardly unknown in other southern states, the story of Arkansas' third-party movement suggests that southern Populists stood no chance of breaking the Democratic Party's stranglehold on political power in the region. When the Democrats failed to maintain power through extralegal or paramilitary means, they were apt to respond with still more force, as when they assassinated John Clayton in 1889 and murdered African Americans to overthrow the biracial Populist-Republican government of Wilmington nearly a decade later. Under such circumstances it is difficult to imagine how the Populists could have possibly risen to and maintained power in the South, even when farmers and laborers, white and black, found the inspiration and courage to make common cause in supporting the third party.

# Appendix 1

Selected Greenback-Labor or Independent Political Leaders in the South, 1874–1884

| Name | State | Party affiliation | Offices held or sought |
|---|---|---|---|
| William M. Lowe | Alabama | Greenback-Labor | Congress, 1879–81, June–Oct. 1882 |
| James L. Sheffield | Alabama | Greenback-Labor | candidate for governor, 1882 |
| Charles Cunningham | Arkansas | Greenback-Labor | candidate for Congress, 1882 |
| | | Agricultural Wheel | candidate for governor, 1886 |
| | | Union Labor | vice presidential candidate, 1888 |
| William H. Felton | Georgia | Independent | Congress, 1875–81 |
| | | Populist | candidate for Congress, 1894 |
| Emory Speer | Georgia | Independent | Congress, 1879–1883 |
| Daniel L. Russell | North Carolina | Greenback-Labor | Congress, 1879–81 |
| | | Republican | governor, 1897–1901 |
| G. W. "Wash" Jones | Texas | Greenback-Labor | Congress, 1879–1883 |
| | | Greenback- Independent | candidate for governor, 1882, 1884 |

Because Lowe had to contest his opponent's election in 1880, he was not seated for his second term until June 1882; he died four months later.

# Appendix 2

Knights of Labor Membership in Southern District Assemblies, 1885–1888

| DA | City | 1885 | 1886 | 1887 | 1888 |
|---|---|---|---|---|---|
| 67 | Nashville | 129 | – | (see DA 183) | (see DA 183) |
| 78 | Galveston | 1,010 | 8,913 | 6,457 | 3,678 |
| 84 | Richmond (white) | – | 3,125 | 1,675 | 495 |
| 92 | Richmond (black) | – | 3,567 | 1,132 | 343 |
| 102 | New Orleans | – | 3,567 | 5,578 | 4,659 |
| 105 | Atlanta | – | 2,827 | 1,370 | 365 |
| 116 | Knoxville | – | 863 | 921 | 449 |
| 120 | Petersburg, Va. | – | 576 | 140 | – |
| 123 | Norfolk, Va. | – | 1,174 | 827 | 255 |
| 131 | Key West, Fla. | – | 773 | 258 | 115 |
| 132 | Chattanooga | – | 1,804 | 859 | 546 |
| 133 | Memphis | – | 1,252 | 322 | 179 |
| 139 | Savannah | – | 1,037 | 945 | 347 |
| 141 | Columbus, Ga. | – | 926 | 405 | 122 |
| 145 | Texarkana, Tex. | – | 555 | 352 | 133 |
| 171 | Waldo, Ark. | – | – | 301 | 62 |
| 176 | Augusta, Ga. | – | – | 987 | 452 |
| 183 | Nashville | – | – | 158 | 148 |
| 187 | Charleston, S.C. | – | – | 209 | 215 |
| 193 | Lynchburg, Va. | – | – | 1,545 | 176 |
| 194 | Berwick City, La. | – | – | 1,807 | 255 |
| 211 | Galveston, Tex. | – | – | 232 | 190 |
| 215 | Pulaski, Va. | – | – | 268 | 143 |
| 227 | Spartanburg, S.C. | – | – | – | 885 |

Sources: *Proceedings of the General Assembly of the Knights of Labor*, annual editions, 1885–88, 173 (1885), 326–28 (1886), 1848–50 (1887), "Report of the General Secretary," 2–4 (1888).

# Appendix 3

Knights of Labor Membership in Southern State Assemblies, 1886–1888

| State assemblies | 1886 | 1887 | 1888 |
|---|---|---|---|
| Alabama State Assembly | – | 3,951 | 1,978 |
| Arkansas State Assembly | 2,986 | 5,385 | 3,035 |
| Florida State Assembly | – | 2,402 | 1,454 |
| Georgia State Assembly | – | 439 | 1,007 |
| Mississippi State Assembly | – | 1,660 | 2,925 |
| North Carolina State Assembly | – | 3,928 | 7,391 |

Sources: *Proceedings of the General Assembly of the Knights of Labor*, annual editions, 1886–88, 328 (1886), 1850 (1887), "Report of the General Secretary," 5 (1888).

# Notes

## Abbreviations

JKL    *Journal of the Knights of Labor*
JUL    *Journal of United Labor*
NYT   *New York Times*

## Introduction

1. David Schenck diary, 8 December 1890, quoted in Ayers, *The Promise*, 246. Schenck served as a judge and was a very successful railroad attorney. See Escott, *Many Excellent People*, 187, 245.

2. Saloutos makes brief mention of the relationship between the Knights of Labor and the Colored Farmers' Alliance and notes the suspicion of some Southern Alliancemen toward the Knights (*Farmer Movements*, 80, 104–5).

3. Goodwyn writes, "As of 1892, neither the Knights of Labor nor any other American working-class institution had been able to create in its own ranks the culture of a people's movement that had animated the Farmers['] Alliance since 1886" (*Democratic Promise*, 309). Later works that did find a "movement culture" within the Knights of Labor include Fink, *Workingmen's Democracy*, and Laurie, *Artisans*.

4. Sanders, *Roots of Reform*, 27–28 (quotes).

5. Johnston, "Peasants, Pitchforks," 396.

6. Commons et al., *History of Labour*, vol. 2; Ware, *Labor Movement*. Both of these studies also mention the involvement of Knights of Labor leaders in the national Greenback and Greenback-Labor parties. These parties are discussed in chapter 1 of this book.

7. Grob, "The Knights of Labor"; Grob, *Workers and Utopia*.

8. McLaurin, *Paternalism*; McLaurin, "The Knights of Labor"; McLaurin, *The Knights of Labor*. Two brief earlier works on the Knights of Labor in the South are Meyers, "The Knights of Labor," and Black, "The Knights of Labor." Black briefly

discusses the Knights' relationship with the Southern Farmers' Alliance and the Populist Party (210–12).

9. Letwin, *The Challenge*; Shapiro, *A New South Rebellion.*

10. C. Vann Woodward made a similar point when he contended that "nearly all the sharply defined economic issues that divided the militant Populists from the Democratic-Conservatives in the nineties were powerful causes of disaffection in the seventies and eighties" (*Origins*, 82).

11. Goodwyn, *Democratic Promise*, 15. On the founding of the National Labor Union see Ware, *Labor Movement*, 6–9.

12. Fite, *Cotton Fields No More*, 32 (quote), 34.

13. Quoted in Woodward, *Origins*, 178.

14. Fite, *Cotton Fields No More*, 32–37; Range, *A Century*, 83–87.

15. McMath, *American Populism*, 61–62; Ayers, *The Promise*, 45; Fite, *Cotton Fields No More*, 27–28, 33.

16. Woodman, "The Political Economy," 808.

17. The eligibility requirements for membership in the Knights of Labor are discussed on p. 48.

18. For an overview of the southern labor force during the late nineteenth century see McLaurin, *The Knights of Labor*, chap. 2.

19. On these strikes see ibid., 74–75, 140–41; Rogers, "Negro Knights of Labor."

20. For various Farmers' Alliance and Populist Party platforms (including the joint St. Louis demands of the Southern Farmers' Alliance and the Knights of Labor put forth in 1889) see Hicks, *The Populist Revolt*, 427–44. For the platforms of the Knights see Ware, *Labor Movement*, 377–80.

21. Woodward, *Tom Watson*, 220.

### Chapter One. Agrarian Discontent and Political Dissent in the South, 1872–1882

1. *Macon (Ga.) Telegraph and Messenger*, 29 June 1873, quoted in the *Marietta (Ga.) Journal*, 4 July 1873. Emphasis in the first quotation is in the original.

2. Ibid.

3. *Macon (Ga.) Telegraph and Messenger*, 3 July 1873. Emphasis is in the original.

4. *Macon (Ga.) Telegraph and Messenger*, 29 June 1873, quoted in the *Marietta (Ga.) Journal*, 4 July 1873. Secondary sources describing these conditions as they developed during this period include, among others, Arnett, *The Populist Movement*, chap. 2, and Hicks, *The Populist Revolt*, chaps. 2–3. See esp. Otto, *The Final Frontiers*, 28–29, on declining cotton prices and the subsequent net losses suffered by cotton farmers in the southern Upcountry.

5. Abramowitz, "The South," 108–9; Woodward, *Origins*, 83–84.

6. *Proceedings of the General Assembly of the Knights of Labor, Eleventh Regular Session* (1887), 1848–50 (membership of the Louisiana Knights of Labor); Hair, *Bourbonism*, 178–85; Foner and Lewis, *The Black Worker*, 3:143–239; Gould, "The Strike of 1887"; Hall, *Labor Struggles*, 49–59; Rodrigue, *Reconstruction*, 183–91.

7. Gardner, *The Grange*, 20–29; Kelley, *Origins*, 328, 422; *Athens (Ga.) Southern Cultivator* 30 (February 1872): 76 (emphasis is in the original); Nordin, *Rich Harvest*, 29–31.

8. Calvert, "The Southern Grange," 42, 44, 147–53; Marti, *Women*, 1–2, 7, 9, 10, 15, 19–28, 58, 62, 96, 108–9, 141; Nordin, *Rich Harvest*, 5; Lester, "Grassroots Reform," 103–4 (quote).

9. *Proceedings of the Second Annual Session*, 31–32.

10. Saloutos, "The Grange," 476–77 (quote on 477); Brittain, "Negro Suffrage," 91.

11. Saloutos, "The Grange," 478; Nordin, *Rich Harvest*, 32; McMath, *American Populism*, 61; Kantrowitz, *Ben Tillman*, 57; Calvert, "The Southern Grange," 48 (quote).

12. Ayers, *The Promise*, 214.

13. Goodwyn, *Democratic Promise*, 44–46 (quote on 45).

14. Woods, *Knights*, xv (first quote), xviii (second quote), xxi (third quote). By 1876 the Grange seemed to be losing much of its "radical energy" in the South as well; see Saloutos, "The Grange," 486–87.

15. Woods, *Knights*, xxi.

16. This declaration of purposes appears in its entirety in the *NYT*, 12 February 1874. For a similar resolution by the Mississippi Grange see the *Proceedings of the Fifth Annual Session*, 19.

17. *Georgia Grange* (Atlanta), October 1874.

18. *NYT*, 12 February 1874.

19. *Proceedings of the Fifth Annual Session*, 19. The National Grange's Declaration of Purposes (1874) also expressed opposition to usury; see the *NYT*, 12 February 1874.

20. *Proceedings of the Fourth Annual Meeting*, 127. While these proceedings were published in 1876, the meeting was held in Sedalia in December 1875.

21. Saloutos, "The Grange," 479–81.

22. Fite, *Cotton Fields No More*, 53–54; Calvert, "The Southern Grange," 231; Rogers, *The One-Gallused Rebellion*, 73; Nordin, *Rich Harvest*, 140–41, 144; Noblin, *Leonidas LaFayette Polk*, 100.

23. Woeste, *The Farmer's Benevolent Trust*, 20–22; Nordin, *Rich Harvest*, 141–42; McMath, *American Populism*, 60.

24. Woeste, *The Farmer's Benevolent Trust*, 21–24.

25. Nordin, *Rich Harvest*, 155, 163; Saloutos, "The Grange," 481; Calvert, "The Southern Grange," 212–13.

26. Calvert, "The Southern Grange," 250–77; Smith, "The Grange Movement," 301; Nordin, *Rich Harvest*, 142; Fite, *Cotton Fields No More*, 52; Woeste, *The Farmer's Benevolent Trust*, 22–23.

27. *Proceedings of the Second Annual Session*, 18 (first four quotes), 48, 49 (fifth quote), 61, 62, 66. Just days earlier the National Grange had adopted a resolution, introduced by the Texas Grange, asking Congress to grant aid for the completion of the Texas Pacific Railroad; see the *NYT*, 14 February 1875.

28. In addition to the evidence presented in this chapter see Calvert, "The Southern Grange," 47, on the Grange as an organization that represented the interests "of the small white farmer and large landholders . . . against merchants and tenants."

29. Range, *A Century*, 83; Woodman, *New South–New Law*, 78–82; Kantrowitz, *Ben Tillman*, 56; *Proceedings of the Fifth Annual Session*, 35.

30. Wynne, *The Continuity*, 79–80.

31. Davis, "The Granger Movement," 351.

32. *NYT*, 12 February 1874.

33. *Utica (N.Y.) Herald*, n.d., quoted in the *Marietta (Ga.) Journal*, 20 June 1873.

34. Woodward, *Origins*, 82.

35. *Macon (Ga.) Telegraph and Messenger*, 3 July 1873; Grantham, *The Life and Death*, 3; Wynne, *The Continuity*, 80 n. 57; Roberts, *Joseph E. Brown*, 95; Arnett, *The Populist Movement*, 31–32; Bartley, *The Creation*, 94–96; McMath, *American Populism*, 157–59, 162, 164–65, 195.

36. Cobb, "Beyond Planters," 55–61 (quotes on 56, 61).

37. Woodward, *Origins*, 21 (first quote), 58–60, 85 (second quote); Grantham, *The Life and Death*, 7.

38. Jacob and Ragsdale, *Biographical Directory*, 515; Kantrowitz, *Ben Tillman*, 54–56, 89 (quotes), 99–100; Simkins, *The Tillman Movement*, 17–18.

39. Woodward, *Origins*, 82; Calvert, "The Southern Grange," 39; Woeste, *The Farmer's Benevolent Trust*, 22; Fite, *Cotton Fields No More*, 53 (quote).

40. Ritter, *Goldbugs and Greenbacks*, 62, 66–69, 94–95, 190–91; Unger, *The Greenback Era*, 339–42; Barrett, *The Greenbacks*, 185–87; Perman, *Road to Redemption*, 271–72; Sanders, *Roots of Reform*, 109.

41. Nordin, *Rich Harvest*, 204. See also Saloutos, "The Grange," 478.

42. Unger, *The Greenback Era*, 292; Buck, *The Granger Movement*, 114.

43. *Proceedings of the Fourth Annual Meeting*, 23–24.

44. Nordin, *Rich Harvest*, 183, 210; National Party platform reprinted in the *NYT*, 23 February 1878.

45. Commons et al., *History of Labour*, 2:167–71; Ritter, *Goldbugs and Greenbacks*, 49; Unger, *The Greenback Era*, 307–8; Jacob and Ragsdale, *Biographical Directory*, 752; Fine, *Labor*, 62–63; *NYT*, 18 May 1876.

46. Woodward, *Origins*, 83.

47. Commons et al., *History of Labour*, 2:187–91, 240; Laurie, *Artisans*, 142–46. Monographs devoted to the strikes of 1877 include Bruce, *1877*; Foner, *The Great Labor Uprising*; Stowell, *Streets*.

48. Ricker, *The Greenback-Labor Movement*, 33–40; Powderly, *The Path I Trod*, vii, 71–73. For a summary of strike activity in Pennsylvania in the summer of 1877 see Brecher, *Strike!* 22–30.

49. Commons et al., *History of Labour*, 2:244 (quote); *NYT*, 23 February 1878.

50. *NYT*, 23 February 1878.

51. Hair, *Bourbonism*, 66, citing the *St. Louis Evening Post*, 26 September 1878.

52. According to Martin, Grange membership in Texas peaked at forty-five thousand (including six thousand women) in 1876 and 1877: "A period of decline set in immediately thereafter, and the State Grange lost heavily and steadily in membership" ("The Grange," 367).

53. Ibid., 369–71; Barr, *Reconstruction*, 27, 41–42, 52.

54. Barr, *Reconstruction*, 26, 35–36; Martin, "The Greenback Party," 165; Dubin, *United States Congressional Elections*, 240. The use of the term "Independent" here should not be confused with the official title of the first Greenback Party; rather, it designates no formal party affiliation.

55. Barr, *Reconstruction*, 44.

56. Winkler, *Platforms*, 179–80.

57. Martin, "The Greenback Party," 165–66.

58. Smith, "The Grange Movement," 301–4; Barr, *Reconstruction*, 56.

59. Barr, *Reconstruction*, 52, 75; Winkler, *Platforms*, 193–98.

60. Winkler, *Platforms*, 180–81, 187–90 (quotes on 181, 188); Barr, *Reconstruction*, 44–45.

61. *Dublin (Ga.) Post*, 23 October 1878; Barr, *Reconstruction*, 43, 47, 53.

62. Barr, *Reconstruction*, 51, 54–55, 59–60, 64; McMath, *Populist Vanguard*, 5–8; Dubin, *United States Congressional Elections*, 247; Richardson et al., *Texas*, 265; Jacob and Ragsdale, *Biographical Directory*, 1278 (quote); Moneyhon, *Republicanism*, 68, 78–79; *Congressional Record*, 1880, vol. 10, pt. 1, 43; 1882, vol. 13, pt. 1, 116.

63. Martin, "The Greenback Party," 169; Barr, *Reconstruction*, 55–56 (quote).

64. Barr, *Reconstruction*, 60, 69, 73; Martin, "The Greenback Party," 175.

65. For the argument that the failure of Farmers' Alliance cooperatives politicized Texas Alliancemen see Goodwyn, *Democratic Promise*, esp. chap. 5.

66. Barr, *Reconstruction*, 62.

67. Winkler, *Platforms*, 207 (1882 quote), 225 (1884 quote), 227–29.

68. Ibid., 206, 262, 298; Dubin, *United States Congressional Elections*, 276.

69. Goodwyn, *Democratic Promise*, 331, 478, 509; Hill, *Dallas*, 40; Barr, *Reconstruction*, 57, 168, 170–71; Dubin, *United States Congressional Elections*, 254, 262, 276, 301, 310.

70. *National Economist Almanac 1890*, 74; Winkler, *Platforms*, 206, 256, 273, 298, 418, 420, 442, 444; Dubin, *United States Congressional Elections*, 276, 284, 319.

71. Davis, "The Granger Movement," 341, 347, 349; John T. Jones to O. H. Kelley, 15 June 1872, in Kelley, *Origins and Progress*, 389; Wheeler, "The People's Party," 83 (quote).

72. Davis, "The Granger Movement," 351–52. On Hughes's career as governor see Readnour, "Simon P. Hughes," in Donovan, Gatewood, and Whayne, *The Governors*, 83–89.

73. Barjenbruch, "The Greenback Political Movement," 108–9 (quote on 109); Kelley, *Origins and Progress*, 431; Wheeler, "The People's Party," 97–99.

74. Graves, *Town and Country*, 107.

75. Barjenbruch, "The Greenback Political Movement," 107–12, 114–18. For an account of the difficulties confronting the "moribund" Arkansas GLP in 1880 despite extensive campaigning in the state by the party's presidential candidate, James B. Weaver, in August of that year see Lause, *The Civil War's Last Campaign*, 111–16 (quote on 115).

76. On organized labor in Arkansas during the Greenback era and its support for the GLP see Moneyhon, *Arkansas*, 79, 83. To the best of my knowledge, no studies exist of organized labor in Arkansas during the 1870s.

77. Barjenbruch, "The Greenback Political Movement," 110–11, 118–22; Wheeler, "The People's Party," 11, 107, 110–11, 114, 281, 381–83; Lloyd, "The Howard County Race Riot," 355; Graves, *Town and Country*, 139–44; Henningson, "Northwest Arkansas"; Henningson, "Root Hog or Die"; *NYT*, 16 August 1886; Elkins, "State Politics," 257.

78. Clark, *Populism*, 24 (first quote); Brittain, "Negro Suffrage," 91 (second quote).

79. Going, *Bourbon Democracy*, 17–19, 92, 103.

80. On the persistent presence of Republicans in the north Alabama hill country during this period and for decades to come see Webb, *Two-Party Politics*. Webb's study of politics in the Alabama hill country from 1874 to 1920 makes no connection between the Grange and the GLP; he describes the former as having been "largely controlled by planter-landlords in the power structure" (87), most likely Democrats. The most comprehensive article on the Alabama Greenback movement–Roberts, "William Manning Lowe"–makes no mention of the Grange.

81. Going, *Bourbon Democracy*, 57–59; Rogers, *The One-Gallused Rebellion*, 54; Webb, *Two-Party Politics*, 61, 66; Hyman, *The Anti-Redeemers*, 22.

82. Flynt, *Poor but Proud*, 138; Letwin, *The Challenge*, 58, 64; Garlock, *Guide*, 5–7; *JUL*, 15 December 1880; Dennis Leahy to T. V. Powderly, 9 August 1880, Powderly Papers, reel 2 (quote).

83. Webb, *Two-Party Politics*, 61, 66; Roberts, "William Manning Lowe," 107, 108, including n. 25, 115–18; Rogers, *The One-Gallused Rebellion*, 223, 284, 315 (maps); Horton, "Testing the Limits," 64–65, 81–82. For a map identifying the different regions of Alabama see Webb, *Two-Party Politics*, xii.

84. Gutman, "Black Coal Miners"; Flynt, *Poor but Proud*, 138, 247–48; Letwin, *The Challenge*, 54–56, 60–63, 66–67; Curtin, *Black Prisoners*, 73.

85. Letwin, *The Challenge*, 59; Gutman, "Black Coal Miners," 509, 521, 523, 535; Roberts, "William Manning Lowe," 111; *Huntsville (Ala.) Weekly Democrat*, 7 July 1880.

86. *National Labor Tribune*, 25 September 1880.

87. Horton, "The Assassination," 83–95 (quote on 94, citing the *Huntsville [Ala.] Advocate*, 30 June 1880); Going, *Bourbon Democracy*, 57–58; Moore et al., *Congressional Quarterly's Guide*, 2:1416; Lause, *The Civil War's Last Campaign*, 93–94, 105–7; *NYT*, 12, 21 August 1880. On James B. Weaver's campaign for the presidency in 1880 see Haynes, *James Baird Weaver*, chap. 9.

88. Horton, "The Assassination," 95–109 (quote on 109; the quote within the quote is taken from the *Tuscumbia [Ala.] North Alabamian*, 11 February 1881).

89. *Huntsville (Ala.) Gazette*, 8, 15 July 1882; Webb, *Two-Party Politics*, 65–66.

90. Moore et al., *Congressional Quarterly's Guide*, 2:1416.

91. Letter from William V. Turner in the *Huntsville (Ala.) Gazette*, 19 August 1882.

92. Webb, *Two-Party Politics*, 66.

93. Going, *Bourbon Democracy*, 59; *NYT*, 9 August 1882; *Huntsville (Ala.) Weekly Democrat*, 13 September 1882. According to the *Report on Population*, pt. 1, 402, blacks constituted 50.6 percent of Madison County's population in 1880; by 1890 that figure had dropped slightly to 49.2 percent.

94. Roberts, "William Manning Lowe," 100–107, 110, 120–21; Going, *Bourbon Democracy*, 59; Flynt, *Poor but Proud*, 249.

95. Roush, "Aftermath," 329–31, 343, 346–47; Dubin, *United States Congressional Elections*, 264; Webb, *Two-Party Politics*, 81–85.

96. *Journal of the House of Representatives of the State of Alabama, Session of 1882–83*, 59–62; *Journal of the House of Representatives of the State of Alabama, Session of 1892–3*, 58, 60, 62; *Journal of the House of Representatives of the State of Alabama, Session of 1894–5*, 98–100; *Journal of the House of Representatives of the State of Alabama, Session of 1896–7*, 110–12.

97. Green, "Ben E. Green"; Jones, "William H. Felton," 46, including n. 38; *NYT,* 15 October 1878.

98. Jones, "William H. Felton," 38, 54, 74, 123–25, 169–70, 242; Ward, "Georgia," 102 (quote); Bartley, "Emory Speer," in Coleman and Gurr, *Dictionary,* 2:915; Hyman, *The Anti-Redeemers,* 105–6.

99. Roberts, "The Public Career"; Talmadge, *Rebecca Latimer Felton,* 33–112; Jones, "William H. Felton," 149–50, 272–73, 278–81, 301–4; *Savannah News,* n.d., quoted in the *Marietta (Ga.) Journal,* 6 March 1879.

100. *Cedartown (Ga.) Record,* 22 August 1874, quoted in Jones, "William H. Felton," 38. Emphasis in the original.

101. Woodward, *Tom Watson,* 69.

102. On Felton's relationship with the Grange see Roberts, "The Public Career," 58–60. Speer's name does not appear on any of the membership lists (or anywhere else) in the records of the Athens Grange. See Patrons of Husbandry Records. Jones, "William H. Felton," 312–13, also questions the linkage between the Grange and the Independent movement in Georgia. On African American support for Felton and Speer (which was stronger for the former) see Roberts, "The Public Career," 89; Shadgett, *The Republican Party,* 63–66, 73–75, 144–45; Hahn, *The Roots,* 231–34; Hyman, *The Anti-Redeemers,* 174, 187.

103. Green, "Ben E. Green," 8–9.

104. At issue was the repeal not of the entire Resumption Act but of its particular clause calling for the resumption of specie payments for greenbacks; on the various clauses of the Resumption Act see Unger, *The Greenback Era,* 254.

105. *Atlanta Daily Constitution,* 20 November 1877 (all quotes except the last); *Cincinnati Gazette,* n.d., quoted in *Atlanta Daily Constitution,* 18 November 1877 (last quote).

106. *The National Cyclopaedia,* 6:161; Bartley, "Emory Speer," in Coleman and Gurr, *Dictionary,* 2:915; *Atlanta Constitution,* 4 March 1883. On the views of the *Atlanta Constitution* on the tariff issue during the 1880s see Davis, *Henry Grady's New South,* 114, 192.

107. Dubin, *United States Congressional Elections,* 257; Shaw, *The Wool-Hat Boys,* 192, 195; Bartley, "Emory Speer," in Coleman and Gurr, *Dictionary,* 2:915–16; *Atlanta Constitution,* 14 December 1918 (Speer's obituary).

108. *JKL,* 27 April 1893; Shaw, *The Wool-Hat Boys,* 168; Curtin, *Black Prisoners,* 178.

109. Roberts, "The Public Career," 236–46, 417–24; Jones, "William H. Felton," 170–74; Talmadge, *Rebecca Latimer Felton,* 86–89; Shaw, *The Wool-Hat Boys,* 116–17.

110. Arnett, *The Populist Movement,* map on unnumbered page opposite 184; Shaw, *The Wool-Hat Boys,* 96, 117, 120; Bartley, *The Creation,* 95–96; Dubin, *United*

*States Congressional Elections,* 295, 304; Felton, *My Memoirs,* 656–77; Roberts, "The Public Career," 424–41; Talmadge, *Rebecca Latimer Felton,* 86–89.

111. Lefler and Newsome, *North Carolina,* 543–45; Steelman, *North Carolina Farmers' Alliance,* 5–6.

112. Crow and Durden, *Maverick Republican,* 34–41, 52–74 (first quote on 36, others on 39). See also Ritter, *Goldbugs and Greenbacks,* 121–22.

113. Hair, *Bourbonism,* 66–69, 72–78.

114. Lewinson, *Race, Class, and Party,* 56–57.

115. *New York Tribune,* 24 September 1878.

116. *NYT,* 28 September 1878.

117. *Natchitoches (La.) People's Vindicator,* 19 October 1878, quoted in Hair, *Bourbonism,* 78.

118. Hair, *Bourbonism,* 72–73, 78–79.

119. Lewinson, *Race, Class, and Party,* 56–57; Woodward, *Origins,* 57; Hair, *Bourbonism,* 78.

120. *NYT,* 22 December 1878.

121. Hair, *Bourbonism,* 70, 73–74, 77, 79–80, 217, 225, 231.

122. Lewinson, *Race, Class, and Party,* 55, 57–58; Zuczek, *State of Rebellion,* chap. 9.

123. Tindall, *South Carolina Negroes,* 51; Kantrowitz, *Ben Tillman,* 99, 102–3, 140; De Santis, *Republicans,* chap. 4 (see 162 on McLane); *NYT,* 29 October 1882 (quote).

124. Tindall, *South Carolina Negroes,* 51; Kantrowitz, *Ben Tillman,* 100, 104.

125. *Charleston News,* 30 September 1882, quoted in the *NYT,* 8 October 1882.

126. *Charleston News and Courier,* 25 September 1882, quoted in Kantrowitz, *Ben Tillman,* 106.

127. Lewinson, *Race, Class, and Party,* 67; Woodward, *Origins,* 56; Tindall, *South Carolina Negroes,* 69–70; Kantrowitz, *Ben Tillman,* 97, 106–7 (quote on 107).

128. Tindall, *South Carolina Negroes,* 114–17; Kremm and Neal, "Clandestine Black Labor Societies"; Hild, "Organizing," 298–99, 310; Baker, "The 'Hoover Scare.'"

129. Kantrowitz, "Ben Tillman and Hendrix McLane," 515–17, 520, 523 (quotes).

130. Ostler, *Prairie Populism,* esp. chap. 9.

131. Hart, *Redeemers,* 33–35, 40–46, 60–69; McGee, *A History,* 239, 242, 244–45; Lester, "Grassroots Reform," 63, 311 n. 2.

132. *NYT,* 2 September 1878; Fine, *Labor,* 65; Hild, "Greenbackers," 74, table 1. No less an authority than Rebecca Felton described her husband, William H. Felton, as "a strong Greenback man" in a private letter in September 1878 (Jones, "William H. Felton," 117).

133. Steven Hahn, of course, makes this argument based upon his examination of the Georgia Upcountry in *The Roots*.

134. It should be noted that Democrats did not possess a monopoly on dirty tactics; for a stark account of Populists using deplorable tactics to influence elections in Georgia during the 1890s see Shaw, *The Wool-Hat Boys*, chap. 5.

135. On the Grange's opposition to the convict lease system see Calvert, "The Southern Grange," 47.

## Chapter Two. Building the Southern Farmer and Labor Movements, 1878–1886

1. Powderly, *Thirty Years*, 238–42; Ware, *Labor Movement*, 23, including n. 1, 55–60; *Record of Proceedings of the General Assembly of the \*\*\*\*\* [Knights of Labor]* (1878), 19. The asterisks appear in the title of the last item in lieu of the words "Knights of Labor" because the Order's name was secret at the time. See Powderly, *The Path I Trod*, 49.

2. Powderly, *Thirty Years*, 242–43; Powderly, *The Path I Trod*, 48–49, including 49 n. 2; Dulles, *Labor in America*, 100–101, 108–10; Grob, *Workers and Utopia*, 15–18, 38–40, 44, 99; Marcus, "The Knights of Labor," 9–13, 100. The National Labor Union did not actually issue a platform in 1866, but its various committee reports amounted to one. See Rayback, *A History*, 116–17.

3. The Reading platform is reprinted in Powderly, *Thirty Years*, 243–45.

4. The National (Greenback-Labor) Party's Toledo platform appears in the *NYT*, 23 February 1878. In 1888 Powderly commented upon the striking similarities between the Reading and Toledo platforms, noting that "it was from that [Reading] preamble that the platform of the Greenback Labor Party sprung" (quoted in James, "American Labor," 464).

5. Powderly, *Thirty Years*, 240; Ware, *Labor Movement*, 43, 50; Powderly, *The Path I Trod*, 71–73; Weir, "Trevellick, Richard F.," in Garraty and Carnes, *American National Biography*, 21:824.

6. Winkler, *Platforms*, 234–37 (Jones is quoted on 234–35; the Cleburne platform is reprinted on 235–37).

7. McMath, *American Populism*, 68.

8. On the predominantly rural composition of the South during this era see the charts listing the percent of rural to total population for each southern state in Dodd and Dodd, *Historical Statistics*.

9. For arguments that the Southwest strike of 1886 severely damaged the Knights of Labor and, hence, the prospects for American farmer-labor political activism see Ware, *Labor Movement*, 149, 360–61, 367–70; Grob, *Workers and Utopia*, 73, 97–98;

Goodwyn, *Democratic Promise*, 65, 165–66, 640 n. 14; McMath, *American Populism*, 76.

10. Smith, "The Farmers' Alliance," 346–51; McMath, *Populist Vanguard*, chap. 1; Garlock, "A Structural Analysis," 235. Two differing accounts by Texas Alliance members themselves placed the organization's founding in either 1874–75 or in September 1877; see McMath, *Populist Vanguard*, 4.

11. Morgan, *History*, 60; letter from Dan Fraser Tomson in the *JUL*, 10 April 1886.

12. For information on the composition of Knights of Labor local assemblies see Garlock, *Guide*.

13. McLaurin, *The Knights of Labor*, 43.

14. Ibid.; Garlock, *Guide*, 7–8; "Constitution of the General Assembly, District Assemblies, and Local Assemblies of the Order of the Knights of Labor of America" (1885), 59, in the Powderly Papers, reel 64 (quotes). The Knights of Labor lifted its ban against doctors in 1884 (Powderly, *The Path I Trod*, 47 n. 1).

15. *Record of the Proceedings of the Third Regular Session of the General Assembly [of the Knights of Labor]* (1879), 110–11; McLaurin, *The Knights of Labor*, 44 (quote); Garlock, "A Structural Analysis," 236; Letwin, *The Challenge*, 67; Garlock, *Guide*, 5–8. McLaurin states that the Knights appointed six southern organizers in 1879. He neglected to count two Texas organizers, perhaps because his study does not cover Texas.

16. *JUL*, 15 December 1880; Dennis Leahy to T. V. Powderly, 9 August 1880, Powderly Papers, reel 2.

17. *JUL*, 15 May 1880.

18. James, "T. V. Powderly," 445–48; Phelan, *Grand Master Workman*, 48.

19. Letwin, *The Challenge*, 1, 69; Head, "The Development," 44, 65; Flynt, *Poor but Proud*, 247–48; *Montgomery (Ala.) Workingmen's Advocate*, 2 March 1879.

20. Garlock, *Guide*, 3–9; Flynt, *Poor but Proud*, 138, 247–49; Letwin, *The Challenge*, 58–66, 69; Roush, "Aftermath," 234; Roberts, "William Manning Lowe"; Webb, *Two-Party Politics*, 61–66; *Huntsville (Ala.) Weekly Democrat*, 13 September 1882. On the GLP and the organizing and political activities of the Knights of Labor in Mobile between 1878 and 1880 see Fitzgerald, *Urban Emancipation*, 239–41.

21. On segregated Greenback clubs in Alabama see Gutman, "Black Coal Miners"; Flynt, *Poor but Proud*, 138, 247; Letwin, *The Challenge*, 63, 67; Curtin, *Black Prisoners*, 72–73.

22. William Wright to Powderly, 11 September 1880, Powderly Papers, reel 2.

23. Powderly to Wright, 19 September 1880, Powderly Papers, reel 44, emphasis in the original.

24. E. P. P. Dunn to Powderly, 15 November 1883, Powderly Papers, reel 6.

Powderly did not respond to Dunn's inquiry. The letter is stamped "No Answer Required."

25. Ibid.

26. Garlock, *Guide*, 3–9. H. J. Sharit Sr., the Knight from New Castle who won election to the Alabama House of Representatives in 1880, was a blacksmith and a farmer (see above). Most likely a number of miners in the Birmingham district who belonged to the Knights at that time practiced farming as well.

27. The border states of Missouri and Kentucky contained fifty-five and twenty local assemblies, respectively, in 1883. The number of locals in Alabama had dropped to six by that year (Garlock, "A Structural Analysis," 236).

28. McLaurin, *The Knights of Labor*, 43–44.

29. Garlock, *Guide*, 235–38, 484–90; letter from Dan Fraser Tomson in the *JUL*, 10 April 1886.

30. *JKL*, 28 July 1892; Gabler, *The American Telegrapher*, 160–61.

31. Garlock, *Guide*; *JUL*, May 1883; *Record of the Proceedings of the Eighth General Assembly [of the Knights of Labor]* (1884), 580. Accounts of the national telegraphers strike of 1883 include McNeill, *The Labor Movement*, 391–92; Ware, *Labor Movement*, 128–30; and the most complete and authoritative account, Gabler, *The American Telegrapher*, 5–29, 162–68. On the telegraphers strike in Georgia see Hild, "A 'Flagrant and High-handed Outrage,'" 37–40.

32. *Record of the Proceedings of the Eighth Regular Session of the General Assembly*, 580.

33. *JUL*, 25 January, 10 March 1885; Phelan, *Grand Master Workman*, 151–54 (quote on 154); Rachleff, *Black Labor*, 118–20.

34. Garlock, "A Structural Analysis," 236.

35. Garlock, *Guide*, 517–27; Rachleff, *Black Labor*, 115–23.

36. Garlock, "A Structural Analysis," 236.

37. Garlock, *Guide*, 52–59; Hild, "A 'Flagrant and High-handed Outrage,'" 41; Hild, "Organizing," 290 (table), 293–94; *Report of the General Executive Board, Thirteenth Regular Session* (1889), 20, included with the *Proceedings of the General Assembly of the Knights of Labor, Twelfth Regular Session* (1888).

38. Garlock, *Guide*, 3–9, 484–90; Shapiro, *A New South Rebellion*, 31; Abernathy, "The Knights of Labor," 45–46; Letwin, *The Challenge*, 73–75.

39. Garlock, *Guide*, 161–67. See also Hair, *Bourbonism*, 176–77.

40. Garlock, "A Structural Analysis," 236. The Knights had less than ten local assemblies in 1885 in each of the four southern states not discussed here (Florida, Mississippi, North Carolina, and South Carolina).

41. Dunning, *Farmers' Alliance History*, 15; Hicks, *The Populist Revolt*, 96–99; McMath, *Populist Vanguard*, 4, 77–79.

42. Dunning, *Farmers' Alliance History*, 15–17; *NYT*, 23 February 1878.

43. Smith, "The Farmers' Alliance," 346.

44. McMath, *Populist Vanguard*, 3 (quote); McMath, "Sandy Land," 206–7, 213.

45. Barr, *Reconstruction*, 54, 59–60; McMath, *Populist Vanguard*, 5–8; Smith, "The Farmers' Alliance," 349.

46. Smith, "The Farmers' Alliance," 348–49.

47. McMath, "Sandy Land," 214–15, 226 n. 30, 227 n. 31.

48. Dunning, *Farmers' Alliance History*, 36 (quote); Smith, "The Farmers' Alliance," 351.

49. Garlock, *Guide*, 491–513; *JUL*, October, December 1882, December 1883.

50. Garlock, *Guide*, 491–513; Barr, *Reconstruction*, map facing 34. The Knights chartered three local assemblies in Houston in 1882, two mixed, and one a trade local of telegraphers, as well as a mixed local at Harrisburg in the same county.

51. Garlock, *Guide*, 504; Barr, *Reconstruction*, 68–69.

52. *Record of the Proceedings of the Third Regular Session of the General Assembly*, 111.

53. *JUL*, June, July 1882; Garlock, *Guide*, 491–513; *Record of the Proceedings of the Sixth Regular Session of the General Assembly [of the Knights of Labor]* (1882), 268, 374; *Proceedings of the First Annual Session*, 12; Garlock, "A Structural Analysis," 236.

54. Morgan, *History*, 99 (second quote), 348–50; Barnes, *Farmers*, 53 (first quote).

55. Hahn, *The Roots*, 135; McMath, "Sandy Land," 219–20; Goodwyn, *Democratic Promise*, 37–39, 42–44, 47–49; Dunning, *Farmers' Alliance History*, 20–38.

56. Rhinehart, *A Way of Work*, 72; Calderon, *Mexican Coal Mining Labor*, 145; Allen, *Chapters*, 91; Garlock, *Guide*, 636.

57. Ware, *Labor Movement*, 139; Buchanan, *The Story*, 143.

58. *JUL*, 10 January 1885; Powderly, *Thirty Years*, 638. Powderly listed DA 78 as being based in Austin, but both the *Journal* and the *Record of the Proceedings of the Ninth Regular Session of the General Assembly [of the Knights of Labor]* (1885), 173, list DA 78 as being based in Galveston.

59. The first subordinate Wheel in Texas was organized in Cleburne on 5 April 1884. The Brothers of Freedom had chartered lodges in Alabama and Texas by 1885. The Texas Alliance did not spread to other states until 1886. See Morgan, *History*, 76; Henningson, "Root Hog or Die," 213; McMath, *Populist Vanguard*, 33.

60. Morgan, *History*, 60–62.

61. Ibid., 62 (quotes); Wheeler, "The People's Party," 117.

62. Morgan, *History*, 63.

63. Ibid., 63–64.

64. Ibid., 64.

65. Dunning, *Farmers' Alliance History*, 209.

66. McMath, *Populist Vanguard*, 15, 44–46; Dunning, *Farmers' Alliance History*, 209 (quote); Holmes, "The Demise," 187, 191–92; Elkins, "The Agricultural Wheel in

Arkansas," 253–54; Wagner, "Farms," 1. The Northern Alliance did admit African Americans, and a few local Wheel chapters accepted black and white members; see Holmes, "The Demise," 191–92. For examples of white Southern Alliance opposition to the Colored Alliance see, among others, Holmes, "The Demise," 199; and Crowe, "Tom Watson," 108–9.

67. Morgan, *History*, 69 (quote); *Biographical and Historical Memoirs of Eastern Arkansas*, 678.

68. Dunning, *Farmers' Alliance History*, 216; Henningson, "Northwest Arkansas," 312; *The National Economist Almanac 1890*, 75; Saloutos, "The Agricultural Wheel," 133–34; Elkins, "State Politics," 252–53; John H. Robertson to W. B. W. Heartsill, 31 August 1896, Heartsill Papers.

69. See the preamble of the Brothers of Freedom's Declaration of Principles in Dunning, *Farmers' Alliance History*, 217, and the Wheel's preamble in Morgan, *History*, 63–65.

70. The sixteen Brothers of Freedom counties in the sample are Boone, Conway, Crawford, Faulkner, Franklin, Johnson, Logan, Marion, Newton, Perry, Pope, Scott, Searcy, Sebastian, Van Buren, and Yell. The fourteen Agricultural Wheel counties are Conway, Faulkner, Garland, Jackson, Lonoke, Pope, Prairie, Pulaski, St. Francis, Sebastian, Van Buren, White, Woodruff, and Yell. These lists of Arkansas counties in which the Brothers or Wheel (or both) were active were compiled from the following sources: Elkins, "Arkansas Farmers"; Elkins, "The Agricultural Wheel: County Politics"; Henningson, "Northwest Arkansas"; Henningson, "Root Hog or Die." The statistical data used in this analysis are drawn from the *Compendium of the Tenth Census*, pt. 1, 687–88, 744–47, and the *Report on Productions*, 32–33. For a map showing the geographical regions of Arkansas see Wheeler, "The People's Party," 5. For a list of the counties in the Arkansas Delta see Otto, *The Final Frontiers*, 16.

71. Henningson, "Northwest Arkansas," 307–10, 313 (quote); Hicks, *The Populist Revolt*, 56 (table on crop prices); Henningson, "Root Hog or Die," 213; Taylor, *The Farmers' Movement*, 206.

72. *Russellville (Ark.) Democrat*, 14 February 1884, quoted in Henningson, "Northwest Arkansas," 320–21 (first quote); Elkins, "Arkansas Farmers," 245, quoting W. Scott Morgan (other quotes).

73. Elkins, "Arkansas Farmers," 245; Elkins, "The Agricultural Wheel: County Politics," 152, 154, 169; Henningson, "Northwest Arkansas," 316–20 (quote on 316, citing the *Russellville [Ark.] Democrat*, 14 February 1884).

74. Elkins, "Arkansas Farmers," 245; Elkins, "The Agricultural Wheel: County Politics," 172, 174; Henningson, "Northwest Arkansas," 316–18; Henningson, "Root Hog or Die," 213; *History of Benton*, 625.

75. Morgan, *History*, 68; Henningson, "Root Hog or Die," 198.

76. Henningson, "Root Hog or Die," 214.

77. Henningson, "Root Hog or Die," 214–15; Barjenbruch, "The Greenback Political Movement," 109, 112.

78. Elkins, "The Agricultural Wheel: County Politics," 159, 161; Woodward, *Origins*, 69; Elkins, "Arkansas Farmers," 241; *Lead Hill (Ark.) Bugle*, 13 September 1884, quoted in Henningson, "Root Hog or Die," 206–7.

79. Henningson, "Root Hog or Die," 200–204 (quote on 201). On the opposition of some Brothers to the organization putting forth Independent tickets, see also J. D. Yant to Secretary of Center Common Council No. 5 (of the Brothers of Freedom), 17 May 1884, Heartsill Papers.

80. Elkins, "The Agricultural Wheel: County Politics," 156–58.

81. Henningson, "Root Hog or Die," 208–9, including 209 n. 41; Elkins, "The Agricultural Wheel: County Politics," 166.

82. The Brothers' county tickets won complete victories in Johnson, Newton, and Van Buren counties and partial victories in Franklin, Perry, Pope, and Searcy counties. Brothers-Republican fusion county tickets won partial victories in Crawford and Scott counties. Agricultural Wheel county tickets won complete victories in Prairie and White counties. A Brothers-Wheel fusion ticket probably won in Conway County. The Brothers' tickets in Logan, Sebastian, and Yell counties lost to the Democratic tickets, as did a Brothers-Wheel fusion ticket in Faulkner County (Henningson, "Root Hog or Die," 209, including n. 41).

83. Ibid.; *Little Rock (Ark.) Gazette*, 16 September 1888, 10 September 1890.

84. Letter from Dan Fraser Tomson in the *JUL*, 25 March 1885.

85. Tomson to Powderly, 12 January 1884, Powderly Papers, reel 6.

86. Tomson to Powderly, 26 September 1884, Powderly Papers, reel 8.

87. Letter from "A Charter Member," 26 May 1884, in the *JUL*, 25 June 1884. See also Tomson to Powderly, 12 January 1884, on Freedom Assembly No. 2447 and Tomson's efforts to assist the assembly.

88. Garlock, "A Structural Analysis," 235–36; Garlock, *Guide*, 11–21.

89. Letter from "A Charter Member."

90. Tomson to Powderly, 26 September 1884.

91. Dodd and Dodd, *Historical Statistics*, 7; *Compendium of the Eleventh Census*, pt. 1, lxxi, 63, 64, 68; Garlock, *Guide*, 11–21.

92. Tomson to Powderly, 26 September 1884. Powderly's handwritten instructions about contacting McCracken and Walter are on this letter.

93. Morgan, *History*, 72–73. The merger of the Brothers of Freedom into the Agricultural Wheel occurred on 15 October 1885 at a session of the Arkansas State Wheel in Greenbriar, Faulkner County.

94. Tomson to Powderly, 24 March 1885, Powderly Papers, reel 9; Garlock, *Guide*, 13, 16, 18.

95. Ware, *Labor Movement*, 134–36; Buchanan, *The Story*, 70–99 (first quote on 75, second quote on 77).

96. Chandler, "The Knights of Labor," 22–24; Klein, *The Life and Legend*, 330; Ware, *Labor Movement*, 139.

97. Chandler, "The Knights of Labor," 24–25.

98. Ibid., 26; Buchanan, *The Story*, 143.

99. Buchanan, *The Story*, 142–45; Chandler, "The Knights of Labor," 26, 28–29, 32, 35; *JUL*, 10 January 1885; Garlock, *Guide*, 491–513. Garlock lists the Denison locals as being mixed or, in the one exception, as consisting of "laborers"; he does not list any of the Galveston locals as consisting of railroad workers. Undoubtedly, locals in both cities did include railroad workers. For confirmation of this in the case of Galveston see Young, *Tracks*, 94.

100. Chandler, "The Knights of Labor," 35–37; Ware, *Labor Movement*, 140. Neither the primary nor secondary sources I examined specify whether the Wabash's retraction of its wage cut entailed keeping the workday at eight hours at an average daily wage of $1.60 or raising that salary from $1.80 to $2.00 for the ten-hour workday that the company had announced. For example, the *NYT* states that the Wabash had announced that "wages would be restored to the figures existing prior to the reduction" (17 March 1885). The *Chicago Tribune* says virtually the same thing: "The General Manager of the Wabash Railroad . . . [announced] that wages would be restored at once to the figure existing before the cut" (17 March 1885).

101. *John Swinton's Paper* (New York), 12 April 1885, quoted in Ware, *Labor Movement*, 140; Phelan, *Grand Master Workman*, 158.

102. Chandler, "The Knights of Labor," 42–43; Ware, *Labor Movement*, 140–41; Phelan, *Grand Master Workman*, 158–59 (quote on 159).

103. Ware, *Labor Movement*, 141–42; Phelan, *Grand Master Workman*, 159–60.

104. Phelan, *Grand Master Workman*, 160; Chandler, "The Knights of Labor," 48 (quote).

105. Ware, *Labor Movement*, 143–44 (quotes on 144); Chandler, "The Knights of Labor," 52–54.

106. McMath, *American Populism*, 74; Chandler, "The Knights of Labor," 34.

107. Chandler, "The Knights of Labor," 34–35.

108. Hicks, *The Populist Revolt*, 104–5; Garlock, "A Structural Analysis," 235–36; Barr, *Reconstruction*, 93; Garlock, *Guide*, 491–513; McMath, *Populist Vanguard*, 23; McMath, "Sandy Land," 220–21. The *Dallas News* claimed that the Knights had thirty thousand members in three hundred local assemblies in Texas on the eve of the Southwest strike of 1886 (4 January 1893). As Ruth Allen noted, however, these

unofficial figures "should be accepted with skepticism." She added that this figure may have reflected the fact that "membership in many farmers' organizations was accepted as membership in the Knights of Labor," which further underscores the close relationship between the Knights and the Farmers' Alliance in Texas at the time (Allen, *Chapters*, 21, including citation of the *Dallas News*).

109. Ware, *Labor Movement*, 366 (quote taken from *John Swinton's Paper*, 30 August 1885); McMath, *American Populism*, 75; McMath, *Populist Vanguard*, 23; Allen, *Chapters*, 91; Rhinehart, *A Way of Work*, 72; Calderon, *Mexican Coal Mining Labor*, 145.

110. *Proceedings of the First Annual Session*, 48, 50–51, 59 (quote). On the Knights' conflict with the Mallory Steamship Line see Cartwright, *Galveston*, 135–36. On the Knights' campaign against the use of convict as well as alien contract laborers in the construction of the state capitol see Allen, *Chapters*, chap. 5.

111. Goodwyn, *Democratic Promise*, 56–58, 61–62; McMath, *Populist Vanguard*, 24; McMath, *American Populism*, 75; Barnes, *Farmers*, 70–71; Garlock, *Guide*, 494–96, 504–6.

112. *Jacksboro (Tex.) Rural Citizen*, 11 March 1886, quoted in Goodwyn, *Democratic Promise*, 59.

113. Simonds and McEnnis, *The Story*, 451; Allen, *The Great Southwest Strike*, 47.

114. Phelan, *Grand Master Workman*, 179.

115. Simonds and McEnnis, *The Story*, 451–52; Allen, *The Great Southwest Strike*, 50; Garlock, *Guide*, 499.

116. Powderly, *The Path I Trod*, 121–22; Allen, *The Great Southwest Strike*, chap. 5 (quotes on 56, 62). Phelan also accepts Powderly's account of the events involving Irons and the strike order, deeming the incident "an inauspicious start to such a critical battle" (*Grand Master Workman*, 179). For a more skeptical judgment see Case, "Free Labor," 297–300.

117. *Proceedings of the First Annual Session*, 52–53; *Record of the Proceedings of the Tenth Regular Session of the General Assembly [of the Knights of Labor]* (1886), 170 (quote); Garlock, *Guide*, 492; Allen, *The Great Southwest Strike*, 45–46. Besides wages, another grievance that spurred the strike was the refusal of railroad officials in the Southwest system to accord the Knights of Labor official recognition as a collective bargaining agent.

118. Cassity, "Modernization," 43–44, 54 (quote).

119. Turner and Rogers, "Arkansas Labor," 31–32.

120. Cassity, "Modernization," 54–59; Turner and Rogers, "Arkansas Labor," 38–39; Allen, *The Great Southwest Strike*, 129; Chandler, "The Knights of Labor," 29–32, 64, 71; Case, "Free Labor," 202–6, 216, 223–26, 306–14, 323.

121. Phelan, *Grand Master Workman*, 180–83. According to Allen, about two thirds of the strikers in Dallas did not get their jobs back, a fate shared by about three fifths of the strikers in St. Louis (*The Great Southwest Strike*, 90–91). According to Turner and Rogers, about 95 percent of the Little Rock strikers did not get their jobs back by the middle of May, even though most of them had applied ("Arkansas Labor," 44–45).

122. The principal studies of the Haymarket riot are David, *The History of the Haymarket Affair*, Avrich, *The Haymarket Tragedy*, and Green, *Death in the Haymarket*.

123. Goodwyn, *Democratic Promise*, 62–63; McMath, *American Populism*, 76; McMath, *Populist Vanguard*, 24; Barnes, *Farmers*, 71.

124. Barnes, *Farmers*, 71.

125. Calvert, "The Southern Grange," 52–53; Smith, "The Farmers' Alliance," 352–54; Smith, "The Grange Movement," 302–4; Goodwyn, *Democratic Promise*, 45–46, 86.

126. Goodwyn, *Democratic Promise*, 55–56, 64; McMath, *American Populism*, 76–77; McMath, *Populist Vanguard*, 24. The quote appears in both of the last two sources.

127. Goodwyn, *Democratic Promise*, 63 (quotes); Smith, "The Farmers' Alliance," 355; *Proceedings of the First Annual Session*, 28.

128. Cassity, *Defending*, 146–47, 164–65; *St. Louis Post-Dispatch*, 3–5 May 1888.

129. *Arkansas Gazette*, 16 May (first quote), 9 June (second quote) 1886; Morgan, *History*, 335–36; *NYT*, 16 August 1886; Moneyhon, *Arkansas*, 81–82, 85; Elkins, "State Politics," 255–57; James, "American Labor," 315 n. 87. Abramowitz claims that Isom P. Langley was black ("The Negro in the Populist Movement," 266–67), but a biographical sketch (with illustration) of him in Morgan clearly shows that Langley was white (*History*, 335–36).

130. Goodwyn, *Democratic Promise*, 66; Turner and Rogers, "Arkansas Labor," 41–42.

131. Winkler, *Platforms*, 236–37; Barr, *Reconstruction*, 96, 98, 114, 118–20.

132. Martin, *The People's Party*, 35–36; Barr, *Reconstruction*, 96, 99.

133. Official annual membership figures from 1882 through 1888 were given as of 1 July. These figures are listed in Ware, *Labor Movement*, 66. Weir estimates that actual, unofficial membership in the Knights of Labor probably surpassed one million in 1886 (*Beyond Labor's Veil*, 12).

134. *Record of the Proceedings of the Tenth Regular Session of the General Assembly [of the Knights of Labor]* (1886), 326–28; *Record of the Proceedings of the Eleventh Regular Session of the General Assembly [of the Knights of Labor]* (1887), 1847–50; and "Report of the General Secretary," 2–5, in *Record of the Proceedings of the Twelfth Regular Session of the General Assembly [of the Knights of Labor]* (1888).

135. The argument presented here is not meant to suggest that the potential national political strength of the labor movement was not diminished by the Haymarket riot and lost strikes in 1886. For counterfactual suggestions about what that political strength may have been had it not been for these setbacks see Fink, "New Labor History," 132–34; McMath, *American Populism*, 76. On the Knights' continued vibrancy in Texas as late as 1896 see Allen, *Chapters*, 21; Garlock, *Guide*, 491–513. See also chap. 5.

136. For evidence of this examine the coverage given by virtually any major U.S. newspaper to the Knights' General Assembly convention in Richmond, Virginia, in October 1886 both before and (especially) after the eruption of the "social equality" controversy centering upon New York City's DA 49 and its African American delegate.

### Chapter Three. The Knights of Labor and Southern Farmer-Labor Insurgency, 1885–1888

1. *Athens (Ga.) Daily Banner-Watchman*, 18 August 1885.

2. *Athens (Ga.) Daily Banner-Watchman*, 18 March 1886; Patrons of Husbandry Records (minutes for 10 September 1873 mention Jennings's initiation, and the list of "Life Members" contained in the folder includes Jennings's name and reveals that he paid twenty dollars for that designation); *Atlanta Constitution*, 8 December 1885; *JUL*, 10 September, 10 October 1885. Additional information on the membership of the two mixed locals in Athens can be gleaned from the expulsion lists in the *JUL*, 25 January, 25 February 1886, which reveal that LA 4141 expelled a shoemaker and a machinist and LA 4273 expelled a blacksmith.

3. *Atlanta Constitution*, 3, 8 December 1885; C. B. Gardner, J. W. Black, and W. H. Haines to Powderly, 22 April 1886, Powderly Papers, reel 15; *Athens (Ga.) Weekly Banner-Watchman*, 26 January 1886 (last quote). The fact that the Athens mayoral election was nonpartisan apparently did not affect voter eligibility.

4. This study focuses primarily upon farmer-labor political alliances in the South. An older but still valuable study that focuses upon farmer-labor political alliances in the Midwest, especially Illinois, is Destler, *American Radicalism*. Studies of late-nineteenth-century farmer-labor politics in specific nonsouthern states include Clinch, *Urban Populism*; Brundage, *The Making of Western Labor Radicalism*; Kolnick, "A Producer's Commonwealth"; Pierce, "The Plow and Hammer."

5. Fink, *Workingmen's Democracy*, 26. Fink's table (28–29) listing Knights of Labor political tickets by state or territory, 1885–88, lists only Macon for Georgia, overlooking not only Athens but also Atlanta, Augusta, Decatur, Marietta, and Savannah, where the Knights ran candidates or complete tickets in elections in

1886. See the *Atlanta Constitution,* 25, 29 September, 2, 6–8 October 1886. Other broad studies dealing with the Knights' political activities in the mid- to late 1880s include Ware, *Labor Movement,* chap. 17; Foner, *History,* chaps. 8, 10; Grob, *Workers and Utopia,* chap. 5; McLaurin, *The Knights of Labor,* chap. 5; Summers, *Party Games,* chap. 13.

6. Ware deals with the Knights of Labor's involvement in farmer-labor politics, primarily at the national level, but minimizes its significance, asserting that by the time the national Order became seriously involved in these efforts its declining strength meant that the Knights' "indorsement of the farmers' demands could help neither the farmers nor themselves" (*Labor Movement,* 365–69, quote on 367). McLaurin deals with the Knights' involvement in farmer-labor politics in the South and at the national level but emphasizes conflicts between the Knights and the farmers' organizations and, like Ware, portrays the Knights' movement toward a political coalition with the Southern Farmers' Alliance as an indication of the Knights' weakness (*The Knights of Labor,* 104–5, 174–79). As mentioned in note 4 above, several studies examine farmer-labor politics during the late nineteenth century in states outside the South.

7. Laurie, *Artisans,* 157; Phelan, *Grand Master Workman,* 175.

8. Powderly to Tomson, 23 January 1886, Powderly Papers, reel 47.

9. Laurie, *Artisans,* 157; Phelan, *Grand Master Workman,* 176–77; Weir, *Beyond Labor's Veil,* 12; *JUL,* 10 April 1886.

10. Garlock, "A Structural Analysis," 235–36.

11. Garlock, *Guide,* 11–21, 491–513.

12. *Record of the Proceedings of the Tenth Regular Session of the General Assembly [of the Knights of Labor]* (1886), 324.

13. Garlock, *Guide,* 52–59, 353–68, 479–81, 517–27.

14. *Charlotte Home-Democrat,* 25 June 1886.

15. Garlock, *Guide,* 53.

16. Whites, "Paternalism," 78, emphasis in the original quote.

17. Letter from Mrs. Ira Campbell in the *JUL,* 21 January 1888.

18. Head, "The Development," 54; Garlock, *Guide,* 3–9.

19. Knights of Labor, Van Buren Assembly, Records, Minute Book, 27 December 1890. On efforts at and discussions about organizing women in this local assembly see 4 November 1886, 10 April, 24 July 1888, 13 July, 3, 10 (?) August 1889, 26 July, 2 August 1890. On the admission of women into LA 6307 see 20 September, 1, 8, 22, 29 November, 6, 27 December 1890, 14 February, 31 March 1891. The minutes of 31 January 1891 reveal that the local assembly elected a woman to the office of almoner.

20. Garlock, *Guide,* 484–90; *Knoxville Daily Journal,* 24, 25, 28 November, 4, 8

December 1885. On the Knights and women see Levine, *Labor's True Woman*; Weir, *Knights Unhorsed*, chap. 6; Ware, *Labor Movement*, chap. 16.

21. Rachleff, *Black Labor*, 118–20; Garlock, *Guide*, 517–27.

22. McLaurin, *The Knights of Labor*, 133; Hild, "The Knights of Labor," 88–91. The Knights later chartered a black women's local in Raleigh. See *JUL*, 10 April 1886.

23. On the weakness of the Farmers' Alliance and the Populist Party in Virginia see Gerteis, "Class," chap. 7.

24. Barr, *Reconstruction*, 99; Hill, *Dallas*, 28–29; McMath, *Populist Vanguard*, 26.

25. Winkler, *Platforms*, 237–40.

26. Barr, *Reconstruction*, 97–98, 104–5, 149; Martin, *The People's Party*, 35 (quote).

27. McMath, *Populist Vanguard*, 25–26 (first quote on 26); Lightfoot, "The Human Party," 28–40 (second quote on 31); Barr, *Reconstruction*, 99.

28. Garlock, *Guide*, 496; Barr, *Reconstruction*, 99–100; Martin, *The People's Party*, 31–32, including 32 n. 3.

29. Parsons, Dubin, and Parsons, *United States Congressional Districts*, 148; Simonds and McEnnis, *The Story*, 455; Smith, "The Farmers' Alliance," 355; Goodwyn, *Democratic Promise*, 63.

30. *NYT*, 2 November 1886. See also the *Dallas Morning News*, 16 October 1886. The term "Dark Lantern" Party was a derisive label used to describe political parties that met secretly, the implication being that they were not "manly" enough to conduct their business out in the open. I am indebted to Gregg Cantrell for clarifying this point.

31. Barr, *Reconstruction*, 100; Garlock, *Guide*, 507. Allen estimates that about two thirds of the participants in the Southwest strike of 1886 in Dallas did not get their jobs back (*The Great Southwest Strike*, 90–91).

32. McMath, *American Populism*, 78–80; Goodwyn, *Democratic Promise*, 63, 77, 79. The Cleburne platform is reprinted in Winkler, *Platforms*, 235–37.

33. Goodwyn, *Democratic Promise*, 82–86; McMath, *Populist Vanguard*, 26–30. See also the article in the *NYT*, 10 October 1886, entitled "Caused by Politics: The Texas Farmers' Alliance Going to Pieces." On Macune's life and career prior to 1886 see an article written by his great-grandson, Macune, "The Wellsprings."

34. Winkler, *Platforms*, 246–47. On Loe's and Martin's involvement with the Union Labor and Populist parties see 262–63, 314, 316, 335, 379. On Martin's role in the state Greenback Party in 1884 see 229. On Loe's activities as a delegate to the first annual session of Knights of Labor DA 78 in January 1886 see the *Proceedings of the First Annual Session*, 4, 25, 27.

35. Barr, *Reconstruction*, 100.

36. On the conservative leanings of the Texas Grange during this period see

Goodwyn, *Democratic Promise*, 44–46; Smith, "The Farmers' Alliance," 356–57. As for the relative size of the Farmers' Alliance and the Grange in Texas, the former claimed two hundred thousand members in the Lone Star State and Indian Territory in January 1887, while the ranks of Texas Grangers amounted to less than nine thousand (Goodwyn, *Democratic Promise*, 86; Hicks, *The Populist Revolt*, 104–5).

37. *NYT*, 3, 4 November 1886; Dubin, *United States Congressional Elections*, 276; Goodwyn, *Democratic Promise*, 76–77 (Farmer quoted on 77), 331, 478, 491, 509; Hill, *Dallas*, 40; *Proceedings of the First Annual Session*, 28, 53; *The National Economist Almanac 1890*, 74. See also Cantrell and Paschal, "Texas Populism," 38, on Kearby's efforts to appeal specifically to Knights as well as Alliancemen during his campaign for Congress in 1886.

38. Winkler, *Platforms*, 262, 297, 298, 380, 424; Dubin, *United States Congressional Elections*, 301, 310, 319.

39. *NYT*, 16 August 1886; Elkins, "State Politics," 255–56.

40. *NYT*, 6, 16 August 1886; Morgan, *History*, 86; Elkins, "State Politics," 253–55. On opposition among Wheelers to nominating a state ticket see Elkins, "State Politics," 250–51, 255; *Arkansas Gazette*, 9 June 1886. On dissent in the Sebastian County Agricultural Wheel in southwestern Arkansas over the issue of involvement in politics see Heartsill to R. B. CarlLee, 7 June 1886; Heartsill to T. W. Newton, 11 June 1886; Isaac McCracken to Heartsill, 10 August 1886; handwritten proceedings of the County Wheel of Sebastian County, ca. 1886, all in the Heartsill Papers.

41. *NYT*, 6, 16 August (first quote), 26 September (second quote) 1886; Elkins, "State Politics," 257. The Wheel failed to nominate a candidate for associate justice, and its nominee for attorney general, J. M. Harrell of Garland County, declined the nomination. The Wheel ticket thus entered the campaign with two empty slots.

42. Dubin, *United States Congressional Elections*, 271; Martis, *The Historical Atlas*, 121; *NYT*, 3 November 1886. Elkins, "State Politics," 254, claims that CarlLee ran as a Union Labor candidate for Congress in 1884 but bases this erroneous statement on a misprint in *Biographical and Historical Memoirs of Eastern Arkansas* that says 1884 where it should say 1886 (237). That CarlLee did not run for Congress in 1884 is confirmed by Dubin, *United States Congressional Elections*, 264. As for the claim that CarlLee ran for Congress as a Union Labor candidate, the National Union Labor Party was not formed until February 1887. Dubin (*United States Congressional Elections*, 271) and the *NYT* (3 November 1886) both call CarlLee a Wheeler candidate; Dubin calls Hitt a Greenback candidate, while the *Times* calls him a Wheeler candidate.

43. Elkins, "State Politics," 254.

44. Dubin, *United States Congressional Elections*, 271.

45. Ibid., 264, 271; Sanders, *Roots of Reform*, 46.

46. Elkins, "State Politics," 255. By the time Langley joined the Knights of Labor he had ended his law practice. The Knights did occasionally admit lawyers, though, despite the fact that doing so violated the organization's constitution. See Beckel, "Roots of Reform," 482; Weir, *Beyond Labor's Veil*, 217, 219–20.

47. Garlock, *Guide*, 12, 17–19; Knights of Labor, Van Buren Assembly, Records, Minute Book, 5 August, 16 September, 28 October, 13 December 1886, 9 May, 21 June, 19 July 1887, 8 February 1890; *Biennial Report, 1886*, 259.

48. Tomson to Powderly, 24 January 1887, Powderly Papers, reel 20.

49. Dubin, *United States Congressional Elections*, 271.

50. On the entrance of the Farmers' Alliance into Georgia and North Carolina see Morgan, *History*, 116, 123–24. Chapter 3 of Morgan's book, which provides a detailed history of the Agricultural Wheel from its founding in 1882 until its merger agreement with the Southern Farmers' Alliance at the end of 1888, makes no mention of the Wheel ever reaching Georgia or North Carolina, but the *Alabama State Wheel* (Moulton) 7 June 1888, reports the organization of subordinate Wheels (local Wheel chapters) in Georgia.

51. James E. Schofield to Powderly, 6 August 1886, Powderly Papers, reel 17; *Atlanta Constitution*, 6, 7 October 1886; *Augusta Chronicle*, 15 September 1886. The *Atlanta Constitution* also reported that "in Columbus [Muscogee County] there is a fight made by the Knights of Labor against . . . one of the [Democratic] nominees" (6 October 1886). The *Columbus Enquirer-Sun*, reporting on the results of the elections for state officers and the local state senator and representatives, noted, however, that "there was no opposition to the [D]emocratic nominees" (7 October 1886).

52. Schofield to Powderly, 6 August 1886; *Macon (Ga.) Telegraph*, 5 August, 7 October 1886.

53. Hild, "The Knights of Labor," 74–88 (quote from the *Savannah Morning News*, 25 September 1886, on 77).

54. *Augusta Chronicle*, 15 September 1886. The standard accounts of the strike-lockout that occurred in Augusta's textile mills in 1886 are McLaurin, *Paternalism*, 91–112, and Reed, "The Augusta Textile Strike."

55. *Augusta Chronicle*, 6 October (quote), 7 October 1886; Cashin, *The Story of Augusta*, 157–58.

56. *Southern Alliance Farmer* (Atlanta), 29 November 1889.

57. Walsh, " 'Horny-Handed Sons of Toil,' " 264; *Atlanta Constitution*, 7 October 1886.

58. *Athens Weekly Banner-Watchman,* 28 September 1886.

59. Fite, *Richard B. Russell, Jr.,* 1–3; *Athens Weekly Banner-Watchman,* 12 October 1886 (quotes); Stewart, "The Urban-Rural Dynamic," 166, 183.

60. *Athens Weekly Banner-Watchman,* 28 September 1886. After this issue the newspaper made no reference to Tucker's candidacy, and the election results in the issue of 12 October 1886 list only Russell, Lowry, and Murrell as having received votes in the election for the state house of representatives.

61. On the demise of the Knights of Labor in Athens see Hild, "The Knights of Labor," 111.

62. Garlock, *Guide,* 52–59. Garlock lists Roswell and Alpharetta, both of which had at least one Knights of Labor local assembly in 1886, as being located in Fulton County. While both of these cities (then small towns) are located in Fulton County today, neither was during the nineteenth century. Roswell was part of Cobb County, while Alpharetta was part of the no longer extant county of Milton. On Roswell see Temple, *The First Hundred Years,* 116. On Alpharetta see Candler and Evans, *Georgia,* 1:53.

63. Garlock, *Guide,* 53, 55.

64. Letter from C.P.F. in the *JUL,* 28 January 1888. This local is identified as the "Gem City" Assembly in H. N. Austin to Powderly, 1 February 1887, Powderly Papers, reel 21.

65. Temple, *The First Hundred Years,* 645; *Record of the Proceedings of the Tenth Regular Session of the General Assembly [of the Knights of Labor]* (1886), 323. On Sanges's activities as a Knights of Labor lecturer and organizer see the *Marietta (Ga.) Journal,* 1 July 1886, 31 March 1887; *Cartersville (Ga.) Courant-American,* 9 August 1888; letter from C.P.F. in the *JUL,* 28 January 1888; letter from James C. Sanges in *JUL,* 20 June 1889; James E. Schofield and James A. Ware to Powderly, 14 October 1887, Powderly Papers, reel 23; Sanges to Powderly, 25 November, 2 December 1889, Powderly Papers, reel 31.

66. *JUL,* 10 September 1886; *Record of the Proceedings of the Tenth Regular Session of the General Assembly [of the Knights of Labor]* (1886), 323.

67. *Marietta (Ga.) Journal,* 9 September (quotes), 14 October 1886; Jacob and Ragsdale, *Biographical Directory,* 788; Garlock, *Guide,* 53, 55; letter from Sanges in the *JUL,* 20 June 1889; *Atlanta Constitution,* 8 October 1886.

68. Schofield to Powderly, 6 August 1886; *Sholes' Directory,* 28–29, 47, 272; *Augusta Chronicle,* 25 July 1888; Hild, "The Knights of Labor," 77, 79–80, 86–87.

69. The Reading platform is reprinted in Powderly, *Thirty Years,* 243–45. The Reading platform called for "the reduction of hours of labor to eight per day," but such a demand would have been impossibly optimistic in the late-nineteenth-century South.

70. Jacob and Ragdale, *Biographical Directory*, 988–89; Ward, "Georgia," 411–31; Roberts, "The Public Career," 306–7, 332–59; Talmadge, *Rebecca Latimer Felton*, 98–99; Davis, *Henry Grady's New South*, 145–48; *Atlanta Constitution*, 20 November 1886, 6–7 October 1887; *JUL*, 8 January 1887; *Macon (Ga.) Telegraph*, 30 July 1887. For Rebecca Felton's account of her and her husband's involvement in the anti-convict lease crusade see Felton, *My Memoirs*, 581–623, and Ansley, *History*, chap. 6. Dr. Felton was not the first future Georgia Populist to oppose the convict lease system; earlier in the 1880s Tom Watson also attacked it during his brief career in the state house of representatives (1882–83) and as early as 1880 in campaign speeches (Woodward, *Tom Watson*, 80, 100, 105–7).

71. Evans, "The History," 410–12, 448–49, 573; *Augusta Chronicle*, 15, 17 September 1887; H. N. Cramer to Powderly, 8 January 1888, Powderly Papers, reel 24 (quote).

72. *Atlanta Constitution*, 4 August, 22 September 1889, 2 January 1890; *Augusta Chronicle*, 17 October, 7 November 1889; Evans, "The History," 412–16; *Acts and Resolutions*, 163–64.

73. McLaurin, "The Knights of Labor"; Edwards, *Gendered Strife*, chap. 6.

74. Garlock, *Guide*, 353–68; John R. Ray to Powderly, 15 March 1885, Powderly Papers, reel 9. The Raleigh local assembly referred to here is Pioneer LA 3282.

75. Garlock, "A Structural Analysis," 236.

76. *Raleigh News and Observer*, 16 April 1886; *JUL*, 10 April 1886.

77. Garlock, *Guide*, 355; *JUL*, 10 June 1886; *National Labor Tribune*, 6 November 1886.

78. McLaurin, "The Knights of Labor," 302.

79. Ray to Powderly, 15, 24 March 1885, Powderly Papers, reel 9; McLaurin, "The Knights of Labor"; Beckel, "Roots of Reform," 399, 429 n. 55, 461, 478, 506 n. 38, 555–56. As Beckel notes, Raleigh LA 3606 included a number of small, aspiring entrepreneurs, some of them Democrats and others Republicans.

80. Knights of Labor, Raleigh Assembly, Minute Book, minutes for 12 July, 2 August 1886; McLaurin, "The Knights of Labor," 299, 301–3.

81. Jacob and Ragsdale, *Biographical Directory*, 1569; Beckel, "Roots of Reform," 55–56 (quote on 56); McLaurin, "The Knights of Labor," 302.

82. Beckel, "Roots of Reform," 32, 36–37, 39; Jacob and Ragsdale, *Biographical Directory*, 1569; McLaurin, "The Knights of Labor," 302–3 (quote on 302).

83. McLaurin, "The Knights of Labor," 302–3; Beckel, "Roots of Reform," 477. On the presence of landowning farmers in Raleigh LA 3606 see Beckel, "Roots of Reform," 399, 466, 551. A local assembly of farmhands, farm laborers, and mechanics (LA 8152) existed at Forestville in Wake County from 1886 until at least 1888 (Garlock, *Guide*, 364). In 1888, however, John Nichols claimed that the

Knights had organized "few field hands" in North Carolina (Beckel, "Roots of Reform," 459). For some evidence to the contrary see above.

84. Dubin, *United States Congressional Elections,* 275; Daniels, *Tar Heel Editor,* 332–36; McLaurin, "The Knights of Labor," 302–4 (first quote on 304); Beckel, "Roots of Reform," 399 (second quote, citing the entry on Sorrell in *Legislative Biographical Sketch Book, Session 1887, North Carolina* [Raleigh: Edwards & Broughton, 1887], 43), 478.

85. McLaurin, "The Knights of Labor," 305–7; Noblin, *Leonidas LaFayette Polk,* 101, 266; Beckel, "Roots of Reform," 440, 486, 542; Jacob and Ragsdale, *Biographical Directory,* 521–22. By 1890 Polk would be traveling and lecturing with Knights of Labor political lobbyist and third-party advocate Ralph Beaumont; see Noblin, *Leonidas LaFayette Polk,* 3–4. McLaurin refers to S. B. Alexander as the president of the North Carolina Farmers' Alliance ("The Knights of Labor," 306), but the Alliance did not enter the state until April 1887, and Alexander did not become the State Alliance president until October 1887, after the modified bureau of labor statistics bill had already passed (Morgan, *History,* 123–24). The North Carolina Farmers' Association, created at a mass convention of farmers in Raleigh in January 1887 (which John Nichols attended), resolved that convict labor should be employed on public roads and condemned the policy of allowing convict labor to "be employed for the benefit of moneyed corporations" (*Winston [N.C.] Progressive Farmer,* 9 February 1887).

86. McLaurin, *The Knights of Labor,* 85–92; Garlock, *Guide,* 519, 522–23; Fink, *Workingmen's Democracy,* 154–69 (quote on 160); Rachleff, *Black Labor,* 150–91. On the controversy regarding the Knights' violation of Jim Crow customs at the Richmond General Assembly see also Miner, "The 1886 Convention," and Foner and Lewis, *The Black Worker during the Era,* pt. 4. For Terence V. Powderly's account and view of the "social equality" controversy at Richmond see Powderly, *Thirty Years,* 651–62.

87. Fink, *Workingmen's Democracy,* 26.

88. McLaurin, who focuses upon the Southeast, states that "in the South, [the Knights'] peak membership probably occurred sometime early in 1887 and then fell rapidly" (*The Knights of Labor,* 170). In Alabama the Knights' membership apparently peaked in late 1887 or early 1888. The membership figures given in appendixes 2 and 3 reflect membership as of 1 July of each given year. During the last quarter of 1887 the Alabama State Assembly of the Knights of Labor reported 5,614 members in good standing. See Abernathy, "The Knights of Labor," 60–62; Head, "The Development," 51–52.

89. Morgan, *History,* 75–85; Rogers, *The One-Gallused Rebellion,* 122.

90. Hair, *Bourbonism,* 142–48.

91. According to contemporary Wheel and Alliance historian W. Scott Morgan, the Texas Alliance had chartered a small number of sub-Alliances in Louisiana (west of the Red River) and Kentucky by the end of 1886 as well as an unspecified number in the Indian Territory (*History*, 119–20, 130–31). Membership figure is taken from Goodwyn, *Democratic Promise*, 82.

92. Morgan, *History*, 77–79, 102–3, 111, 115–18, 120–28, 130–31; Dunning, *Farmers' Alliance History*, 64–65; Hair, *Bourbonism*, 149–52.

93. On these points regarding the more radical character of the Wheel in comparison to the Southern Alliance see, in addition to the evidence presented in this study, Saloutos, *Farmer Movements*, 60–64, 67–68; McMath, *Populist Vanguard*, 36, 44, 58–60; McMath, *American Populism*, 62, 87–88, 130, 172.

94. *Progressive Farmer*, 9 February 1887.

95. McMath, *Populist Vanguard*, 39; Knights of Labor, Raleigh Assembly, Minute Book, 6 June, 1 August 1887.

96. Beckel, "Roots of Reform," 551.

97. McLaurin, *The Knights of Labor*, 125–26; Beckel, "Roots of Reform," 465, 470; *JUL*, 10 August 1886; *Fayetteville (N.C.) Messenger*, 23 March 1888.

98. Knights of Labor, Raleigh Assembly, Minute Book, 7 April 1890.

99. *Fayetteville Messenger*, 13 January 1888.

100. Letter from "B" in *Fayetteville Messenger*, 13 April 1888.

101. McLaurin, "The Knights of Labor," 308.

102. Letter from L.D. in the *JUL*, 12 November 1887.

103. McMath, "Southern White Farmers," 118–19; Steelman, *North Carolina Farmers' Alliance*, 188 (quote), 263–64.

104. Letter from M.W. (perhaps meaning Master Workman) in the *JUL*, 2 August 1888. McLaurin also cites this letter and states that its author was a "black farm worker" ("The Knights of Labor," 308). Given the composition of this local assembly (LA 10491), McLaurin is probably correct about the author's race, although the letter does not make this clear. Garlock does not list the assembly as a black or biracial local but misses many such locals (*Guide*, 363).

105. Noblin, *Leonidas LaFayette Polk*, 199–200.

106. Rogers, *The One-Gallused Rebellion*, 121–22, 131; McMath, *Populist Vanguard*, 33; Horton, "Testing the Limits," 63–74; *Alabama Sentinel*, 10 August 1889. On the national consolidation of the Southern Farmers' Alliance and the Agricultural Wheel into the former under the short-lived moniker "Farmers' and Laborers' Union of America" see McMath, *Populist Vanguard*, 58–60.

107. Abernathy, "The Knights of Labor," 29–39, 50–53; Garlock, *Guide*, 3–9; Webb, *Two-Party Politics*, xii (map); letter from T. H. White in the *JUL*, 18 February 1888 (quote); *Alabama Sentinel*, 16 August 1890. Garlock incorrectly lists LA

10,092 as being located in Hale County (*Guide,* 5). While no statistics appear to be available on the number of "colored" (or white) subordinate Wheels in Alabama, the *Alabama State Wheel* announced that a meeting would be held later that month near Mount Hope (Lawrence County) for the organization of a State Colored Agricultural Wheel (4 January 1888).

108. On the Agricultural Wheel and African Americans in Alabama see Rogers, *The One-Gallused Rebellion,* 127–28, 146; Horton, "Testing the Limits," 64, 73–80, 83–84. On the Knights of Labor and African Americans in Alabama see Abernathy, "The Knights of Labor," 54–56; Head, "The Development," 56–57; Hild, "Dixie Knights Redux," 38–40, 45; Letwin, *The Challenge,* 73, 75–83, 86; McLaurin, *The Knights of Labor,* 136–38, 145–47.

109. Horton, "Testing the Limits," 63–67; Rogers, "The Agricultural Wheel," 6–7 (quote on 7).

110. Letwin, *The Challenge,* 43–44, 69–71.

111. McKiven, *Iron and Steel,* 79; DuBose, *Jefferson County,* 308–9. The Alabama State Assembly of the Knights of Labor subsumed DA 173 upon the larger body's formation in March 1887. On the formation of the Alabama State Assembly, in which Birmingham Knights played a prominent role, see Abernathy, "The Knights of Labor," 58–59; Head, "The Development," 48–49.

112. *Alabama State Wheel* (Isbell), n.d., quoted in the *JUL,* 2 July 1887. The holdings of the *Alabama State Wheel* at the Alabama Department of Archives and History in Montgomery begin with the issue of 18 November 1887, by which time the paper was being published at Moulton.

113. *NYT,* 23–24 February 1887; *Alabama Sentinel,* 3 September 1887 (reprints the Union Labor Party platform adopted at Cincinnati); McMath, *American Populism,* 170–71. The *NYT* reported that "about 300 delegates" attended the Cincinnati convention, while Alabama delegate J. J. Woodall claimed that over six hundred had attended (23 February 1887); see the *Alabama Sentinel,* 6 August 1887.

114. *NYT,* 25 February 1887; *Alabama Sentinel,* 6 August 1887.

115. *Journal of Proceedings,* 4; Rogers, *The One-Gallused Rebellion,* 77, 126–27.

116. *Alabama Sentinel,* 6 August, 17 September (quote) 1887.

117. Head, "The Development," 70; Rogers, *The One-Gallused Rebellion,* 127; *Alabama Sentinel,* 24 September 1887 (quotes); Webb, *Two-Party Politics,* 68, 88–89, 135; letter from J.P.V. in the *JUL,* 28 April 1888.

118. Abernathy, "The Knights of Labor," 73; Head, "The Development," 70–72; *Alabama Sentinel,* 31 March 1888 (second and third quotes); Rogers, *The One-Gallused Rebellion,* 154–57; *Montgomery Advertiser,* n.d., quoted in the *Alabama State Wheel,* 29 March 1888 (first quote). According to the *Alabama Sentinel,* Gaither also represented two Knights of Labor local assemblies from Etowah County (31 March 1888).

119. Abernathy, "The Knights of Labor," 73–74; Head, "The Development," 71; McKiven, *Iron and Steel,* 80–81.

120. Letter from S.J.B. in the *JUL,* 9 June 1888; Abernathy, "The Knights of Labor," 74.

121. Head, "The Development," 72; Webb, *Two-Party Politics,* 90, first quote citing the *Clanton (Ala.) Chilton View,* 12 April 1888, second quote citing the *Clanton (Ala.) Chilton View,* 18 October 1888.

122. *Dallas (Tex.) Southern Mercury,* 10 May 1888.

123. Rogers, *The One-Gallused Rebellion,* 206. See also McMath, *Populist Vanguard,* 128, on Gaither's pioneering role in establishing the Populist Party in Alabama.

124. McLaurin, "The Knights of Labor," 310–14 (quote on 313, citing the *Raleigh News and Observer,* 20 September 1888); *Fayetteville Messenger,* 3 February, 19 October (letter from "Wage-Worker"), 26 October 1888; Beckel, "Roots of Reform," 502 n. 26, 560–61, 566–67; Dubin, *United States Congressional Elections,* 282; Beatty, *Alamance,* 202–3. For evidence of support for the Union Labor Party from North Carolina Farmers' Alliance members see the *Fayetteville Messenger,* 13 July, 7 September (letter from S.A.H.), 14, 21 September (letter from "71st White Gentlemen"), 28 September (letter from "Flea Hill White Men"), 5 October (letter from "Flea Hill Convert") 1888. But this evidence must not have represented the mainstream Alliance view of the Union Labor Party in North Carolina, since the State Alliance claimed 42,000 members in August 1888, while the Union Labor presidential candidate, A. J. Streeter, received an official total of only 299 votes in North Carolina. This figure undoubtedly represented an undercount, as the *Fayetteville Messenger* charged, but nevertheless no more than a minute percentage of North Carolina Alliancemen voted for Streeter. Even if some Alliancemen voted for local ULP candidates and a major party presidential candidate, the ULP clearly garnered nothing more than rather minor Alliance support in this state (Morgan, *History,* 124; *Fayetteville Messenger,* 30 November 1888).

125. Hild, "The Knights of Labor," 101.

126. Ibid., 57–66; Walsh, " 'Horny-Handed Sons of Toil,' " 267.

127. *Marietta (Ga.) Journal,* 14 October 1886, 2, 9, 16 August, 11 October 1888; Garlock, *Guide,* 53.

128. Hyman, *The Anti-Redeemers,* 18 (table 2).

129. Scott, "Cobb County," 101.

130. Winkler, *Platforms,* 262; Martin, *The People's Party,* 34; Barr, *Reconstruction,* 104.

131. Letter from R.S. in the *JUL,* 20 August 1887 (letter dated 25 July 1887).

132. Letter from N.J.C. in the *JUL,* 3 March 1888. See also letters in the issues dated 29 October 1887, 5 May, 2, 9, 16, 23 June 1888.

133. Ware, *Labor Movement,* 364.

134. Letter from J.H.W. in the *JUL*, 19 November 1887. The author of this letter resided in Groesbeck, which current atlases show to be in Limestone County, but the quoted excerpt makes it clear that the author lived in another county.

135. Letter from R.S. in the *JUL*, 20 August 1887.

136. Letter from W. E. Farmer in the *JUL*, 20 June 1889; McMath, *Populist Vanguard*, 66.

137. Letter from J. M. Clure in the *Southern Mercury*, 31 July 1888.

138. Letter from "Renter" in the *Southern Mercury*, 7 August 1888.

139. Garlock, *Guide*, 11–21, 353–67; McLaurin, "The Knights of Labor," 301, 308.

140. On Georgia see Garlock, *Guide*, 52–59, and, for a map of the Georgia Upcountry in the 1880s see Hahn, *The Roots*, 8. On the racial composition of the Georgia Upcountry see the *Report on Population*, pt. 1, 406–7. On locals in other southern states that included landless farmers see Garlock, *Guide*.

141. Garlock, *Guide*, 491–513. For a sampling of letters from Texas Knights that mention or suggest the presence of landless farmers in their local assemblies see the *JUL*, 16 July, 29 October, 19 November 1887, 7 January, 2 June, 12 July, 25 October 1888.

142. *Record of the Proceedings of the Tenth Regular Session of the General Assembly [of the Knights of Labor]* (1886), 314; Garlock, *Guide*, 14–15. One of the local assemblies of planters in Jefferson County, Arkansas, consisted of African Americans.

143. Letter from W.J.M. in the *JUL*, 12 November 1887.

144. W. E. Farmer to Powderly, 24 January 1887, Powderly Papers, reel 20; letter from J. W. Iley in the *JUL*, 20 September 1888; *The National Economist Almanac 1890*, 74.

145. *Southern Mercury*, 19 April 1888; Winkler, *Platforms*, 256 (quotes); Smith, "The Farmers' Alliance," 352–53, 356–57, 360–64.

146. *Southern Mercury*, 6 November 1888; Martin, *The People's Party*, 32; Smith, "The Farmers' Alliance," 360; Winkler, *Platforms*, 256–57 (quotes).

147. Letter from James Hurst in the *Southern Mercury*, 31 May 1888.

148. Letter from S. J. Dott in the *Southern Mercury*, 18 September 1888. See also letters in the issues dated 4, 11 September, 2, 9 October 1888. On the position of the *Southern Mercury* toward the ULP see the issue dated 13 November 1888, which editorialized, "If a new party can win the fight, let the new party enter the arena."

149. Winkler, *Platforms*, 260–63; *Southern Mercury*, 6 November 1888; Barr, *Reconstruction*, 145; McMath, *American Populism*, 170–71.

150. Winkler, *Platforms*, 199, 260–63; Goodwyn, *Democratic Promise*, 101, 218, 279–80 (quote on 279); Dann, "Black Populism," 60–61; *Southern Mercury*, 12 July 1888.

151. Goodwyn, *Democratic Promise*, 141–42; McMath, *Populist Vanguard*, 30–31; *NYT*, 26 August 1888; Barr, *Reconstruction*, 104–5; Buenger, *The Path*, 9, 11 (quote); Winkler, *Platforms*, 646. Buenger suggests that voting fraud and Martin's stance on prohibition may have cost the challenger votes from black and white rural insurgents (*The Path*, 11–12). Even those factors, however, probably did not fully account for the large margin by which Martin lost (250,338 votes for Ross to Martin's 98,447).

152. *NYT*, 1 November 1888; Dubin, *United States Congressional Elections*, 276, 284; Goodwyn, *Democratic Promise*, 279–80.

153. Barr (*Reconstruction*, 105–6) makes this point but incorrectly reports that the Streeter-Cunningham ticket received 33,384 votes in Texas. Winkler (*Platforms*, 649) and Fine (*Labor*, 70) both list the Texas ULP presidential vote as 29,459. Fine lists the third-party presidential vote state by state for the elections of 1880, 1884, and 1888. On Streeter see Ware, *Labor Movement*, 364; McMath, *American Populism*, 104, 109; and a brief biographical sketch in the *Fayetteville Messenger*, 29 June 1888.

154. Martin, *The People's Party*, 32–33; *Southern Mercury*, 25 September 1888.

155. Fine, *Labor*, 70; Burnham, *Presidential Ballots*, 275.

156. The Union Laborites and the Republicans fused under the ULP banner in the elections for the state offices in 1888. In the four Arkansas congressional races in which the two parties agreed not to compete with each other, two candidates ran as Union Laborites, one ran as a Republican, and one ran as an Independent.

157. Otto, *The Final Frontiers*, 16, 117 (table 9); letter from J.T.L. in the *JUL*, 3 December 1887.

158. Letter from H.M. in the *JUL*, 10 March 1888.

159. *Arkansas Gazette*, 11 April (quoting the *Marianna [Ark.] Index*, n.d.), 1 May 1888; Morgan, *History*, 318–19.

160. Wheeler, "The People's Party," 143; *Arkansas Gazette*, 1 May 1888 (quote). The National Farmers' Alliance was actually the name of the Northern, not the Southern, Farmers' Alliance, although the passage quoted here undoubtedly referred to the latter organization, which entered Arkansas in late 1886 (McMath, *Populist Vanguard*, 33).

161. *Alabama Sentinel*, 31 March 1888.

162. *St. Louis Post-Dispatch*, 1 May 1888; *Arkansas Gazette*, 14 August 1888, quoted in Paisley, "Political Wheelers," 4.

163. *Arkansas Gazette*, 1 May 1888; *St. Louis Post-Dispatch*, 1 May 1888; *Biographical and Historical Memoirs of Pulaski*, 439.

164. *JUL*, 16 August 1888.

165. James, "T. V. Powderly," 452–54.

166. Paisley, "Political Wheelers," 6–7 (quotes on 6, citing the *Arkansas Gazette*, 21 June 1888); Moneyhon, *Arkansas*, 87.

167. Paisley, "Political Wheelers," 8; Bayliss, "Public Affairs," 301.

168. Barnes, *Who Killed John Clayton?* 70–71.

169. *JUL*, 30 June 1888. For a list of district assemblies chartered between the Knights' General Assembly meeting of October 1887 and that of November 1888, including seven in Arkansas (most of which were attached to the State Assembly of the Arkansas Knights of Labor) see Powderly, *Thirty Years*, 647–48. See also Hild, "Labor, Third-Party Politics," 36, on support for Union Labor candidates in Arkansas Knights of Labor strongholds in 1888.

170. Martis, *The Historical Atlas*, 123; Dubin, *United States Congressional Elections*, 279.

171. Knights of Labor, Van Buren Assembly, Records, Minute Book, 14 February 1888.

172. See the *JUL*, 17 March (letter from A.C.L.), 28 April (letter from J. H. Robertson), 26 July (letter from R.A.A.), 9 August (letters from W.M.T. and J.L.L. and editor's report on Mountainburg, Arkansas), 23 August (letter from J.M.) 1888. See also the issues of 20 December 1888 (letter from H. H. Dill, Arkansas Knights of Labor State Statistician) on the glum financial condition of many Arkansas Knights, and 30 June and 6 September 1888 on a Knights of Labor miners strike in Coal Hill, Arkansas.

173. Knights of Labor, Van Buren Assembly, Records, Minute Book, 5 June 1888.

174. Quoted in Moneyhon, *Arkansas*, 86.

175. Paisley, "Political Wheelers," 13 (first quote, citing the *Arkansas Gazette*, 3 August 1888), 17–18 (second quote, citing the *Arkansas Gazette*, 7 October 1888).

176. *Biennial Report, 1888*, 41.

177. R. B. CarlLee to G. W. Pike, n.d. This letter was intended for publication, and Pike circulated it to the press. Among the newspapers that published it were the *Arkansas Gazette*, 22 September 1888, and the *Fayetteville (N.C.) Messenger*, 12 October 1888.

178. Barnes, *Who Killed John Clayton?* 96. For similar assessments see Paisley, "Political Wheelers," 17–18; Moneyhon, *Arkansas*, 87; Summers, "Party Games," 426, 428. See also the letter from Charles M. B. Cox of Rector, Arkansas, in the *JUL*, 22 August 1889, for charges that Norwood "was elected, but counted out."

179. Dubin, *United States Congressional Elections*, 271, 279; Morgan, *History*, 319; Barnes, *Who Killed John Clayton?* 65 (quote); Paisley, "Political Wheelers," 4–8; Martis, *The Historical Atlas*, 123.

180. Letter from Charles M. B. Cox in the *JUL*, 22 August 1889; Powderly,

*Thirty Years*, 647. Powderly listed DA 223 as being based in Paragould, whereas the Order's official "Report of the General Secretary" (1888, 4) had the district assembly based about twenty miles northeast of Paragould in Rector. The district's headquarters probably relocated sometime after the summer of 1888. The "Report of the General Secretary" is included with the *Record of the Proceedings of the Twelfth Regular Session of the General Assembly [of the Knights of Labor]* (1888).

181. Dubin, *United States Congressional Elections*, 286 nn. 2, 3; Barnes, *Who Killed John Clayton?* 7, 32, 65, 75–81.

182. Fine, *Labor*, 70.

183. Cassity, *Defending*, 146–47, 165; *St. Louis Post-Dispatch*, 3 May 1888; *JUL*, 18 February (letter from G.W.L.), 31 March (letter from J.L.F.); unidentified newspaper clipping (dateline Rolla, Missouri, 1 February 1888) in Knights of Labor, Phillipsburg, Missouri, Records; Clevenger, "The Farmers' Alliance," 28; Dubin, *United States Congressional Elections*, 281, 298, 307, 316, 325, 333, 351, 369; Ostler, *Prairie Populism*, 10 (quote), 77–78, 112–13; Goodwyn, *Democratic Promise*, 100–102; Fink, *Workingmen's Democracy*, 135–36; Hicks, *The Populist Revolt*, 154–56. For evidence of third-party supporters among the Knights of Labor in Phillipsburg, Missouri, in 1890 see Knights of Labor, Phillipsburg, Missouri, Records, Minute Book, 5, 19 April 1890.

184. Fine, *Labor*, 70.

## Chapter Four. *Toward a Third Party in the South and Nation, 1889–1892*

1. Morgan, *History*, 90–92 (quote on 92).

2. McMath, *Populist Vanguard*, 59–60; Wheeler, "The People's Party," 162, 164; Gerteis, "Class," 152–53; Holmes, "The Demise," 191–92. Holmes notes that in Alabama and Tennessee African Americans "continued to maintain chapters of the Agricultural Wheel long after" the merger between the Wheel and the Southern Alliance (188).

3. C. W. Macune to Powderly, 10 January 1889, Powderly Papers, reel 28.

4. R. F. Gray to Powderly, 10 June 1889, Powderly Papers, reel 30.

5. Isaac McCracken to Powderly, 24 June 1889, Powderly Papers, reel 30.

6. Morgan, *History*, 72–73. See above.

7. For secondary accounts that emphasize the weakness of the Knights of Labor during the late 1880s and early 1890s as an obstacle to constructing a farmer-labor coalition see Ware, *Labor Movement*, 367–70; Grob, *Workers and Utopia*, 96–98; Goodwyn, *Democratic Promise*, 65, 165–66; McLaurin, *The Knights of Labor*, 174–79; Phelan, *Grand Master Workman*, 249. For accounts of the Knights' decline after 1886 see Foner, *History*, chap. 11; Laurie, *Artisans*, 164–75; Phelan, *Grand Master Work-*

*man*, 196–215, 227–58. On the Order's decline in the South see McLaurin, *The Knights of Labor*, chap. 9. For Knights of Labor membership figures see Ware, *Labor Movement*, 66; Oestreicher, "A Note," 106–8.

8. Laurie, *Artisans*, 164–65; Fink, *Workingmen's Democracy*, 19; Ware, *Labor Movement*, 83. Laurie states that Ralph Beaumont was the first chief of the Knights' national legislative committee, but in fact the position was first held by another labor reform veteran, George McNeill (Phelan, *Grand Master Workman*, 182, 190).

9. McCracken to Powderly, 24 June 1889.

10. Laurie, *Artisans*, 176–83. Historian Julie Greene has argued that the early, Gompers-led AFL was not apolitical but that the organization followed Gompers's insistence that "only trade union members and leaders should determine the shape of American labor politics" and that "party politics must be kept out of the trade unions." Both of these tenets precluded an alliance between the AFL (as long as Gompers was its president) and an agrarian-based third party (Greene, *Pure and Simple Politics*, 3 [first quote], 61 [second quote]).

11. The Knights reported 220,607 members in 1889, while the AFL reported 200,000. Knights membership cited in Ware, *Labor Movement*, 66; AFL membership cited in the *Report of Proceedings of the Twenty-Fourth Annual Convention*, 16. The AFL membership figure is given in rounded numbers on a graph showing annual membership. Foner, *History*, 171 n., states that the official AFL membership figures from this period are exaggerated.

12. See chap. 5.

13. It is unclear whether the Knights' choice of Atlanta as the site of the General Assembly meeting of 1889 reflected a desire on the part of Knights leaders to increase the Order's ties with the Southern Farmers' Alliance. While the Knights' General Executive Board chose Atlanta in July 1889 after Alliance and Agricultural Wheel leaders had contacted Powderly, the Knights' previous General Assembly, meeting in Indianapolis in November 1888, had already decided that the following year's meeting would be held in either Atlanta, New Orleans, or Albany, New York. See the *Atlanta Constitution*, 28 November 1888, 17 July 1889. Atlanta was the home to an important Southern Alliance newspaper, the *Southern Alliance Farmer*, and the Georgia Farmers' Alliance state cooperative exchange, which enabled Alliance members to purchase agricultural supplies and other staple goods at discounted prices. Of the nine Georgia counties with more than a thousand Alliance members in 1890, seven were within forty miles of Atlanta. On the Alliance state exchange and its establishment in Atlanta see McMath, *Populist Vanguard*, 49; Davis, *Henry Grady's New South*, 128. On the Georgia counties with the greatest Alliance membership in 1890 see the *Atlanta Constitution*, 19–20 August 1890.

14. *Atlanta Constitution*, 13–16 November 1889 (quote from 13 November issue).

15. Birmingham, "The Knights of Labor," 10–11.

16. *JKL*, 16 January 1890. On Beaumont's third-party advocacy during 1889 and 1890 see Phelan, *Grand Master Workman*, 250; Birmingham, "The Knights of Labor," 29.

17. Hicks, *The Populist Revolt*, 113–20; McMath, *Populist Vanguard*, 86–87; Steiner, "Toilers," 406–7, 410.

18. Hicks, *The Populist Revolt*, 119–21; McMath, *Populist Vanguard*, 87; Morgan, *History*, 180–81; Steiner, "Toilers," 407–8.

19. Steiner, "Toilers," 410–15; McMath, *Populist Vanguard*, 86; Phelan, *Grand Master Workman*, 249.

20. The complete text of the agreement between the Southern Alliance and the Knights is reprinted in Morgan, *History*, 171–73.

21. Birmingham, "The Knights of Labor," 23–24; McMath, *Populist Vanguard*, 94; Grob, *Workers and Utopia*, 85; Phelan, *Grand Master Workman*, 182, 190.

22. Ayers, *The Promise*, 245–46 (first quote on 246, citing the David Schenck diary, 8 December 1890); *Tarboro (N.C.) Tarborough Southerner*, 30 January 1890 (all other quotes); Knights of Labor, Raleigh Assembly, Minute Book, 27 January 1890; Steelman, *North Carolina Farmers' Alliance*, 55; Phelan, *Grand Master Workman*, 275; Garlock, *Guide*, 362–63.

23. Garlock, "A Structural Analysis," 235; Garlock, *Guide*, 353–68. On the growth of the Knights in North Carolina in 1890 see also the *Wilson (N.C.) Advance*, 1 May 1890. In this article Knights State Secretary-Treasurer Tonnoffski is reported as saying that "the confederation of the Knights and the Alliance upon certain lines has had the effect of allaying a great deal of the once very strong feeling against the Knights," and he makes the rather doubtful assertion that the North Carolina Knights then had 20,000 members in 275 local assemblies, "the membership . . . about equally divided between the races." See also H. H. Perry to Elias Carr, 2 May 1890, quoted in Ali, "Black Populism," 54, for anecdotal evidence of the growth of the Knights among African Americans in North Carolina at that time.

24. Letter from Sanges in the *JUL*, 20 June 1889; Sanges to Powderly, 2 December 1889 (quote), Powderly Papers, reel 31.

25. According to Oestreicher ("A Note," 107), the national Order's dues-paying membership rose from about 120,000 for the quarter ending 1 January 1890 to nearly 140,000 for the quarter ending 1 July 1890.

26. *Report on Population*, pt. 1, 168; letter from John L. Flynn in the *JKL*, 3 April 1890 (quotes); Hair, *Bourbonism*, 155, 184–85.

27. Brittain, "Negro Suffrage," 93.

28. *Alabama Sentinel*, 27 July 1889.

29. *Alabama Sentinel*, 10 August 1889.

30. *Alabama Sentinel,* 7 April 1888, 2 November (second quote), 9 November (letter from F. L. Fielder, third and fourth quotes), 16 November (letter from E.M., fifth and sixth quotes), 7 December (first quote) 1889; see also the letter from Mrs. Ira Campbell in the *JUL,* 28 November 1889.

31. Letter from John Staybolt in the *Alabama Sentinel,* 7 December 1889.

32. *Alabama Sentinel,* 11 January 1890.

33. Letter from George W. Hull in the *JKL,* 10 July 1890. See also a letter from J. J. Ragsdale in *JKL,* 22 May 1890; *Alabama Sentinel,* 28 June 1890.

34. Brittain, "Negro Suffrage," 93.

35. Rogers, *The One-Gallused Rebellion,* chap. 8.

36. *Alliance Journal* (Montgomery), December 1889, quoted in Saloutos, *Farmer Movements,* 105.

37. *Alliance Journal* (Montgomery), n.d., quoted in *Carrollton (Ala.) West Alabamian,* 12 February 1890, quoted in Rogers, *The One-Gallused Rebellion,* 139.

38. *Alliance Journal* (Montgomery), n.d., quoted in *Centreville (Ala.) Bibb Blade,* 28 February 1890, quoted in Rogers, *The One-Gallused Rebellion,* 144.

39. Rogers, *The One-Gallused Rebellion,* 78, 266–67.

40. *Alabama Sentinel,* 26 April 1890. Subsequent events would prove the *Sentinel*'s faith in Johnston to have been ill founded; elected governor in 1896, Johnston, according to a recent study of convict labor in Alabama, "talked reform, but when it came to prisons, his administration set improvement back thirty years," and the state did not abolish the convict lease system until 1928 (Curtin, *Black Prisoners,* 164 [quote], 167). For a sketch of Johnston's life and career see Perman, "Joseph F. Johnston," in Webb and Armbrester, *Alabama Governors,* 127–33.

41. Head, "The Development," 147.

42. *JKL,* 24 July 1890.

43. Letter from John H. Robertson in *JKL,* 5 June 1890.

44. Wheeler, "The People's Party," 166; *Arkansas Gazette,* 11 June 1890 (quote). On the rise (albeit a slight one) and fall of the National Union Labor Party see Andrew D. McNitt, "Union Labor Party, 1887–1888," in Ness and Ciment, *The Encyclopedia,* 3:569–71.

45. *Arkansas Gazette,* 11 June 1890.

46. *Arkansas Gazette,* 11, 12 June 1890; *Biographical and Historical Memoirs of Eastern Arkansas,* 282; letter from Charles M. B. Cox in the *JUL,* 22 August 1889 (quote).

47. Bayliss, "Public Affairs," 316; Dubin, *United States Congressional Elections,* 271, 286 n. 3, 287.

48. Bayliss, "Public Affairs," 315–16; letter from Robertson in the *JKL,* 5 June 1890 (quote).

49. Moneyhon, *Arkansas,* 89.

50. *Biennial Report, 1892,* 50. This report includes the results of the gubernatorial elections of 1890 and 1892.

51. Dubin, *United States Congressional Elections,* 287; Wheeler, "The People's Party," 156; Schlesinger, *The Almanac,* 370. The Lodge Election Bill, or "Force Bill," passed in the House of Representatives but failed in the Senate.

52. Dubin, *United States Congressional Elections,* 286 n. 2; Wheeler, "The People's Party," 168; *Congressional Record,* 1890, vol. 21, pt. 4, 3276, pt. 9, 8840–41, pt. 11, 10456; 1891, vol. 22, pt. 2, 1503, pt. 4, 3516 (quote); Nixon, "The Cleavage," 28–31. Featherston's bill "to increase the volume of money on a real estate . . . basis" was a call for the enactment of the "land loan" proposal that the Southern Farmers' Alliance had added to the subtreasury plan; see Saloutos, *Farmer Movements,* 122. On the circumstances surrounding Featherston's election to the U.S. House of Representatives see above.

53. Wheeler, "The People's Party," 168; Dubin, *United States Congressional Elections,* 279, 285, 287. For a brief discussion of election contests during the Gilded Age that underscores the unlikelihood of legislative bodies unseating a member of the majority party see Summers, *Party Games,* 114–15.

54. D. F. Tomson, H. H. Wilson, J. W. McSlarrow, H. H. Dill, and J. Frank Williams to Powderly, 2 January 1889, Powderly Papers, reel 28. Someone other than Tomson must have signed his name to this letter, since it is misspelled as "Thompson." See also the letter from Dill in the *JUL,* 1 November 1888, and the letters from John H. Robertson in the issues dated 22 November and 20 December 1888. Knights of Labor General Secretary-Treasurer John W. Hayes claimed that nationally the Knights' involvement in the political campaigns of 1888 cost the Order some 55,000 members (Phelan, *Grand Master Workman,* 250–51).

55. *JUL,* 28 February, 28 March, 11, 18, 25 April (letter from J. M. Temple), 9, 16 May, 6 June (letter from J. C. Hollingsworth) 1889; *Arkansas Gazette,* 20 August 1890 (quote); Tomson et al. to Powderly, 2 January 1889; *JKL,* 11 September 1890.

56. Woodward, *Origins,* 235–37; Goodwyn, *The Populist Moment,* 144; Holmes, "The Southern Farmers' Alliance"; McMath, *Populist Vanguard,* 96; McMath, *American Populism,* 130, 147 (quote).

57. Woodward, *Origins,* 204, 238; Kantrowitz, *Ben Tillman,* 147–49.

58. Woodward, *Origins,* 238; Barr, *Reconstruction,* 118; letter from John C. Roach in the *JKL,* 11 December 1890. Woodward wrote that during Hogg's first several months in office the state legislature approved a law "abolishing the convict lease." In fact, however, the convict lease system did not end in Texas until 1912. See Walker, *Penology for Profit,* 188–89.

59. Powderly to John W. Hayes, 20 April 1890, quoted in McLaurin, *The Knights of Labor,* 177.

264 Notes to Chapter Four

60. Birmingham, "The Knights of Labor," 29, 35, 38; Phelan, *Grand Master Workman*, 250, 266 n. 75; *Proceedings of the Fourteenth Regular Session of the General Assembly [of the Knights of Labor]* (1890), 70–71 (quote on 71); *JKL*, 16 October, 25 December 1890.

61. McMath, *Populist Vanguard*, 94, 107–10; Hicks, *The Populist Revolt*, 207–8; Goodwyn, *Democratic Promise*, 227–30; Argersinger, *Populism and Politics*, 81; Birmingham, "The Knights of Labor," 39, 41 (quote); Rogers, *The One-Gallused Rebellion*, 195; *Toccoa (Ga.) News and Piedmont Industrial Journal*, 19 September 1891.

62. McMath, *Populist Vanguard*, 110–11.

63. Argersinger, *Populism and Politics*, 81–82; Goodwyn, *The Populist Moment*, 151.

64. Birmingham, "The Knights of Labor," 40, 50 (quote, citing the *National Economist*, 4 April 1891).

65. Ibid., 52–53; Hicks, *The Populist Revolt*, 212–13; Goodwyn, *Democratic Promise*, 245–46; McMath, *American Populism*, 145–46; *Atlanta Constitution*, 20 May 1891 (first quote); *NYT*, 20 May 1891 (second quote).

66. Hicks, *The Populist Revolt*, 213–15; Goodwyn, *Democratic Promise*, 247–48; McMath, *American Populism*, 146; *Atlanta Constitution*, 21 May 1891; *NYT*, 21 May 1891.

67. *NYT*, 21 May 1891; Goodwyn, *Democratic Promise*, 40–41, 174, 246; McMath, *Populist Vanguard*, 127–28; Rodriquez, "Urban Populism," 113–14; *JKL*, 12 February 1891; McMath, *American Populism*, 144–45.

68. Hill, *Dallas*, 33–34; Winkler, *Platforms*, 293, 297; McMath, *Populist Vanguard*, 71; *Southern Mercury*, 6 November 1888. McMath notes that Louisiana, Texas, and Alabama were the first southern states to establish "nuclei of the People's party" in 1891 (*Populist Vanguard*, 128). The Louisiana People's Party held its first state convention in October 1891 (Hair, *Bourbonism*, 216–19), while the Alabama People's Party did not hold a state convention until June 1892 (Webb, *Two-Party Politics*, 105–6).

69. Winkler, *Platforms*, 293–97 (quotes on 297).

70. Hill, *Dallas*, 35–37; Rodriquez, "Urban Populism," 268, 332, including n. 44; Cantrell, *Kenneth and John B. Rayner*, 203–5 (quote on 204, citing Rayner to Macune, 12 November 1891).

71. T. P. Towns to Powderly, 8 June 1890, Powderly Papers, reel 33; John T. Braud to Powderly, 22 July 1890, Powderly Papers, reel 33 (quote, original spelling unaltered); letter from J.F.F. (James F. Foster) in the *JUL*, 16 June 1888; Dubin, *United States Congressional Elections*, 287. Both of these letters to Powderly are stamped "NO ANSWER REQUIRED." Historian George L. Jones notes that "Felton's opposition to the Alliance's subtreasury scheme virtually doomed his chances of success" in 1890 ("William H. Felton," 313). At least one sub-Alliance in the Seventh District unanimously passed a resolution "disapprov[ing] all bolting

and independentism" and pledging to "support the [D]emocratic nominee, R. W. Everett, for [C]ongress," the Alliance's supposed nonpartisan character notwithstanding. See the letter from J.W.B. in the *Southern Alliance Farmer*, 14 October 1890. On Felton's efforts to abolish the convict lease system in Georgia see above.

72. Holmes, "The Georgia Alliance Legislature," 497; *Journal of the House of Representatives of the State of Georgia*, 1134; Bonner, "The Alliance Legislature," 169; McLaurin, *Paternalism*, 125.

73. Shapiro, *A New South Rebellion*, 79 (quote), 81, 84, 86–87.

74. Ibid., 8, 89–90, 123.

75. *Nashville Weekly Toiler*, 21 November (letter from Thomas F. Carrick), 12 December 1888 (letter from S. W. Beddingfield [quotes]), 14 August 1889 (letter from Carrick).

76. Hart, *Redeemers*, 173–75, 189; Shapiro, *A New South Rebellion*, 103–4, 130–31, 139–43, 179–81; Lester, "Grassroots Reform," 306–7.

77. *Macon (Ga.) Telegraph*, 3 December 1886.

78. Holmes, "Arkansas Cotton Pickers Strike"; Foner and Lewis, *The Black Worker during the Era*, 286, 330–64; Biegert, "Legacy of Resistance"; Gaither, *Blacks*, 13–16; Ali, "Black Populism," 82, 111–17. According to Holmes, some black pickers struck on one farm near Palestine, Texas, but the farm owner fired them, and that settled the matter ("Arkansas Cotton Pickers Strike," 113–14). Gaither notes that a "minor strike was reported in the area of Florence and Orangeburg, South Carolina" (*Blacks*, 15).

79. Holmes, "The Demise," 194; *JKL*, 27 August 1891; Ali, "Black Populism," 118.

80. Holmes, "Leflore County Massacre."

81. Ayers, *The Promise*, 146–49; Perman, *Struggle for Mastery*, 72–74, 83–87. As Perman notes, the Farmers' Alliance played a major role in calling for the constitutional convention that produced the disfranchisement measures, and Alliancemen numbered 55 of the 134 delegates at the convention. On the other hand, as J. Morgan Kousser has pointed out, Mississippi Farmers' Alliance leader and future Populist gubernatorial candidate Frank Burkitt, a delegate at the constitutional convention, "refused to sign the constitution" because he "opposed disfranchising anyone, white or black" (Kousser, *The Shaping*, 140, 142 [quotes]).

82. Kousser, *The Shaping*, 124–30; Graves, *Town and Country*, 164–74, 282 n. 19 (statistics on illiteracy are taken from the U.S. census of 1890, quoted on 166); Perman, *Struggle for Mastery*, 62–64.

83. Palmer, *"Man over Money,"* 169.

84. Hart, *Redeemers*, 173.

85. The *NYT* noted that Gompers "has been here [at the Cincinnati conference]

observing the course of events." "He does not predict," the report added, "but it is surmised that the federation [the AFL] may decide to join the People's Party in the campaign" (21 May 1891). On the membership of the Knights of Labor during the early 1890s, which fluctuated between January 1890 and January 1892 at levels far below those of the Order's heyday and then entered a steady decline, see Oestreicher, "A Note," 107.

86. The only northeastern states to send representatives to the Ocala convention of the Southern Farmers' Alliance in December 1890 were New York and Pennsylvania (Dunning, *Farmers' Alliance History*, 294). Alliance membership figures for July 1890 included only three northeastern states, New York, New Jersey, and Pennsylvania, each of which reportedly had only five hundred Alliance members at that time (*Appleton's Annual Cyclopaedia . . . 1890*, n.s. 15, 301). Membership statistics for the Knights of Labor by district or state assembly are not available after 1888, but available figures indicate a sharp decline in the Knights' membership in the Northeast by that date, and the Knights' ongoing decline after that date suggests that membership figures in the Northeast did not recover. On the decline of the Knights' membership in northern (as well as some southern and midwestern) district assemblies between July 1886 and July 1888 see Sanders, *Roots of Reform*, 52 (table 3.2). See also the *New York Tribune* on the "disheartening" decline of the Knights "in the industrial and manufacturing centres" of New England, the mid-Atlantic states, and the West (13 August 1889).

87. Hicks, *The Populist Revolt*, 223–30 (226 n. 58 lists the number of delegates sent to the St. Louis conference by each major organization represented); McMath, *American Populism*, 160–63; Shaw, *The Wool-Hat Boys*, 52–53.

88. Birmingham, "The Knights of Labor," 69–70 (platform quote on 69); *St. Louis Post-Dispatch*, 24 February 1892. On the relationship between the Knights of Labor and the Woman's Christian Temperance Union, including Frances Willard's involvement with the Knights and the Knights' support for woman's suffrage, see Dyer, "Combatting," chaps. 3–5.

89. Abramowitz, "The Negro," 263; Gaither, *Blacks*, 36–37; Shaw, *The Wool-Hat Boys*, 54. These accounts differ slightly in details but agree on the important points of this episode.

90. Gaither, *Blacks*, 41. Gaither writes, "It appears that there were only four black delegates [at the Omaha convention], one each from Kansas and Virginia, and two members with the Texas Committee." At least two other southern state People's Parties, those of Alabama and Arkansas, appointed a black delegate, although it is unclear if either actually attended the Omaha convention. On Alabama see Webb, *Two-Party Politics*, 106. On Arkansas see Wheeler, "The People's Party," 238 n. 36.

91. James, "American Labor," 480.

92. Knights (or former Knights) from Texas who served as delegates to Omaha included William R. Lamb and H. S. P. "Stump" Ashby. See Birmingham, "The Knights of Labor," 74; Winkler, *Platforms,* 314; *Southern Mercury,* 6 November 1888. The Arkansas delegation at Omaha included at least three men who were members of the Knights of Labor at that time: Thomas Fletcher, J. W. Dollison, and J. B. Suttler. See the *Arkansas Gazette,* 22 June 1892, 23 March 1894; letter from Charles M. B. Cox in the *JUL,* 22 August 1889; J. B. Suttler to Powderly, 30 September 1892, Powderly Papers, reel 39; John H. Robertson to W. B. W. Heartsill, 17 May 1894, Heartsill Papers. The Georgia delegation included at least two men who had been members of the Knights of Labor during the 1880s, Charles C. Post and Silas C. Reed Jr. See the *Atlanta People's Party Paper,* 10 March, 1 July 1892; Powderly to C. C. Post, 5 August 1884, Powderly Papers, reel 46; Walsh, " 'Horny-Handed Sons of Toil,' " 267.

93. Birmingham, "The Knights of Labor," 74–75; Grob, *Workers and Utopia,* 96. Powderly's refusal to accept delegate's credentials from the Pennsylvania People's Party may have stemmed in part from his ties to that state's Republican Party; see James, "T. V. Powderly," 455–56; Weir, *Knights Unhorsed,* 165–66.

94. *JKL,* 7 July 1892.

95. The Omaha resolutions are reprinted in Hicks, *The Populist Revolt,* 443–44.

96. Birmingham, "The Knights of Labor," 74–75. For a written sample of Donnelly's rhetorical skills see McMath, *American Populism,* 161–62.

97. The Omaha platform is reprinted in Hicks, *The Populist Revolt,* 439–43.

98. Birmingham, "The Knights of Labor," 72 (Powderly quote), 75.

99. By May 1892 it had become painfully apparent to Powderly himself that Gompers had usurped him as the leader of the American labor movement. During that month Powderly ruefully noted to John W. Hayes that "Sam Gompers is to orate at the trade union picnic" at Powderly's hometown of Scranton, Pennsylvania, while "I am to occupy a place on the sidewalk" (Powderly to Hayes, 1 May 1892, quoted in Ware, *Labor Movement,* 374).

100. On the founding of the Tennessee People's Party by former Union Laborites see Hart, *Redeemers,* 185.

101. Letter from W.F. in the *Nashville Weekly Toiler,* 4 May 1892. On the Democrats' nomination of Turney see Lester, "Grassroots Reform," 310, 313, 317–40; Hart, *Redeemers,* 179–89. Unfortunately, the letter from W.F. does not indicate which city, town, or district he lived in, although the author does make reference to "my miner friends," which might suggest that he lived in a mining region of east or middle Tennessee.

102. On the conversion of the *Nashville Weekly Toiler* (and its editor, L. K. Taylor) to Populism in the spring of 1892 see Lester, "Grassroots Reform," 334–36; Hart, *Redeemers*, 185.

## Chapter Five. *Southern Labor and Southern Populism, 1892–1896*

1. *People's Party Paper*, 10 March 1892.

2. Oestreicher, "A Note," 106–7; *JKL*, 2 June 1892; Gompers, "Organized Labor," 93–94. Emphasis is in the original quote.

3. McLaurin, *The Knights of Labor*, 179.

4. Newby, *Plain Folk*, esp. chaps. 1–3; Hall et al., *Like a Family*, 31–45, 52–53, 56, 146–47, 153–54; Tullos, *Habits of Industry*, 175–77; Letwin, *The Challenge*, 26–27, 59; Beatty, *Alamance*, 172–73, 175–76, 181–83; Walsh, " 'Horny-Handed Sons of Toil,' " 27, 46, 63–64, 71–72, 77–78, 191, 194, 286–89. On the composition of southern Knights of Labor local assemblies see Garlock, *Guide*. A rare surviving Knights of Labor local assembly minute book provides detailed information about the membership of LA 239 in the coal-mining community of Greenwood, Arkansas, upon its formation in February 1892. The thirty-two charter members included twenty-one miners, two farmers, two grocers, one grocer's clerk, another clerk, one engineer, one coal weighman, one teamster, one painter, and one member for whom no occupation is listed. Two more members, a farmer and a printer, were initiated at the assembly's first meeting. Greenwood Knights of Labor Minute Book, 1892–95, minutes of 20 February 1892, Heartsill Papers.

5. Flamming, *Creating the Modern South*, 73–74; Walsh, " 'Horny-Handed Sons of Toil,' " 286–88.

6. Shaw, *The Wool-Hat Boys*, 170; McLaurin, *Paternalism*, 121–22.

7. See the *Kosciusko (Miss.) Clod-Hopper*, n.d., quoted in the *National Economist*, 6 September 1890, and the *Searcy Arkansas Economist*, n.d., quoted in the *National Economist*, 27 June 1891, for such defenses of the subtreasury plan. For more on this point see Palmer, *"Man over Money,"* 107, 109–10. For a specific example of a Georgia town laborer expressing opposition to the subtreasury plan on the grounds mentioned here see John T. Braud to Powderly, 22 July 1890, Powderly Papers, reel 33.

8. For a discussion of the relative strength or weakness of the People's Party in the various southern states see Ayers, *The Promise*, 275–81. See also the state-by-state listing of popular votes for Populist presidential candidate James B. Weaver in 1892 in Goldinger, *Presidential Elections*, 117. On the sparse activity of the Greenback-Labor Party in Georgia see Green, "Ben E. Green."

9. Winkler, *Platforms*, 293–99 (quote on 299).

10. Ibid., 300–301, 314–16; Barr, *Reconstruction*, 128–29, 141. The Populist state ticket initially included a railroad worker, C. C. Drake of Fort Worth, as the nominee for state comptroller. Drake subsequently withdrew from the ticket, however, and ran for the U.S. House of Representatives as a Republican. See Saunders, "The Ideology," 30–31, 43.

11. *JKL*, 31 December 1891, 18 August 1892; Rodriquez, "Urban Populism," 142, 184–85; Hill, *Dallas*, 38. The Texas State Federation of Labor was formed in 1889; see Hill, *Dallas*, 64.

12. *Alabama Sentinel*, 20 February 1892; *JKL*, 14 April 1892 (quotes); *Report on Population*, pt. 1, 54.

13. *Alabama Sentinel*, 4 June 1892; *JKL*, 26 May 1892 (quotes).

14. Head, "The Development," 51–52, 131–32, 135, 143–47; Garlock, *Guide*, 3–9; *Birmingham Labor Advocate*, 4 June 1892.

15. Head, "The Development," 69–72; Abernathy, "The Knights of Labor," 73–74; Rogers, *The One-Gallused Rebellion*, 206–7; Webb, *Two-Party Politics*, 104; *JKL*, 14 April 1892; *Alabama Sentinel*, 31 March 1888, 4 June 1892 (quote); *Labor Advocate*, 4 June 1892. Jere Dennis edited and published the *Labor Advocate* at this time; on his activities as a Populist see above.

16. Steelman, *North Carolina Farmers' Alliance*, 259–60; *Report on Population*, pt. 1, 423–24; Garlock, *Guide*, 353–68.

17. Grob, *Workers and Utopia*, 96.

18. Garlock, *Guide*, 361, 366.

19. *JKL*, 11 February 1892 (quotes). The demand for the issue of a national circulating currency directly to the people is referred to in this article as "the fourteenth section of the principles of the Knights of Labor." For a list of those principles, expressed in the Order's platform preamble, see *JKL*, 30 January 1890. The Populists' Cincinnati platform of 1891 is reprinted in Hicks, *The Populist Revolt*, 433–35.

20. *JKL*, 5 May (quote), 2 June 1892; Garlock, *Guide*, 362–63; Steelman, *North Carolina Farmers' Alliance*, 216–17.

21. Noblin, *Leonidas LaFayette Polk*, 284–93; *NYT*, 6 July 1892.

22. Israel, *Student's Atlas*, 76–77; Birmingham, "The Knights of Labor," 77 (Powderly quote).

23. *Appleton's Annual Cyclopaedia . . . 1892*, 626–27; Krause, *The Battle*, chap. 1; Phelan, *Grand Master Workman*, 258. The figures on fatalities given here are taken from *Appleton's* and differ from those given by Krause on page 3 of his book. Laurie gives yet another set of figures (*Artisans*, 202). The Omaha resolutions are reprinted in Hicks, *The Populist Revolt*, 443–44.

24. Watson quoted in Woodward, *Tom Watson*, 206. Historian Norman Pollack has suggested that Watson was less a champion of labor than these comments might

suggest. According to Pollack, Watson "placed his opposition to Pinkertons within a broader context of public order which pronounced equally unacceptable the supposed excesses of working people" (*The Just Polity*, 204–5).

25. *JKL*, 28 July 1892. The Knights of Labor General Executive Board members present at the hearings were John Devlin, A. W. Wright, and John W. Hayes.

26. *National Economist*, 16 July (second quote), 30 July (first quote) 1892.

27. *JKL*, 4 August, 1, 29 September, 6 October, 3 November 1892; James, "T. V. Powderly," 455–56.

28. *JKL*, 3 November 1892.

29. Grob, *Workers and Utopia*, 96; Ware, *Labor Movement*, 369; Israel, *Student's Atlas*, 88–89.

30. For evidence of the continuity between the Union Labor Party and the People's Party in Arkansas see the coverage of the Populist state convention in the *Arkansas Gazette*, 22 June 1892. Many of the Populist leaders mentioned therein were former Union Laborites, including Charles E. Cunningham (an old Granger and Greenbacker), L. P. Featherston, Isaac McCracken, J. W. Dollison, Reuben CarlLee, and John H. Robertson.

31. The members of the Arkansas People's Party campaign committee of 1892 are identified on the letterhead of John H. Robertson to Powderly, 31 August 1892, Powderly Papers, reel 39. In addition to Robertson and Fletcher, J. B. Suttler and J. W. Dollison both belonged to the Knights of Labor as well. On the membership of these men in the Knights see the letter from Charles M. B. Cox in the *JUL*, 22 August 1889; *JKL*, 17 September 1891, 6 October 1892; Suttler to Powderly, 30 September 1892, Powderly Papers, reel 39; *Arkansas Gazette*, 23 March 1894; Robertson to W. B. W. Heartsill, 17 May 1894, 31 August 1896, Heartsill Papers.

32. Letter from M. S. Richey in the *JKL*, 21 July 1892.

33. Suttler to Heartsill, 29 February 1892, Heartsill Papers.

34. Baskett, "Miners Stay Away!" 111–13.

35. Horace Addis to Heartsill, 10 August 1890, Heartsill Papers.

36. Heartsill to C. R. Breckenridge, 23 February 1885, Heartsill Papers, emphasis in original. Heartsill wrote to Democratic congressman Breckenridge seeking help in obtaining the position of register of the land office at Dardanelle, Arkansas. In 1892 Heartsill ran against Breckenridge for the latter's congressional seat.

37. Greenwood Knights of Labor Minute Book, 12 March 1892, Heartsill Papers.

38. Suttler to Heartsill, 29 March 1892 (first of two letters of that date), Heartsill Papers.

39. Suttler to Powderly, 30 September 1892.

40. Suttler to Heartsill, 11 August 1892, Heartsill Papers.

41. *JKL*, 6 October 1892.

42. *JKL*, 27 October 1892, 19 September 1895.

43. Wheeler, "The People's Party," 235 (quote from the People's Party platform), 326.

44. A number of historians have examined convict labor in the late-nineteenth- and early-twentieth-century South. See, for example, Ayers, *Vengeance and Justice*; Walker, *Penology for Profit*; Lichtenstein, *Twice the Work*; Mancini, *One Dies*; Oshinsky, *Worse than Slavery*; Curtin, *Black Prisoners*.

45. This platform appears in the *Arkansas Gazette*, 22 June 1892.

46. Wheeler, "The People's Party," 272 (quoting the *Arkadelphia [Ark.] Siftings*, n.d., as quoted in the *Arkansas Gazette*, 16 July 1892).

47. Edwards, *Gendered Strife*, chap. 6; letter from R.J.C. in the *JUL*, 11 June 1887 (quote). For more on white southern Democrats' use of propaganda about the specter of black men raping white women as a political weapon against their opponents of both races see Gilmore, *Gender and Jim Crow*, 82–89, 91–92; Kantrowitz, *Ben Tillman*, 105–6.

48. *JKL*, 22 September 1892.

49. Degler, *The Other South*, 338.

50. See chaps. 3 and 4 above.

51. *Conway (Ark.) Faulkner County Wheel*, n.d., quoted in the *People's Party Paper*, 5 August 1892. See also Graves, *Town and Country*, 210–11, 214, on the Republicans' nomination of a state ticket in 1892.

52. Moore et al., *Congressional Quarterly's Guide*, 2:1419; J. B. Weaver to Powderly, 9 September 1892, Powderly Papers, reel 39.

53. Wheeler, "The People's Party," 304.

54. For the official results of the congressional elections of 1892 in Arkansas see Dubin, *United States Congressional Elections*, 295.

55. Wheeler, "The People's Party," 200–201; Dubin, *United States Congressional Elections*, 295; Martis, *The Historical Atlas*, 127; Henningson, "Northwest Arkansas"; Henningson, "Root Hog or Die."

56. Greenwood Knights of Labor Minute Book, 10 September 1892, Heartsill Papers; Dubin, *United States Congressional Elections*, 295; Martis, *The Historical Atlas*, 127; Baskett, "Miners Stay Away!" 114–16; Robertson to Heartsill, 4 October 1893, Heartsill Papers; *NYT*, 12 September 1892.

57. Heartsill to Suttler, 6 March 1892; Suttler to Heartsill, 5 May (first quote), 3 October (second quote), 6 October (third quote) 1892, Heartsill Papers.

58. The lack of campaign funds would continue to plague the People's Party in Arkansas and at the national level as well. See Durden, *The Climax of Populism*, 63. On the poll tax amendment to the state constitution that voters approved in 1892 see Kousser, *The Shaping of Southern Politics*, 125–27, 129; Graves, *Town and Country*, 185–94; Perman, *Struggle for Mastery*, 64–67.

59. Barr, *Reconstruction*, 131–40 (quote on 137).

60. Ibid.; Woodward, *Origins,* 204, 238; Barnes, *Farmers,* 138–39, 142–43.

61. Barr, *Reconstruction,* map inserted between 130 and 131, 139–40; Smith, "The Farmers' Alliance," 348–49, 351, 355, 360; Winkler, *Platforms,* 260, 646; Barnes, *Farmers,* 142 (quote); Garlock, *Guide,* 491–513; Saunders, "Ideology," 44 n. 90; Rodriquez, "Urban Populism," 183.

62. Cantrell and Barton, "Texas Populists," 661–62 (first quote on 662), 664; Abramowitz, "The Negro in the Populist Movement," 269 (other quotes).

63. Rogers, *The One-Gallused Rebellion,* 167–85, 198, 201–5, 207–20.

64. Ibid., 215.

65. Ibid., 140, 196–97, 209, 215; McMath, *Populist Vanguard,* 122.

66. *Alabama Sentinel,* 23 July 1892.

67. Rogers, *The One-Gallused Rebellion,* 213–14; Rogers et al., *Alabama,* 310 (quote, citing the *Union Springs [Ala.] Herald,* 15 June 1892).

68. *Alabama Sentinel,* 23 July 1892.

69. Rogers, *The One-Gallused Rebellion,* 221–22, 224 (first quote on 222, second on 224). The Republican Party did not nominate a state ticket in Alabama in 1892.

70. For a map showing which counties each candidate carried in Alabama's gubernatorial election in 1892 see ibid., 223. On counties that the Greenback-Labor Party, Independents, or the Labor Party of Alabama carried in Alabama elections in the late 1870s or 1880s see Roberts, "William Manning Lowe," 104, 108 n. 25, 119, 120, 121 n. 63; Webb, *Two-Party Politics,* 66, 71–72, 83–84; Flynt, *Poor but Proud,* 247–49; Abernathy, "The Knights of Labor," 74; Head, "The Development," 72; *NYT,* 9 August 1882; *Huntsville (Ala.) Weekly Democrat,* 13 September 1882; *Huntsville (Ala.) Gazette,* 30 September 1882. On the support of white laborers for the Democratic Party in Jefferson County during this period see McKiven, *Iron and Steel,* chap. 5; Letwin, *The Challenge,* 66–67, 97–99; *Alabama Sentinel,* 15 February, 29 March 1890, 28 November 1891, 13 February, 23 April, 13 August, 22 October 1892. On the results of the gubernatorial election of 1892 in the Jefferson County mining beats see *Alabama Sentinel,* 13 August 1892; Saunders, "Ideology," 41; Letwin, *The Challenge,* 99.

71. Shaw, *The Wool-Hat Boys,* 29–30, 37–38, 66; *People's Party Paper,* 25 February 1892 (quotes).

72. *People's Party Paper,* 25 February (all quotes except first), 5 August (letter from Charles S. Abney) 1892. The quotes and information from the issue of 25 February are drawn from three letters, one signed by Knights of Labor Local Assembly 5030, another by G. C. Williams, and the third by M. M. Conner (whose name was sometimes spelled "Connor" by others) and Sam G. Crouch. On Watson's decision not to enter the Democratic caucus but to join the first People's Party caucus instead see Woodward, *Tom Watson,* 190–93. On M. M. Conner's role in the

strike-lockout of 1886 see McLaurin, *Paternalism*, 100, 108, 111; Reed, "Augusta Textile Mills," 242; Hild, "The Knights of Labor," 47, 50–51; Walsh, "'Horny-Handed Sons of Toil,'" 255–56. The Knights of Labor motto was "That is the most perfect government in which an injury to one is the concern of all." See Powderly, *Thirty Years*, 248.

73. Woodward, *Tom Watson*, 205–7; *JKL*, 3 November 1892; *Congressional Record*, 52nd Cong., 1st sess., 1892, vol. 23, pt. 6, 5723.

74. Woodward, *Tom Watson*, 178 (third quote), 227, 234 (first two and last three quotes); Walsh, "'Horny-Handed Sons of Toil,'" 299 (fourth quote); Thomas E. Watson to Powderly, 8 October 1892; Watson to H. E. Taubeneck, 8 October 1892; Taubeneck to Powderly, 11 October 1892, Powderly Papers, reel 39.

75. Woodward, *Tom Watson*, 211–15, 241–42, 257–58 (quote on 257); *Augusta Chronicle*, 10 November 1892; Arnett, *The Populist Movement*, 145–46, 153–55; Saunders, "Ideology," 49–50; Shaw, *The Wool-Hat Boys*, 75–76; Walsh, "'Horny-Handed Sons of Toil,'" 316–19. As Arnett (*The Populist Movement*, 155), Woodward (*Tom Watson*, 241), and Shaw (*The Wool-Hat Boys*, 76) all point out, Populists in the Tenth District and elsewhere in Georgia also engaged in voting fraud, but they were unable to do so on the massive scale that the Democrats did.

76. Although Roswell lies in Fulton County, Georgia, today, it was part of Cobb County during this period. *Report of the General Executive Board [of the Knights of Labor], Thirteenth Regular Session* (1889), 20, Powderly Papers, reel 67; James F. Foster to John W. Hayes, 19 July 1890, 24 May 1891, Hayes Papers, reel 8.

77. Temple, *The First Hundred Years*, 453–56, 460–61; Scott, "Cobb County, Georgia," 101–3; *Marietta (Ga.) Journal*, 10 November 1892; *Atlanta Constitution*, 7 November 1894.

78. On the backlash engendered by the Knights of Labor's failed political campaigns in Athens see Hild, "The Knights of Labor," 111.

79. Stewart, "The Urban-Rural Dynamic," 174 (quote, citing the *Athens Weekly Banner*, 21 January 1890), 179–84.

80. Of the nineteen Georgia counties that historian Barton C. Shaw identified as "Populist strongholds," the Knights of Labor formed local assemblies in at least seven during 1886–87: Columbia, Forsyth, Gordon, Jefferson, Paulding, Taliaferro, and Warren. The Knights' membership in all of these counties included farmers or farm laborers. As well as can be determined, the Knights formed local assemblies in 37 percent of the state's counties that later became Populist strongholds but in only 27 percent of the Georgia counties (37 out of 136) that existed during the late nineteenth century. Shaw, *The Wool-Hat Boys*, x (map); Garlock, *Guide*, 52–59.

81. Horton, "Testing the Limits," 64–65; Foster with Scott, *Paulding County*, 33, 42; Hahn, *The Roots*, 131.

82. Hahn, *The Roots*, 137, 140; Foster with Scott, *Paulding County*, 230; Garlock, *Guide*, 57.

83. The precise date of the Alliance's entry into Georgia is uncertain, but according to Morgan, the first Alliance organizer to enter Georgia arrived in March 1887 (*History*, 116). On the Alliance in Paulding County see Foster with Scott, *Paulding County*, 237 (quote).

84. Letter from J.F.F. (James F. Foster) in the *JUL*, 16 June 1888; Garlock, *Guide*, 57. See also Hild, "The Knights of Labor," 132–34.

85. Dubin, *United States Congressional Elections*, 279; Shadgett, *The Republican Party*, 64–65, 110; Foster with Scott, *Paulding County*, 174–75, 202, 230–33; *Report on Population*, pt. 1, 407.

86. Garlock, *Guide*, 57; Foster with Scott, *Paulding County*, 237; Foster to Hayes, 14 August 1892, Hayes Papers, reel 8.

87. Foster with Scott, *Paulding County*, 238; *Dallas (Ga.) Paulding New Era*, 18 November 1892; Redmond, *Cemeteries*, 33; *JKL*, 4 August 1892; Hahn, *The Roots*, 280–81 (quote). The *JKL* article, a report on a meeting of the Georgia Knights of Labor State Assembly, spells Brintle's last name as "Brintts," but this undoubtedly is an error. The editor or compositor must have misread "Brintle," written in longhand, as "Brintts." A letter from James C. Sanges in the *JUL*, 20 June 1889, correctly spells Brintle's name and mentions that he is from Roxana (Paulding County) and an officer in the Knights of Labor State Assembly.

88. On the lack of votes received by Populist presidential candidate James B. Weaver and gubernatorial candidate William L. Peek in the urban counties of Georgia in 1892 relative to the rest of the state see Saunders, "Ideology," 42, 197 (chart 1), 198 (chart 2). See also Soule, "Populism," 445, on the lack of support for Populist candidates in the state's manufacturing areas.

89. Russell, *Atlanta*, 209, 213; *People's Party Paper*, 8 July, 12 August 1892; J. C. Sanges to Powderly, 16 July 1888, Powderly Papers, reel 27; H. N. Cramer to Powderly, 13 July 1889, Powderly Papers, reel 30; Hild, "A 'Flagrant and High-handed Outrage,'" 44–45; Shaw, *The Wool-Hat Boys*, 24, 72; Dubin, *United States Congressional Elections*, 295; *Atlanta Constitution*, 9 November 1892; Deaton, "James G. Woodward," 12–13. Russell refers to Cramer as "H.M.," but Cramer's letters to Powderly are clearly signed "H.N." Furthermore, *Weatherbe's Atlanta, Ga., Duplex City Directory 1886* lists only one Cramer whose first name begins with the letter H, one "Henry N. Cramer" (157).

90. Hild, "The Knights of Labor," chap. 3; J. F. Brown to Powderly, 4 July 1892, Powderly Papers, reel 38 (first quote); M. J. Lee to Powderly, 20 August 1892, Powderly Papers, reel 39; Powderly to Lee, 14 September 1892, Powderly Papers, reel 39; *JKL*, 1 September 1892 (last two quotes).

91. Garlock, *Guide*, 353–68; *JKL*, 2, 9 May 1895; Martis, *The Historical Atlas*, 127;

Dubin, *United States Congressional Elections,* 299; Steelman, *North Carolina Farmers' Alliance,* 110, 249; McLaurin, "The Knights of Labor," 313.

92. On Ray and Tonnoffski as Populists see Beckel, "Roots of Reform," 614 n. 97, 622. Garlock gives no evidence of any Knights of Labor local assemblies still existing in Raleigh in 1892 (*Guide,* 364), but a report in the *JKL* suggests that the Order was active in a soap manufactory in the city at that time (11 February 1892).

93. Dubin, *United States Congressional Elections,* 299.

94. Steelman, *North Carolina Farmers' Alliance,* 258–59; Garlock, *Guide,* 353–68; *JKL,* 1 September 1892 (letter from E.W. [quote]), 2, 9 May 1895.

95. Goldinger, *Presidential Elections,* 117; Webb, *Two-Party Politics,* 112. Webb notes that some Alabama Populists feared that the Republican state committee's endorsement of Weaver represented a deliberate strategy to take electoral votes away from Cleveland. Historians have debated whether Terence V. Powderly and other national Knights of Labor leaders were involved in such a Republican strategy in the South, sending GOP-funded Knights organizers into the region to drum up support for Weaver. The evidence that such a scheme was implemented is circumstantial at most, and at any rate Cleveland carried all eleven ex-Confederate states. See McLaurin, *The Knights of Labor,* 179; McMath, *Populist Vanguard,* 144; James, "T. V. Powderly," 455–56. McLaurin claims that "efforts by the Knights' national leadership on [Reuben F.] Kolb's behalf . . . were designed to encourage a large Populist turnout which could result in split ticket balloting at the presidential level and would thus throw the state's electors to the Republican presidential candidate, Benjamin Harrison." The veracity of this assertion seems doubtful, however, given that the Alabama gubernatorial election of 1892 occurred three months before the presidential election.

96. Steelman, *North Carolina Farmers' Alliance,* 249–50; Goldinger, *Presidential Elections,* 117; Dubin, *United States Congressional Elections,* 299.

97. Goldinger, *Presidential Elections,* 117.

98. Hicks, *The Populist Revolt,* 269.

99. Oestreicher, "A Note," 105 (quote), 107.

100. Falzone, *Terence V. Powderly,* 163–67; Phelan, *Grand Master Workman,* 245–48, 250–51; Weir, "Dress Rehearsal," 21–42.

101. Powderly to Hayes, 10 May 1893, quoted in Ware, *Labor Movement,* 375.

102. Phelan, *Grand Master Workman,* 251 (quote), 255–57; Weir, *Knights Unhorsed,* 161, 173–74; Falzone, *Terence V. Powderly,* 169–71. For Powderly's own account of his resignation see Powderly, *The Path I Trod,* 365–67. For an insider's view of the turbulent General Assembly meeting of 1893 and the circumstances surrounding Powderly's resignation see Robertson to Heartsill, 7 December 1893, Heartsill Papers.

103. *JKL,* 10 May 1894; *Statement of T. V. Powderly, to the Order of the Knights of*

*Labor* (Scranton, Pa.: Self-published, 31 May 1894), 34 (quote), in Heartsill Papers; Oestreicher, "A Note," 107. On Powderly's suspension from the Order in May 1894 see the *JKL*, 24 May 1894; Ware, *Labor Movement*, 375; Phelan, *Grand Master Workman*, 257; Weir, *Knights Unhorsed*, 176.

104. Foster to Hayes, 20 February 1894, Hayes Papers, reel 8.

105. Hayes to Foster, 9 June (quote), 21 June 1894, Hayes Papers, reel 8.

106. Letter from "An Observer" in the *Birmingham Hot Shots*, 23 September 1899, reprinted in the *JKL*, June 1900 (quote); Abernathy, "The Knights of Labor," 85–86.

107. List of current and suspended local assemblies in Arkansas, ca. 1894, Heartsill Papers; William Murray to Heartsill, 13 January 1894, Heartsill Papers (first quote); W. L. Lancaster to Heartsill, 22 October 1893, Heartsill Papers (second quote).

108. For a brief account of the national miners strike of 1894 see Fox, *United We Stand*, 44–47. Two recent books examine the Pullman strike of that year: Papke, *The Pullman Case*, and Schneirov, Stromquist, and Salvatore, *The Pullman Strike*.

109. Wheeler, "The People's Party," 322; Moneyhon, *Arkansas*, 110; Baskett, "Miners Stay Away!" 127–28. Fox notes, "Though there were only 13,000 union miners [in the UMWA nationwide], 100,000 men stopped work on April 21, 1894" (*United We Stand*, 45).

110. Wheeler, "The People's Party," 322; *Arkansas Gazette*, 12 July 1894. The governor referred to here is William M. Fishback. For a detailed account of the Pullman strike of 1894 see Ginger, *The Bending Cross*, chaps. 6–7.

111. Wheeler, "The People's Party," 326, including n. 26, 346–47 (quote on 347, citing the *Arkansas Gazette*, 21 July 1894).

112. Studies that deal at length with the depression that began in 1893 include Hoffman, *The Depression*, and Steeples and Whitten, *Democracy in Desperation*.

113. Robertson to Heartsill, 15 February 1894, Heartsill Papers (first quote); letter from R.S. in the *JKL*, 3 May 1894 (second quote); Foster to Heartsill, 1 May 1894, Heartsill Papers (third quote); J. W. Dollison to Heartsill, 23 June 1894, Heartsill Papers; Robertson to Heartsill, 27 July 1894, Heartsill Papers. It is not clear that Heartsill played any active role in the People's Party in 1894, but the letter from R.S. in the *JKL*, 3 May 1894, suggests that Heartsill was still a Populist at that time.

114. Wheeler, "The People's Party," 374; Dubin, *United States Congressional Elections*, 304. The Democratic gubernatorial candidate in 1894 was James P. Clarke.

115. Goldstein, "Labor Unrest," 88–90; Head, "The Development," 94–96; Ward and Rogers, *Labor Revolt*, 51–54; Letwin, *The Challenge*, 99.

116. Goldstein, "Labor Unrest," 95–99, 103; Head, "The Development," 96–98; Ward and Rogers, *Labor Revolt*, 59–67; Letwin, *The Challenge*, 101–2; Fox, *United We Stand*, 44–45.

117. Clark, *Populism*, 152; Goldstein, "Labor Unrest," 98–99; Ward and Rogers, *Labor Revolt*, 47 (Sovereign quote), 120–21; Hackney, *Populism*, 60–61; Flynt, *Poor but Proud*, 252; *JKL*, 15 March 1894.

118. Goldstein, "Labor Unrest," 105–12, 147; Ward and Rogers, *Labor Revolt*, 76–86, 91–92, 99–100, 119, 131–32; Hackney, *Populism*, 59–62; Huggins, "Bourbonism," 279 (quote); *JKL*, 24 May, 2 August 1894. Goldstein alone among the sources listed above says that Governor Jones sent troops to Camp Forney on 26 May ("Labor Unrest," 112).

119. Goldstein, "Labor Unrest," 126–37; Head, "The Development," 111–12; Ward and Rogers, *Labor Revolt*, 104–7 (Jones quoted on 106).

120. Goldstein, "Labor Unrest," 138–47; Ward and Rogers, *Labor Revolt*, 108–27; Hackney, *Populism*, 60–62; Letwin, *The Challenge*, 109–10; *NYT*, 1 August 1894; *JKL*, 9 August 1894 (on Sovereign in Alabama). The *JKL* merely reported that Sovereign had been "delivering addresses and organizing Local Assemblies" in Alabama, but given the timing of his visit, his pro-Jeffersonian Democratic/Populist statements during his March trip to the state (see above), and the strong pro-Kolb, anti-Oates editorial statements made in the *JKL* on 24 May and 2 August 1894, there can be little doubt that Sovereign spoke in favor of Kolb during his addresses.

121. Ward and Rogers, *Labor Revolt*, 128–29 (quote on 129).

122. Rogers, *The One-Gallused Rebellion*, 284 (map); Ward and Rogers, *Labor Revolt*, 129; Letwin, *The Challenge*, 111.

123. Goldstein, "Labor Unrest," 148–50; Head, "The Development," 103–6; Ward and Rogers, *Labor Revolt*, 130–36; Letwin, *The Challenge*, 111–16; Fox, *United We Stand*, 47.

124. Dubin, *United States Congressional Elections*, 304, 311, 312 n. 2; Martis, *The Historical Atlas*, 127.

125. Douty, "Early Labor Organization," 265; Dubin, *United States Congressional Elections*, 308; Martis, *The Historical Atlas*, 127.

126. Crow and Durden, *Maverick Republican*, 43–53 (quote on 50); Escott, *Many Excellent People*, 249, 251–52; Beatty, *Alamance*, 139–40; *Report on Population*, pt. 1, 423–24. On western North Carolina Republicans and fusion see also McKinney, *Southern Mountain Republicans*, 158–66.

127. Crow and Durden, *Maverick Republican*, 50; Dubin, *United States Congressional Elections*, 308, 312 n. 19.

128. Crow and Durden, *Maverick Republican*, 49; Beckel, "Roots of Reform," 645, 656; McMath, *Populist Vanguard*, 148. Butler's membership in the Knights of Labor is mentioned in Robertson to Heartsill, 31 August 1896, Heartsill Papers. It is unknown when Butler joined the Knights, but whatever local assembly he belonged to (most likely in Sampson County, his home) probably already existed by 1894, since few locals were organized later than that. Moreover, Butler's correspondence with

James R. Sovereign in 1894 would suggest that Butler was a member of the Order by then. On Butler's communications with General Master Workman Sovereign in 1894 see above.

129. David Schenck diary, 8 December 1890 (first quote), 12 December 1894 (second quote), quoted in Ayers, *The Promise,* 246 (first quote), 292 (second quote).

130. Crow and Durden, *Maverick Republican,* 49–50; Kousser, *The Shaping,* 185–87 (quote on 187); Ayers, *The Promise,* 293.

131. Honey, "Class, Race, and Power," 169 (first two quotes); Beeby, "'Equal Rights to All,'" 186 (third quote).

132. *JKL,* 28 September 1893 (quote), 4, 11 October, 22, 29 November 1894, 3 January 1895. For portrayals of the Knights of Labor as a moribund organization nationally by this time see (among others) Dubofsky and Dulles, *Labor in America,* 135–36, and in the South see McLaurin, *The Knights of Labor,* chap. 9.

133. *JKL,* 4 October 1894, 7, 21, 28 February, 7, 28 March, 11, 25 April, 2, 9, 23 May 1895; *Proceedings of the General Assembly of the Knights of Labor, Twentieth Regular Session* (1896), 118.

134. McLaurin, *The Knights of Labor,* 180–81; *JKL,* 23 January, 24 April (letter from Ellen Williams), 24 July, 7 August (letter from Sarah F. Law), 11 September (letter from Treaser Hill), 2 October (letter from Claborn Speller Jr.), 9, 23 October (letter from Betty E. Smallwood), 11 December (letter from Fannie Smith) 1890, 5 February (letter from H. W. Cherry), 12 February (letter from S. H. Fagins), 5 March (letter from D. H. Cherry), 23 April (letter from Betty C. [*sic*?] Smallwood), 11 June (letter from Fannie Smith), 13 August (letter from Bettie Marshall), 1, 29 October, 24, 31 December 1891, 28 January 1892, 14, 28 September, 16 November, 7 December 1893, 12 July, 23 August, 13 September 1894, 28 March, 11 April 1895.

135. *JKL,* 28 September 1893.

136. McMath, *American Populism,* 79, observes that "the Cleburne demands [of the Texas Farmers' Alliance] stand as a direct antecedent of the great Populist platforms of the 1890s" and that "all but four of the fifteen demands made at Cleburne were essentially the same as points addressed in the 1878 Reading preamble of the Knights of Labor, which was itself a recapitulation of earlier antimonopoly platforms." Key demands of the Populists' Omaha platform of 1892 that were already part of the Knights' platform include the issue by the federal government of circulating currency without the intervention of banks, the graduated income tax, postal savings banks, government ownership of railroads, telegraphs, and the telephone system, and similar demands regarding land reform (except that the Populists did not follow the Knights in endorsing the single tax upon land). For the Knights' Reading platform and subsequent revisions see Ware, *Labor Movement,* 377–80. For the Populists' Omaha platform see Hicks, *The Populist Revolt,* 439–43.

137. Hunt, "Marion Butler," 223, 244. The *JKL*, 4 October 1894, issued the same reminder to southern laborers in response to a report of low wages in North Carolina.

138. On North Carolina counties where the Knights had locals in 1894 see Garlock, *Guide*, 353–68; *JKL*, 2, 9 May 1895. The *JKL* articles list the counties covered by District Assemblies 80 and 81, which were formed in 1894. For a map showing which North Carolina counties belonged to which congressional districts at this time see Beeby, " 'Equal Rights,' " 167. On the congressional elections referred to here see Dubin, *United States Congressional Elections*, 308.

139. Beeby, " 'Equal Rights,' " 167–68; Dubin, *United States Congressional Elections*, 299, 308; Beckel, "Roots of Reform," 614 n. 97, 622, 650–51, 656–57, 670.

140. Martin, *The People's Party*, 67–68 (quote on 68).

141. Dubin, *United States Congressional Elections*, 301; Goodwyn, *Democratic Promise*, 331, 491, 509; Hill, *Dallas*, 40; Barr, *Reconstruction*, 57, 136–37, 139, 158–59; *NYT*, 3 November 1886.

142. Martin, *The People's Party*, 217; Powderly, *Thirty Years*, 244; Hill, *Dallas*, 38.

143. *JKL*, 29 June, 7 September (letter from S. B. Willyerd) 1893, 9 August 1894. DA 21 encompassed the following counties: Fannin, Grayson, Cook, Montague, Denton, and Collin. DA 21 held its district meetings at the Alliance Hall in Bonham. Regarding Beaumont's bid for Congress, since Oklahoma was a territory at that time, not a state, the position that he sought was not that of a congressional representative but rather that of a congressional delegate. On his unsuccessful campaign see Miller, *Oklahoma Populism*, 108–10, 116.

144. *JKL*, 19 February 1891 (letter from Charles W. Marsh), 28 September 1893 (quote); Garlock, *Guide*, 497–98. For a similar pro-Populist resolution from LA 1196 of Hopkins County, Texas, see the *JKL*, 21 September 1893.

145. Rodriquez, "Urban Populism," 295–96.

146. *JKL*, 5 October 1893, 22 March 1894 (letter from M. J. Gomes).

147. Letter from J. P. Diffey in *JKL*, 25 January 1894.

148. Letter from N. W. Ward in *JKL*, 8 March 1894.

149. Letter from M. J. Gomes in *JKL*, 21 June 1894.

150. Letter from W. I. Bralley in *JKL*, 22 November 1894.

151. *Record of the Proceedings of the Eighteenth Regular Session of the General Assembly [of the Knights of Labor]* (1894), 89–90; Garlock, *Guide*, 491–513.

152. Miles Crowley to Powderly, 2 December 1892, Powderly Papers, reel 39; Jacob and Ragsdale, *Biographical Directory*, 851. Crowley became a lawyer in 1892, but this did not make him the first lawyer to belong to the Knights of Labor, despite the fact that the Order's constitution barred lawyers from membership. See Weir, *Beyond Labor's Veil*, 217, 219–20; Beckel, "Roots of Reform," 482.

153. Hill, *Dallas*, 38–39; Rodriquez, "Urban Populism," 280–83; letters from James Fitzgerald in the *JKL*, 12 April (all quotes except the last), 14 June (last quote), 23 August 1894.

154. Letter from James Fitzgerald in *JKL*, 23 August 1894.

155. Martin, *The People's Party*, 68. See also Barr, *Reconstruction*, 157, 159; Saunders, "Ideology of Southern Populists," 113; and, on labor support for the People's Party in Fort Worth and Dallas in 1894, Rodriquez, "Urban Populism," 296–305, 309.

156. *JKL*, 13 September, 8 November 1894. Sovereign also addressed a joint meeting of laborers and Populists at the Dallas city hall auditorium on 31 October and then traveled north to Denison, Texas, to address labor organizations (Rodriquez, "Urban Populism," 305).

157. Barr, *Reconstruction*, 157–59; Cantrell and Barton, "Texas Populists," 672; Abramowitz, "The Negro in the Populist Movement," 269–70; Cantrell, *Kenneth and John B. Rayner*, 204–5, 208–12, 215–20; Dubin, *United States Congressional Elections*, 310.

158. Martin, *The People's Party*, 221 n. 47; Cantrell and Paschal, "Texas Populism," 31, including n. 2, 64–65. Davis filed a notice of contest with the U.S. House of Representatives but neglected to follow through by providing evidence to support his case.

159. Martin, *The People's Party*, 184–85, including 185 n. 72, 221 n. 47; Goodwyn, *Democratic Promise*, 332; Cantrell and Barton, "Texas Populists," 668–69, 671–72. Historians Gregg Cantrell and Kristopher B. Paschal offer a more circumspect judgment of the election involving Jerome Kearby, concluding that Kearby "may well have been a victim of . . . [Democratic] fraud, but if he was, the Democrats covered their tracks so well that neither Kearby's lawyers nor today's historians can prove it" ("Texas Populism," 66–67).

160. Letter from W. I. Bralley in the *JKL*, 22 November 1894.

161. Shaw, *The Wool-Hat Boys*, 101, 105, 107, 115–16, 167–70, 181–82; Palmer, *"Man over Money,"* 170–73.

162. Arnett, *The Populist Movement*, 180 (quote), 182–84; Shaw, *The Wool-Hat Boys*, 106–8, 115–16, 169; Felton, *My Memoirs*, 660; *JKL*, 1 November 1894. The number of Populist legislators elected in Georgia in 1894 varies according to the source. The *JKL* gives the figure fifty-three, while Arnett (*The Populist Movement*, 184) says fifty-two and Shaw (*The Wool-Hat Boys*, 126 n. 6) says forty-seven.

163. Dubin, *United States Congressional Elections*, 304. For a map showing the congressional districts of Georgia at this time see Shaw, *The Wool-Hat Boys*, unnumbered page opposite 1. Georgia Populist congressional candidates officially

received more than 40 percent of the vote in five districts in 1894, while Tom Watson's official figure of 39.3 percent would have been higher if not for fraud.

164. Felton, *My Memoirs*, 11, 644–53, 659–60; Roberts, "The Public Career," 408–24; Talmadge, *Rebecca Latimer Felton*, 40–42, 46–48, 62–66, 86; Jones, "William H. Felton," 313; Palmer, *"Man over Money,"* 169, 174; William H. Felton to S. J. McKnight, 25 August 1894 (quote), Felton Collection, reel 3. For similar rhetoric from Felton in 1877 see above.

165. Dubin, *United States Congressional Elections*, 257, 287, 304. Felton received 1,537 votes (23 percent of the total cast) in the Seventh District congressional election of 1886 but never declared himself a candidate that year (Dubin, *United States Congressional Elections*, 272; see also Jones, "William H. Felton," 299).

166. *Marietta (Ga.) Journal*, 6 November 1890, 8 November 1894; *Hustler of Rome* (Ga.), 8 November 1894; Garlock, *Guide*, 52–59.

167. Felton, *My Memoirs*, 654–77; John D. Cunningham to W. H. Felton, 8 November 1894, Felton Collection, reel 3; letter from Seaborn Wright in the *People's Party Paper*, 16 November 1894; Roberts, "The Public Career," 424–41; Talmadge, *Rebecca Latimer Felton*, 86–89; Shaw, *The Wool-Hat Boys*, 117–20.

168. Dubin, *United States Congressional Elections*, 304, 311; Woodward, *Tom Watson*, 269–77; Shaw, *The Wool-Hat Boys*, 117–18, 120–22; letter from F. B. Fitch ("Frauds Worse Than Ever") in the *People's Party Paper*, 9 November 1894; *Augusta Chronicle*, 3 October 1895. Watson contested his defeat in the October 1895 election but without success.

169. *Philadelphia Press*, n.d., quoted in the *JKL*, 24 January 1895; *Proceedings of the General Assembly of the Knights of Labor, Nineteenth Regular Session* (1895), 121, 123. Page 121 lists Sovereign's place of residence as Sulphur Springs, while page 123 lists Des Moines as his place of residence. But a letter written by Sovereign dated 29 December 1895 and published in the *JKL* on 23 January 1896 gives Sulphur Springs as his place of residence. For a lower estimate of the Knights' national membership in January 1895 than the one given here see Oestreicher, "A Note," 107.

170. Letwin, *The Challenge*, 112–13, 115–16; Fox, *United We Stand*, 47–48; Ginger, *The Bending Cross*, 172, 178–81; Currie, *Eugene V. Debs*, 25–28, 32, 36, 38; Salvatore, *Eugene V. Debs*, 138–39, 145–46.

171. Oestreicher, "A Note," 106; Ware, *Labor Movement*, 66.

172. *Report of Proceedings of the Sixteenth Annual Convention*, iii–v. The AFL counted its annual convention of 1896 as its sixteenth because the count included the conventions of its predecessor, the Federation of Organized Trades and Labor Unions, which dated back to 1881.

173. "List of Organizations Affiliated with the American Federation of Labor, International, National, State, Central, Local," enclosed with a letter from Samuel Gompers to Marion Butler, 17 February 1897, Butler Papers, reel 5.

174. Kaufman, "Samuel Gompers," 49–50 (quote from "political programme" plank ten on 50); Foner, *History*, 287–88; Pierce, "The Populist President," 14; *American Federationist* 1 (November 1894): 205–6. Incidentally, the coalition that deposed Terence V. Powderly as the General Master Workman of the Knights of Labor at the Knights' General Assembly in Philadelphia in November 1893 also consisted chiefly of midwestern Populists and eastern Socialists; see above.

175. Foner, *History*, 290–93, 324; Kaufman, "Samuel Gompers," 51–52; Greene, *Pure and Simple Politics*, 63–64; Pierce, "The Populist President," 16–19, 23 (McBride quoted on 19; AFL resolution quoted on 23).

176. Mandel, *Samuel Gompers*, 168.

177. Salvatore, *Eugene V. Debs*, 158–61; Eugene V. Debs to William Jennings Bryan, 27 July 1896, in Constantine, *Letters*, 120; Niswonger, *Arkansas Democratic Politics*, 78; J. R. Sovereign to Butler, 24 September 1896, Butler Papers, reel 2; Sanders, *Roots of Reform*, 54, 58–59, 144.

178. Phelan, *Grand Master Workman*, 15, 258–59; Falzone, *Terence V. Powderly*, 174; Sanders, *Roots of Reform*, 53–55.

179. Unger, *These United States*, 489–93 (Bryan quoted on 490); Nicholson, *Labor's Story*, 139–40 (last quote on 139).

180. *JKL*, 30 April, 6 August (quote) 1896; Garlock, *Guide*, 361.

181. *JKL*, 31 January, 7, 21, 28 February, 7, 28 March, 11, 25 April, 2, 9, 23 May 1895, 28 May, 30 July, 13, 27 August 1896.

182. Beeby, "Revolt," 345–46; *Gubernatorial Elections*, 71. The North Carolina Populists nominated a gubernatorial candidate, William A. Guthrie, in 1896, but Guthrie, who had expected Russell to withdraw from the race, ultimately withdrew himself one week before the election. He then asked Populists to vote for the Democratic candidate, Cyrus Watson. Guthrie nevertheless received 9.4 percent of the vote. The rest of the would-be Populist vote was probably split closely between Russell and Watson. See *Gubernatorial Elections*, 71; Hunt, *Marion Butler*, 108–9, 111–12, 121; Beeby, "Revolt," 328, 341–42, 345.

183. *JKL*, 14 February (letter from H. Howington [quote]), 14 March (letter from W. Howington) 1895, 6 August 1896; Garlock, *Guide*, 4. It is unclear if H. and W. Howington were actually two different people or if the first initial of the name was misprinted beneath one of the letters.

184. Mrs. Ira Campbell to Butler, 26 September 1896, Butler Papers, reel 2. As a Knight of Labor Campbell frequently contributed enthusiastic letters to the *JUL* (see, e.g., the issue of 28 November 1889) and the *Alabama Sentinel* (see, e.g., the issue of 17 March 1888).

185. Hild, "Dixie Knights Redux," 38–39; Hackney, *Populism*, 102–4; *Birmingham Labor Advocate*, 4 June 1892; Gompers to Jere Dennis, 23 September 1896, in Kaufman, Albert, and Palladino, *The Samuel Gompers Papers*, 231–32, including 232 n. 1; Head, "The Development," 132–33; *Journal of the House of Representatives of the State of Alabama, Session of 1896–7*, 110–12. The town of Talladega is located in Talladega County.

186. *JKL*, 2 January, 18 June 1896. It is uncertain whether DA 145 of northeast Texas remained active in 1896; the last reference to it in the *JKL* appears in the issue dated 25 July 1895.

187. Letter from James Fitzgerald in *JKL*, 16 May 1895.

188. Letter from R. D. Cross in *JKL*, 23 May 1895.

189. *JKL*, 2 January 1896; Rodriquez, "Urban Populism," 334 (quote, citing the *Dallas Morning News*, 21 January 1896).

190. *JKL*, 25 July, 22 August, 17 October 1895.

191. Martin, *The People's Party*, 217–18 (first quote on 218); Barr, *Reconstruction*, 171 (second quote).

192. Winkler, *Platforms*, 646; Dubin, *United States Congressional Elections*, 319.

193. Rodriquez, "Urban Populism," 363; Barr, *Reconstruction*, 158–59.

194. Rodriquez, "Urban Populism," 365 (Kearby quote, citing the *Dallas Morning News*, 10 December 1896); Martin, *The People's Party*, 243–44; Cantrell and Barton, "Texas Populists," 676–90.

195. Robertson to Heartsill, 29 August 1895, Heartsill Papers; *JKL*, 12 December 1895, 23 July, 13 August 1896.

196. Robertson to Heartsill, 31 August 1896, Heartsill Papers. The actions of James R. Sovereign at the St. Louis convention gave at least some credence to Robertson's claims; the General Master Workman delivered the seconding speech for the vice presidential nomination of Tom Watson. See Niswonger, *Arkansas Democratic Politics*, 57. According to Niswonger (*Arkansas Democratic Politics*, 57) and Wheeler ("The People's Party," 434), the Arkansas delegation to St. Louis consisted of twenty-five delegates, not twenty-seven, as Robertson claimed.

197. *American Federationist* 1 (November 1894): 197.

198. Wheeler, "The People's Party," 445, 456.

199. Kantrowitz, *Ben Tillman*, 149; Kantrowitz, "Ben Tillman," 523 (quote); Goldinger, *Presidential Elections*, 117. On the Greenback-Labor Party in South Carolina and the Democratic rhetoric and violence that it faced see above.

200. Shugg, "The New Orleans General Strike"; Hair, *Bourbonism*, 227; Hall, *Labor Struggles*, 32–46; Ettinger, "John Fitzpatrick," 351; Jackson, *New Orleans*, 225. Hall, a Louisiana labor activist, claimed decades later that the Populists "had a large following among New Orleans workers" (*Labor Struggles*, 44), but the other sources contradict this assertion.

201. Weaver to Powderly, 9 September 1892; J. W. McFarland to Powderly, 14 September 1892, both in Powderly Papers, reel 39; Hair, *Bourbonism*, 185; Shugg, "The New Orleans General Strike," 553; Hall, *Labor Struggles*, 39; Garlock, *Guide*, 161–67.

202. On the Greenback and Independent movements in Louisiana see above. On Louisiana GLP or Independent leaders who became Populist leaders see Hair, *Bourbonism*, 70, 217, 225, 231.

203. Ibid., chap. 10 (quote from an unnamed Louisiana state trooper on 261); Goodwyn, *Democratic Promise*, 333–37.

204. Hart, *Redeemers*, 180–81, 185, 187; Shapiro, *A New South Rebellion*, 167–69; *Nashville Weekly Toiler*, 30 March 1892 (first quote); Lester, "Grassroots Reform," 325–26 (Buchanan quoted on 326).

205. Hart, *Redeemers*, 188–90; Shapiro, *A New South Rebellion*, 179–90; Lester, "Grassroots Reform," 339–41, 343–44, 347–48.

206. Letter from W.F. in the *Nashville Weekly Toiler*, 4 May 1892 (first quote); Hart, *Redeemers*, 181.

207. Letter from Statistician in the *JKL*, 19 April 1894.

208. Saunders, "The Ideology," 42–43; Lester, "Grassroots Reform," 327.

209. On the Greenback-Labor Party in Tennessee see above.

210. Letter from T.H.D. in the *JUL*, 25 March 1885.

211. *Sparta (Ga.) Ishmaelite*, 3 September 1886; Connie L. Lester, "Knights of Labor," in West, *The Tennessee Encyclopedia*, 505.

212. See, for example, the *JUL*, 25 July 1885, 30 June (letter from J.D.M.), 8 November (letters from John A. Gann and from J. D. McCormick, S. M. Morton, and C. B. Woodward) 1888.

213. Key, *Southern Politics*, 75; Lester, "Grassroots Reform," 311 n. 2.

214. On the Knights' role in laying the groundwork for and launching the People's Party in Kansas see Nugent, *The Tolerant Populists*, 50–51, 66; Argersinger, *Populism*, 29, 35, 56; Fink, *Workingmen's Democracy*, 135–36; Ostler, *Prairie Populism*, 78, 122, 210 n. 28.

215. On the continuing decline of the Knights of Labor after 1896 see Oestreicher, "A Note," 106 (table 3); Foner, *History*, 168; Phelan, *Grand Master Workman*, 258; Weir, *Knights Unhorsed*, 178. On the demise of the Alliances see Hicks, *The Populist Revolt*, 269–70; McMath, *Populist Vanguard*, 148–49.

216. On Watson see Woodward, *Tom Watson*, 330–31; on Kearby see Rodriquez, "Urban Populism," 366. "Forgotten Alternatives" is the title of chap. 2 of Woodward, *The Strange Career*, in which he discusses alternative philosophies of race relations that held credence in the late-nineteenth-century South until the turn of the century, when, according to Woodward, the doctrine of extreme racism became

dominant in the region. On Woodward's Arkansas background see Woodward, *Thinking Back*, 9, 85; Roper, *C. Vann Woodward, Southerner*, chap. 1; O'Brien, "From a Chase," 235.

## Chapter Six. Southern Farmer and Labor Movements after the Populist Defeat of 1896

1. Miller, "Building," 164–65 (Kearby quoted on 164).

2. Woodward, *Tom Watson*, 330, citing the *People's Party Paper*, 13 November 1896.

3. Crow and Durden, *Maverick Republican*, 49–50 (quote on 49).

4. Ibid., chap. 7; Prather, *We Have Taken a City*, chaps. 2–5; Honey, "Class, Race, and Power," 175–76.

5. Woodward, *The Strange Career*, 84, 97; Kousser, *The Shaping*, 189–95; Perman, *Struggle*, 162–72.

6. Haley, "Race," 220.

7. Perman, *Struggle*, 172; Honey, "Class, Race, and Power," 178.

8. Goodwyn, "Populist Dreams"; Barr, *Reconstruction*, chap. 13; Kousser, *The Shaping*, 196–209; Perman, *Struggle*, 271–81.

9. Ayers, *The Promise*, 304, 309; Woodward, *The Strange Career*, 83–85; Kousser, *The Shaping*; Perman, *Struggle*. See also Redding, who asserts that "by 1912 blacks and many poor whites, particularly in those areas [of the South] with higher rates of [farm] tenancy, manufacturing employment, . . . and former Populist support, simply could not or did not vote" (*Making Race, Making Power*, 29).

10. Woodward, *The Strange Career*, 98.

11. Ibid., chap. 3; Williamson, *The Crucible*, 6, 111–323. Rebecca Felton served in the U.S. Senate for two days in 1922, becoming the nation's first female senator. She was the interim replacement for Tom Watson, who won election to the Senate in 1920 as a Democrat and died two years later. On the election of Watson see Woodward, *Tom Watson*, 473; on Felton's appointment and brief service in the Senate see Talmadge, *Rebecca Latimer Felton*, 139–49.

12. See Durden, *The Climax of Populism*, which portrays fusion in a fairly favorable light but nevertheless clearly explains the difficult position in which the Democrats' nomination of Bryan placed the Populists that year. See also Hicks, *The Populist Revolt*, 354, 356–59, 366–77, 399–400; McMath, *American Populism*, 202–6.

13. Shaw, *The Wool-Hat Boys*, 118–20 (quote on 118). On the Georgia Democratic and Populist parties and the issue of lynching see also Brundage, *Lynching*, 194–97.

14. Barjenbruch, "The Greenback Political Movement," 109; Bayliss, "Public Affairs," 315–16, 333–34; Wheeler, "The People's Party," 326, 333–35, 412–13.

On the Arkansas state legislature's abolishment of the convict lease system in 1893 see above.

15. Martin, *The People's Party*, 242.

16. Palmer, *"Man over Money,"* 143, 146–47, 149, 176–78; Shaw, *The Wool-Hat Boys*, 100, 143; McMath, *Populist Vanguard*, 148.

17. McMath, *Populist Vanguard*, 46, 58–60, 144, 146–50; McMath, *American Populism*, 178–79; Martin, *The People's Party*, 157–59, 250 n. 42. Martin emphasizes the "martial aspects" of the Industrial Legion, likening the organization to "a Populist army" (*The People's Party*, 158).

18. Brennan, "Sawn Timber," 55–61; Drobney, *Lumbermen*, 127–41; Hild, "Dixie Knights Redux"; *Report of Proceedings of the Twenty-Fourth Annual Convention*, 16.

19. Ware, *Labor Movement*, xi; Foner, *History*, 168.

20. AFL southern membership statistics for this period are not available, since the AFL, unlike the Knights of Labor during its heyday, did not publish those statistics for individual cities or states.

21. *Report of Proceedings of the Twenty-Fourth Annual Convention*, 132.

22. Evans, "The History," 36 (table 14), 41 (table 18); Hild, "The Knights of Labor," 13.

23. Douty, "Early Labor Organization," 266, citing the North Carolina Bureau of Labor and Printing, *Annual Report* (1901), 386; Garlock, "A Structural Analysis," 236.

24. Barr, *Reconstruction*, 93; Allen, *Chapters*, 152. The Texas State Federation of Labor reported 12,478 members in 1910.

25. *Thirteenth Census*, 24.

26. Head, "The Development," 131, 135–36.

27. Montgomery, *The Fall*, 172; Letwin, *The Challenge*, 127; Hild, "Dixie Knights Redux," 39–40; Head, "The Development," 184–86; Taft, *Organizing Dixie*, 31–33.

28. Hild, "Organizing," 298; Baker, "The 'Hoover Scare,' " 261; unidentified Charlotte, North Carolina, newspaper clippings included with H. F. Hover to Powderly, 22 May 1886, Powderly Papers, reel 16; letter from C. L. Lindsey in the *Concord (N.C.) Times*, 15 April 1886; letter from John R. Ray in the *Salisbury (N.C.) Carolina Watchman*, 29 April 1886; Knights of Labor, Raleigh Assembly, Minute Book, 3 May 1886.

29. Kremm and Neal, "Clandestine Black Labor Societies," 229–31; Hild, "Organizing," 298–301; Baker, "The 'Hoover Scare,' " 262, 264. Other southern Knights of Labor organizers endured rough treatment and threats of violence as well. See McLaurin, *The Knights of Labor*, 152, on the case of John R. Ray, and Hild, "Organizing," 298, on the case of Victor E. St. Cloud.

30. See, for example, Tindall, *The Emergence*, 525–30; Ingalls, "The Wagner Act."

31. Kremm and Neal, "Clandestine Black Labor Societies," 228; Head, "The Development," 62–63. Kremm and Neal suggest that these laws were aimed at "groups attempting to organize black agricultural laborers," but the Georgia law that they refer to, discussed above, as well as the Alabama law described by Head clearly had broader aims than that, which would suggest that the other state laws probably did as well.

32. Hild, "The Knights of Labor," 61–62 (quotes on 62, citing the *Augusta [Ga.] Chronicle*, 25 July 1888).

33. Hackney, *Populism,* 249; Taft, *Organizing Dixie,* 38, 40, 51.

34. On "right-to-work" laws in the South during the twentieth century see Marshall, *Labor,* 242, 319–20, 326, 329; Tindall, *The Emergence,* 711; Bartley, *The New South,* 49–50, 158, 210, 403.

35. Laurie, *Artisans,* 192, 198–99, 210; Foner, *History,* 345–46, 349, 368; Taft, *The A.F. of L.,* 97–99, 101–3. The only delegate from Georgia to attend the AFL annual convention in Birmingham in 1891 was G. E. Stillman of Atlanta, who represented the Street Railway Employees, No. 5586 (*Report of Proceedings of the Eleventh Annual Convention,* 7–8).

36. Laurie, *Artisans,* 192–98 (quote on 197); Foner, *History,* 346–55, 358–61, 364–68; Taft, *The A.F. of L.,* 308–17. A study conducted under the supervision of W. E. B. DuBois in 1902 estimated that only 40,000 of the AFL's 1,025,300 members were black (Foner, *History,* 350; *Report of Proceedings of the Twenty-Third Annual Convention,* 37). By contrast, African American membership in the Knights of Labor reportedly reached 90,000 in mid-1887, at which time the Knights' official total membership was 548,239 (*New York Sun,* 26 June 1887; *New Orleans Weekly Pelican,* 23 July 1887; Ware, *Labor Movement,* 66).

37. Farmers in Blocton, Alabama, reportedly made plans to organize an AFL Farmers' Union in early 1902, but no evidence exists that these plans came to fruition. See the *Laborer's Banner* (Brewton, Ala.), 15 February 1902. This would not have been the same organization as the Farmers' Union organized in Texas that year.

38. Taylor, *The Farmers' Movement,* 336–38; Saloutos, *Farmer Movements,* 184–88; Miller, "Building," 176; Sanders, *Roots of Reform,* 150 (quote). The Farmers' Union admitted American Indians but not African Americans. On debates within the Farmers' Union over the race issue and the establishment of two black counterpart organizations see Saloutos, *Farmer Movements,* 192–94.

39. Woodward, *Origins,* 413; Taylor, *The Farmers' Movement,* 344–50; Saloutos, *Farmer Movements,* 189–90; Miller, "Building," 176–78.

40. Saloutos, *Farmer Movements,* chap. 12; Taylor, *The Farmers' Movement,* 349–64; Woodward, *Origins,* 413–15; Sanders, *Roots of Reform,* 150–52.

41. Allen, *Chapters*, 129.

42. Ibid., 129–30; Sanders, *Roots of Reform*, 98, 152. On Gompers's appearance before the National Farmers' Union see also the *American Federationist* 15 (October 1908): 869–71, 891–94.

43. Barr, *Reconstruction*, 247–48; Green, *Grass-Roots Socialism*, 56; Miller, "Building," 163, 177–81 (quote on 181). See also Marshall (*Labor*, 36–37) and Green ("The Texas Labor Movement," 12–14) on the political accomplishments of the farmer-labor coalition in Texas during the early twentieth century.

44. Green, *Grass-Roots Socialism*, 67, 119–20 (quote on 120).

45. Taft, *Organizing Dixie*, 38, 40, 60; Flynt, *Alabama*, 52–54; Flynt, *Poor but Proud*, 327–28, 349–52. On the Populist O. M. Mastin see Webb, *Two-Party Politics*, 135 and above. Historian Bruce E. Field contends that the Alabama Farmers' Union's charter was revoked as part of a "purge" by National Farmers' Union president James Patton of "those elements who, by refusing to support President Truman's Cold War policies, brought negative publicity to the [national] organization" (*Harvest of Dissent*, 141–43 [quotes on 142]).

46. Wright, *Old South, New South*, 118 (table 4.6). See also Woodward, *Origins*, 415.

47. On Socialism in Oklahoma see Burbank, *When Farmers Voted Red*; Bissett, *Agrarian Socialism*.

48. Allen, *The Great Southwest Strike*, 145–49; Green, *Grass-Roots Socialism*, 15, 20–21 (first quote on 20, second quote on 21); *Laborer's Banner*, 24 November (third quote), 22 December 1900.

49. Martin, *The People's Party*, 67, including n. 14, 79, including n. 28; Green, *Grass-Roots Socialism*, 7, 15, 19–20, 38, 40, 56, 67 (quote), 138, 295; Winkler, *Platforms*, 275, 314, 332, 380, 418, 420, 442, 444, 470, 472, 484, 513–14, 564, 647–48. Martin contends that the Rhodes brothers "ran each in turn as the Socialist candidate for Governor" (*The People's Party*, 79 n. 28). If this assertion is correct, then only Jake actually received the party's nomination and represented the Socialists in a gubernatorial election. See Winkler, *Platforms*, 646–48; *Gubernatorial Elections*, 81.

50. Martin, *The People's Party*, 79–80 (quote on 80), 81 (table 3).

51. Winkler, *Platforms*, 296, 315, 474, 566–67 (quote from the platform of the Socialist state convention of 1912 on 567).

52. Wheeler, "The People's Party," 482–83, 489; Green, *Grass-Roots Socialism*, 17; Niswonger, *Arkansas Democratic Politics*, 57, 75, 224.

53. Kiser, "The Socialist Party," 123–25, 127–34, 136–38, 141–43, 146, 149, 152; Green, *Grass-Roots Socialism*, 248.

54. Baskett, "Miners Stay Away!" 113, 114, including n. 28, 115, 117, 132; Green,

*Grass-Roots Socialism*, 30, 33, 77, 123–24, 200, 247–48, 292; Kiser, "The Socialist Party," 126–27, 133, 137–38, 143, 145–46, 148–50; Robertson to Heartsill, 30 April 1895, Heartsill Papers; Niswonger, *Arkansas Democratic Politics*, 224. See also n. 4, chap. 5, on the Knights of Labor in Sebastian County.

55. Green, *Grass-Roots Socialism*, 194, 200; Kiser, "The Socialist Party," 148.

56. Kiser, "The Socialist Party," 127, 131, 133, 139–40 (first quote on 139, citing the *Little Rock Union Labor Bulletin*, 12 August 1906), 142–43 (second quote on 142), 146, 148–50; Green, *Grass-Roots Socialism*, 77, 248; Niswonger, *Arkansas Democratic Politics*, 224; *Gubernatorial Elections*, 41.

57. On the return of many former rank-and-file Texas Populists to the Democratic Party along with former Populist leaders such as H. S. P. "Stump" Ashby and James H. "Cyclone" Davis see Barr, *Reconstruction*, 173–74; Miller, "Building." On Davis's and Ashby's post-Populist careers see also Goodwyn, *Democratic Promise*, 559–61. On the return of Arkansas third-party men to the Democratic Party, including such leaders as Charles M. Norwood, David E. Barker, and W. B. W. Heartsill, see Wheeler, "The People's Party," 480–81, 485–91; Niswonger, *Arkansas Democratic Politics*, 74–79.

58. Green, *Grass-Roots Socialism*, 405–6, 414, 423, 425.

59. Lewinson, *Race, Class, and Party*, 165 (table 2).

60. On increasing rates of farm tenancy in the Alabama hill country, a predominantly white region, during the late nineteenth and early twentieth centuries see Flynt, *Poor but Proud*, 70–72; Webb, *Two-Party Politics*, 61, 120.

61. Paul, "Rebels of the New South, 1897–1920," 22, 68–70, 80–82, 95, 97–100; Paul, "Rebels of the New South, 1892–1920," 20, 35, 149; Letwin, *The Challenge*, 128.

62. Paul, "Rebels of the New South, 1892–1920," 72; Webb, *Two-Party Politics*, 190–91, 207; Webb, "From Independents," 731. On these three counties as long-time centers of farmer-labor anti-Democratic insurgency see, in addition to evidence presented in this study, Horton, "Testing the Limits," on Lawrence County; Webb, "From Independents" on Chilton County; and, on Shelby County, Webb, *Two-Party Politics*, 74, 78–85, 94–96, 104–5, 111, 134, 148, 156, 164–65, 181–84, 191–93, 205–10, 216; Head, "The Development," 72.

63. Webb, *Two-Party Politics*, 207–8; Hackney, *Populism*, 115 (quote).

64. Webb, *Two-Party Politics*, chap. 8 (quote and Jemison election results on 209).

65. Foster with Scott, *Paulding County*, 312–13. On Watson's presidential campaign in 1904 see Woodward, *Tom Watson*, 357–63.

66. Shaw, *The Wool-Hat Boys*, 171–73, 184 (quote). See also Saunders, "The Ideology," 162–64; Palmer, *"Man over Money,"* 176–77; Woodward, *Tom Watson*, 405–8. Woodward quotes (on 404) Georgia's Populist executive secretary as noting Pop-

ulist defections to the Socialists in 1905, but the Populist Party was practically defunct by then; see Shaw, *The Wool-Hat Boys*, chap. 11.

67. Paul, "Rebels of the New South, 1897–1920," 66–68 (quote on 66–67). See also Kuhn, *Contesting*, 24–25, 27.

68. Paul, "Rebels of the New South, 1897–1920," 33; Shaw, *The Wool-Hat Boys*, 171.

69. Shaw, *The Wool-Hat Boys*, 150, 208; *Atlanta Constitution*, 5 October 1900; *Laborer's Banner*, 29 March 1902.

70. Woodward, *Tom Watson*, 373–78 (Hines quoted on 374); Shaw, *The Wool-Hat Boys*, 201–2, 204, 208; Arnett, *The Populist Movement*, 218–21.

71. Arnett, *The Populist Movement*, 220–23 (quote on 222–23); Shaw, *The Wool-Hat Boys*, 200–202; Woodward, *Tom Watson*, 370–72, 384–86.

72. For arguments claiming continuity between Populism and progressivism in Alabama see Webb, *Two-Party Politics*, chap. 8; in Georgia, Arnett, *The Populist Movement*, 221–23, 226–28; Shaw, *The Wool-Hat Boys*, 207–8; in Texas, Martin, *The People's Party*, 266–68; Miller, "Building," esp. 179–82. For a powerful argument against continuity between Populism and progressivism in Alabama see Hackney, *Populism*. For a more ambivalent assessment of the continuity between Populism and progressivism in Georgia than that presented by Arnett and Shaw see Jones, "Progressivism," 5–7.

73. Sanders, *Roots of Reform*, 159 (first quote), 413 (second quote). For another argument stressing continuity between Populism and progressivism at the national level see Hicks, *The Populist Revolt*, chap. 15. For arguments that stress the differences rather than the similarities between Populism and progressivism, either at the national or southern regional levels, see Woodward, *Origins*, 371, 392–93; Wiebe, *The Search*, 178; Goodwyn, *Democratic Promise*, 518–21, 535–37, 550; McMath, *American Populism*, 209–10; Hunt, *Marion Butler and American Populism*, 188–89; Holmes, "Reflections," 281–82. McMath has since moved closer to the continuity position on this issue, suggesting that "we may profitably consider a long agrarian moment stretching at least from the 1860s through the rise of southern Progressivism and reaching the peak of its national influence during the presidency of Woodrow Wilson" ("C. Vann Woodward," 758).

74. For the Knights' Reading platform of 1878 see Powderly, *Thirty Years*, 243–45.

75. Flynt, *Poor but Proud*, 101, 118–20, 154–55; Cobb, *Industrialization*, 72–73; Hall et al., *Like a Family*, 58–60, 77; Flamming, *Creating*, 130, 170; Tindall, *The Emergence*, 213, 320–23. Company stores did become less common in southern mill villages during the Progressive Era, and South Carolina's state legislature of 1915–16 outlawed mill owners' practices of paying operatives in store goods and discounting mill checks. But in some parts of the South mill owners continued

to pay workers in scrip redeemable only at company stores well into the 1930s. See Hall et al., *Like a Family*, 130–31; Tindall, *The Emergence*, 326; Carlton, *Mill and Town*, 258; Cobb, *Industrialization*, 73. For a close examination of child labor reform in Progressive Era Alabama see Sallee, *The Whiteness*.

76. On these strikes see, among others, Mitchell, *Textile Unionism*; Tippett, *When Southern Labor Stirs*; Hall et al., *Like a Family*; Irons, *Testing*; Salmond, *The General Textile Strike*.

77. Wright, *Old South, New South*, 117–19; Fite, *Cotton Fields No More*, 84, 88; Hicks, *The Populist Revolt*, 407–8, 414–22; Arnett, *The Populist Movement*, 227; Range, *A Century*, 248–51; Goodwyn, *Democratic Promise*, 519–20. Some Populist demands became law during the Progressive Era without being diluted, such as the direct election of U.S. senators and the imposition of a graduated income tax, but these were not agricultural demands per se. On the Knights' and Populists' land reform planks see Powderly, *Thirty Years*, 244; Hicks, *The Populist Revolt*, 443.

78. Tindall, *The Emergence*, 52, 354 (quoting David R. Coker); Wright, *Old South, New South*, 117–19.

79. Kolnick, "A Producer's Commonwealth," 133, 138–44, 211–14, 219–20, 255, 261, 275, 277–79, 299.

80. Fink, *Workingmen's Democracy*, 115–16, 135–40 (quote on 139).

81. Woodward, *Origins*, 297–99.

82. Summers, "Party Games."

83. Woodward, *Tom Watson*, 220 (emphasis and capitalization appear here as reproduced by Woodward).

84. On the Minnesota Farmer-Labor Party see Gieske, *Minnesota Farmer-Laborism*; Valelly, *Radicalism*.

85. Brief assessments of the roles played by southern Populists in disfranchisement appear in Woodward, *Origins*, 323–24; Woodward, *The Strange Career*, 89–90; McMath, *American Populism*, 206–7; Hahn, *A Nation*, 446. See also Feldman, *The Disfranchisement Myth*, esp. 23–32, for an in-depth examination of the involvement of Populists (or former Populists) in the enactment of disfranchisement in Alabama.

86. Goodwyn, "Populist Dreams," 1450.

87. Bartley, *The New South*, 148–52, 157–58; Cobb, *Industrialization*, 40–41, 105, 140–41.

88. Crow and Durden, *Maverick Republican*, 49–50.

89. Works that discuss these ideologies (under various labels) and their decline include, among others, Fink, *Workingmen's Democracy*; Hahn, *The Roots*; Laurie, *Artisans*; Voss, *The Making*.

90. See the remarks made by Jerome Kearby in 1896, quoted above. See also remarks made by North Carolina's fusionist U.S. senators, Marion Butler and Jeter

Pritchard, in 1900, quoted in Crow and Durden, *Maverick Republican*, 154. Also, though he was neither a southerner nor, ultimately, a committed third-party supporter, see T. V. Powderly to N. B. Stack, 29 June 1901, quoted in Abernathy, "The Knights of Labor," 98–99, in which Powderly suggested that the American labor movement had lost its sense of "brotherhood" and "spirit of fraternity." He also lamented the Knights' failure while expressing hope that "in the *distant* future, the work we did may be appreciated" (emphasis added).

91. David Schenck diary, 8 December 1890, quoted in Ayers, *The Promise*, 246.

92. Goodwyn, *Democratic Promise*, 310.

93. In Arkansas the Brothers of Freedom also played an important role in farmer-labor third-party (or Independent) politics before merging with the Agricultural Wheel in 1885.

94. Shaw, *The Wool-Hat Boys*, 167.

# Bibliography

PRIVATE PAPERS AND MANUSCRIPT COLLECTIONS

Butler, Marion. Papers. Microfilm. Southern Historical Collection, University of North Carolina at Chapel Hill.

Felton, Rebecca Latimer. Collection. Microfilm. Hargrett Rare Book and Manuscript Library, University of Georgia, Athens.

Hayes, John W. Papers. Microfilm. Glen Rock, N.J.: Microfilming Corporation of America, 1974.

Heartsill, W. B. W. Papers. Archives and Special Collections Department, University of Arkansas at Little Rock Library.

Knights of Labor. Phillipsburg, Missouri, Records (Local Assembly 1009), 1888–96. Microfilm. Western Historical Manuscript Collection, University of Missouri, Rolla.

———. Raleigh Assembly, [No. 3606] Minute Book, 1886–90. North Carolina State Archives, North Carolina Division of Archives and History, Raleigh.

———. Van Buren Assembly, No. 6307 Records, 1886–92. Special Collections Division, University of Arkansas Libraries, Fayetteville.

Patrons of Husbandry. Georgia State Grange, Grange No. 101 (Athens) Records, 1873–77. Hargrett Rare Book and Manuscript Library, University of Georgia, Athens.

Powderly, Terence V. Papers. Microfilm. Glen Rock, N.J.: Microfilming Corporation of America, 1974.

PROCEEDINGS

*Journal of Proceedings of the Third Annual Session of the Alabama State Grange, Patrons of Husbandry, Held in Montgomery, Ala., November 30th–December 3rd, 1875.* Montgomery: Southern Plantation Printing and Binding, 1875.

*Proceedings of the Fifth Annual Session of the State Grange of Mississippi, of the Patrons of*

*Husbandry. Held at Kosciusko, Miss., September 14th, 1875.* Jackson: Farmers' Vindicator Print, 1875.

*Proceedings of the First Annual Session of District Assembly No. 78, Knights of Labor, Held
at Galveston, Texas, Jan. 4–9, 1886.* Fort Worth: Labor Siftings Cooperative Publishing Co., 1886.

*Proceedings of the Fourth Annual Meeting of the Missouri State Grange of the Patrons of Hus-
bandry.* St. Louis: Levison & Blythe, 1876.

*Proceedings of the General Assembly of the Knights of Labor,* annual eds., 1878–96. Microfilm. Madison: State Historical Society of Wisconsin, 1950.

*Proceedings of the Second Annual Session of the Tennessee State Grange, Patrons of Hus-
bandry, Held at Knoxville, Tennessee, February 17, 18, 19 and 20, 1875.* Nashville:
N.p., 1875.

*Report of Proceedings of the Eleventh Annual Convention of the American Federation of La-
bor, Held at Birmingham, Ala., December 14–19, 1891.* New York: Concord Cooperative Printing Co., 1892.

*Report of Proceedings of the Sixteenth Annual Convention of the American Federation of La-
bor, Held at Cincinnati, O., December 14th to 21st, 1896.* Cincinnati: Ohio Valley
Co., n.d.

*Report of Proceedings of the Twenty-Fourth Annual Convention of the American Federation
of Labor, Held at San Francisco, California, November 14 to 26, Inclusive, 1904.* Washington, D.C.: Law Reporter Printing Co., 1904.

*Report of Proceedings of the Twenty-Third Annual Convention of the American Federation of
Labor, Held at Boston, Massachusetts, November 9 to 23, Inclusive, 1903.* Washington,
D.C.: Law Reporter Printing Co., 1903.


NEWSPAPERS AND PERIODICALS

*Alabama Sentinel* (Birmingham), 1887–92

*Alabama State Wheel* (Moulton), 1888

*American Federationist* (New York; Indianapolis), 1894, 1908

*Arkansas Gazette* (Little Rock), 1886, 1888, 1890, 1892, 1894

*Athens (Ga.) Daily Banner-Watchman,* 1885–86

*Athens (Ga.) Southern Cultivator,* 1872

*Athens (Ga.) Weekly Banner-Watchman,* 1886

*Atlanta Constitution* (superseded the *Atlanta Daily Constitution*), 1883, 1885–92, 1894,
1900, 1918

*Atlanta Daily Constitution,* 1877

*Augusta (Ga.) Chronicle,* 1886–89, 1892, 1895

*Birmingham Labor Advocate,* 1892

*Brewton (Ala.) Laborer's Banner,* 1900, 1902

*Cartersville (Ga.) Courant-American,* 1888

*Charlotte Home-Democrat,* 1886

*Chicago Tribune,* 1885

*Columbus (Ga.) Enquirer-Sun,* 1886

*Concord (N.C.) Times,* 1886

*Dallas (Ga.) Paulding New Era,* 1892

*Dallas (Tex.) Morning News,* 1886

*Dallas (Tex.) Southern Mercury,* 1888

*Dublin (Ga.) Post,* 1878

*Fayetteville (N.C.) Messenger,* 1888

*Georgia Grange* (Atlanta), 1874

*Huntsville (Ala.) Gazette,* 1882

*Huntsville (Ala.) Weekly Democrat,* 1880, 1882

*Hustler of Rome* (Ga.), 1894

*Journal of the Knights of Labor* (Philadelphia; Washington, D.C.) (superseded the *Journal of United Labor*), 1890–96, 1900

*Journal of United Labor* (Marblehead, Mass.; Pittsburgh; Philadelphia), 1880, 1882–89

*Knoxville Daily Journal,* 1885

*Macon (Ga.) Telegraph* (superseded the *Macon [Ga.] Telegraph and Messenger*), 1886–87

*Macon (Ga.) Telegraph and Messenger,* 1873

*Marietta (Ga.) Journal,* 1873, 1879, 1886, 1888, 1890, 1892, 1894

*Montgomery (Ala.) Workingmen's Advocate,* 1879

*Nashville Weekly Toiler,* 1888–89, 1892

*National Economist* (Washington, D.C.), 1890–92

*National Labor Tribune* (Pittsburgh), 1880, 1886

*New Orleans Weekly Pelican,* 1887

*New York Sun,* 1887

*New York Times,* 1874–76, 1878, 1880, 1882, 1885–88, 1891–92, 1894

*New York Tribune,* 1878, 1889

*People's Party Paper* (Atlanta), 1892, 1894

*Raleigh (N.C.) News and Observer,* 1886

*St. Louis Post-Dispatch,* 1888, 1892

*Salisbury (N.C.) Carolina Watchman,* 1886

*Southern Alliance Farmer* (Atlanta), 1889–90

*Sparta (Ga.) Ishmaelite,* 1886

*Tarboro (N.C.) Tarborough Southerner,* 1890

*Toccoa (Ga.) News and Piedmont Industrial Journal,* 1891

*Wilson (N.C.) Advance,* 1890

*Winston (N.C.) Progressive Farmer,* 1887

GOVERNMENT DOCUMENTS

*Acts and Resolutions of the General Assembly of the State of Georgia, 1889.* Atlanta: Franklin Publishing House, 1890.

*Biennial Report of the Secretary of State of the State of Arkansas, 1886.* Little Rock: A. M. Woodruff, State Printer, 1886.

*Biennial Report of the Secretary of State of the State of Arkansas, 1888.* Little Rock: Press Printing Co., 1888.

*Biennial Report of the Secretary of State of the State of Arkansas, 1892.* Little Rock: Press Printing Co., 1893.

*Compendium of the Tenth Census (June 1, 1880).* Pt. 1. Washington, D.C.: U.S. Government Printing Office, 1883.

*Compendium of the Eleventh Census: 1890.* Pt. 1. Washington, D.C.: U.S. Government Printing Office, 1892.

*Congressional Record,* various volumes and years. Washington, D.C.: U.S. Government Printing Office.

*Journal of the House of Representatives of the State of Alabama, Session of 1882–83.* Montgomery: W. D. Brown & Co., 1883.

*Journal of the House of Representatives of the State of Alabama, Session of 1892–3.* Montgomery: Brown Printing Co., 1893.

*Journal of the House of Representatives of the State of Alabama, Session of 1894–5.* Montgomery: Roemer Printing Co., 1895.

*Journal of the House of Representatives of the State of Alabama, Session of 1896–7.* Montgomery: Roemer Printing Co., 1897.

*Journal of the House of Representatives of the State of Georgia, at the Adjourned Session of the General Assembly, at Atlanta, Wednesday, July 8, 1891.* Atlanta: Geo. W. Harrison, State Printer, 1891.

*Report on Population of the United States at the Eleventh Census: 1890.* Pt. 1. Washington, D.C.: U.S. Government Printing Office, 1895.

*Report on Productions of Agriculture as Returned at the Tenth Census (June 1, 1880).* Washington, D.C.: U.S. Government Printing Office, 1883.

*Thirteenth Census of the United States, Taken in the Year 1910: Abstract of the Census.* Washington, D.C.: U.S. Government Printing Office, 1913.

BOOKS AND ARTICLES

Ansley, Mrs. J. J. [Lula Barnes]. *History of the Georgia Woman's Christian Temperance Union from Its Organization, 1883 to 1907.* Columbus, Ga.: Gilbert Printing Co., 1914.

*Appleton's Annual Cyclopaedia and Register of Important Events of the Year 1890.* New York: D. Appleton and Co., 1891.

*Appleton's Annual Cyclopaedia and Register of Important Events of the Year 1892.* New York: D. Appleton and Co., 1893.

*Biographical and Historical Memoirs of Eastern Arkansas.* Chicago: Goodspeed Publishing Co., 1890.

*Biographical and Historical Memoirs of Pulaski, Jefferson, Lonoke, Faulkner, Grant, Saline, Perry, Garland, and Hot Springs Counties, Arkansas.* Chicago: Goodspeed Publishing Co., 1889. Repr. Easley, S.C.: Southern Historical Press, 1978.

Buchanan, Joseph R. *The Story of a Labor Agitator.* Orig. pub. 1903. Repr. Freeport, N.Y.: Books for Libraries Press, 1971.

Constantine, J. Robert, ed. *Letters of Eugene V. Debs.* Vol. 1. Urbana: University of Illinois Press, 1990.

Daniels, Josephus. *Tar Heel Editor.* Chapel Hill: University of North Carolina Press, 1939.

DuBose, John W. *Jefferson County and Birmingham, Alabama: Historical and Biographical, 1887.* Birmingham: Teeple and Smith, 1887. Repr. Easley, S.C.: Southern Historical Press, 1976.

Dunning, N. A., ed. *The Farmers' Alliance History and Agricultural Digest.* Washington, D.C.: Alliance Publishing Co., 1891.

Felton, Mrs. William H. [Rebecca L.] *My Memoirs of Georgia Politics.* Atlanta: Index Printing Co., 1911.

Foner, Philip S., and Ronald L. Lewis, eds. *The Black Worker during the Era of the Knights of Labor.* Vol. 3 of *The Black Worker.* Philadelphia: Temple University Press, 1978.

Gompers, Samuel. "Organized Labor in the Campaign." *North American Review* 155 (July 1892): 91–96.

*History of Benton, Washington, Carroll, Madison, Crawford, Franklin, and Sebastian Counties, Arkansas.* Chicago: Goodspeed Publishing Co., 1889. Repr. Easley, S.C.: Southern Historical Press, 1978.

Kaufman, Stuart B., Peter J. Albert, and Grace Palladino, eds. *The Samuel Gompers Papers.* Vol. 4. Urbana: University of Illinois Press, 1991.

Kelley, O. H. *Origins and Progress of the Order of the Patrons of Husbandry in the United States; a History from 1866 to 1873.* Philadelphia: A. Wagenseller, 1875.

McNeill, George E., ed. *The Labor Movement: The Problem of Today.* New York: M. W. Hazen Co., 1892.

Morgan, W. Scott. *History of the Wheel and Alliance, and the Impending Revolution.* 3rd ed. Orig. pub. 1891. Repr. New York: Burt Franklin, 1968.

*The National Cyclopaedia of American Biography.* Vol. 6. New York: James T. White & Co., 1896.

*The National Economist Almanac 1890: National Farmers Alliance and Industrial Union Hand-Book.* Washington, D.C.: National Economist Print, 1890.

Powderly, Terence V. *The Path I Trod: The Autobiography of Terence V. Powderly.* Ed. Harry J. Carman, Henry David, and Paul N. Guthrie. New York: Columbia University Press, 1940. Repr. New York: AMS Press, 1968.

———. *Thirty Years of Labor.* Columbus, Ohio: Excelsior Publishing House, 1889.

*Sholes' Directory of the City of Augusta, 1886.* Augusta, Ga.: Chronicle Book and Job Rooms, 1886.

Simonds, John Cameron, and John T. McEnnis. *The Story of Manual Labor in All Lands and Ages: Its Past Condition, Present Progress, and Hope for the Future.* Chicago: R. S. Peale & Co., 1887.

*Weatherbe's Atlanta, Ga., Duplex City Directory 1886.* Atlanta: Dunlop & Cohen, 1886.

Winkler, Ernest W., ed. *Platforms of Political Parties in Texas.* Bulletin of the University of Texas No. 53. Austin: University of Texas, 1916.


*Secondary Sources*

Abernathy, John H., Jr. "The Knights of Labor in Alabama." M.S. thesis, University of Alabama, 1960.

Abramowitz, Jack. "The Negro in the Populist Movement." *Journal of Negro History* 38 (July 1953): 257–89.

———. "The South: Arena for Greenback Reformers." *Social Education* 17 (March 1953): 108–10.

Ali, Omar H. "Black Populism in the New South, 1886–1898." Ph.D. diss., Columbia University, 2003.

Allen, Ruth. *Chapters in the History of Organized Labor in Texas.* University of Texas Publication No. 4143. Austin: Bureau of Research in the Social Sciences, University of Texas, 1941.

———. *The Great Southwest Strike.* University of Texas Publication No. 4214. Austin: University of Texas, 1942.

Argersinger, Peter H. *Populism and Politics: William Alfred Peffer and the People's Party.* Lexington: University Press of Kentucky, 1974.

Arnett, Alex M. *The Populist Movement in Georgia: A View of the "Agrarian Crusade" in the Light of Solid-South Politics.* New York: Columbia University, 1922.

Avrich, Paul. *The Haymarket Tragedy.* Princeton, N.J.: Princeton University Press, 1984.

Ayers, Edward L. *The Promise of the New South: Life after Reconstruction.* New York: Oxford University Press, 1992.

———. *Vengeance and Justice: Crime and Punishment in the Nineteenth-Century American South.* New York: Oxford University Press, 1984.

Baker, Bruce E. "The 'Hoover Scare' in South Carolina, 1887: An Attempt to Organize Black Farm Labor." *Labor History* 40 (Fall 1999): 261–82.

Barjenbruch, Judith. "The Greenbacker Political Movement: An Arkansas View." *Arkansas Historical Quarterly* 36 (Summer 1977): 107–22.

Barnes, Donna A. *Farmers in Rebellion: The Rise and Fall of the Southern Farmers Alliance and the People's Party in Texas.* Austin: University of Texas Press, 1984.

Barnes, Kenneth C. *Who Killed John Clayton? Political Violence and the Emergence of the New South, 1861–1893.* Durham, N.C.: Duke University Press, 1998.

Barr, Alwyn. *Reconstruction to Reform: Texas Politics, 1876–1906.* Austin: University of Texas Press, 1971.

Barrett, Don C. *The Greenbacks and Resumption of Specie Payments, 1862–1879.* Cambridge, Mass.: Harvard University Press, 1931.

Bartley, Numan V. *The Creation of Modern Georgia.* 2nd ed. Athens: University of Georgia Press, 1990.

———. *The New South, 1945–1980.* Baton Rouge: Louisiana State University Press, 1995.

Baskett, Thomas S., Jr. "Miners Stay Away! W. B. W. Heartsill and the Last Years of the Arkansas Knights of Labor, 1892–1896." *Arkansas Historical Quarterly* 42 (Summer 1983): 107–33.

Bayliss, Garland E. "Public Affairs in Arkansas, 1874–1896." Ph.D. diss., University of Texas at Austin, 1972.

Beatty, Bess. *Alamance: The Holt Family and Industrialization in a North Carolina County, 1837–1900.* Baton Rouge: Louisiana State University Press, 1999.

Beckel, Deborah. "Roots of Reform: The Origins of Populism and Progressivism as Manifest in Relationships among Reformers in Raleigh, North Carolina, 1850–1905." Ph.D. diss., Emory University, 1998.

Beeby, James M. " 'Equal Rights to All and Special Privileges to None': Grass-Roots Populism in North Carolina." *North Carolina Historical Review* 78 (April 2001): 156–86.

———. "Revolt of the Tar Heelers: A Socio-Political History of the North Carolina Populist Party, 1892–1901." Ph.D. diss., Bowling Green State University, 1999.

Biegert, M. Langley. "Legacy of Resistance: Uncovering the History of Collective Action by Black Agricultural Workers in Central East Arkansas from the 1860s to the 1930s." *Journal of Social History* 32 (Fall 1998): 73–99.

Birmingham, Alphonse J. "The Knights of Labor and the Farmers' Alliances." M.A. thesis, Catholic University of America, 1955.

Bissett, Jim. *Agrarian Socialism in America: Marx, Jefferson, and Jesus in the Oklahoma Countryside, 1904–1920.* Norman: University of Oklahoma Press, 1999.

Black, Paul V. "The Knights of Labor and the South: 1876–1893." *Southern Quarterly* 1 (April 1963): 201–12.

Boles, John B., and Bethany L. Johnson, eds. *"Origins of the New South" Fifty Years*

*Later: The Continuing Influence of a Historical Classic.* Baton Rouge: Louisiana State University Press, 2003.

Bonner, James C. "The Alliance Legislature of 1890." In *Studies in Georgia History and Government,* ed. James C. Bonner and Lucien E. Roberts, 155–71. Athens: University of Georgia Press, 1940.

Bonner, James C., and Lucien E. Roberts, eds. *Studies in Georgia History and Government.* Athens: University of Georgia Press, 1940.

Brecher, Jeremy. *Strike!* Rev. and updated ed. Cambridge, Mass.: South End Press, 1997.

Brennan, James R. "Sawn Timber and Straw Hats: The Development of the Lumber Industry in Escambia County, Alabama, 1880–1910." *Gulf Coast Historical Review* 11 (Spring 1996): 41–67.

Brittain, Joseph M. "Negro Suffrage and Politics in Alabama since 1870." Ph.D. diss., Indiana University, 1958.

Bruce, Robert V. *1877: Year of Violence.* Indianapolis: Bobbs-Merrill, 1959.

Brundage, David. *The Making of Western Labor Radicalism: Denver's Organized Workers, 1875–1905.* Urbana: University of Illinois Press, 1994.

Brundage, W. Fitzhugh. *Lynching in the New South: Georgia and Virginia, 1880–1930.* Urbana: University of Illinois Press, 1993.

Buck, Solon J. *The Granger Movement: A Study of Agricultural Organization and Its Political, Economic and Social Manifestations, 1870–1880.* Cambridge, Mass.: Harvard University Press, 1913.

Buenger, Walter L. *The Path to a Modern South: Northeast Texas between Reconstruction and the Great Depression.* Austin: University of Texas Press, 2001.

Burbank, Garin. *When Farmers Voted Red: The Gospel of Socialism in the Oklahoma Countryside, 1910–1924.* Westport, Conn.: Greenwood Press, 1976.

Burnham, W. Dean, comp. *Presidential Ballots, 1836–1892.* Baltimore, Md.: Johns Hopkins Press, 1955.

Calderon, Roberto R. *Mexican Coal Mining Labor in Texas and Coahuila, 1880–1930.* College Station: Texas A&M University Press, 2000.

Calvert, Robert A. "The Southern Grange: The Farmer's Search for Identity in the Gilded Age." Ph.D. diss., University of Texas at Austin, 1969.

Candler, Allen D., and Clement A. Evans, eds. *Georgia: Comprising Sketches of Counties, Towns, Events, Institutions, and Persons, Arranged in Cyclopedic Form.* 4 vols. Atlanta: State Historical Association, 1906.

Cantrell, Gregg. *Kenneth and John B. Rayner and the Limits of Southern Dissent.* Urbana: University of Illinois Press, 1993.

Cantrell, Gregg, and D. Scott Barton. "Texas Populists and the Failure of Biracial Politics." *Journal of Southern History* 55 (November 1989): 659–92.

Cantrell, Gregg, and Kristopher B. Paschal. "Texas Populism at High Tide: Jerome C. Kearby and the Case of the Sixth Congressional District, 1894." *Southwestern Historical Quarterly* 109 (July 2005): 30–70.

Carlton, David L. *Mill and Town in South Carolina, 1880–1920.* Baton Rouge: Louisiana State University Press, 1982.

Cartwright, Gary. *Galveston: A History of the Island.* New York: Athenaeum, 1991.

Case, Theresa A. "Free Labor on the Southwestern Railroads: The 1885–1886 Gould System Strikes." Ph.D. diss., University of Texas at Austin, 2002.

Cashin, Edward J. *The Story of Augusta.* Augusta, Ga.: Richmond County Board of Education, 1980.

Cashin, Edward J., and Glenn T. Eskew, eds. *Paternalism in a Southern City: Race, Religion, and Gender in Augusta, Georgia.* Athens: University of Georgia Press, 2001.

Cassity, Michael. *Defending a Way of Life: An American Community in the Nineteenth Century.* Albany: State University of New York Press, 1989.

———. "Modernization and Social Crisis: The Knights of Labor and a Midwest Community, 1885–1886." *Journal of American History* 66 (June 1979): 41–61.

Cecelski, David S., and Timothy B. Tyson, eds. *Democracy Betrayed: The Wilmington Race Riot of 1898 and Its Legacy.* Chapel Hill: University of North Carolina Press, 1998.

Chandler, Jerry W. "The Knights of Labor and the Southwestern Strikes." M.A. thesis, Florida State University, 1970.

Clark, John B. *Populism in Alabama.* Auburn, Ala.: Auburn Printing Co., 1927.

Clevenger, Homer. "The Farmers' Alliance in Missouri." *Missouri Historical Review* 39 (October 1944): 24–44.

Clinch, Thomas A. *Urban Populism and Free Silver in Montana: A Narrative of Ideology in Political Action.* Missoula: University of Montana Press, 1970.

Cobb, James C. "Beyond Planters and Industrialists: A New Perspective on the New South." *Journal of Southern History* 54 (February 1988): 45–68.

———. *Industrialization and Southern Society, 1877–1984.* Lexington: University Press of Kentucky, 1984.

Coleman, Kenneth, and Charles Stephen Gurr, eds. *Dictionary of Georgia Biography.* 2 vols. Athens: University of Georgia Press, 1983.

Commons, John R., David J. Saposs, Helen L. Sumner, E. B. Mittelman, H. E. Hoagland, John B. Andrews, and Selig Perlman. *History of Labour in the United States.* Vol. 2. New York: Macmillan, 1926.

Crow, Jeffrey J., and Robert F. Durden. *Maverick Republican in the Old North State: A Political Biography of Daniel L. Russell.* Baton Rouge: Louisiana State University Press, 1977.

Crowe, Charles. "Tom Watson, Populists, and Blacks Reconsidered." *Journal of Negro History* 55 (April 1970): 99–116.

Currie, Harold W. *Eugene V. Debs.* Boston: Twayne Publishers, 1976.

Curtin, Mary E. *Black Prisoners and Their World, Alabama, 1865–1900.* Charlottesville: University Press of Virginia, 2000.

Dann, Martin. "Black Populism: A Study of the Colored Farmers' Alliance through 1891." *Journal of Ethnic Studies* 2 (Fall 1974): 58–71.

David, Henry. *The History of the Haymarket Affair: A Study in the American Social-Revolutionary and Labor Movements.* New York: Farrar and Rinehart, 1936.

Davis, Granville D. "The Granger Movement in Arkansas." *Arkansas Historical Quarterly* 4 (Winter 1945): 340–52.

Davis, Harold E. *Henry Grady's New South: Atlanta, a Brave and Beautiful City.* Tuscaloosa: University of Alabama Press, 1990.

Deaton, Thomas M. "James G. Woodward: The Working Man's Mayor." *Atlanta History: A Journal of Georgia and the South* 31 (Fall 1987): 11–23.

Degler, Carl N. *The Other South: Southern Dissenters in the Nineteenth Century.* New York: Harper & Row, 1974.

De Santis, Vincent P. *Republicans Face the Southern Question: The New Departure Years, 1877–1897.* Baltimore, Md.: Johns Hopkins University Press, 1959.

Destler, Chester M. *American Radicalism, 1865–1901: Essays and Documents.* New London: Connecticut College, 1946.

Dodd, Donald B., and Wynelle S. Dodd. *Historical Statistics of the South, 1770–1970.* University: University of Alabama Press, 1973.

Donovan, Timothy P., Willard B. Gatewood, Jr., and Jeannie M. Whayne, eds. *The Governors of Arkansas: Essays in Political Biography.* 2nd ed. Fayetteville: University of Arkansas Press, 1995.

Douty, H. M. "Early Labor Organization in North Carolina, 1880–1900." *South Atlantic Quarterly* 34 (July 1935): 260–68.

Drobney, Jeffrey A. *Lumbermen and Log Sawyers: Life, Labor, and Culture in the North Florida Timber Industry, 1830–1930.* Macon, Ga.: Mercer University Press, 1997.

Dubin, Michael J., comp. *United States Congressional Elections, 1788–1997: The Official Results of the Elections of the 1st through 105th Congresses.* Jefferson, N.C.: McFarland & Co., 1998.

Dubofsky, Melvyn, and Foster Rhea Dulles. *Labor in America: A History.* 7th ed. Wheeling, Ill.: Harlan Davidson, 2004.

Dulles, Foster Rhea. *Labor in America: A History.* 3rd ed. New York: Thomas Y. Crowell Co., 1966.

Durden, Robert F. *The Climax of Populism: The Election of 1896.* Lexington: University of Kentucky Press, 1965.

Dyer, Dawn M. "Combatting the 'Fiery Flood': The Woman's Christian Temperance Union's Approach to Labor and Socialism." Ph.D. diss., Auburn University, 1998.

Edwards, Laura F. *Gendered Strife and Confusion: The Political Culture of Reconstruction.* Urbana: University of Illinois Press, 1997.

Elkins, F. Clark. "The Agricultural Wheel: County Politics and Consolidation, 1884–1885." *Arkansas Historical Quarterly* 29 (Summer 1970): 152–75.

———. "The Agricultural Wheel in Arkansas, 1887." *Arkansas Historical Quarterly* 40 (Autumn 1981): 249–60.

———. "Arkansas Farmers Organize for Action: 1882–1884." *Arkansas Historical Quarterly* 13 (Autumn 1954): 231–48.

———. "State Politics and the Agricultural Wheel." *Arkansas Historical Quarterly* 38 (Autumn 1979): 248–58.

Escott, Paul D. *Many Excellent People: Power and Privilege in North Carolina, 1850–1900.* Chapel Hill: University of North Carolina Press, 1985.

Ettinger, Brian G. "John Fitzpatrick and the Limits of Working-Class Politics in New Orleans, 1892–1896." *Louisiana History* 26 (Fall 1985): 341–67.

Evans, Mercer G. "The History of the Organized Labor Movement in Georgia." Ph.D. diss., University of Chicago, 1929.

Falzone, Vincent J. *Terence V. Powderly: Middle Class Reformer.* Washington, D.C.: University Press of America, 1978.

Feldman, Glenn. *The Disfranchisement Myth: Poor Whites and Suffrage Restriction in Alabama.* Athens: University of Georgia Press, 2004.

Field, Bruce E. *Harvest of Dissent: The National Farmers Union and the Early Cold War.* Lawrence: University Press of Kansas, 1998.

Fine, Nathan. *Labor and Farmer Parties in the United States, 1828–1928.* New York: Rand School of Social Science, 1928. Repr. New York: Russell and Russell, 1961.

Fink, Leon. "The New Labor History and the Powers of Historical Pessimism: Consensus, Hegemony, and the Case of the Knights of Labor." *Journal of American History* 75 (June 1988): 115–36.

———. *Workingmen's Democracy: The Knights of Labor and American Politics.* Urbana: University of Illinois Press, 1983.

Fite, Gilbert C. *Cotton Fields No More: Southern Agriculture, 1865–1980.* Lexington: University Press of Kentucky, 1984.

———. *Richard B. Russell, Jr., Senator from Georgia.* Chapel Hill: University of North Carolina Press, 1991.

Fitzgerald, Michael W. *Urban Emancipation: Popular Politics in Reconstruction Mobile, 1860–1890.* Baton Rouge: Louisiana State University Press, 2002.

Flamming, Douglas. *Creating the Modern South: Millhands and Managers in Dalton, Georgia, 1884–1984.* Chapel Hill: University of North Carolina Press, 1992.

Flynt, Wayne. *Alabama in the Twentieth Century.* Tuscaloosa: University of Alabama Press, 2004.

———. *Poor but Proud: Alabama's Poor Whites.* Tuscaloosa: University of Alabama Press, 1989.

Foner, Philip S. *The Great Labor Uprising of 1877.* New York: Monad Press, 1977.

———. *History of the Labor Movement in the United States.* 2nd ed. Vol. 2. New York: International Publishers, 1975.

Foster, W. A., Jr., with Thomas A. Scott. *Paulding County: Its People and Places.* Roswell, Ga.: W. H. Wolfe Associates, 1983.

Fox, Maier B. *United We Stand: The United Mine Workers of America, 1890–1990.* Washington, D.C.: United Mine Workers of America, 1990.

Gabler, Edwin. *The American Telegrapher: A Social History, 1860–1900.* New Brunswick, N.J.: Rutgers University Press, 1988.

Gaither, Gerald H. *Blacks and the Populist Revolt: Ballots and Bigotry in the "New South."* University: University of Alabama Press, 1977.

Gardner, Charles M. *The Grange–Friend of the Farmer.* Washington, D.C.: National Grange, 1949.

Garlock, Jonathan, comp. *Guide to the Local Assemblies of the Knights of Labor.* Westport, Conn.: Greenwood Press, 1982.

———. "A Structural Analysis of the Knights of Labor: A Prolegomenon to the History of the Producing Classes." Ph.D. diss., University of Rochester, 1974.

Garraty, John A., and Mark C. Carnes, eds. *American National Biography.* 24 vols. New York: Oxford University Press, 1999.

Gerteis, Joseph. "Class and the Color Line: The Sources and Limits of Interracial Class Coalition, 1880–1896." Ph.D. diss., University of North Carolina at Chapel Hill, 1999.

Gieske, Millard L. *Minnesota Farmer-Laborism: The Third-Party Alternative.* Minneapolis: University of Minnesota Press, 1979.

Gilmore, Glenda E. *Gender and Jim Crow: Women and the Politics of White Supremacy in North Carolina, 1896–1920.* Chapel Hill: University of North Carolina Press, 1996.

Ginger, Ray. *The Bending Cross: A Biography of Eugene Victor Debs.* New Brunswick, N.J.: Rutgers University Press, 1949.

Going, Allen J. *Bourbon Democracy in Alabama, 1874–1890.* University: University of Alabama Press, 1951.

Goldinger, Carolyn, ed. *Presidential Elections since 1789.* 5th ed. Washington, D.C.: Congressional Quarterly Press, 1991.

Goldstein, Harold J. "Labor Unrest in the Birmingham District, 1871–1894." M.A. thesis, University of Alabama, 1951.

Goodwyn, Lawrence. *Democratic Promise: The Populist Moment in America.* New York: Oxford University Press, 1976.

———. "Populist Dreams and Negro Rights: East Texas as a Case Study." *American Historical Review* 76 (December 1971): 1435–56.

———. *The Populist Moment: A Short History of the Agrarian Revolt in America.* New York: Oxford University Press, 1978.

Gould, Jeffrey. "The Strike of 1887: Louisiana Sugar War." *Southern Exposure* 12 (November–December 1984): 45–55.

Grantham, Dewey W. *The Life and Death of the Solid South: A Political History.* Lexington: University Press of Kentucky, 1988.

Graves, John W. *Town and Country: Race Relations in an Urban-Rural Context, 1865–1905.* Fayetteville: University of Arkansas Press, 1990.

Green, Fletcher M. "Ben E. Green and Greenbackism in Georgia." *Georgia Historical Quarterly* 30 (March 1946): 1–13.

Green, George N. "The Texas Labor Movement, 1870–1920." *Southwestern Historical Quarterly* 108 (July 2004): 1–25.

Green, James R. *Death in the Haymarket: A Story of Chicago, the First Labor Movement, and the Bombing That Divided Gilded Age America.* New York: Pantheon, 2006.

———. *Grass-Roots Socialism: Radical Movements in the Southwest, 1895–1943.* Baton Rouge: Louisiana State University Press, 1978.

Greene, Julie. *Pure and Simple Politics: The American Federation of Labor and Political Activism, 1881–1917.* Cambridge: Cambridge University Press, 1998.

Grob, Gerald N. "The Knights of Labor, Politics, and Populism." *Mid-America* 40 (January 1958): 3–21.

———. *Workers and Utopia: A Study of Ideological Conflict in the American Labor Movement, 1865–1900.* Evanston, Ill.: Northwestern University Press, 1961.

*Gubernatorial Elections, 1787–1997.* Washington, D.C.: Congressional Quarterly Press, 1998.

Gutman, Herbert G. "Black Coal Miners and the Greenback-Labor Party in Redeemer Alabama, 1878–1879: The Letters of Warren D. Kelley, Willis Johnson Thomas, 'Dawson,' and Others." *Labor History* 10 (Summer 1969): 506–35.

Hackney, Sheldon. *Populism to Progressivism in Alabama.* Princeton, N.J.: Princeton University Press, 1969.

Hahn, Steven. *A Nation under Our Feet: Black Political Struggles in the Rural South from Slavery to the Great Migration.* Cambridge, Mass.: Belknap Press of Harvard University Press, 2003.

———. *The Roots of Southern Populism: Yeoman Farmers and the Transformation of the Georgia Upcountry, 1850–1890*. New York: Oxford University Press, 1983.

Hahn, Steven, and Jonathan Prude, eds. *The Countryside in the Age of Capitalist Transformation: Essays in the Social History of Rural America*. Chapel Hill: University of North Carolina Press, 1985.

Hair, William I. *Bourbonism and Agrarian Protest: Louisiana Politics, 1877–1900*. Baton Rouge: Louisiana State University Press, 1969.

Haley, John. "Race, Rhetoric, and Revolution." In *Democracy Betrayed: The Wilmington Race Riot of 1898 and Its Legacy*, ed. David S. Cecelski and Timothy B. Tyson, 207–24. Chapel Hill: University of North Carolina Press, 1998.

Hall, Covington. *Labor Struggles in the Deep South and Other Writings*. Ed. David R. Roediger. Chicago: Charles H. Kerr Publishing Co., 1999.

Hall, Jacquelyn Dowd, James Leloudis, Robert Korstad, Mary Murphy, Lu Ann Jones, and Christopher B. Daly. *Like a Family: The Making of a Southern Cotton Mill World*. Chapel Hill: University of North Carolina Press, 1987.

Hart, Roger L. *Redeemers, Bourbons & Populists: Tennessee, 1870–1896*. Baton Rouge: Louisiana State University Press, 1975.

Haynes, Fred E. *James Baird Weaver*. Iowa City: State Historical Society of Iowa, 1919.

Head, Holman. "The Development of the Labor Movement in Alabama Prior to 1900." M.B.A. thesis, University of Alabama, 1955.

Henningson, Berton E., Jr. "Northwest Arkansas and the Brothers of Freedom: The Roots of a Farmer Movement." *Arkansas Historical Quarterly* 34 (Winter 1975): 304–24.

———. "Root Hog or Die: The Brothers of Freedom and the 1884 Arkansas Election." *Arkansas Historical Quarterly* 45 (Autumn 1986): 197–216.

Hicks, John D. *The Populist Revolt: A History of the Farmers' Alliance and the People's Party*. Minneapolis: University of Minnesota Press, 1931. Repr. Westport, Conn.: Greenwood Press, 1981.

Hild, Matthew. "Dixie Knights Redux: The Knights of Labor in Alabama, 1898–1902." *Gulf South Historical Review* 17 (Fall 2001): 36–51.

———. "A 'Flagrant and High-handed Outrage': The Knights of Labor and Skilled Workers in Atlanta, 1882–1886." *Atlanta History: A Journal of Georgia and the South* 43 (Fall 1999): 35–47.

———. "Greenbackers, Knights of Labor, and Populists: Farmer-Labor Insurgency in the Late-Nineteenth-Century South." Ph.D. diss., Georgia Institute of Technology, 2002.

———. "The Knights of Labor in Georgia." M.A. thesis, University of Georgia, 1996.

————. "Labor, Third-Party Politics, and New South Democracy in Arkansas, 1884–1896." *Arkansas Historical Quarterly* 63 (Spring 2004): 24–43.

————. "Organizing across the Color Line: The Knights of Labor and Black Recruitment Efforts in Small-Town Georgia." *Georgia Historical Quarterly* 81 (Summer 1997): 287–310.

Hill, Patricia E. *Dallas: The Making of a Modern City.* Austin: University of Texas Press, 1996.

Hoffman, Charles. *The Depression of the Nineties: An Economic History.* Westport, Conn.: Greenwood Publishing, 1970.

Holmes, William F. "The Arkansas Cotton Pickers Strike of 1891 and the Demise of the Colored Farmers' Alliance." *Arkansas Historical Quarterly* 32 (Summer 1973): 107–19.

————. "The Demise of the Colored Farmers' Alliance." *Journal of Southern History* 41 (May 1975): 187–200.

————. "The Georgia Alliance Legislature." *Georgia Historical Quarterly* 68 (Winter 1984): 479–515.

————. "The Leflore County Massacre and the Demise of the Colored Farmers' Alliance." *Phylon* 34 (September 1973): 267–74.

————. "Reflections on Woodward's *Origins.*" In *"Origins of the New South" Fifty Years Later: The Continuing Influence of a Historical Classic,* ed. John B. Boles and Bethany L. Johnson, 278–85. Baton Rouge: Louisiana State University Press, 2003.

————. "The Southern Farmers' Alliance and the Georgia Senatorial Election of 1890." *Journal of Southern History* 50 (May 1984): 197–224.

Honey, Michael. "Class, Race, and Power in the New South: Racial Violence and the Delusions of White Supremacy." In *Democracy Betrayed: The Wilmington Race Riot of 1898 and Its Legacy,* ed. David S. Cecelski and Timothy B. Tyson, 163–84. Chapel Hill: University of North Carolina Press, 1998.

Horton, Paul. "The Assassination of Rev. James Madison Pickens and the Persistence of Anti-Bourbon Activism in North Alabama." *Alabama Review* 57 (April 2004): 83–109.

————. "Testing the Limits of Class Politics in Postbellum Alabama: Agrarian Radicalism in Lawrence County." *Journal of Southern History* 57 (February 1991): 63–84.

Huggins, Carolyn R. "Bourbonism and Radicalism in Alabama: The Gubernatorial Administration of Thomas Goode Jones, 1890–1894." M.A. thesis, Auburn University, 1968.

Hunt, James L. *Marion Butler and American Populism.* Chapel Hill: University of North Carolina Press, 2003.

————. "Marion Butler and the Populist Ideal, 1863–1938." Ph.D. diss., University of Wisconsin–Madison, 1990.

Hyman, Michael R. *The Anti-Redeemers: Hill-Country Political Dissenters in the Lower South from Redemption to Populism.* Baton Rouge: Louisiana State University Press, 1990.

Ingalls, Robert P. "The Wagner Act on Trial: Vigilante Violence and the Struggle to Organize Textile Workers in Fitzgerald, Georgia, 1937–1940." *Georgia Historical Quarterly* 81 (Summer 1997): 370–94.

Irons, Janet. *Testing the New Deal: The General Textile Strike of 1934 in the American South.* Urbana: University of Illinois Press, 2000.

Israel, Fred L. *Student's Atlas of American Presidential Elections, 1789–1996.* Washington, D.C.: Congressional Quarterly Press, 1997.

Jackson, Joy J. *New Orleans in the Gilded Age: Politics and Urban Progress, 1880–1896.* Baton Rouge: Louisiana State University Press, 1969.

Jacob, Kathryn Allamong, and Bruce A. Ragsdale, eds. *Biographical Directory of the United States Congress, 1774–1989.* Washington, D.C.: U.S. Government Printing Office, 1989.

James, Edward T. "American Labor and Political Action, 1865–1896: The Knights of Labor and Its Predecessors." Ph.D. diss., Harvard University, 1954.

————. "T. V. Powderly, a Political Profile." *Pennsylvania Magazine of History and Biography* 99 (October 1975): 443–59.

Johnston, Robert D. "Peasants, Pitchforks, and the (Found) Promise of Progressivism." *Reviews in American History* 28 (September 2000): 393–98.

Jones, Alton D. "Progressivism in Georgia, 1898–1918." Ph.D. diss., Emory University, 1963.

Jones, George L. "William H. Felton and the Independent Democratic Movement in Georgia, 1870–1890." Ph.D. diss., University of Georgia, 1971.

Kantrowitz, Stephen. "Ben Tillman and Hendrix McLane, Agrarian Rebels: White Manhood, 'The Farmers,' and the Limits of Southern Populism." *Journal of Southern History* 66 (August 2000): 497–524.

————. *Ben Tillman & the Reconstruction of White Supremacy.* Chapel Hill: University of North Carolina Press, 2000.

Kaufman, Stuart B. "Samuel Gompers and the Populist Movement." M.A. thesis, University of Florida, 1964.

Key, V. O. *Southern Politics in State and Nation.* New York: Alfred A. Knopf, 1949.

Kiser, G. Gregory. "The Socialist Party in Arkansas, 1900–1912." *Arkansas Historical Quarterly* 40 (Summer 1981): 119–53.

Klein, Maury. *The Life and Legend of Jay Gould.* Baltimore, Md.: Johns Hopkins University Press, 1986.

Kolnick, Jeffrey D. "A Producer's Commonwealth: Populism and the Knights of Labor in Blue Earth County, Minnesota, 1880–1892." Ph.D. diss., University of California, Davis, 1996.

Kousser, J. Morgan. *The Shaping of Southern Politics: Suffrage Restriction and the Establishment of the One-Party South, 1880–1910.* New Haven, Conn.: Yale University Press, 1974.

Krause, Paul. *The Battle for Homestead, 1880–1892.* Pittsburgh: University of Pittsburgh Press, 1992.

Kremm, Thomas W., and Diane Neal. "Clandestine Black Labor Societies and White Fear: Hiram F. Hoover and the 'Co-operative Workers of America' in the South." *Labor History* 19 (Spring 1978): 226–37.

Kuhn, Clifford M. *Contesting the New South Order: The 1914–1915 Strike at Atlanta's Fulton Mills.* Chapel Hill: University of North Carolina Press, 2001.

Laurie, Bruce. *Artisans into Workers: Labor in Nineteenth-Century America.* New York: Hill and Wang, 1989.

Lause, Mark A. *The Civil War's Last Campaign: James B. Weaver, the Greenback-Labor Party & the Politics of Race & Section.* Lanham, Md.: University Press of America, 2001.

Lefler, Hugh T., and Albert R. Newsome. *North Carolina: The History of a Southern State.* 3rd ed. Chapel Hill: University of North Carolina Press, 1973.

Lester, Connie L. "Grassroots Reform in the Age of Bourbon Democracy and New South Agriculture: The Agricultural Wheel, the Farmers' Alliance, and the People's Party in Tennessee, 1884–1892." Ph.D. diss., University of Tennessee, Knoxville, 1998.

Letwin, Daniel. *The Challenge of Interracial Unionism: Alabama Coal Miners, 1878–1921.* Chapel Hill: University of North Carolina Press, 1998.

Levine, Susan. *Labor's True Woman: Carpet Weavers, Industrialization, and Labor Reform in the Gilded Age.* Philadelphia: Temple University Press, 1984.

Lewinson, Paul. *Race, Class, and Party: A History of Negro Suffrage and White Politics in the South.* New York: Russell & Russell, 1932. Repr. New York: Grosset & Dunlap, 1965.

Lichtenstein, Alex. *Twice the Work of Free Labor: The Political Economy of Convict Labor in the New South.* London: Verso, 1996.

Lightfoot, B. B. "The Human Party: Populism in Comanche County, 1886." *West Texas Historical Association Year Book* 31 (October 1955): 28–40.

Lloyd, Peggy S. "The Howard County Race Riot of 1883." *Arkansas Historical Quarterly* 59 (Winter 2000): 353–87.

Macune, Charles W., Jr. "The Wellsprings of a Populist: Dr. C. W. Macune before 1886." *Southwestern Historical Quarterly* 90 (October 1986): 139–58.

Mancini, Matthew J. *One Dies, Get Another: Convict Leasing in the American South, 1866–1928.* Columbia: University of South Carolina Press, 1996.

Mandel, Bernard. *Samuel Gompers: A Biography.* Yellow Springs, Ohio: Antioch Press, 1963.

Marcus, Irwin M. "The Knights of Labor: Reform Aspects." Ph.D. diss., Lehigh University, 1965.

Marshall, F. Ray. *Labor in the South.* Cambridge, Mass.: Harvard University Press, 1967.

Marti, Donald B. *Women of the Grange: Mutuality and Sisterhood in Rural America, 1866–1920.* Westport, Conn.: Greenwood Press, 1991.

Martin, Roscoe C. "The Grange as a Political Factor in Texas." *Southwestern Political and Social Science Quarterly* 6 (March 1926): 363–83.

———. "The Greenback Party in Texas." *Southwestern Historical Quarterly* 30 (January 1927): 161–77.

———. *The People's Party in Texas: A Study in Third Party Politics.* Bulletin of the University of Texas No. 3308. Austin: University of Texas, 1933. Repr. University of Texas Press, 1970.

Martis, Kenneth C. *The Historical Atlas of United States Congressional Districts, 1789–1983.* New York: Free Press, 1982.

McGee, Gentry R. *A History of Tennessee from 1663 to 1930.* Orig. pub. 1930. Repr. Nashville: Charles Elder, 1971.

McKinney, Gordon B. *Southern Mountain Republicans, 1865–1900: Politics and the Appalachian Community.* Chapel Hill: University of North Carolina Press, 1978.

McKiven, Henry M., Jr. *Iron and Steel: Class, Race, and Community in Birmingham, Alabama, 1875–1920.* Chapel Hill: University of North Carolina Press, 1995.

McLaurin, Melton. "The Knights of Labor in North Carolina Politics." *North Carolina Historical Review* 49 (July 1972): 298–315.

———. *The Knights of Labor in the South.* Westport, Conn.: Greenwood Press, 1978.

———. *Paternalism and Protest: Southern Cotton Mill Workers and Organized Labor, 1875–1905.* Westport, Conn.: Greenwood Publishing, 1971.

McMath, Robert C., Jr. *American Populism: A Social History, 1877–1898.* New York: Hill and Wang, 1993.

———. "C. Vann Woodward and the Burden of Southern Populism." *Journal of Southern History* 67 (November 2001): 741–68.

———. *Populist Vanguard: A History of the Southern Farmers' Alliance.* Chapel Hill: University of North Carolina Press, 1975.

———. "Sandy Land and Hogs in the Timber: (Agri)cultural Origins of the Farmers' Alliance in Texas." In *The Countryside in the Age of Capitalist Transformation:*

*Essays in the Social History of Rural America*, ed. Steven Hahn and Jonathan Prude, 205–29. Chapel Hill: University of North Carolina Press, 1985.

————. "Southern White Farmers and the Organization of Black Farm Workers: A North Carolina Document." *Labor History* 18 (Winter 1977): 115–19.

Meyers, Frederic. "The Knights of Labor in the South." *Southern Economic Journal* 6 (April 1940): 479–87.

Miller, Worth Robert. "Building a Progressive Coalition in Texas: The Populist–Reform Democrat Rapprochement, 1900–1907." *Journal of Southern History* 52 (May 1986): 163–82.

————. *Oklahoma Populism: A History of the People's Party in the Oklahoma Territory.* Norman: University of Oklahoma Press, 1987.

Miner, Claudia. "The 1886 Convention of the Knights of Labor." *Phylon* 44 (June 1983): 147–59.

Mitchell, George S. *Textile Unionism and the South.* Chapel Hill: University of North Carolina Press, 1931.

Moneyhon, Carl H. *Arkansas and the New South, 1874–1929.* Fayetteville: University of Arkansas Press, 1997.

————. *Republicanism in Reconstruction Texas.* Austin: University of Texas Press, 1980.

Montgomery, David. *The Fall of the House of Labor: The Workplace, the State, and American Labor Activism, 1865–1925.* Cambridge: Cambridge University Press, 1987.

Moore, John L., Jon P. Preimesberger, and David R. Tarr, eds. *Congressional Quarterly's Guide to U.S. Elections.* 4th ed. 2 vols. Washington, D.C.: Congressional Quarterly Press, 2001.

Ness, Immanuel, and James Ciment, eds. *The Encyclopedia of Third Parties in America.* 3 vols. Armonk, N.Y.: Sharpe Reference, 2000.

Newby, I. A. *Plain Folk in the New South: Social Change and Cultural Persistence, 1880–1915.* Baton Rouge: Louisiana State University Press, 1989.

Nicholson, Philip Y. *Labor's Story in the United States.* Philadelphia: Temple University Press, 2004.

Niswonger, Richard L. *Arkansas Democratic Politics, 1896–1920.* Fayetteville: University of Arkansas Press, 1990.

Nixon, Herman C. "The Cleavage within the Farmers' Alliance Movement." *Mississippi Valley Historical Review* 15 (June 1928): 22–33.

Noblin, Stuart. *Leonidas LaFayette Polk, Agrarian Crusader.* Chapel Hill: University of North Carolina Press, 1949.

Nordin, D. Sven. *Rich Harvest: A History of the Grange.* Jackson: University Press of Mississippi, 1974.

Nugent, Walter T. K. *The Tolerant Populists: Kansas Populism and Nativism.* Chicago: University of Chicago Press, 1963.

O'Brien, Michael. "From a Chase to a View: The Arkansan." In *C. Vann Woodward: A Southern Historian and His Critics,* ed. John Herbert Roper, 234–52. Athens: University of Georgia Press, 1997.

Oestreicher, Richard. "A Note on Knights of Labor Membership Statistics." *Labor History* 25 (Winter 1984): 102–8.

Oshinsky, David M. *Worse Than Slavery: Parchman Farm and the Ordeal of Jim Crow Justice.* New York: Free Press, 1996.

Ostler, Jeffrey. *Prairie Populism: The Fate of Agrarian Radicalism in Kansas, Nebraska, and Iowa, 1880–1892.* Lawrence: University Press of Kansas, 1993.

Otto, John S. *The Final Frontiers, 1880–1930: Settling the Southern Bottomlands.* Westport, Conn.: Greenwood Press, 1999.

Paisley, Clifton. "The Political Wheelers and Arkansas' Election of 1888." *Arkansas Historical Quarterly* 25 (Spring 1966): 3–21.

Palmer, Bruce. *"Man over Money": The Southern Populist Critique of American Capitalism.* Chapel Hill: University of North Carolina Press, 1980.

Papke, David R. *The Pullman Case: The Clash of Labor and Capital in Industrial America.* Lawrence: University Press of Kansas, 1999.

Parsons, Stanley B., Michael J. Dubin, and Karen Toombs Parsons. *United States Congressional Districts, 1883–1913.* Westport, Conn.: Greenwood Press, 1990.

Paul, Brad A. "Rebels of the New South: The Socialist Party in Dixie, 1892–1920." Ph.D. diss., University of Massachusetts, Amherst, 1999.

———. "Rebels of the New South: The Socialist Party in Dixie, 1897–1920." M.A. thesis, Georgia State University, 1994.

Perman, Michael. "Joseph F. Johnston, 1896–1900." In *Alabama Governors: A Political History of the State,* ed. Samuel L. Webb and Margaret E. Armbrester, 127–33. Tuscaloosa: University of Alabama Press, 2001.

———. *The Road to Redemption: Southern Politics, 1869–1879.* Chapel Hill: University of North Carolina Press, 1984.

———. *Struggle for Mastery: Disfranchisement in the South, 1888–1908.* Chapel Hill: University of North Carolina Press, 2001.

Phelan, Craig. *Grand Master Workman: Terence Powderly and the Knights of Labor.* Westport, Conn.: Greenwood Press, 2000.

Pierce, Michael C. "The Plow and Hammer: Farmers, Organized Labor and the People's Party in Ohio." Ph.D. diss., Ohio State University, 1999.

———. "The Populist President of the American Federation of Labor: The Career of John McBride, 1880–1895." *Labor History* 41 (February 2000): 5–24.

Pollack, Norman. *The Just Polity: Populism, Law, and Human Welfare.* Urbana: University of Illinois Press, 1987.

Prather, H. Leon, Sr. *We Have Taken a City: Wilmington Racial Massacre and Coup of 1898.* Rutherford, N.J.: Fairleigh Dickinson University Press and Associated University Presses, 1984.

Rachleff, Peter J. *Black Labor in the South: Richmond, Virginia, 1865–1890.* Philadelphia: Temple University Press, 1984.

Range, Willard. *A Century of Georgia Agriculture, 1850–1950.* Athens: University of Georgia Press, 1954, 1969.

Rayback, Joseph G. *A History of American Labor.* Rev. ed. New York: Free Press, 1966.

Readnour, Harry W. "Simon P. Hughes, 1885–1889." In *The Governors of Arkansas: Essays in Political Biography,* ed. Timothy P. Donovan, Willard B. Gatewood, Jr., and Jeannie M. Whayne, 83–89. 2nd ed. Fayetteville: University of Arkansas Press, 1995.

Redding, Kent. *Making Race, Making Power: North Carolina's Road to Disfranchisement.* Urbana: University of Illinois Press, 2003.

Redmond, LaGroon, ed. *Cemeteries of Paulding County, Georgia.* Roswell, Ga.: Wolfe Publishing, 1995.

Reed, Merl E. "The Augusta Textile Mills and the Strike of 1886." *Labor History* 14 (Spring 1973): 228–46.

Rhinehart, Marilyn D. *A Way of Work and a Way of Life: Coal Mining in Thurber, Texas, 1888–1926.* College Station: Texas A&M University Press, 1992.

Richardson, Rupert N., Adrian Anderson, Cary D. Wintz, and Ernest Wallace. *Texas: The Lone Star State.* 8th ed. Upper Saddle River, N.J.: Prentice-Hall, 2001.

Ricker, Ralph R. *The Greenback-Labor Movement in Pennsylvania.* Bellefonte, Pa.: Pennsylvania Heritage, 1966.

Ritter, Gretchen. *Goldbugs and Greenbacks: The Antimonopoly Tradition and the Politics of Finance in America, 1865–1896.* Cambridge: Cambridge University Press, 1997.

Roberts, Derrell C. *Joseph E. Brown and the Politics of Reconstruction.* University: University of Alabama Press, 1973.

Roberts, Frances. "William Manning Lowe and the Greenback Party in Alabama." *Alabama Review* 5 (April 1952): 100–121.

Roberts, William P. "The Public Career of Doctor William Harrell Felton." Ph.D. diss., University of North Carolina at Chapel Hill, 1952.

Rodrigue, John C. *Reconstruction in the Cane Fields: From Slavery to Free Labor in Louisiana's Sugar Parishes, 1862–1880.* Baton Rouge: Louisiana State University Press, 2001.

Rodriquez, Alicia E. "Urban Populism: Challenges to Democratic Party Control in Dallas, Texas, 1887–1900." Ph.D. diss., University of California, Santa Barbara, 1998.

Rogers, William Warren. "The Agricultural Wheel in Alabama." *Alabama Review* 20 (January 1967): 5–16.

———. "The Negro Alliance in Alabama." *Journal of Negro History* 45 (January 1960): 38–44.

———. *The One-Gallused Rebellion: Agrarianism in Alabama, 1865–1896.* Baton Rouge: Louisiana State University Press, 1970.

Rogers, William Warren, Robert David Ward, Leah Rawls Atkins, and Wayne Flynt. *Alabama: The History of a Deep South State.* Tuscaloosa: University of Alabama Press, 1994.

Roper, John Herbert, ed. *C. Vann Woodward: A Southern Historian and His Critics.* Athens: University of Georgia Press, 1997.

———. *C. Vann Woodward, Southerner.* Athens: University of Georgia Press, 1987.

Roush, Gerald L. "Aftermath of Reconstruction: Race, Violence, and Politics in Alabama, 1874–1884." M.A. thesis, Auburn University, 1973.

Russell, James M. *Atlanta, 1847–1890: City Building in the Old South and the New.* Baton Rouge: Louisiana State University Press, 1988.

Sallee, Shelley. *The Whiteness of Child Labor Reform in the New South.* Athens: University of Georgia Press, 2004.

Salmond, John A. *The General Textile Strike of 1934.* Columbia: University of Missouri Press, 2002.

Saloutos, Theodore. "The Agricultural Wheel in Arkansas." *Arkansas Historical Quarterly* 2 (March 1943): 127–40.

———. *Farmer Movements in the South, 1865–1933.* Berkeley: University of California Press, 1960.

———. "The Grange in the South, 1870–1877." *Journal of Southern History* 19 (November 1953): 473–87.

Salvatore, Nick. *Eugene V. Debs: Citizen and Socialist.* Urbana: University of Illinois Press, 1982.

Sanders, Elizabeth. *Roots of Reform: Farmers, Workers, and the American State, 1877–1917.* Chicago: University of Chicago Press, 1999.

Saunders, Robert M. "The Ideology of Southern Populists, 1892–1895." Ph.D. diss., University of Virginia, 1967.

Schlesinger, Arthur M., Jr., ed. *The Almanac of American History.* New York: G. P. Putnam's Sons, 1983.

Schneirov, Richard, Shelton Stromquist, and Nick Salvatore, eds. *The Pullman Strike and the Crisis of the 1890s: Essays on Labor and Politics.* Urbana: University of Illinois Press, 1999.

Scott, Thomas A. "Cobb County, Georgia, 1880–1900: A Socioeconomic Study of an Upper Piedmont County." Ph.D. diss., University of Tennessee, Knoxville, 1978.

Shadgett, Olive Hall. *The Republican Party in Georgia: From Reconstruction through 1900.* Athens: University of Georgia Press, 1964.

Shapiro, Karin A. *A New South Rebellion: The Battle against Convict Labor in the Tennessee Coalfields, 1871–1896.* Chapel Hill: University of North Carolina Press, 1998.

Shaw, Barton C. *The Wool-Hat Boys: Georgia's Populist Party.* Baton Rouge: Louisiana State University Press, 1984.

Shugg, Roger W. "The New Orleans General Strike of 1892." *Louisiana Historical Quarterly* 21 (April 1938): 547–60.

Simkins, Francis Butler. *The Tillman Movement in South Carolina.* Durham, N.C.: Duke University Press, 1926.

Smith, Ralph. "The Farmers' Alliance in Texas, 1875–1900: A Revolt against Bourbon and Bourgeois Democracy." *Southwestern Historical Quarterly* 48 (January 1945): 346–69.

———. "The Grange Movement in Texas, 1873–1900." *Southwestern Historical Quarterly* 42 (April 1939): 297–315.

Soule, Sarah A. "Populism and Black Lynching in Georgia, 1890–1900." *Social Forces* 71 (December 1992): 431–49.

Steelman, Lala Carr. *The North Carolina Farmers' Alliance: A Political History, 1887–1893.* Greenville, N.C.: East Carolina University Publications, 1985.

Steeples, Douglas, and David O. Whitten. *Democracy in Desperation: The Depression of 1893.* Westport, Conn.: Greenwood Press, 1998.

Steiner, Michael J. "Toilers of the Cities and Tillers of the Soil: The 1889 St. Louis 'Convention of the Middle Classes.'" *Missouri Historical Review* 93 (July 1999): 397–416.

Stewart, Bruce E. "The Urban-Rural Dynamic of the Southern Farmers' Alliance: Relations between Athens Merchants and Clarke County Farmers, 1888–1891." *Georgia Historical Quarterly* 89 (Summer 2005): 157–84.

Stowell, David O. *Streets, Railroads, and the Great Strike of 1877.* Chicago: University of Chicago Press, 1999.

Summers, Mark Wahlgren. *Party Games: Getting, Keeping, and Using Power in Gilded Age Politics.* Chapel Hill: University of North Carolina Press, 2004.

———. "Party Games: The Art of Stealing Elections in the Late-Nineteenth-Century United States." *Journal of American History* 88 (September 2001): 424–35.

Taft, Philip. *The A.F. of L. in the Time of Gompers.* New York: Harper & Brothers, 1957.

———. *Organizing Dixie: Alabama Workers in the Industrial Era.* Rev. and ed. Gary M. Fink. Westport, Conn.: Greenwood Press, 1981.

Talmadge, John E. *Rebecca Latimer Felton: Nine Stormy Decades.* Athens: University of Georgia Press, 1960.

Taylor, Carl C. *The Farmers' Movement, 1620–1920.* New York: American Book Co., 1953.

Temple, Sarah Blackwell Gober. *The First Hundred Years: A Short History of Cobb County in Georgia.* Atlanta: Walter W. Brown Publishing Co., 1935.

Tindall, George B. *The Emergence of the New South, 1913–1945.* Baton Rouge: Louisiana State University Press, 1967.

———. *South Carolina Negroes, 1877–1900.* Columbia: University of South Carolina Press, 1952.

Tippett, Tom. *When Southern Labor Stirs.* New York: Jonathan Cape and Harrison Smith, 1931.

Tullos, Allen. *Habits of Industry: White Culture and the Transformation of the Carolina Piedmont.* Chapel Hill: University of North Carolina Press, 1989.

Turner, Ralph V., and William Warren Rogers. "Arkansas Labor in Revolt: Little Rock and the Great Southwestern Strike." *Arkansas Historical Quarterly* 24 (Spring 1965): 29–46.

Unger, Irwin. *The Greenback Era.* Princeton, N.J.: Princeton University Press, 1964.

———. *These United States: The Questions of Our Past.* Concise combined ed. Upper Saddle River, N.J.: Prentice-Hall, 1999.

Valelly, Richard M. *Radicalism in the States: The Minnesota Farmer-Labor Party and the American Political Economy.* Chicago: University of Chicago Press, 1989.

Voss, Kim. *The Making of American Exceptionalism: The Knights of Labor and Class Formation in the Nineteenth Century.* Ithaca, N.Y.: Cornell University Press, 1993.

*Wagner, MaryJo. "Farms, Families, and Reform: Women in the Farmers' Alliance and Populist Party." Ph.D. diss., University of Oregon, 1986.*

*Walker, Donald R. Penology for Profit: A History of the Texas Prison System, 1867–1912.* College Station: Texas A&M University Press, 1988.

Walsh, Julia M. " 'Horny-Handed Sons of Toil': Workers, Politics, and Religion in Augusta, Georgia, 1880–1910." Ph.D. diss., University of Illinois at Urbana-Champaign, 1999.

Ward, Judson C. "Georgia under the Bourbon Democrats, 1872–1890." Ph.D. diss., University of North Carolina at Chapel Hill, 1947.

Ward, Robert David, and William Warren Rogers. *Labor Revolt in Alabama: The Great Strike of 1894.* University: University of Alabama Press, 1965.

Ware, Norman J. *The Labor Movement in the United States, 1860–1895: A Study in Democracy.* New York: D. Appleton and Co., 1929.

Webb, Samuel L. "From Independents to Populists to Progressive Republicans:

The Case of Chilton County, Alabama, 1880–1920." *Journal of Southern History* 59 (November 1993): 707–36.

———. *Two-Party Politics in the One-Party South: Alabama's Hill Country, 1874–1920.* Tuscaloosa: University of Alabama Press, 1997.

Webb, Samuel L., and Margaret E. Armbrester, eds. *Alabama Governors: A Political History of the State.* Tuscaloosa: University of Alabama Press, 2001.

Weir, Robert E. *Beyond Labor's Veil: The Culture of the Knights of Labor.* University Park: Pennsylvania State University Press, 1996.

———. "Dress Rehearsal for Pullman: The Knights of Labor and the 1890 New York Central Strike." In *The Pullman Strike and the Crisis of the 1890s: Essays on Labor and Politics,* ed. Richard Schneirov, Shelton Stromquist, and Nick Salvatore, 21–42. Urbana: University of Illinois Press, 1999.

———. *Knights Unhorsed: Internal Conflict in a Gilded Age Social Movement.* Detroit: Wayne State University Press, 2000.

West, Carroll Van, ed. *The Tennessee Encyclopedia of History & Culture.* Nashville: Rutledge Hill Press, 1998.

Wheeler, John M. "The People's Party in Arkansas, 1891–1896." Ph.D. diss., Tulane University, 1975.

Whites, LeeAnn. "Paternalism and Protest in Augusta's Cotton Mills: What's Gender Got to Do with It?" In *Paternalism in a Southern City: Race, Religion, and Gender in Augusta, Georgia,* ed. Edward J. Cashin and Glenn T. Eskew, 68–84. Athens: University of Georgia Press, 2001.

Wiebe, Robert H. *The Search for Order, 1877–1920.* New York: Hill and Wang, 1967.

Williamson, Joel. *The Crucible of Race: Black-White Relations in the American South since Emancipation.* New York: Oxford University Press, 1984.

Woeste, Victoria Saker. *The Farmer's Benevolent Trust: Law and Agricultural Cooperation in Industrial America, 1865–1945.* Chapel Hill: University of North Carolina Press, 1998.

Woodman, Harold D. *New South–New Law: The Legal Foundations of Credit and Labor Relations in the Postbellum Agricultural South.* Baton Rouge: Louisiana State University Press, 1995.

———. "The Political Economy of the New South: Retrospects and Prospects." *Journal of Southern History* 67 (November 2001): 789–810.

Woods, Thomas A. *Knights of the Plow: Oliver H. Kelley and the Origins of the Grange in Republican Ideology.* Ames: Iowa State University Press, 1991.

Woodward, C. Vann. *Origins of the New South, 1877–1913.* Baton Rouge: Louisiana State University Press, 1951.

———. *The Strange Career of Jim Crow.* Rev. 3rd ed. New York: Oxford University Press, 1974.

————. *Thinking Back: The Perils of Writing History.* Baton Rouge: Louisiana State University Press, 1986.

————. *Tom Watson, Agrarian Rebel.* New York: Macmillan, 1938. Repr. New York: Oxford University Press, 1963.

Wright, Gavin. *Old South, New South: Revolutions in the Southern Economy since the Civil War.* New York: Basic Books, 1986.

Wynne, Lewis N. *The Continuity of Cotton: Planter Politics in Georgia, 1865–1892.* Macon, Ga.: Mercer University Press, 1986.

Young, Earle B. *Tracks to the Sea: Galveston and Western Railroad Development, 1866–1900.* College Station: Texas A&M University Press, 1999.

Zuczek, Richard. *State of Rebellion: Reconstruction in South Carolina.* Columbia: University of South Carolina Press, 1996.

# Index

Adams, Samuel M., 154

Agricultural Wheel, 80, 121, 135, 159; African Americans and, 59, 100, 103–4, 122, 239n66; cooperative enterprises of, 61, 115; expansion of, 77, 88, 90, 99, 103, 104, 166, 239n59; membership requirements, 59; merger with the Brothers of Freedom, 88, 163, 241n93; merger with the Farmers' Alliance, 122; origins of, 48, 58, 66; partisan politics and, 4, 62–63, 75–76, 77, 84, 88–90, 107, 108, 112, 114, 115–17, 134, 145, 195, 198, 204, 219, 241n82; platform of, 58–59, 60, 61; women and, 59–60. *See also under* Knights of Labor, Noble and Holy Order of the

Alabama State Federation of Labor, 205, 208

Alexander, S. B., 97

Alliance Democrats: in Georgia, 19, 109, 136, 139, 140–41, 167, 170, 188; in North Carolina, 102, 108, 173; in South Carolina, 136, 203; in Tennessee, 141–43, 198; in Texas, 77, 84–85, 136–37, 164–65

"Alliance yardstick," 136–37

American Federation of Labor (AFL), 154, 196; Farmers' Union and, 208;

membership of, 150, 189, 204, 205, 206–7; origins of, 125; Populism and, 125, 145, 150, 189–91, 193

American Railway Union (ARU), 174, 180, 186, 189, 210

Anti-Monopoly Party, 86–87

anti-union laws, 206, 287n31

Arkansas State Federation of Labor, 211

Ashby, H. S. P. ("Stump"), 140, 184, 289n57

Barker, D. E., 134, 289n57

Barnett, J. W., 87–88

Beaumont, Ralph: Farmers' Alliance and, 126, 127–28, 131, 137, 252n85; Greenback-Labor Party and, 46; Populism and, 138, 139, 160, 184, 279n143

Birmingham Alliance Labor Conference, 154–55, 193

Black, James C. C., 169, 188–89

Bourbon Triumvirate, 19, 136

Bralley, W. I., 185, 187

Brintle, O. F., 172, 274n87

Broiles, H. S., 75, 86, 87, 112, 113, 140, 165

Brothers of Freedom, 60–63, 77, 88, 159, 163, 239n59, 241n82, 241n93

Brown, Joseph E., 19, 94

Grange (Patrons of Husbandry)
(*continued*)
   agricultural employer-employee
   relationship and, 17–18, 230n28;
   cooperative enterprises and, 15–16,
   207; Declaration of Purposes of, 14,
   18; decline of, 132, 164, 229n11,
   231n58, 247n36; origins and growth
   of, 9–10, 12; partisan politics and,
   9–10, 18–26 passim, 29–30, 31,
   36, 75, 77, 84, 112, 120, 136, 164;
   railroads and, 16–17; Southwest
   strike of 1886 and, 74; women and,
   13, 183; mentioned, 59, 61, 105,
   106, 129, 130, 132, 214. *See also under*
   Greenback-Labor Party (GLP)
Gray, Reuben F., 123, 126
Greenback-Labor Party (GLP): African
   Americans and, 30, 32, 34, 39,
   40–41, 43, 50, 196; in Alabama,
   31–35, 42–43, 49–50, 104, 199, 219;
   in Arkansas, 29–31, 43, 199, 203,
   210, 219; assessment of success in
   the South, 42–44; as a forerunner
   of Populism, 2, 3, 4, 11–12, 108,
   109, 120, 151, 152, 153, 167, 178;
   in Georgia, 35–36; Grange and,
   21–22, 25–26, 29–30, 31; Knights
   of Labor and, 32, 46–47, 49–50,
   104; in Louisiana, 39, 43, 196; in
   Missouri, 75; in North Carolina,
   37–38; origins and growth of, 19–24;
   presidential campaigns and, 64,
   157; in Tennessee, 41–42, 43, 198;
   in Texas, 24–29, 42–43, 199, 219;
   Toledo platform of, 4, 22, 23, 36, 46,
   73, 105, 112, 123, 128; mentioned,
   214, 218

Harris, G. B., 209–10
Harrison, Benjamin, 162, 168, 174–75
Hayes, John W., 137, 147, 171, 175, 176
Hayes, Rutherford B., 40
Heartsill, W. B. W., 159, 163–64, 194,
   289n57
Hines, James K., 187, 214
Hitt, L. H., 89, 133, 248n42
Hogan, Dan, 211
Hogg, James S., 136–37, 164–65, 208
Homestead (Pa.) massacre, 157–58, 168
Hover, Hiram F., 205–6
Hughes, Simon, 29–30
Humphrey, R. M., 113, 114, 123, 138,
   139, 143, 147

Independent politics and politicians:
   in Alabama, 31, 34, 130–31, 167; in
   Arkansas, 63, 119; in Georgia, 31,
   35–37, 91–92, 188; Knights of Labor
   and, 75, 80, 84, 85, 91–97 passim,
   108–10, 130–31, 165; in Louisiana,
   38–40, 196; in Mississippi, 31; in
   North Carolina, 94–95, 95–97,
   108–9; in South Carolina, 40–41; in
   Tennessee, 197; in Texas, 75, 85, 87,
   109–10, 114, 165, 184, 187
Industrial Workers of the World, 210
Irons, Martin, 72–73, 160, 209–10

Jeffersonian Democrats, 108, 153, 166,
   179
Johnston, Joseph F., 132, 262n40
Jones, Evan, 85, 113–14, 122, 126, 127
Jones, G. W. (Wash), 25, 27–28, 38,
   54–55, 113
Jones, John T., 29–30
Jones, Thomas G., 166–67, 179, 180

subtreasury plan and, 204; as victim of election fraud, 169–70, 174, 188–89

White, T. H., 131, 132

Willard, Frances, 146

Willyerd, S. L., 184

Wilmington (N.C.) coup d'état of 1898, 202, 216, 218, 221

Wilson, Woodrow, 213

Woman's Christian Temperance Union (WCTU), 94, 146

women's suffrage, 105–6, 113, 146–47, 203

Woodall, J. J. (Jonce), 106, 108

Wright, A. W., 126, 128, 137

Wright, Seaborn, 214